Discourse 2.0

Georgetown University Round Table on Languages and Linguistics Series
Selected Titles

Crosslinguistic Research in Syntax and Semantics: Negation Tense and Clausal Architecture
RAFFAELLA ZANUTTINI, HÉCTOR CAMPOS, ELENA HERBURGER, PAUL H. PORTNER, EDITORS

Discourse and Technology: Multimodal Discourse Analysis
PHILIP LEVINE AND RON SCOLLON, EDITORS

Educating for Advanced Foreign Language Capacities: Constructs, Curriculum, Instruction, Assessment
HEIDI BYRNES, HEATHER D. WEGER-GUNTHARP, AND KATHERINE A. SPRANG, EDITORS

Implicit and Explicit Language Learning: Conditions, Processes, and Knowledge in SLA and Bilingualism
CRISTINA SANZ AND RONALD P. LEOW, EDITORS

Language in Use: Cognitive and Discourse Perspectives on Language and Language Learning
ANDREA E. TYLER, MARI TAKADA, YIYOUNG KIM, AND DIANA MARINOVA, EDITORS

Little Words: Their History, Phonology, Syntax, Semantics, Pragmatics, and Acquisition
RONALD P. LEOW, HÉCTOR CAMPOS, AND DONNA LARDIERE, EDITORS

Sustaining Linguistic Diversity: Endangered and Minority Languages and Language Varieties
KENDALL A. KING, NATALIE SCHILLING-ESTES, LYN WRIGHT FOGLE, JIA JACKIE LOU, AND BARBARA SOUKUP, EDITORS

Telling Stories: Language, Narrative, and Social Life
DEBORAH SCHIFFRIN, ANNA DE FINA, AND ANASTASIA NYLUND, EDITORS

DISCOURSE 2.0
Language and New Media

Deborah Tannen and Anna Marie Trester, Editors

GEORGETOWN UNIVERSITY PRESS
Washington, DC

Library of Congress Cataloging-in-Publication Data

Discourse 2.0 : language and new media / Deborah Tannen and Anna Marie Trester, editors.

p. cm.

Includes bibliographical references and index.

ISBN 978-1-58901-954-6 (pbk. : alk. paper)

1. Discourse analysis--Social aspects. 2. Mass media and language. 3. Social media. 4. Digital media. 5. Conversation analysis. 6. Sociolinguistics. I. Tannen, Deborah. II. Trester, Anna Marie. III. Title: Discourse two.

P302.84.D54 2012

401'.41--dc23   2012016626

♾ This book is printed on acid-free paper meeting the requirements of the American National Standard for Permanence in Paper for Printed Library Materials.

15 14 13   9 8 7 6 5 4 3 2
First printing

Printed in the United States of America

Contents

Acknowledgments

The chapters in this volume are drawn from the nearly two hundred presentations given and workshops conducted at the 2011 Georgetown University Round Table on Languages and Linguistics (GURT), "Discourse 2.0: Language and New Media." Given the constraints of space inherent in a volume of this sort, it was necessary to reject many worthy papers. We are grateful to all those who submitted their papers for consideration, and to all those who were involved in the conference. To all who participated, we continue to be inspired by your work. Finally, for invaluable assistance in preparing the manuscript for publication, we are deeply grateful to Gwynne Mapes.

Introduction

DEBORAH TANNEN AND ANNA MARIE TRESTER
Georgetown University

OUR LIVES NOW, in ways we are only beginning to understand, are lived with and through electronic media: We get news on the internet, read books on Kindle, find old friends on Facebook and new loves on OKCupid and Match.com. We network on LinkedIn, and create, enhance, and share images with Instagram; we "tweet," "friend," and "follow"; "post," "pin" and "like"; and sometimes "#fail." As we seek to understand these new ways of using language in our lives, the new worlds of words they entail in turn provide new means of understanding who we are and how we connect through language.

The chapters in this volume are drawn from the sixty-third annual meeting of the Georgetown University Round Table on Languages and Linguistics (GURT), "Discourse 2.0: Language and New Media," which is also the title of this volume. Included here are the five plenary addresses as well as selected papers by workshop leaders, panel organizers, and paper presenters, all of whom turn the attention of discourse analysis, broadly defined, to emerging and rapidly evolving new media platforms for interpersonal interaction. In this introduction we suggest some connections among the chapters as well as some focal themes of the volume.

In chapter 1, Susan Herring sets the stage for the volume by defining and describing Web 2.0, placing it in the historical context of computer-mediated discourse analysis (CMDA) and showing that it can be understood through the lens of the tripartite classification suggested in her title, "Discourse in Web 2.0: Familiar, Reconfigured, and Emergent." Considering a wealth of data sources such as Second Life, YouTube, Twitter, wikis, games, Skype, and texting, she outlines her CMDA toolkit, providing a set of methods grounded in discourse analysis, which may be used to uncover patterns of structure and meaning in networked communications.

The chapters that follow begin to provide the range of research that Herring calls for in her conclusion. In chapter 2, "Polities and Politics of Ongoing Assessments: Evidence from Video-Gaming and Blogging," Hervé Varenne, Gillian "Gus" Andrews, Aaron Chia-Yuan Hung, and Sarah Wessler develop and integrate the notion of "assessment" from the disparate fields of education, mental health, and conversation analysis, by exploring three examples of the phenomenon as played out in electronic discourse: first, an interaction at a video-game design camp in which an expert child takes over the controls from an incompetent adult; next, a group of four young Chinese friends playing video games in New York City, wherein three of the young men were expert, but the fourth, a young woman, was a novice; and, finally, a series of multiparty exchanges in which a number of people mistakenly tried to cancel AOL accounts by posting messages to the blog of an individual who had written humorously about difficulties encountered when attempting to cancel an AOL account. In all of these contexts, the authors examine the linguistic means by which incompetence or expertise is assessed by participants in the interactions, considering how such "indexical propositions and their interpretation" are shaped by synchronicity (in face-to-face encounters), or in the asynchronicity exemplified in the blog data.

In chapter 3, "Participatory Culture and Metalinguistic Discourse: Performing and Negotiating German Dialects on YouTube," Jannis Androutsopoulos considers the asynchronous interactive nature of Web 2.0 discourse in a very different context: videos on YouTube that feature the Berlin dialect. Adopting a discourse-as-social-practice perspective, he proposes the concept of "participatory spectacle" to focus on the relationship between the videos and the viewers who comment on them, zeroing in on the ways that Web 2.0 discourse combines unique capabilities of video spectacle with the ability of viewers to voice reactions.

Chapter 4 shares concerns with the preceding chapters while focusing on yet another very different electronic platform. In "'My English Is So Poor . . . So I Take Photos': Metalinguistic Discourses about English on Flickr," Carmen Lee examines the self-assessments of their linguistic ability by nonnative speakers of English who use the language on Flickr, the photosharing website. She then examines the assumptions about and attitudes toward English, and toward its role in web discourse, that their comments reveal.

Visual images are also at the heart of chapter 5, "'Their Lives Are So Much Better Than Ours!' The Ritual (Re)construction of Social Identity in Holiday Cards." This chapter contributes to an understanding of meaning-making in popular culture by exploring how a website and its use reflect and affect social forces in contemporary society. The holiday cards that are the focus of Jenna Mahay's analysis are samples available on two websites that allow individuals to order personalized yet professionally printed holiday cards by uploading their own family photos to the website and selecting from a range of designs and greeting options provided. Mahay explores what one might identify, using Androutsopoulos's term the "participatory spectacle," by which the individuals create their own social identities, especially with respect to class and status, while reinforcing an idealized image of family happiness based on a heterosexual, two-parent family with young children.

Chapters 6–13 examine the use of electronic media in interpersonal interaction. In chapter 6, "The Medium Is the Metamessage: Conversational Style in New Media Interaction," Deborah Tannen reminds us that the concept of "discourse" is invaluable as a "corrective to the tendency to think of spoken and written language as separate and fundamentally different." She presents examples of (written) new media discourse in the form of email, Facebook, instant messaging, and text message exchanges among family and friends. She suggests that use of such conventions as capitalization, emphatic punctuation, repetition, and speed of reply constitute new media analogs to conversational style features in spoken conversation, with analogous risks of miscommunication and mutual misjudgment in interaction among women and men, as well as among members of different age groups. She also suggests that, given the availability of multiple potential media, the choice of medium itself carries meaning (in her terms, sends metamessages), and that the risk of miscommunication is sometimes built into the mechanics of a given medium, such as a tag line automatically appended to text messages that is visible to the receiver but not to the sender.

In chapter 7, "Bringing Mobiles into the Conversation: Applying a Conversation Analytic Approach to the Study of Mobiles in Co-present Interaction," Stephen M. DiDomenico and Jeffrey Boase examine a segment of a video recording of a naturally occurring social gathering among three women friends in which the participants oscillated between attention to the people in the room and attention to their mobile devices. In their first example, drawing on Gibson's concept of "technological affordance," the authors demonstrate the importance of the asynchronous nature of texting in relation to the turn-taking organization of the face-to-face interaction. Their second example illustrates the blurring of boundaries between the two attention foci, as two of the participants become effective bystanders to an interaction between the third participant and the sender of a text message who is not in the room. This study thus demonstrates how new media discourse is integrated into face-to-face interaction, exemplifying how norms about such use are interactionally negotiated.

Continuing the exploration of interactional norms in chapter 8, "Facework on Facebook: Conversations on Social Media," Laura West and Anna Marie Trester examine interaction on Facebook to uncover how politeness norms are negotiated. Specifically, the authors explore the discursive means by which participants manage what Brown and Levinson characterize in their politeness schema as face-threatening acts (FTAs). Drawing from an ongoing ethnography, the authors contrast, on the one hand, fake Facebook interactions that create humor by featuring FTAs that violate politeness norms, with, on the other hand, naturally occurring Facebook interactions collected from users' walls, in which FTAs are largely avoided. With particular focus on how intertextuality is implicated in facework, the authors focus on the core practices of friending, posting, and replying, as well as some of the conversational rituals that Facebook has sought to operationalize: issuing invitations and sending birthday greetings. The authors thus consider how users navigate the balancing of face needs in this medium. Beginning and ending the discussion with the playful negotiation of norms surrounding one of the newer features on the site (tagging), this chapter sets the stage for the one that follows; together, the chapters demonstrate that ludic discursive practices are critical to the creation and navigation of interactional meaning in online contexts.

Whereas the chapters thus far have applied theoretical and methodical frameworks of anthropology (chapter 2), sociology (chapters 5 and 7), interactional sociolinguistics (chapter 6), and politeness theory (chapter 8), in chapter 9, "Mock Performatives in Online Discussion Boards: Toward a Discourse-Pragmatic Model of Computer-Mediated Communication," Tuija Virtanen applies and contributes to the semantic theory of performativity by examining the use of the word "hereby" in what she characterizes as "mock performatives" on a discussion board devoted to beauty and fashion. She introduces the term "discourse transformer" to highlight the way that these mock performatives signal a shift into a "play mode" by referencing a familiar institutional script. She ends by suggesting that her analysis provides a discourse pragmatic model for the study of performativity in computer-mediated communication.

Chapter 10, "Re- and Pre-authoring Experiences in Email Supervision: Creating and Revising Professional Meanings in an Asynchronous Medium," by Cynthia Gordon and Melissa Luke, focuses on the commonly practiced but little studied use of email in exchanges between student interns and their supervisors in a counselor education and training program. Drawing on and developing Bakhtin's notion of dialogue, the authors show that supervisors' "reinforcement" and "reframing" of interns' discourse constitutes a kind of "re-authorship," while their practice of advice giving constitutes a kind of "pre-authorship." The authors' analysis identifies the linguistic devices by which these goals are accomplished, thereby documenting how email is used in the development of professional identity within this educational environment.

An educational context is also the subject of chapter 11, "Blogs: A Medium for Intellectual Engagement with Course Readings and Participants," by Marianna Ryshina-Pankova and Jens Kugele. The data for this chapter are blog entries written by students in a college course as part of an online discussion of course readings. The authors apply the systemic-functional framework of ENGAGEMENT to identify the linguistic strategies the students use, and the extent to which these strategies evidence learning—that is, knowledge construction and sharing. The Bakhtinian concept of dialogicality enables them to provide insight into how students use interactive blogs to account for their positions, establish authority, integrate information from various sources in intersubjective stancetaking, and accomplish tasks and activities that the authors identify as being essential to academic learning and knowledge construction. This chapter thus illustrates how interactive blogs can function in a college course, and offers evidence for their efficacy as a vehicle for learning.

Chapter 12, "Reading in Print or Onscreen: Better, Worse, or About the Same?" is the third to focus on an educational context. Naomi Baron begins with a survey and discussion of print culture, then examines how electronic books change one's conception as well as use of written texts. She then describes and presents the results of a pilot study she conducted to compare college students' reading in these two media, in order to answer the question posed by her title: What respective advantages and disadvantages do the students report with regard to reading on paper and on screens? She concludes with a discussion of how the frequent use of electronic reading material is transforming students' attitudes toward and assumptions about texts as well as their tendencies to multitask. In exploring the effects of the internet upon cognition, Baron's chapter thus addresses issues of global import to individuals' lives and to society at large.

That broader perspective characterizes the final chapter as well. In chapter 13, "Fakebook: Synthetic Media, Pseudo-sociality, and the Rhetorics of Web 2.0," Crispin Thurlow offers a global word of caution about the "often hyperbolic claims about 'social media' made in the context of education, the media, commerce, and politics." Aligning himself with the subfield of critical discourse studies and other approaches that address the role of language in societal power relations, Thurlow shows that entities with institutional power and commercial motives, such as advertisers, corporations, and politicians, invoke "highly stylized, commoditized notions of language and communication" to create a false impression of sociality. Much as Baron cautions about some negative effects of reading online, Thurlow concludes by cautioning that the institutional use of discourse that mimics the social functions of talk in interpersonal interaction threatens to blur distinctions between "the public and private, the personal and institutional, and the corporate and social."

To bring this overview full circle, we conclude by observing that, taken together, the chapters in this volume, like the many papers presented at GURT 2011, support Susan Herring's observation that if this work "demonstrates only one thing, it should be that Discourse 2.0 offers a rich field of investigation for discourse analysts"—and, we might add, that the field of discourse analysis offers a rich source of insight into the language of new media and the way it is shaping human lives.

1

Discourse in Web 2.0: Familiar, Reconfigured, and Emergent

SUSAN C. HERRING

Indiana University Bloomington

Introduction

FROM CONTROVERSIAL BEGINNINGS, the term Web 2.0 has become associated with a fairly well-defined set of popular web-based platforms characterized by social interaction and user-generated content. Most of the content on such sites is human discourse, via text, audio, video, and static images. It is therefore, in principle, of theoretical and practical interest to scholars of computer-mediated discourse. Yet although discourse-focused studies of individual Web 2.0 environments such as Facebook, Flickr, Twitter, and YouTube are starting to appear (see, for example, the chapters in Thurlow and Mroczek 2011), systematic consideration of the implications of Web 2.0 for computer-mediated discourse analysis (CMDA) as a whole is lacking. Does discourse in these new environments call for new methods of analysis? New classificatory apparatuses? New theoretical understandings? In this chapter I attempt to address these questions.

After defining Web 2.0 and reviewing its development over the past decade, the CMDA paradigm developed by the author (Herring 2004) is briefly reviewed, with the ultimate goal of determining whether—and if so, in what ways—it needs to be revised in light of Web 2.0. As a heuristic to address this goal, I introduce a three-part classification of Web 2.0 discourse phenomena: phenomena *familiar* from older computer-mediated discourse (CMD) modes such as email, chat, and discussion forums that appear to carry over into Web 2.0 environments with minimal differences; CMD phenomena that adapt to and are *reconfigured* by Web 2.0 environments; and new or emergent phenomena that did not exist—or if they did exist, did not rise to the level of public awareness—prior to the era of Web 2.0. This classification is loosely inspired by Crowston and Williams's (2000) broad classification of web pages into "reproduced" versus "emergent" genres, but with a focus on discourse, rather than genre.

I suggest that this three-way classification can provide insight into why particular discourse phenomena persist, adapt, or arise anew in technologically mediated environments over time. In so doing, I invoke technological factors such as multimodality and media convergence, social factors at both the situational and cultural levels, and inherent differences among linguistic phenomena that make them variably sensitive to technological and social effects. Suggestions are also made of practical ways in which the classification might guide researchers to frame their studies and select certain methods of analysis. While the reconfigured and emergent categories are especially attractive in that they present new phenomena and raise special challenges for analysts of CMD, I argue that researchers should not neglect what appears familiar in favor of pursuing newness or novelty: all three categories merit research attention, for different reasons.

Background

The World Wide Web itself is not new. It was pitched as a concept by physicist Tim Berners-Lee to his employers at the European Organization for Nuclear Research (CERN) in 1990, implemented by 1991, and attracted widespread attention after the first graphical browser, Mosaic, was launched in 1993.[1] The early websites of the mid-1990s tended to be single-authored, fairly static documents; they included personal homepages, lists of frequently asked questions (FAQs), and ecommerce sites. The late 1990s saw a shift toward more dynamic, interactive websites, however: notably blogs (Herring et al. 2004) and online newssites (Kutz and Herring 2005), the content of which could be—and often was—updated frequently and which allowed users to leave comments on the site. These sites foreshadowed what later came to be called Web 2.0.

What Is Web 2.0?

The term "Web 2.0" was first used in 2004 when Tim O'Reilly, a web entrepreneur in California, decided to call a conference he was organizing for "leaders of the Internet Economy [to] gather to debate and determine business strategy" the "Web 2.0 Conference" (Battelle and O'Reilly 2010; O'Reilly 2005). At the time, the meaning of the term was vague—more aspirational and inspirational than descriptive. As a business strategy, Web 2.0 was supposed to involve viral marketing rather than advertising and a focus on services over products. One of O'Reilly's mantras is "Applications get better the more people use them" (Linden 2006). Today the term refers, according to Wikipedia (2011b) and other online sources, to *changing trends in, and new uses of,* web technology and web design, especially involving participatory information sharing; user-generated content; an ethic of collaboration; and use of the web as a social platform. The term may also refer to the *types of sites* that manifest these uses, such as blogs, wikis, social network sites, and media-sharing sites.

From the outset, the notion of Web 2.0 was controversial. Critics claimed that it was just a marketing buzzword, or perhaps a meme—an idea that is passed electronically from one internet user to another—rather than a true revolution in web content and use as its proponents claimed. They questioned whether the web was qualitatively different in recent years than it had been before, and whether the applications grouped under the label Web 2.0—including such diverse phenomena as online auction sites, photosharing sites, collaboratively authored encyclopedias, social bookmarking sites, news aggregators, and microblogs—formed a coherent set. Tim Berners-Lee's answer to these questions was no—for the inventor of the web, the term suffered from excessive hype and lack of definition (Anderson 2006).

■ Table 1.1
Web 2.0 vs. Web 1.0 phenomena (adapted from O'Reilly 2005)

Web 1.0	Web 2.0
Personal websites	Blogging
Publishing	Participation
Britannica Online	Wikipedia
Content-management systems	Wikis
Stickiness	Syndication
Directories (taxonomies)	Tagging (folksonomies)

In response to such criticisms, O'Reilly (2005) provided a chart to illustrate the differences between Web 2.0 and what he retroactively labeled "Web 1.0." This is shown in modified and simplified form in table 1.1. The phenomena in the second column are intended to be the Web 2.0 analogs of the phenomena in the first column.

This is no more than a list, however; it does not provide a principled way to determine what should or should not be included as "Web 2.0." An alternative approach to conceptualizing Web 2.0 is from a temporal perspective. Most Web 2.0 phenomena emerged over the last decade; indeed, one criticism of the concept is that it seems to mean nothing more than "recent websites"—paving the way for "Web 3.0," Web 4.0," etc., to describe ever-newer web-based phenomena in the future. Figure 1.1 situates phenomena that exhibit characteristics of "Web 2.0" along a timeline for roughly the first decade of the twenty-first century. The phenomena included in the figure are not intended to be exhaustive in any sense; however, an attempt has been made to include important exemplars of a range of phenomena. In the figure, applications that run on a platform other than the web but otherwise have characteristics of Web 2.0 are indicated in lighter text; Web 2.0 sites that were launched before O'Reilly coined the term in 2004 are indicated in black type; and Web 2.0 sites launched since 2004 are in bold type.[2]

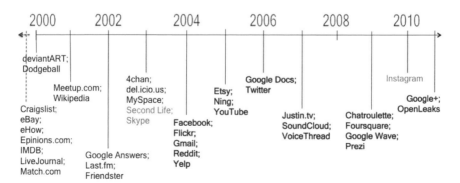

■ Figure 1.1 Web 2.0 timeline (selective).

The most recent decade of collaborative communicative technologies is not a perfect match with Web 2.0 in the strict sense. Not all of the applications mentioned in figure 1.1 are based in the web—for example, Second Life (a three-dimensional graphical world) and Skype (a form of internet telephony) are applications that run on the internet but not on the web, and Instagram, a recently introduced photosharing application, runs on mobile phones (although it can share with web-based social network sites). Moreover, a number of sites commonly considered to be Web 2.0 were launched before 2004, and some—such as eBay, blog-hosting sites (such as LiveJournal), and online dating sites—go back to the 1990s. Nonetheless, with these exceptions, and together with the characteristics of the sites themselves, the timeline suggests some conceptual coherence that can be attributed to these phenomena. Thus, for the purpose of this chapter, the following redefinition of Web 2.0 is proposed: web-based platforms that emerged as popular in the first decade of the twenty-first century, and that incorporate user-generated content and social interaction, often alongside or in response to structures or (multimedia) content provided by the sites themselves.

Computer-Mediated Discourse Analysis, Media Convergence, and "Discourse 2.0"

The second key background component of this chapter is discourse analysis and, specifically, the approach to analyzing online discourse that I have developed over the past seventeen years, CMDA. CMDA is an approach to the analysis of computer-mediated communication (CMC) focused on language and language use; it is also a set of methods (a toolkit) grounded in linguistic discourse analysis for mining networked communication for patterns of structure and meaning, broadly construed (Herring 2004).[3]

The term "computer-mediated discourse analysis" was first used as the name of a GURT workshop I organized in 1994. Since then it has evolved into a model organized around four levels of CMDA: structure, meaning, interaction management, and social phenomena (Herring 2004). The organizational principle of the CMDA toolkit is fairly simple: The basic idea is to adapt existing methods, primarily from linguistics (but in principle from any relevant discipline that analyzes discourse), to the properties of digital communication media. The methods and the phenomena, along with broader issues they address, are then loosely mapped onto four levels of hierarchy, from the microlinguistic, more context-independent level of structure to the macrolevel of contextualized social phenomena, as summarized in table 1.2. (A nonlinguistic level—participation—is sometimes included as well.)

However, in the time since the CMDA approach was originally conceptualized, CMC itself has been undergoing a shift, from occurrence in stand-alone clients such as emailers and instant messaging programs to juxtaposition with other content, often of an information or entertainment nature, in converged media platforms, where it is typically secondary, by design, to other information or entertainment-related activities (Herring 2009; Zelenkauskaite and Herring 2008). This phenomenon, which I refer to as convergent media computer-mediated communication (CMCMC), is especially common on Web 2.0 sites. Examples include text comments on photosharing sites; text (and video) responses to YouTube videos; text (and voice) chat dur-

Table 1.2
Four levels of CMDA (adapted from Herring 2004)

Levels	Issues	Phenomena	Methods
Structure	Orality, formality, complexity, efficiency, expressivity, genre characteristics, etc.	Typography, orthography, morphology, syntax, discourse schemata, formatting conventions, etc.	Structural/descriptive linguistics, text analysis, stylistics
Meaning	What is intended, what is communicated, what is accomplished	Meaning of words, utterances (speech acts), exchanges, etc.	Semantics, pragmatics
Interaction management	Interactivity, timing, coherence, repair, interaction as co-constructed, etc.	Turns, sequences, exchanges, threads, etc.	Conversation analysis, ethnomethodology
Social phenomena	Social dynamics, power, influence, identity, community, cultural differences, etc.	Linguistic expressions of status, conflict, negotiation, face-management, play, discourse styles/lects, etc.	Interactional sociolinguistics, critical discourse analysis, ethnography of communication

ing multiplayer online games; and text messages from mobile phones posted to interactive TV programs. Less prototypically (because it involves the convergence of text with text rather than the convergence of text with another mode), CMCMC is also illustrated by reader comments on news stories; "talk" pages associated with Wikipedia articles; status updates and comments (and for that matter, chat and inbox exchanges) on Facebook profiles; and interpersonal and group exchanges on Twitter.[4]

In fact, the overlap between CMCMC and Web 2.0 is considerable. Almost all so-called Web 2.0 sites feature CMCMC, and almost all CMCMC applications are on the web. An exception to the former is social bookmarking sites such as del.icio.us, which do not contain CMC; an exception to the latter is text chat in multiplayer online games such as World of Warcraft, which are not hosted on the web. However, the trend is for increasing convergence, and it would not be surprising if these distinctions disappeared in the future. In what follows, it is assumed that Web 2.0 generally involves CMCMC.

The discourse in these new environments—what we might call convergent media computer-mediated discourse (CMCMD) or Discourse 2.0—raises many issues for CMDA. There are new types of *content* to be analyzed: status updates, text annotations on video, tags on social bookmarking sites, and edits on wikis. New *contexts* must also be considered—for example, social network sites based on geographic location—as well as new (mass media) audiences, including in other languages and cultures. (Facebook, for example, now exists in localized versions in well over one hundred languages [Lenihan 2011].) Discourse 2.0 manifests new *usage patterns,* as well, such as media coactivity, or near-simultaneous multiple activities on a single platform (Herring et al. 2009) and multiauthorship, or joint discourse production (Androutsopoulos 2011; Nishimura 2011). The above reflect, in part, new *affordances* made available by new communication technologies: text chat in multiplayer online games (MOGs); collaboratively editable environments such as wikis; friending and friend circles on social network sites; social tagging and recommender systems; and so forth. Last but not least, Discourse 2.0 includes *user adaptations* to circumvent the constraints of Web 2.0 environments, such as interactive uses of @ and #, as well as retweeting, on Twitter (boyd, Golder, and Lotan 2010; Honeycutt and Herring 2009) and performed interactivity on what are, in essence, monologic blogs (Peterson 2011; Puschmann 2013). Each of these issues deserves attention, and some are starting to be addressed, but on a case-by-case, rather than a systemic, basis.

In the face of so many apparently new phenomena, one might question whether Discourse 2.0 should continue to be called CMD. The term "computer-mediated" originally referenced the term "computer-mediated communication," which is still preferred by communication scholars. But communication technologies are increasingly moving beyond computers. Mobile phones can be considered honorary computers, but voice calls, for example, challenge that characterization, as does television-mediated conversation via text messages (Zelenkauskaite and Herring 2008). Some recent discourse-focused publications use such alternative terms as "digital media" and "new media" discourse. However, the term "new media" is lacking in historical perspective, and "digital media" is too broad, referring as it does to video games as well as communication devices, although "digital discourse" (Thurlow and Mroczek 2011) makes clear that discourse is in focus. Conversely, the term "keyboard-to-screen communication" proposed by Jucker and Dürscheid (2012) is too narrow, in that it excludes communication input via audio and video technologies. It well may be that in the coming years, the dust will settle and a descriptive term that is neither too narrow nor too broad will emerge as the obvious candidate. For now, CMD and CMDA still seem useful terms, in that they make the link to CMC transparent and are based on established tradition, so they will continue to be used in the remainder of this chapter.

Discourse in Web 2.0: An Organizational Lens

As a conceptual aid to making sense of Discourse 2.0 on a larger scale, I propose a three-part organizational lens, a broad categorization scheme according to which discourse in Web 2.0 environments can be classified. This scheme challenges the prima facie assumption that all phenomena that seem new actually are new, classifying them instead in relation to their antecendents (or lack of antecedents) as *familiar, reconfigured,* or *emergent.* At first blush, the scheme may appear simply to reproduce chronology—older phenomena might be expected to be familiar, and new ones to be emergent—but in fact it does not. As the discussion below shows, the reverse pattern sometimes holds.

Web Genre Classification

The Discourse 2.0 classification scheme proposed here was inspired by Crowston and Williams (2000), who in the mid-1990s were among the first scholars to attempt to classify genres of web pages. They proposed a simple, two-way classification—reproduced versus emergent—but noted that some pages could be classified as adaptations of reproduced genres.

The following are examples of Crowston and Williams's categories applied to traditional web content. Reproduced content (sometimes referred to as "shovelware") includes course syllabi, scholarly articles, and meeting minutes, which in the early years of the web (and sometimes still) were often created with word processing software offline and simply uploaded to the web. Adapted genres include news sites, genealogy sites, and ejournals, which have tended to preserve the basic genre conventions of their offline precursors—but with adaptations, such as user commenting and hyperlinking, that leverage the affordances of the web. As examples of emergent genres, Crowston and Williams mention hotlists of links and personal homepages; blogs and wikis have also been claimed to be indigenous to the web (Blood 2002; Wagner 2004). In the case of blogs, however, several scholars (Herring et al. 2004; Miller and Shepherd 2004) have pointed out the continuities between paper diary writing, for example, and blogging—such that nowadays most blog researchers would consider blogs to be an adapted genre. As this last case illustrates, there is a general ahistoricity that characterizes much new media research and a tendency to claim newness when historical precedents in fact exist; this is a risk associated with applying Crowston and Williams's classification. The scheme can also be somewhat subjective, depending on what facets of a web genre one chooses to focus on and the familiarity of the researcher with previous genres. Nonetheless, the classification can lead to interesting insights.

One such insight is that there appears to be a trend over time for web genres to shift along a continuum from reproduced to adapted to emergent, with the seemingly paradoxical effect that as genres age, they move along the continuum in the direction of "emergence." An example is online news sites, which tended to be *reproduced* from print newspapers in the early days but have become increasingly *adapted* to the web with the inclusion of user comments, multimedia, hyperlinks, and other interactivity and navigation features (Eriksen and Ihlström 2000). Similarly, the social network site Facebook initially combined the format of "face books" from Harvard University dormitories with web-based features such as commenting (Wikipedia 2011c) and was thus *adapted,* but over time it has added and combined so many features (including embedded graphics, games, polls, and various modes of CMC) that it can now arguably be considered *emergent.* This is not just because of the number of features, but because the whole is qualitatively different from the sum of its parts, and it has no single offline or online precedent.

This trend is consistent with the observation in media studies that new information and communication technologies (ICTs) are first put mainly to old uses, and uses that take advantage of the full potential of the technologies emerge only later, if at all (Winston 1998). In the case of web genres, the mechanisms underlying this shift are, on the one hand, the incorporation of new media affordances into familiar text types, and on the other hand, increasing media convergence. When familiar media combine, they often do so in ways that result in qualitatively different phenomena that can be considered new or emergent.

In the present classification scheme, the term "familiar" is used rather than "reproduced" to suggest continuities in (rather than copies of earlier) discourse phenomena. Familiar patterns are presumed to have manifested more or less continuously on the web from the 1990s until the present, albeit not necessarily on the same sites. The term "reconfigured," rather than "adapted," is used to highlight the structural reshaping of some discourse phenomena that takes place in Web 2.0 environments. To be sure, users adapt to changes in ICTs, but their adaptations are only relevant to CMDA when they manifest in tangible discourse behaviors. However, the term "emergent" is preserved from Crowston and Williams (2000), in that new web genres and discourse phenomena can equally be described as emerging—that is, becoming evident where previously there was no general awareness of their existence.

A Three-Part Classification Scheme
In the following sections the proposed rubric of familiar-reconfigured-emergent is applied to classify examples of Web 2.0 discourse phenomena, with discussion of some of the challenges each category raises for CMDA.

Familiar Aspects of Web 2.0 Discourse   Contrary to the impression conveyed by much new media research that almost everything on the web today is new and different, a great deal—and perhaps the majority—of Web 2.0 discourse phenomena are familiar. For one thing, text remains the predominant channel of communication among web users, whether in blogs, microblogs, wikis, comments on news sites, or web discussion forums. The latter, in particular, remain very popular and illustrate many of the same kinds of phenomena as did asynchronous online forums in the 1990s. These include nonstandard typography and orthography, code switching, gender differences, flaming, and email hoaxes and scams.[5]

Contemporary practices, especially when situated in new environments, may not seem familiar at first blush. Vaisman (2011) recently documented a creative typographic practice among Israeli preteen girl bloggers that she calls "Fakatsa" style (*fakatsa* means a silly, fashion-conscious girl), in which letters of the Hebrew alphabet are replaced by characters of similar appearance, including numbers, symbols, and letters from the roman alphabet. Vaisman gives the following example, the user ID of one of the bloggers, which translates as "Gal [a Hebrew name] the hot babe":

$$\sim\text{תי}§!¢\text{ה}\sim5\text{ג}°:\bullet$$

In standard Hebrew typography, this name would be written גל הכוסית. The section symbol (§) in the Fakatsa version replaces the Hebrew letter that resembles (in this font) a small O, the cent symbol (¢) replaces the Hebrew letter that looks like a backward C, and the Arabic numeral 5 substitutes for the Hebrew letter *lamed* (ל); these substitutions are based loosely on graphical resemblance. Moreover, the Fakatsa version of the word includes extra symbols—such as a tilde (~) in two places and the dots on the right—that are purely decorative.

On the face of it, Fakatsa writing appears novel and exotic. Although nonstandard typography and orthography are familiar characteristics of CMC (netspeak expressions such as "ur gr8" [You're great] themselves have antecedents in offline writing [Crystal 2008]), Fakatsa seems to take this practice to a new level, including requiring norms of reading that differ from those for netspeak. Yet as Vaisman points out, Fakatsa shows many parallels with *leetspeak* or *leet*, an English subcultural variety that originated with computer hackers in the 1980s. Leet replaces letters from the roman alphabet with non-alphabetic characters and symbols based on visual resemblance, similar to Fakatsa, as illustrated in the following example: "1 k4n 7¥p3 1337" (I can type leet). The similarities between the two varieties do not appear to be due to any direct contact between them; rather, they share a common generative principle that appears to have been exploited spontaneously in the two different writing systems (for further examples of graphic-based substitutions in computer-mediated Arabic and Greek typography, see Danet and Herring 2007). This example illustrates the first level of CMDA: structure.

Historical continuities in CMD are also evident on the broader level of social interaction. Gender differences in discourse style were documented in public online discussion forums and chat rooms throughout the 1990s that showed males to be more assertive, insulting, sarcastic, and profane, and females to be more accommodating, supportive, affectionate, and upbeat (Cherny 1994; Herring 1993, 2003a). These patterns reproduced gender styles in spoken conversation as described by Tannen (1990). Moreover, despite a tendency of scholars and lay people alike to imagine that such stylistic differences reflect outmoded gender role differences that have tended to disappear over time, a recent study of teen chat sites (Kapidzic and Herring 2011a) found similar differences in message tone: In 2011, males were still significantly more aggressive and flirtatious and tended to be more sexual, whereas females were significantly more friendly in their chat messages. Girls also still used more emoticons, especially those representing smiles and laughter, than boys did (Kapidzic and Herring 2011b), as shown in figure 1.3. Similar to the findings of earlier research (such as Wolf 2000), the only emoticon that boys used more was the winking face, which is associated with both sarcasm and flirtation.

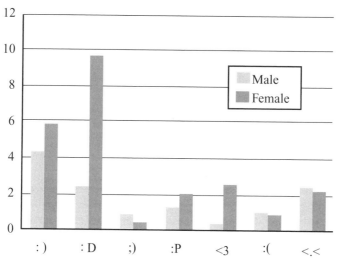

Figure 1.3 Emoticon use in teen chat by gender per 1000 words (Kapidzic and Herring 2011b).

Familiar Discourse 2.0 phenomena lend themselves readily to CMDA in its current form, since they are the kinds of phenomena the paradigm was designed to address. The challenges they pose mainly concern identification: familiar phenomena may be mistaken for new (as a researcher unfamiliar with leet might be tempted to do with Fakatsa) or assumed to be different by virtue of the passage of time (as in the case of online gender styles). There is a need to trace relevant antecedents to gain perspective where familiar online discourse phenomena are concerned, in order to do conscientious research. This, in turn, requires some familiarity with earlier CMDA research. Alternatively, familiar phenomena may simply be passed over by researchers in favor of newer, more exotic CMD phenomena.

Reconfigured Aspects of Web 2.0 Discourse   Although Discourse 2.0 may not be as different as popular belief holds, changes have taken place in both technology and communicative practices. These have resulted in the reconfiguration or reshaping of a number of aspects of CMD. Examples include personal status messages, quoting others' messages, small stories,[6] and customized advertising spam—which might on the surface appear new but have traceable online antecedents—as well as reconfigurations of such familiar phenomena as topical coherence, turn-taking, threading, and intertextuality.

As a first illustration, let us consider personal status updates of the sort that have been popularized on Facebook and Twitter, in response to a generic prompt such as "What are you doing?" "What's on your mind?" or "What's happening?" The issues raised by the analysis of status updates involve the CMDA levels of structure (syntax), meaning (semantics and pragmatics), and interaction management. Lee (2011) provides the following examples in her study of Hong Kong users of Facebook, which compares the communicative functions of status updates produced before and after Facebook changed the default response format from "[Name] is" (with the third-person singular form of the verb "to be") to simply "[Name]":

1. Amy is in a good mood.
2. Snow is "I've seen you in the shadow."
3. Kenneth quitting facebook.
4. Ariel thinks that no news is good news.
5. Katy: ?

Example 1 is a grammatical sentence formed from the prompt "Amy [name of user] is." Example 2 is also built on the "name is" prompt, but what follows ("I've seen you in the shadow") is a song lyric; the result is not a grammatical sentence. Status update 3 ("Kenneth quitting facebook") is also ungrammatical, but for a different reason: it lacks the auxiliary verb "is," which by this time had been omitted from the default Facebook prompt. The presence, explicit or implicit, of "is" in the Facebook response format thus results in some status descriptions that are syntactically nonstandard.

The update in 4 ("Ariel thinks that no news is good news"), in contrast, is syntactically well formed, but pragmatically appropriate in the simple present tense only if Ariel's thinking is generally true, which is not the most likely interpretation in this context (it is more likely that Ariel is responding to some specific news, or lack thereof).

This use of simple present tense is presumably a carryover of the simple present tense of the former "is" in the prompt. Its use in place of, say, the present progressive lends the utterance a performative feel, as if Ariel performs the act of thinking that no news is good news by typing it. Finally, if Katy's status update in 5—consisting of only a question mark (presumably to indicate that she is confused or does not know what to say)— is treated as an utterance, it is both syntactically and pragmatically ill formed.[7]

In fact, these kinds of utterances have characterized CMC since the early days of Internet Relay Chat (IRC [Werry 1996]) and MUDs and MOOs (text-based virtual reality environments [Cherny 1994, 1995, 1999]). Those chat environments made available special commands (called "action descriptions" on IRC and "emotes" on MUDs and MOOs) that produced third-person present tense descriptions of first-person actions and states, such as "Chris is in a bad mood" and "Lynn waves." These often had a performative flavor, especially when used to describe actions rather than states (for further discussion of performativity in CMD, see Virtanen (2013) and chapter 9, this volume. Utterances that play with the convention itself, analogous to example 5 above, were also common in early chat environments (in a perfect parallel, Cherny 1999 gives examples of MOO utterances consisting solely of "[Name] ?" as well as "null-emotes," emotes left intentionally blank such that only the username appears).

However, status updates do not simply reproduce these earlier practices. Rather, they have been structurally and functionally reconfigured in comparison to action descriptions and emotes. Syntactically, the inclusion of "is" in an earlier version of Facebook has led to a greater use of "is" constructions, even when these are not prescriptively correct. One of my Facebook friends has continued to start each of his updates with "[Name] is," inserting the "is" as a stylistic affectation even when another finite verb is present in the utterance, e.g., "[Name] is has a headache." Functionally, status updates on Twitter and Facebook serve as prompts that trigger comment threads, unlike the earlier constructions, which were single utterances.

The second example of a reconfigured phenomenon also involves interaction management—specifically, repeating parts of another participant's message in one's own message to create cross-message coherence. "Retweeting" on Twitter is the inclusion of a previous message ("tweet") in a new message, sometimes with a comment added. boyd, Golder, and Lotan (2010) give the following typical example:

RT @StopAhmadi Bring down Khomeini's website

Here, the (unidentified) user makes use of the abbreviation RT to retweet wholesale a tweet that was originally addressed to StopAhmadi (on the uses of @ as an addressivity marker, see Honeycutt and Herring 2009). Presumably the retweeter does this for the purpose of spreading further the sentiment expressed in the original tweet, *Bring down Khomeini's website.*

Another example of retweeting given by boyd, Golder, and Lotan is more complex, in that it contains multiple levels of embedding:

@AndreaJarrell: Via @mStonerblog: RT @zephoria: new blog post "Is Facebook for old people?" socioecon and race are most interesting here http://bit.ly/v0aPS.

In this tweet the user is addressing to AndreaJarrell a message originally received from mStonerblog, who in turn retweeted a message from zephoria ("new blog post 'Is Facebook for old people?' http://bit.ly/v0aPS"). (The latter two instances of @ conventionally signal that what follows is a Twitter username and can effectively be ignored for the purposes of understanding this tweet.) To complicate the message further, the user inserts a comment of his or her own ("socioecon and race are most interesting here") before zephoria's link.

On the face of it, retweeting might seem a prime example of a discourse phenomenon that is new and that has arisen in response to the novel affordances and constraints of Twitter. In fact, retweeting is a modern form of the older practice in textual CMC of "quoting" in asynchronous messages (Severinson Eklundh 2010; Severinson Eklundh and Macdonald 1994). Quoted and retweeted segments are both flagged by a conventional symbol (an angle bracket [>] preceding each quoted line in Usenet, where the convention originated; RT in Twitter). Both incorporate the words of others in one's own message (intertextuality, to establish context), and embedded quotations such as those in Twitter example 2 above can occur in both CMC modes. The following schematic from Severinson Eklundh (2010) illustrates multiple embeddings in a traditional asynchronous system (fig. 1.4).

Although some systems include quoted text automatically when the user responds using the reply function, users can also set the default such that quoted text is not included or edit the quoted text selectively. Evidence of the latter can be seen in the message in figure 1.4, especially where B had previously responded to A point by point, interleaving his text (at two levels of embedding) with text by A (at three levels of embedding).

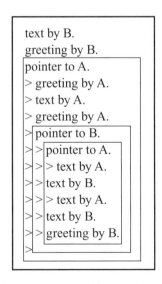

text by B.
greeting by B.
pointer to A.
> greeting by A.
> text by A.
> greeting by A.
> pointer to B.
> > pointer to A.
> > > text by A.
> > text by B.
> > > text by A.
> > text by B.
> > greeting by B.
>

Figure 1.4 Schematic structure of a message received by A with three levels of quotation (Severinson Eklundh 2010).

As the figure suggests, in quoting the repeated material is set off on a separate line, whereas on Twitter, because of the character limit on tweets, quoted and non-quoted material appear together without line breaks, giving the two practices different surface appearances. Retweeting can thus be considered a form of quoting that is adapted to, and reconfigured by, the Twitter environment. The reconfiguration involves condensing quoted content to fit within 140 characters, including omitting information and reducing URLs to abbreviated bit.ly links, and using new (user-generated) conventions for referring or attributing, resulting in a visually very different format (that includes a small image of the sender, as well) but with a similar underlying function.

The third and last example of a reconfigured phenomenon also involves interaction management, this time with a focus on topical coherence. Conversational exchanges on many Web 2.0 platforms tend to be prompt focused—that is, comments respond to an initial prompt, such as a news story, a photo, or a video, more often than to other users' responses. Although this pattern was attested in older CMD, notably in online learning contexts in which students responded to an instructor's prompt, it was not common in public discourse on the internet. Rather, patterns of topical development tended to involve stepwise digression away from the original topic in multiparty exchanges in chat rooms (Herring 1999) and discussion forums (Lambiase 2010). These differing patterns are illustrated in figure 1.5 using the Visual DTA (Dynamic Topic Analysis) tool developed by Herring and Kurtz (2006). The diagram on the left, showing the prompt-focused pattern, represents a Flickr (photosharing site) community comment thread in response to a photograph of a dog in a party hat (Herring 2009), and the diagram on the right, showing stepwise topical digression, represents a conversation on a recreational IRC channel (Herring 2003b). In the diagrams, messages are numbered in chronological order along the y axis, and the x axis represents cumulative semantic distance from the initiating message.

Both diagrams illustrate thematically coherent patterns of interaction involving multiple participants that begin with an initial prompt, but in the Flickr comment thread (and much other Discourse 2.0) responses are mostly directed to the prompt throughout, resulting in limited topical development, whereas in the IRC example the topic shifts progressively from the upper left to the lower right through interaction among participants. The former pattern can be considered an adaptation of topical coherence to CMCMC environments in which entertainment and news content is presented for users to consume and comment on. As a consequence of this adaptation, patterns of interaction are reconfigured not just at the individual level but at the group level.

Because they may appear quite different on the surface, reconfigured phenomena are at an even greater risk than familiar phenomena of being mistaken for emergent CMD, with consequent loss of comparative insight. An additional challenge posed by reconfigured phenomena for CMDA is the need to abstract common structures, functions, or social dynamics across different media affordances in order to identify what they are reconfigured from and the reasons for the reconfigurations.

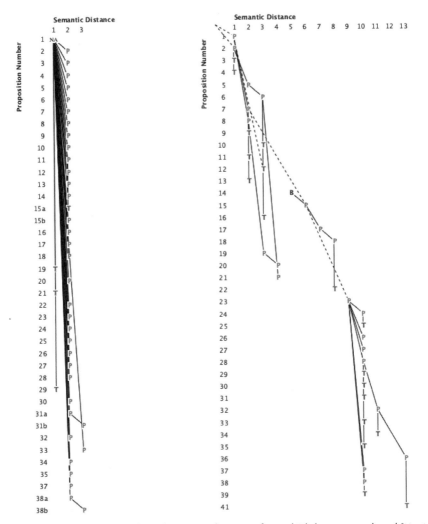

■ Figure 1.5 Two patterns of topical development. Left: prompt focused (Flickr comment thread [Herring 2009]). Right: stepwise progression (Internet Relay Chat [Herring 2003b]).

Emergent Aspects of Web 2.0 Discourse   Given that much of what has been claimed to be un-precedented on the web has been found, upon deeper examination, to have online or offline antecedents (or both), caution must be exercised in asserting that any phenom-enon is entirely new. This section tentatively identifies several Web 2.0 discourse phe-nomena that appear to be emergent and unprecedented, at least as common practices.[8] These include the dynamic collaborative discourse that takes place on wikis, along with conversational video exchanges, conversational exchanges via image texts, and multimodal conversation more generally. In the domain of non-bona fide discourse, the phenomena of sock puppets and link building are also mentioned.

Collaborative text production of the sort that takes place on Wikipedia represents a new kind of online discourse. It is democratic and anarchic: There is no central organization, and anyone can contribute to any part of a text. It is massively multi-authored by internet users who usually do not know one another. It leaves a manifest trace both front stage, in article pages, and backstage (Goffman 1959) in talk and user pages. Moreover, every addition, deletion, or alteration of the text is preserved in history pages, which in themselves constitute a new kind of text. It is process focused rather than product focused (Wagner 2004); even its most stable content, articles, are dynamic documents subject to frequent updating. To be sure, texts such as group reports are sometimes constructed collaboratively in offline contexts, but typically each person is responsible for one part; the number of contributors is limited; their talk about the task is ephemeral; the tasks are centrally coordinated; and at some point, the product is deemed complete and no further editing takes place. The anarchic nature of contribution to Wikipedia, in combination with the platform's ease of updating and technical affordances that make process visible, results in a discourse context that seems qualitatively unprecedented.

Interestingly, despite being arrived at by entirely different means, the text of Wikipedia articles can be strikingly similar to that of traditional print encyclopedias, both in quality of content (Giles 2005) and in style (Emigh and Herring 2005). In a corpus-based analysis of structural markers of formality and informality in fifteen articles in four corpora—Wikipedia, Everything2 (an online knowledge repository in which articles are individually authored), a traditional print encyclopedia, and Wikipedia talk pages—Emigh and Herring found that the degree of formality in Wikipedia and the traditional encyclopedia was statistically identical, whereas Everything2 and the talk pages were significantly less formal. As an explanation for this counterintuitive result, Emigh and Herring suggested that Wikipedia contributors have internalized cultural norms of encyclopedic style, which includes formality. However, this does not explain how the collaborative editing process takes place over time, or how hundreds of strangers come to an apparent consensus. A tool for visualizing the creation of Wikipedia articles over time has been developed by Viégas, Wattenberg, and Dave (2004), but it has yet to be applied by discourse analysts.

Another emergent Discourse 2.0 phenomenon is the use of channels other than text, and semiotic systems other than verbal language, to carry on conversational exchanges. Exchanges in which the turn unit is a video created by an individual and uploaded to a website have been analyzed by Pihlaja (2011) for YouTube, with a focus on verbal metaphor development; and by Kendall (2007) for a user-created animation sharing site, with a focus on the role of visual themes in creating cross-video coherence. McDonald (2007) analyzed conversational exchanges of still webcam images on a graphical community blog, describing four strategies used to create coherence across images: positional play (for example, showing a picture in which a person is pointing to another picture on the site that is outside the picture frame), animation, text-in-image, and image quotes. In image quotes, a picture or part of a picture posted by a previous contributor is used, sometimes with modification, in a response, as illustrated in the sequence in figure 1.6 (from McDonald 2007).

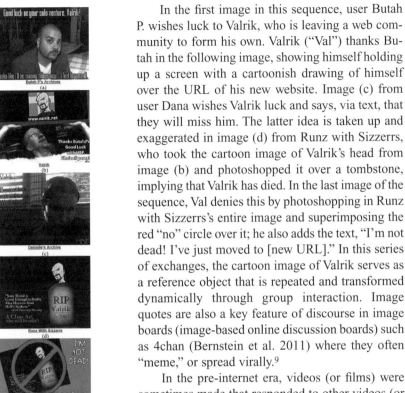

Figure 1.6 A conversation with image quotes from a community blog (Mc-Donald 2007).

In the first image in this sequence, user Butah P. wishes luck to Valrik, who is leaving a web community to form his own. Valrik ("Val") thanks Butah in the following image, showing himself holding up a screen with a cartoonish drawing of himself over the URL of his new website. Image (c) from user Dana wishes Valrik luck and says, via text, that they will miss him. The latter idea is taken up and exaggerated in image (d) from Runz with Sizzerrs, who took the cartoon image of Valrik's head from image (b) and photoshopped it over a tombstone, implying that Valrik has died. In the last image of the sequence, Val denies this by photoshopping in Runz with Sizzerrs's entire image and superimposing the red "no" circle over it; he also adds the text, "I'm not dead! I've just moved to [new URL]." In this series of exchanges, the cartoon image of Valrik serves as a reference object that is repeated and transformed dynamically through group interaction. Image quotes are also a key feature of discourse in image boards (image-based online discussion boards) such as 4chan (Bernstein et al. 2011) where they often "meme," or spread virally.[9]

In the pre-internet era, videos (or films) were sometimes made that responded to other videos (or films), but this practice was restricted mostly to artistic contexts due to the cost and special equipment required. Video is now cheaper and easier to create, enabling qualitatively different kinds of communication to take place. And although images with text have been around since the first illuminated manuscripts and include such familiar genres as comics and children's books, dynamic image texts that develop collaboratively, as in figure 1.6, appear to be a recent phenomenon—one enabled by popular access to drawing and photo modification software.

Media convergence is also resulting in a trend for multiple modes of verbal communication to coexist in the same platform. For example, an individual may respond (asynchronously) to a YouTube video either via text comments or video; may chat (synchronously) while playing World of Warcraft via text or voice; and may send text messages (either synchronous or asynchronous, depending on whether the addressee is logged on at the same time) and speak (synchronously) to an interlocutor over Skype. On these platforms the mode options are accessed somewhat differently and tend to be used for different communicative purposes (Newon 2011; Pihlaja 2011; Sindoni 2011), although they may be used contemporaneously. On the multimodal discussion site voicethread.com, in contrast, asynchronous conversations

("VoiceThreads") take place in which comments via text, audio, and video are fully integrated within a single interface display, as shown in figure 1.7. In the figure, the three modes of commenting are displayed as they appear when each type of message is played back in the VoiceThread interface. The case in point involves discussion of a video (in the center of the screen) about the dangers of speeding as part of a high school driver education class (from Herring and Demarest 2011).

The contents of the three comments in figure 1.7 are as follows.

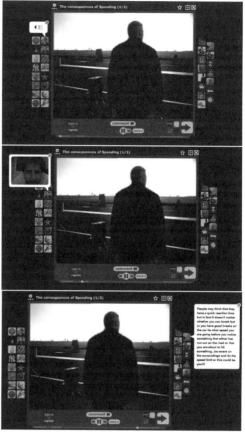

Figure 1.7 An audio comment (top), a video comment (middle), and a text comment (bottom) in a VoiceThread (Herring and Demarest 2011).

AUDIO [teacher]: Hey ya' guys, welcome to . . . VoiceThread. I want you to watch this video clip and give your feedback, either through a video recording or a voice recording. It's a short clip on speeding, and I'm interested to hear your thoughts.

VIDEO [teacher]: Hey hey! It's not actually Steve Perry, it's just me . . . checking this thing out. Uh, this video clip . . . is pretty neat, I think . . . I especially enjoy his Australian accent, and I know it's Australian bec- for a few reasons, uh . . . the biggest one of them obviously being that the car's steering wheel . . . is on the right hand side of the car! So. Another cool thing that I . . . liked about this video, other than the information in it, was the special effects they used, he—he's sorta walked out in front of the car, uh which . . . I wouldn't think anybody would normally do, but he did it! And, uh, Steve Perry—come back for us all, please!

TEXT [student]: People may think that they have a quick reaction time but in fact it doesn't matter whether you can break fast or you have good breaks [sic] on the car its what speed you are going before you notice something that either has run out on the road or that you are about to hit something. . . . Be aware on the surroundings and do the speed limit or this could be you!!!

Herring and Demarest argue that voicethread.com provides an unprecedented, authentic environment for research into mode choice, and they profit from it to analyze the effects of mode on participation by gender, expression of positive or negative attitude, and use of metadiscourse to index social awareness, all of which are found to vary according to mode. Audio and video comments in VoiceThreads are made more often by males than by females and contain more self-reference than text comments, whereas the text comments use more negative language than audio and video comments.

Some Web 2.0 sites take the trend towards convergence further by allowing users to embed text directly into video. An example is collaborative video annotations on YouTube, an innovation that came about when some users discovered that the URL to the interface that allows the person who uploads a video to add textual annonations to it could be shared with other users.[10] Howard (2011) analyzed the referents, tenor, and functional moves performed through such textual annotations posted by education students on videos of teachers teaching a class (see fig. 1.8), with the aim of determining the effectiveness of the environment in fostering critical discussion. His findings were mixed; critical moves were evident, but contributors made little reference to each others' comments, hence the discourse was not very interactive.

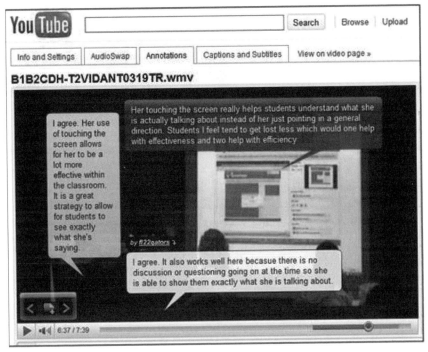

Figure 1.8 Collaborative text annotation on a YouTube video (Howard 2011).

Finally, in the domain of non-bona fide communication, artificial intelligence (AI) agents (or bots) have been present in online chat spaces since the early days of the public internet, and they have occasionally succeeded in fooling some people into thinking they were human (Turkle 1995). But recent developments have largely by-passed sophisticated AI, creating fraudulent participants in online forums through the manipulation, computational or otherwise, of simpler notions such as frequency and timing of participation. For example, multiple fake online personas called "sock pup-pets" are generated automatically and, posing as real people, made to join online fo-rums for various purposes, including posting comments to create the illusion of consensus on controversial issues (Romm 2011). Another practice, link building, in-volves unobtrusively inserting links to a company in web forums in order to boost the company's search engine ranking. One strategy for doing this is to infiltrate a fo-rum and post messages, and after the discussion has moved on to another topic (and the forum moderator is presumably no longer paying attention), edit one's posts to include the links (Haltom 2011). These practices raise the question of how the dis-course of non-bona fide participants (including and in addition to their participation patterns) differs from that of real participants, a question that CMD analysts are well qualified to address, and one that has practical implications for fraud detection.

With the exception of the articles cited above, however, little analysis of these new discourse phenomena has been conducted. A general challenge for emergent me-dia environments is that they need to be analyzed descriptively first before more so-phisticated, theoretically informed analyses can be carried out; this often results in a lag between the emergence of new environments and scholarly understanding of them. The discourse that takes place in emergent environments also raises numerous challenges for the CMDA paradigm. Non-bona fide discourse participants call for new ways of understanding participation. Wikis call for new conceptual understandings of what constitutes a text, what can be data for analysis, and what authorship means. Finally, multimodal discourse requires the analyst to devise new analytical methods and to draw from theoretical frameworks outside linguistics (such as visual semiotics). This last point leads to the question of whether multimodal discourse requires a new level of analysis in the CMDA toolkit, or whether it can be accommodated within the existing paradigm with the addition of semiotic methods to address each level. If the latter, at what level does integrative analysis of the meanings and functions of the com-plex whole take place, and what theories and methods exist to guide it? Table 1.3 sug-gests one possible format for incorporating multimodal discourse into the existing CMDA paradigm, as a new level.

Practically speaking, there is also a need to devise parallel transcription and vi-sualization displays for textual and nontextual communication, which differ in a num-ber of respects, including temporality. (Newon [2011] offers one approach to this in her study of text and voice chat in World of Warcraft.) Such displays should include the representation of silences, and the new norms and meanings surrounding them, in multimodal environments. Finally, it is likely that some apparently emergent phe-nomena will have antecedents that one is not aware of. Given the inherent difficulty of supporting a claim (of newness) that requires negative evidence, researchers need to be circumspect in making such claims.

■ Table 1.3
Multimodal communication as an additional level of CMDA

Level	Issues	Phenomena	Methods
Multimodal communication	Mode effects, cross-mode coherence, reference and address management, generation and spread of graphical meaning units, media coactivity, etc.	Mode choice, text-in-image, image quotes, spatial and temporal positionality and deixis, animation, etc.	Social semiotics, visual content analysis, film studies (?)

Implications

The tripartite familiar–reconfigured–emergent classification presented above raises questions that have the potential to lead to new theoretical insight. Why, for example, do some discourse phenomena persist, others adapt, and others arise anew in technologically mediated environments?

I have previously (Herring 2007) emphasized the importance of taking into account facets of the technological medium and the social context in analyzing CMD. In the case of Discourse 2.0, technological facets that are especially relevant are media convergence and multimodality, including use of images and channel choice. Social facets that continue to be especially relevant include number of participants, anonymity, communicative setting, and cultural context. To these two faceted dimensions I propose adding a linguistic dimension, based on the observation that different linguistic phenomena appear to be variably sensitive to technological and social effects. One tentative generalization that follows from the examples presented above is that social phenomena such as gender styles (level 4 of CMDA) seem most resistant to technological reshaping, perhaps because they exist at a higher level of abstraction and their expression is not bound to a specific communicative modality. In contrast, interactional phenomena (level 2 of CMDA) seem most likely to be reconfigured. This is understandable, in that changes in system design often affect turn-taking, yet conversational exchanges persist even on platforms not primarily designed to support them (Herring 2009; Herring et al. 2009; Kendall 2007; Zelenkauskaite and Herring 2008), necessitating reconfigured strategies of interaction.[11] However, emergent phenomena do not appear to be associated with any particular linguistic level; the analyses cited above involve all four CMDA levels: structure (such as formality markers), meaning (such as functional moves), interactional coherence (such as cross-turn reference), and social phenomena (such as expressions of sociability and negativity), as well as the nonlinguistic level of participation. Even if a new level is posited for CMDA to capture the semiotics of multimodal communication, as in table 1.2, discourse constructed collaboratively through online multimodal systems is only emergent at the present time; in the future it will be familiar or perhaps reconfigured by newer multimodal systems. Thus it is difficult to link emergence with any specific aspect of language use; rather, in the examples presented here, emergence is tied to technological developments.

Classifying online discourse phenomena in terms of their novelty can make explicit what phenomena are new and in need of basic descriptive research; these low-hanging fruit can be attractive objects of study. Reconfigured phenomena can suggest interesting comparative studies that shed light on the effects of technological change on online discourse. Familiar phenomena can be rewarding to analyze, too, especially when familiar patterns are thought to no longer exist or when they are incorrectly labeled as new. Recognizing what is familiar or reconfigured as such is an important antidote to the tendency towards ahistoricity in new media studies. The three-way classification scheme also has other practical benefits. Once a topic for research has been selected, the scheme can be used to frame a research study, select literature for review, determine appropriate methods of analysis, and make interpretive comparisons. However, the scheme should not be applied too strictly; it is coarse grained and intended as a first-pass classification of discourse phenomena, subject to refinement from further investigation.

Summary and Conclusion

Discourse in Web 2.0 environments is mostly CMCMD; that is, it occurs on converged media platforms. CMCMD still has a strong textual component, and many CMD phenomena carry over into CMCMD. At the same time, CMCMD increasingly co-occurs with information in other semiotic, especially graphical, modes, leading to the emergence of new converged CMD phenomena. These differences notwithstanding, and although multimodal online discourse presents special challenges, CMDA remains a useful lens through which to analyze new social media.

This last point becomes more evident when discourse-focused approaches to contemporary web phenomena are contrasted with Web 2.0 approaches. Each is a lens with a central focus and a periphery, and certain phenomena are outside the scope of each. Web 2.0 as a lens has centrally in its sights phenomena such as user-created content, user control of content, collaborative processes, and folksonomies. Social interaction and communication are on the periphery, and CMD in contexts other than Web 2.0 sites lies outside its scope. In contrast, CMCMD as a lens focuses on language, communication, conversation, social interaction, and media coactivity as they occur anywhere online (including via mobile phones), with collaboration on the periphery; noninteractive content is outside its scope. Each lens is valuable, but CMCMD focuses more squarely on phenomena of interest to discourse analysts. At the same time, it overlaps considerably with Web 2.0 and thus remains a timely lens through which to examine online communicative content.

If this chapter demonstrates one thing, it is that Discourse 2.0 offers a rich field of investigation for discourse analysts. Especially urgently needed in future research is integrated multimodal analysis. Longitudinal analysis is also needed, and it is increasingly feasible given the preservation of digital records and computer-assisted corpus analysis methods. Finally, large-scale automated analysis can and should coexist, in my view, with ethnographic case studies. Indeed, it seems likely that in the short term, integrated analyses of multimodal communication will be qualitative and ethnographic in nature, at least until the interplay of different semiotic systems in online environments is understood well enough to distill parameters that can be subjected to systematic, quantitative analysis.

ACKNOWLEDGMENTS
I am grateful to Deborah Tannen and Anna Marie Trester for their helpful comments on an earlier version of this chapter. Any shortcomings that remain are my responsibility alone.

NOTES

1. On the creation of the web, see Wikipedia (2011a).
2. With the possible exception of WikiLeaks, which is the most recent, all of these sites (and many more) can be found in lists of Web 2.0 sites available online (see, e.g., www.sacredcowdung.com /archives/2006/03/all_things_web.html and edudemic.com/2011/11/best-web-tools).
3. For some proposed expansions to CMDA methodology, see the articles in Androutsopoulos and Bießwenger (2008).
4. These are considered to be CMCMC environments because in each case, the site's original purpose was something other than conversational exchange.
5. Herring (2001) provides an overview of many of these practices in the CMD of the 1990s. For discussion of the offline historical predecessors of English-language CMC, see Baron (2000).
6. Small stories are nontraditional narratives and are often personal rather than fictionalized. In Web 2.0 environments they are reconfigured from their offline antecedents in that they tend to be interactive, hypertextual, and collaborative (see Georgakopoulou 2013).
7. It is syntactically ill formed because "Katy: ?" is not a grammatical sentence, and pragmatically ill formed because the default expectation of a Facebook status update is that it provide information about what the user is doing or thinking.
8. These examples are advanced with the caveat that more astute researchers may find plausible antecedents to them. Some could be argued to have antecedents in specialized offline contexts; however, to the best of my knowledge, none have previously existed as common communicative practices online or offline.
9. An example of this is "lolcat" images—photographs of cats with text superimposed (in misspelled and ungrammatical English [e.g., "I can haz cheezburger"])—which originated on 4chan and spread subsequently to other online environments (Bernstein et al. 2011).
10. Craig Howard, email communication, January 8, 2012.
11. Numerous examples of this can be found in the CMD literature (e.g., Cherny 1999; Herring 1999). For an extreme example of reconfigured turn-taking in a synchronous chat system, see Anderson, Beard, and Walther (2010).

REFERENCES

Anderson, Nate. 2006. Tim Berners-Lee on Web 2.0: "[N]obody even knows what it means." *Ars Technica.* arstechnica.com/business/news/2006/09/7650.ars.

Anderson, Jeffrey F., Fred K. Beard, and Joseph B. Walther. 2010. Turn-taking and the local management of conversation in a highly simultaneous computer-mediated communication system. *Language@ Internet* 7, article 7. www.languageatinternet.org/articles/2010/2804.

Androutsopoulos, Jannis. 2011. From variation to heteroglossia in the study of computer-mediated discourse. In *Digital discourse: Language in the new media,* ed. Crispin Thurlow and Kristine Mroczek, 277–98. New York: Oxford University Press.

Androutsopoulos, Jannis, and Michael Beißwenger, eds. 2008. Data and methods in computer-mediated discourse analysis. *Language@Internet* 5, article 2. www.languageatinternet.org/articles/2008.

Baron, Naomi S. 2000. *Alphabet to email: How written English evolved and where it's heading.* London and New York: Routledge.

Battelle, John, and Tim O'Reilly. 2010. Web 2.0 Summit is a wrap. *Web 2.0 Summit.* www.web2 summit.com/web2010.

Bernstein, Michael S., Andrés Monroy-Hernández, Drew Harry, Paul André, Katrina Panovich, and Greg Vargas. 2011. 4chan and /b/: An analysis of anonymity and ephemerality in a large online community. In *Proceedings of the Fifth International Conference on Weblogs and Social Media,* 50–57. Menlo Park, CA: AAAI Press.

Blood, Rebecca. 2002. *The weblog handbook: Practical advice on creating and maintaining your blog.* Cambridge, MA: Perseus.

boyd, danah, Scott Golder, and Gilad Lotan. 2010. Tweet tweet retweet: Conversational aspects of retweeting on Twitter. In *Proceedings of the 43rd Hawaii International Conference on System Sciences,* ed. Ralph Sprague. Los Alamitos, CA: IEEE Press. csdl.computer.org/dl/proceedings/hicss/2010/3869/00/03-06-04.pdf.

Cherny, Lynn. 1994. Gender differences in text-based virtual reality. In *Cultural performances: Proceedings of the Third Berkeley Women and Language Conference, April 8, 9, and 10, 1994,* ed. Mary Bucholtz, Anita C. Liang, Laurel A. Sutton, and Caitlin Liang, 102–15. Berkeley: Berkeley Women and Language Group, University of California.

———. 1995. The modal complexity of speech events in a social mud. *Electronic Journal of Communication* 5. fragment.nl/mirror/Cherny/The_modal_complexity.txt.

———. 1999. *Conversation and community: Chat in a virtual world.* Stanford, CA: CSLI.

Crowston, Kevin, and Michelle Williams. 2000. Reproduced and emergent genres of communication on the World-Wide Web. *The Information Society* 16, no. 3:201–16.

Crystal, David. 2008. *Txtng: The gr8 db8.* New York: Oxford University Press.

Danet, Brenda, and Susan C. Herring, eds. 2007. *The multilingual internet: Language, culture, and communication online.* New York: Oxford University Press.

Emigh, William, and Susan C. Herring. 2005. Collaborative authoring on the Web: A genre analysis of online encyclopedias. In *Proceedings of the 38th Hawaii International Conference on System Sciences,* ed. Ralph Sprague. Los Alamitos, CA: IEEE Press. ella.slis.indiana.edu/~herring/wiki.pdf.

Eriksen, Lars B., and Carina Ihlström. 2000. Evolution of the web news genre: The slow move beyond the print metaphor. In *Proceedings of the 33rd Hawaii International Conference on System Sciences,* ed. Ralph Sprague. Los Alamitos, CA: IEEE. csdl.computer.org/dl/proceedings/hicss/2000/0493/03/04933014.pdf.

Georgakopoulou, Alexandra. 2013. Narrative and computer-mediated communication. In *Handbook of pragmatics of computer-mediated communication,* ed. Susan C. Herring, Dieter Stein, and Tuija Virtanen. Berlin: Mouton de Gruyter.

Giles, Jim. 2005. Internet encyclopaedias go head to head. *Nature* 438:900–901. www.u.arizona.edu/~trevors/nature_15dec2005_wikipedia.pdf

Goffman, Erving. 1959. *The presentation of self in everyday life.* New York: Doubleday.

Haltom, Aaron. 2011. How to spot a link builder. Unpublished manuscript.

Herring, Susan C. 1993. Gender and democracy in computer-mediated communication. *Electronic Journal of Communication* 3, no. 2. ella.slis.indiana.edu/~herring/ejc.doc.

———. 1999. Interactional coherence in CMC. *Journal of Computer-Mediated Communication* 4, no. 4. jcmc.indiana.edu/vol4/issue4/herring.html.

———. 2001. Computer-mediated discourse. In *The handbook of discourse analysis,* ed. Deborah Schiffrin, Deborah Tannen, and Heidi Hamilton, 612–34. Oxford: Blackwell.

———. 2003a. Gender and power in online communication. In *The handbook of language and gender,* ed. Janet Holmes and Miriam Meyerhoff, 202–28. Oxford: Blackwell.

———. 2003b. Dynamic topic analysis of synchronous chat. In *New research for new media: Innovative research methodologies symposium working papers and readings.* Minneapolis: University of Minnesota School of Journalism and Mass Communication. ella.slis.indiana.edu/~herring/dta.2003.pdf.

———. 2004. Computer-mediated discourse analysis: An approach to researching online behavior. In *Designing for virtual communities in the service of learning,* ed. Sasha A. Barab, Rob Kling, and James H. Gray, 338–76. New York: Cambridge University Press.

———. 2007. A faceted classification scheme for computer-mediated discourse. *Language@Internet* 4, article 1. www.languageatinternet.org/articles/2007/761.

———. 2009. New directions in CMC research: CMCMC. Plenary speech, Illinois Language and Linguistic Society Conference (ILLS 1), Urbana, May 31. flash.atlas.illinois.edu/Video.html?src=/ling/ling-v-2009-2/Keynote-Herring&player=SDNC.

Herring, Susan C., and Bradford Demarest. 2011. Mode choice in multimodal comment threads: Effects on participation, sociability, and attitude. Unpublished manuscript.

Herring, Susan C., and Andrew Kurtz. 2006. Visualizing dynamic topic analysis. In *Proceedings of CHI '06.* New York: ACM. ella.slis.indiana.edu/~herring/chi06.pdf.

Herring, Susan C., Daniel O. Kutz, John C. Paolillo, and Asta Zelenkauskaite. 2009. Fast talking, fast shooting: Text chat in an online first-person game. In *Proceedings of the 42nd Hawaii International Conference on System Sciences,* ed. Ralph Sprague. Los Alamitos, CA: IEEE Press. ella.slis.indiana.edu/~herring/hicss.bzflag.pdf.

Herring, Susan C., Lois Ann Scheidt, Sabrina Bonus, and Elijah Wright. 2004. Bridging the gap: A genre analysis of weblogs. In *Proceedings of the 37th Hawaii International Conference on System Sciences,* ed. Ralph Sprague. Los Alamitos, CA: IEEE Press. ella.slis.indiana.edu/~herring/herring.scheidt.2004.pdf.

Honeycutt, Courtenay, and Susan C. Herring. 2009. Beyond microblogging: Conversation and collaboration via Twitter. In *Proceedings of the 42nd Hawaii International Conference on System Sciences,* ed. Ralph Sprague. Los Alamitos, CA: IEEE Press. ella.slis.indiana.edu/~herring/honeycutt.herring.2009.pdf.

Howard, Craig. 2011. Collaborative video annotation as critical discourse. Paper presented at the Georgetown University Round Table on Languages and Linguistics, Washington, DC, March 12.

Jucker, Andreas H., and Christa Dürscheid. 2012. The linguistics of keyboard-to-screen communication: A new terminological framework. *Linguistik Online.* vol. 56, no. 6, www.linguistik-online.org/56_12/juckerDuerscheid.html.

Kapidzic, Sanja, and Susan C. Herring. 2011a. Gender, communication, and self-presentation in teen chatrooms revisited: Have patterns changed? *Journal of Computer-Mediated Communication* 17, no. 1:39–59.

———. 2011b. Gender, innovation, and non-standardness in teen chat language. Paper presented at the Georgetown University Round Table on Languages and Linguistics, Washington, DC, March 12.

Kendall, Lori. 2007. Colin Mochrie vs. Jesus H. Christ: Messages about masculinities and fame in online video conversations. In *Proceedings of the 40th Hawaii International Conference on Systems Sciences,* ed. Ralph Sprague. Los Alamitos, CA: IEEE Press. www.ideals.illinois.edu/bitstream/handle/2142/705/co?sequence=2.

Kutz, Daniel O., and Susan C. Herring. 2005. Micro-longitudinal analysis of Web news updates. In *Proceedings of the 38th Hawaii International Conference on System Sciences,* ed. Ralph Sprague. Los Alamitos, CA: IEEE Press. ella.slis.indiana.edu/~herring/news.pdf.

Lambiase, Jacqueline J. 2010. Hanging by a thread: Topic development and death in an online discussion of breaking news. *Language@Internet* 7, article 9. www.languageatinternet.org/articles/2010/2814.

Lee, Carmen. 2011. Texts and practices of micro-blogging: Status updates on Facebook. In *Digital discourse: Language in the new media,* ed. Crispin Thurlow and Kristine Mroczek, 110–28. New York: Oxford University Press.

Lenihan, Aoife. 2011. "Join our community of translators": Language ideologies and Facebook. In *Digital discourse: Language in the new media,* ed. Crispin Thurlow and Kristine Mroczek, 48–64. New York: Oxford University Press.

Linden, Greg. 2006. Tim O'Reilly and defining Web 2.0. *Geeking with Greg,* May 14. glinden.blogspot.com/2006/05/tim-oreilly-and-defining-web-20.html.

McDonald, David. 2007. Visual conversation styles in web communities. In *Proceedings of the 40th Hawaii International Conference on System Sciences,* ed. Ralph Sprague. Los Alamitos, CA: IEEE Press. www.pensivepuffin.com/dwmcphd/papers/McDonald.HICSS-40.preprint.pdf.

Miller, Caroline R., and Dawn Shepherd. 2004. Blogging as social action: A genre analysis of the weblog. In *Into the blogosphere: Rhetoric, community, and culture of weblogs,* ed. Laura J. Gurak, Smiljana Antonijevic, Laurie Johnson, Clancy Ratliff, and Jessica Reyman. Minneapolis: University of Minnesota Libraries. blog.lib.umn.edu/blogosphere/blogging_as_social_action_a_genre_analysis_of_the_weblog.html.

Newon, Lisa. 2011. Multimodal creativity and identities of expertise in the digital ecology of a World of Warcraft guild. In *Digital discourse: Language in the new media,* ed. Crispin Thurlow and Kristine Mroczek, 131–53. New York: Oxford University Press.

Nishimura, Yukiko. 2011. Japanese *keitai* novels and ideologies of literacy. In *Digital discourse: Language in the new media,* ed. Crispin Thurlow and Kristine Mroczek, 86–109. New York: Oxford University Press.

O'Reilly, Tim. 2005. What is Web 2.0? Design patterns and business models for the next generation of software. *O'Reilly Network,* September 30. oreilly.com/web2/archive/what-is-web-20.html.

Peterson, Eric. 2011. How conversational are weblogs? *Language@Internet* 8, article 8. www.languageat internet.org/articles/2011/Peterson.

Pihlaja, Stephen. 2011. Cops, popes, and garbage collectors: Metaphor and antagonism in an atheist/Christian YouTube video thread. *Language@Internet* 8, article 1. www.languageatinternet.org/articles/2011/3044.

Puschmann, Cornelius. 2013. Blogging. In *Handbook of pragmatics of computer-mediated communication,* ed. Susan C. Herring, Dieter Stein, and Tuija Virtanen. Berlin: Mouton de Gruyter, 83–108.

Romm, Joe. 2011. Denier-bots live! Why are online comments' sections over-run by the anti-science, pro-pollution crowd? *Think Progress,* February 20. thinkprogress.org/romm/2011/02/20/207554/denier-bots-live-why-are-online-comments-sections-over-run-by-the-anti-science-pro-pollution-crowd/.

Severinson Eklundh, Kerstin. 2010. To quote or not to quote: Setting the context for computer-mediated dialogues. *Language@Internet* 7, article 5. www.languageatinternet.org/articles/2010/2665.

Severinson Eklundh, Kerstin, and Clare Macdonald. 1994. The use of quoting to preserve context in electronic mail dialogues. *IEEE Transactions on Professional Communication* 37, no. 4:97–202.

Sindoni, Maria Grazia. 2011. "Mode-switching": Speech and writing in videochats. Paper presented at the Georgetown University Round Table on Languages and Linguistics, Washington, DC, March 11.

Tannen, Deborah. 1990. *You just don't understand: Women and men in conversation.* New York: Morrow.

Thurlow, Crispin, and Kristine Mroczek, eds. 2011. *Digital discourse: Language in the new media.* New York: Oxford University Press.

Turkle, Sherry. 1995. *Life on the screen: Identity in the age of the internet.* New York: Simon and Schuster.

Vaisman, Carmel. 2011. Performing girlhood through typographic play in Hebrew blogs. In *Digital discourse: Language in the new media,* ed. Crispin Thurlow and Kristine Mroczek, 177–96. New York: Oxford University Press.

Viégas, Fernanda B., Martin Wattenberg, and Dave Kushal. 2004. Studying cooperation and conflict between authors with history flow visualizations. In *Proceedings of the 2004 Conference on Human Factors in Computing Systems,* 575–82. New York: ACM.

Virtanen, Tuija. 2013. Performativity in computer-mediated communication. In *Handbook of pragmatics of computer-mediated communication,* ed. Susan C. Herring, Dieter Stein, and Tuija Virtanen. Berlin: Mouton de Gruyter, 269–90.

Wagner, Christian. 2004. Wiki: A technology for conversational knowledge management and group collaboration. *Communications of the Association for Information Systems* 13:265–89.

Werry, Christopher C. 1996. Linguistic and interactional features of Internet Relay Chat. In *Computer-mediated communication: Linguistic, social, and cross-cultural perspectives,* ed. Susan C. Herring, 47–63. Amsterdam and Philadelphia: John Benjamins.

Wikipedia. 2011a. *History of the World Wide Web.* en.wikipedia.org/wiki/History_of_the_World_Wide_Web.

———. 2011b. *Web 2.0.* en.wikipedia.org/wiki/Web_2.0.

———. 2011c. *Facebook.* en.wikipedia.org/wiki/.

Winston, Brian. 1998. *Media, technology, and society, a history: From the telegraph to the internet.* London: Routledge.

Wolf, Alecia. 2000. Emotional expression online: Gender differences in emoticon use. *CyberPsychology and Behavior* 3:827–33.

Zelenkauskaite, Asta, and Susan C. Herring. 2008. Television-mediated conversation: Coherence in Italian iTV SMS chat. In *Proceedings of the 41st Hawaii International Conference on System Sciences,* ed. Ralph Sprague. Los Alamitos, CA: IEEE Press. ella.slis.indiana.edu/~herring/hicss08.pdf.

2

Polities and Politics of Ongoing Assessments: Evidence from Video-Gaming and Blogging

HERVÉ VARENNE, GILLIAN "GUS" ANDREWS, AARON CHIA-YUAN
HUNG, AND SARAH WESSLER
Teachers College, Columbia University

Prologue

> But the point is that between what Ryle calls the "thin description" of what the rehearser (parodist, winker, twitcher . . .) is doing ("rapidly contracting his right eyelids") and the "thick description" of what he is doing ("practicing a burlesque of a friend faking a wink to deceive an innocent into thinking a conspiracy is in motion") lies the object of ethnography: a stratified hierarchy of meaningful structures in terms of which twitches, winks, fake-winks, parodies, rehearsals of parodies are produced, perceived, and interpreted, and without which they would not (not even the zero-form twitches, which, as a cultural category, are as much nonwinks as winks are nontwitches) in fact exist, no matter what anyone did or didn't do with his eyelids. (Geertz 1973, 7)

THIS MOST FAMOUS of Geertz's flights of anthropological writing introduces what he labels an "interpretive theory of culture." It eventually led him and many of his students to radical skepticism about the possibility of anthropology, and—he would have added—sociology, linguistics, conversational analysis. At about the same time Garfinkel, Sacks, and others argued that social life with its twitches and winks is "discoverable . . . not imaginable" (Garfinkel 2002, 96). The analyst need not interpret because, in the real life of sheep raids, school classrooms, and video game playing, a muscular event around the eye is always twitch *or* wink, for *these* people, at *this* time, and for *this* political purpose. Anyone who follows the publicizing of this event will know how it *was* taken if only because of the controversy, or lack thereof, about the event.

No spasms occur without the consequences of the ongoing assessment of the spasm.

Introduction

The term "assessment" has several histories. We consider three, given our desire to build more robust analytic tools to identify what we call the emerging polities of any assessment. In everyday life, people continually find themselves establishing the practical import of earlier statements or moves (or discovering that some *thing* has happened). They find themselves meting out consequences or living with consequences others are meting out. And then everyone has to deal with what has happened.[1] We are thus also concerned with the politics of any assessment. As it happens, new technologies offer interesting cases for exploring these classical issues.[2] The affordances of video games and blogging both expand and disrupt interactional processes in ways that may help us trace more carefully how the distant, in time and place, enters into the here and now, as well as how the here and now can transform, or not, the distant.

The several speech communities or, in our vocabulary, "speech polities" that have made their history around the term "assessment" are quite distinct. The term appears extensively in the discursive traditions of schooling, mental health, and conversational analysis. There is little overlap in the literatures that trace the development, uses, and controversies surrounding the term. But all three address the issue of figuring out what happened to allow an act or a person to be identified as *this* or *that.* They are all in the business of assessing whether a spasm was a twitch or a wink, of fitting this assessment within a political process of significance for a particular polity, and then of justifying consequences. But the differences in the placing of assessment in each tradition bring out fundamental matters. In the worlds of clinical psychology and schooling, the concern with assessing a child individually can be traced, among other sources, and somewhat ironically to John Dewey's belief that "the child's own instincts and powers furnish . . . the starting point for all education" (1959, 20). This leads to the question that keeps moving clinical psychology and schooling: How do we figure out what those instincts and powers might be?

In conversational analysis and ethnomethodology, the term "assessment" may have first appeared in a paper by Harvey Sacks on "police assessment of moral character" (1972) which had been titled, when it was first written in 1965, "Methods in Use for the Production of a Social Order" (1972, 280). Sacks's paper, for many, showed a way that might allow us to trace how instincts and powers are identified but with no concern as to whether these are real outside the settings in which they are identified, or for other purposes than those constituted by the activities of the participants in the settings. These methodological strictures have made conversational analysis of limited value for clinical and school assessors. *Their* task is not analytic but political. They are responsible for producing assessments so powerful that a person's career may be changed. To fulfill this political task, assessors must do it in just such a way as to establish that the assessment is independent of setting or assessor—as the particular polities who might challenge the assessment understand "independence." This political responsibility, of course, places clinical and school assessors in a kind of Catch-22: they must produce social orders that abstract their own social characteristics as they discriminate in the technical, statistical sense.

Various social scientific traditions in anthropology and sociology have established that abstracting the social to reach the real is fundamentally impossible. But few before Sacks—and Garfinkel, of course—had systematically looked at the methods by which routine assessments are made in the daily life of any profession and then used their findings as a way to address the classical issues. In 1973 Geertz was rather typical in his reaction to the evidence that classifications of actions and people, as well as the related consequences, were indefinitely multiple—the occasion for controversy, debate, power plays, if not violence (symbolic or otherwise). Anthropologists in general were altogether convinced, as they continue to be, that it would be impossible to reach universally valid classifications of people or acts, or to invent methods for producing these. As Lévi-Strauss said, "natural species are not chosen [as totems] because they are 'good to eat' but because they are 'good to think'" (1966, 89). This would apply, as he argued in his next work (Lévi-Strauss 1966), to all classifications, including, of course, the classification of psychological "instincts and powers."[3]

But Geertz did not trust any of the then-extant methods to establish how any assessment, anywhere, is done, and Lévi-Strauss does not appear to have been much interested in the matter.[4] Sociologists documented how social consequences are distributed in ways that correlate with any number of classifications (including social class, race, ethnicity, gender). But the exact way these correlations are produced, in the details of everyday lives, remained obscure.

In contrast, Sacks, Garfinkel, their colleagues and students (Pomerantz 1984; Goodwin and Goodwin 1987, 1992), as well as those who were inspired by their work, started giving us a sense of how, for example, a child becomes known as "not knowing how to read" or as "having" or "being with" this or that clinical label (McDermott 1993; Mehan 1996; Mehan, Hertwerk, and Meihls 1986). We seek to continue this work by exploring the linkages between routine assessments and the extraordinary ones that may transform a person's status and her relationships. We are concerned, to paraphrase Garfinkel (1956), with "successful" (de)gradation moments when a spasm is determined to be a twitch, a wink, or a sign that the performer is sick, funny, dangerous, or any *thing* else. Conversational analysis and ethnomethodology have often been criticized for their apparent failure to address significant social processes affecting masses rather than the immediate participants in a local event (Bourdieu 1990; Gellner 1975; Hanks 1996). Many researchers in these fields have demonstrated otherwise, if not quite convincingly. Given the methodological strictures for conversational analysis, it can be difficult to show the linkages between a particular conversational exchange and the general conditions that make it *this* kind of exchange rather than another. It can be even more difficult to link the exchange to its consequences. It can be particularly hard to specify the people, or polity, who have participated in setting the conditions or in meting out consequences.

The set of research projects on which we report here were designed to contribute to the further development of the analytic tools needed to help us trace, in detail, how people get entangled into large-scale historical processes. We start the chapter with a brief illustration of our concerns by reporting on an expert child taking over the controls of a video game from an incompetent adult. We continue with a more detailed analysis of a similar case, in which a group of four video game players handles the incompetence of one of them. Our goal is to move away from a concern with differentiated individual competence so that the focus can be placed instead on the host of others who set the stage for the *particular* issues about which the person might then be assessed as being either expert or incompetent. The third case study traces the sequencing of apparent errors in blog comments. By exploring various indices internal to the technologies, we demonstrate that gaming and blogging are interactional processes that bring together people from various walks of life. Whatever their personal or professional interests, these people must, however briefly, live with what each has created and with the consequences. In conclusion, we suggest that a similar approach would help us understand what can happen when assessments, in school or clinics, are not matters of game.

"Marta Can't Play": Assessments and Consequences

The setting for the first case study is that of a video game design camp for children and adolescents. In her pilot research, Wessler was present when a competitive game was played between two teams in different parts of the country. Each team had to include both children and adults. In this instance Marta—the adult, and one of the teachers—had never played the game *Counter-Strike: Source.* This game is a first-person multiplayer shooting game and Marta was altogether uncomfortable with the genre.[5] But she had to be one of the players. This meant that her body had to face the monitor and her hands had to control keyboard and mouse. She did have a child advisor, Brad, sitting at her side. Brad was heavily invested in winning the game and kept telling her, "Click," "Move left," or "Shoot!" As the game progressed, telling became yelling as more and more of the adult's moves were assessed by the child as being "wrong." In fact, and as their team began to lose, little by little the child took over mouse and keyboard and the adult sat back and watched.

Things came to a head toward the end of the game. The team was down 2–0 and—partially because of her incompetence—Marta was still alive and all but one of the other players had died. It was her job to protect the other player, but she did not know that. At that point, at least four other students were now watching Marta, instructing her, and assessing what should be done next.[6]

8	ROMA: [to Marta]	*Now look to your right, look to your right!*
9	FEFFER: [to Marta]	*Turn your mouse to your right*
10	ROMA: [to Marta]	*Turn your mouse to the right*
11	MR. AWESOME:	*Your right*
12	FEFFER:	*A little bit more Marta!*
13	ROMA:	*Marta turn your mouse! Turn your mouse!*
14	MUNCHKIN:	*Turn!*
15	MR. AWESOME:	*Turn right!*
16	ROMA:	*Your mouse!* [Laughs]
17	FEFFER:	*Turn your mouse to turn Marta!*
18	MR. AWESOME:	*Yeah!*

19   MARTA: *Where?*

20   MR. AWESOME: *Go!*

21   ROMA: *Yo someone should totally* [quietly] *go play for Marta* [Laughs].

22   MR. AWESOME: [Claps Hands] *Ooooh!* [Groans in frustration].

The team lost.

Formally the event, as it progressed, involved two kinds of assessments. The first consisted of assessments of the two previous statements in a sequence of (1) "game as it has progressed so far" (S1), (2) "keyboard move in response to S1" (S2), and (3) "instruction on how to move next" (S3). The second type of assessment was a totalizing one summarizing all the moves-so-far and leading to a change in social organization: the adult is incompetent and cannot be trusted to win the game; she should be replaced. The first kind of assessments could be discussed in terms of turn-taking and adjacency pairs. These are the assessments that concerned Mehan in his work on classroom lessons (1979). The second kind of assessments takes us on to matters like those Sacks investigated in his paper on a joke's telling (1974). We are concerned with the game's playing, but with a twist. We are looking at what can happen *after* it has been assessed that the joke was told incorrectly, or a game was played badly. Sacks did not explore this latter stage specifically. But we can imagine that in joking as in gaming, one's authority to "joke/play next" may change as one's capabilities are assessed *for this new purpose and this polity.*

Formally, we have observed these assessments thus far:

1. The previous move was wrong and next move should be this; and
2. The player is incompetent and the next game should be played by another player.

But, in the instance Wessler studied, there actually is a *third* level of assessment that encompasses these narrower assessments. At a summer camp that is for these intents and purposes a School, a teacher's incompetence at playing video games has *no consequences* on her status as Teacher.[7] Some might find it strange that a teacher in a technology camp should be so incompetent in comparison to the students.[8] Our own concern is to explore the implications of two types of assessments that identify performance within whole ritualized sequences as *this* rather than *that.* There are assessments that, possibly temporarily, indicate a participant is, say, incompetent, *but are of little consequence in terms of future participation.* And there are other assessments that reconstitute much earlier assessments that, say, a person is now Teacher for certain intents and purposes. In such cases the local participants have little power to change the relationship that may make some teachers and some students. In such cases even the assessment that a particular teacher was incompetent may be surprising precisely *because* the person was, is, and will be a Teacher—for all relevant intents and purposes.[9] But, of course, at other times, within other polities, under different circumstances, a person might lose the status of Teacher if she were to be fired from her position.

Not-So-Personal Assessing Instructions

Our second case study builds on Aaron Hung's recent work (Hung 2011). The case is that of four youths from Cantonese- and Mandarin-speaking areas of China playing various video games in New York City. Hung made a three-and-one-half-hour video recording of their playing. During one of the games, *Super Smash Brothers Melee,* the four organized themselves into two competing teams. There was a problem, however. Three of the four (Andrew, Jason, and Kevin) were expert players, and were boys. The fourth (Li) had never played the game, was a girl, and often complained that the boys were not playing fair. She was also primarily a Mandarin speaker, and the boys were primarily Cantonese speakers. She and one of the boys seemed to be in the early stages of some kind of relationship. At the time the status of their relationship was not clearly stated, but it may explain why she was present on that day. Still, her main attribute, for the purpose of game playing, may have been that she could serve as the needed fourth player. The three boys would just have to make do with her other characteristics.

Making do, of course, revealed which of the characteristics made what kind of difference. As they played, all four also assessed what was going wrong and attempted to correct it so that they could continue playing. At certain times the characteristic that mattered was the Cantonese-Mandarin divide. This one appears to have been dealt with easily enough.[10] Most bothersome was the girl's lack of expertise and the moves she was making, or failing to make. We focus on the latter and particularly on the organization of the assessments and instructions that the other players gave her. In brief, the three boys shifted from expressions of dismay to a delegation of instructional duties. After a while, one of the boys took it upon himself to be the chief instructor when the need arose. As he did so, two subsidiary issues appeared to make the most difference. One had to do with the manipulation of the buttons on the controller. The other had to do with the interpretation of the heads-up displays on the screen. It took the boys a while, for example, to figure out that the girl interpreted an increase in one of the indices as a sign that she was winning when just the opposite was the case:

LI: *Damn! I went from 130 something to 0!*

ANDREW: *It is not good to have a higher number.* (Hung 2011, 100)[11]

Figure 2.2 is a screenshot taken while the game was being played. There are four numbers at the bottom, presented as percentages. Even expert players are not quite sure what they are percentages of, or what is the range (given that it can go over 100 percent). These matters may be explained somewhere in the manual, but knowing them does not appear to have an impact on the game. What does have an impact is figuring out which of the four figures represent one's performance, whether an increase is good or bad, and whether the other players are doing better or worse than oneself. Expert players do track all four figures. Li had not yet figured it all out. For observers, what is most noteworthy here is that the numbers are not a matter of interpretation or negotiation as far as playing *this* game is concerned.[12] The girl had to accept that *this* was the "it" she had to attend to. If she did not, then she was not playing, and no playing could take place.

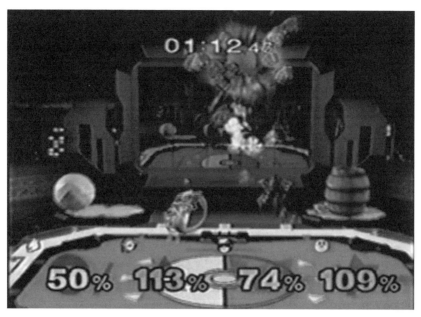

■ Figure 2.2 Screenshot of *Super Smash Brothers Melee* (Hung 2011).

The scoring problem was solved by direct verbal instruction.[13] The problems posed by the controller (fig. 2.3) were more difficult to address. Here is one instance in which the controller becomes the explicit focus:

LI: *Wait, show me for a second what button you press.*

ANDREW: *Let me see what moves this character had*

KEVIN: *Let me teach you a move. . . . Come over here. I'll teach you one move.*

LI: *How do I use it?*

KEVIN: *I'll teach you a move.*

JASON: *Jump up, and then press this button.*

LI: *Do you have to move this?*

JASON: *Jump up, press the up button, then the "B" button.*

[about a minute passes]

JASON: *This one? Press down.*

LI: *What are you doing?*

JASON: *Andrew, let me, let me, Andrew, let me show her a few moves. Let me show her a few things. . . . Press the down button.* (Hung 2011, 121–23)

In such cases, direct, discursive instruction did not quite work, partially because the instructions had to be deictic and partially because they involved muscle control. In

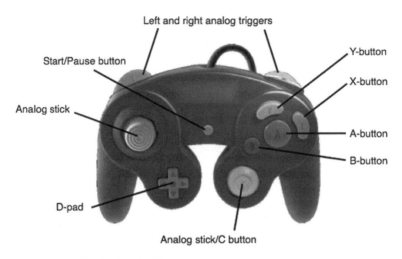

Figure 2.3 Game Controller (*Wikipedia* 2010).

order to fight adequately, one had always to press *this* rather than *that* button—without looking at the controller or one's hands.[14] Given the pace of the game, one did not have time to think about what one was doing, either. And yet there were times when it was impossible not to shift to explicit instruction which revealed the host of problems one has to face when playing such a game. One of the problems was rooted partially in classic conversational difficulties related to the making of indexical propositions and their interpretation. Another problem was a matter of controller design and muscle coordination. This can be said to be a matter of literally "embodying" a cultural arbitrary and to be related to what Marcel Mauss called "techniques of the body" (1979, 114–15). In a world of cyborgs, it can also be said to be a matter of the so-called en-machining of a cultural arbitrary. In any event, habituating one's thumbs to various engineers' design choices is not easy to teach or to do.

Bruno Latour (2005) is famous for stating boldly that things have agency. In our case it would be more technically useful to say that things (controller design, screen display, or programming decisions on the relationship between handling of the controller and changes on the screen) are the mediating interface in an asynchronous interaction between designers and users when neither can assess, and then possibly correct, what the others are doing while they are doing it. A player can try to teach the other player something he discovers she cannot do, but he cannot report his discoveries back to the designers.[15]

This asynchronicity between the actors of far-flung and heavily differentiated polities is of course what makes the task of designers intractable to simple rationalism. The users must imagine what the engineers might have intended, but they will never meet them. The engineers must imagine what users might do, but they cannot meet all of them. As Garfinkel has argued (2002, chapter 6) regarding the writing of instruction manuals, the engineers' task, if it is presented as building universally accessible machines, is impossible in principle; engineers cannot imagine all the possible settings and participants that might use the machine. Thus machines as things have a similar relationship to future action as any verbal statement. Machines suggest particular possibilities while remaining open to assessments that might transform the machines as statement into literally some *thing* else. A machine, like a muscle spasm, can become twitch or wink, and *that* is what it will be for the duration, and for the polity.

Suchman (2007) has extensively explored the peculiarities of human-machine configurations. For our purposes we emphasize only that the crowd of people who imagine, design an interface, program the whole, and eventually play the games in real time, produce only one thing for future reference: the playing (well or not, and satisfactorily or not) of *this* game rather than any other one. The earlier uncertainties get resolved by a political process that produces not so much a consensus as a practical acknowledgment that future struggles will invoke the playing of *that* game *that* day. The game that was played may not have been the game the designer envisioned. For example, Hung's corpus includes two of the expert players' exploration of alternative games made possible by the design of *Super Smash Brothers Melee* (2011, chapter 6). And, of course, personal relationships may be established or transformed. In the process, new forms of political-arbitrary (in Bourdieu's sense) get produced for all those who will find themselves involved: two boys can now say, "*We* are now playing *this* (alternative to the) game," or a boy and a girl can say, "*We* are now a couple" and make it a reality to all who care about either of them.

In other words, at all stages, history gets made through the assessment that *this* happened for the intents and purposes of people who emerge as a polity to each other because of their engagement with the assessment. Mutual engagement, it must be emphasized again, is not at all equivalent to acceptance of an assessment as the only possible one, or even to a recognition or agreement that one now finds oneself in the same polity. The most reluctant participant may actually be the most aware of the arbitrariness, if not symbolic violence (Bourdieu and Passeron 1977) that faced her and within which she was caught.

The Politics of Getting Caught in Complex Polities
The preceding case studies illustrate how new technologies, as they enter everyday life, can reveal classical processes in a new light. Wessler and Hung showed participants in very local politics. They also showed how the peculiar affordances of video games linked the ostensible participants to many others. Determining the boundaries of a polity is not an easy task for either the analyst or the actors.[16] The ethnomethodological tradition has made it plain that analysts should follow the actors for guidance. As Garfinkel put it, "It is the working of the phenomenon that exhibits among its other details the population that staffs it" (2002, 93). The principle is simple, but not easy to use—particularly when the actors are as confused as the analysts as to who is participating and to what effect. The problem was once dramatized in the movie *Taxi Driver,* in which Robert de Niro famously asks, "You talkin' to me? . . . Well, I'm the only one here. Who the f——do you think you're talking to?" Who, indeed is talking to whom when four youths play a video game? In *Taxi Driver,* the irony lies in the character being shown alone in his room, talking to his image in a mirror. Actually, it would be more ethnographically exact to answer that we see an actor

talking to a camera and, thus, to some audience in a movie theater. But even this answer is inadequate in that it does not mention the director, the maker of the camera, or the corporations that fund the film and distribute it.

Our concern now is with the determination of the "here," "who," and "what" when none is self-evident or when it appears that people are alone, writing for invisible audiences that they hope are accessible and might help them accomplish a practical task, or just having fun. In Andrews's setting (2010), blogging, the here would appear readily apparent: it is the web page one has opened. Who would appear to be the owner, identified someplace more or less prominently. What is sometimes specified by formal statements, or by the apparent implicature of opening posts. But all this may not be quite as clear as it seems. The markings of where one has been directed, who is the author of the page, and what it is about can be difficult to assess. Look, for example, at figure 2.4, a screenshot of the blog we treat in this case study:[17]

It is only by clicking on the seventh tab ("info") in the list of words on the second line that we find Jonathan Coulton introducing himself:

> My name is Jonathan Coulton and I'm a musician, a singer-songwriter and an internet superstar. This site is chock full of music, news and me-related merchandise—if you're not that familiar with who I am and what I do you can use the links above to get started. (Coulton 2006)

But many, when first arriving on a page suggested by some search engine, will not then look for an info page. This may be the most proximate reason for the common complaint of expert bloggers that people regularly post responses or comments which appear to imply that they are constructing another what for the blog, or another kind

Jonathan Coulton

music   shows   store   forums   wiki   photos   info   contact

Please Please Cancel My Account
June 13th, 2006

Here's a recording (if that link's swamped, here's a mirror) of a guy trying to cancel his AOL account. Now THAT is funny. Thanks Dr. Smith...

80 Responses to "Please Please Cancel My Account"

« Older Comments

cjohnson
November 14, 2007 at 12:43 am

OH GOD HOW DID I GET HERE I AM NOT GOOD WITH THE COMPUTER

Figure 2.4 Screenshot of Jonathan Coulton's blog including the original post and one of the latter comments (#51).

of person than the info page attempts to describe. Whether the posting of such comments is a symptom of ignorance or of design error is a matter of continuing debate among the expert bloggers themselves. Andrews focuses instead on the peculiar affordances of blogging, as well as of the search engines that lead people to a here that is not the one they were trying to reach, and that get them to interact with people with whom they have no interest in interacting.

Of all textual genres, blogging seems closest to essay writing. Like this chapter, a comment on a blog has a specified author or authors and various stylistic means to place the comment within a discursive tradition and its polities. Yet blogging, like essay writing, is concretely performed away from members of these polities in both time and place. Such genres (which also include letter writing and email) are interactionally asynchronous. Synchronicity (in face-to-face or telephone conversations) allows for ongoing assessments (feedback) of the relative efficacy of the stylistic means to establish that the text is actually being heard or read, that it is decipherable, that it does address an earlier statement in a conversation or discursive tradition, or that it does contribute something that other members of the polities might wish to criticize. In face-to-face conversation all this can be done on the fly and in parallel to the statement. At the other extreme, in book publishing, for example, assessments might come weeks, months, or years after publication (when the text is made public). Book authors may never learn what these assessments are, including what else might have been done with their text that they could not have imagined and that might have dismayed them.

It is on this last matter that blogging is interestingly different from other forms of text-making. Readers of blogs are encouraged by the software and the authors to comment and to have these comments made public. Consider this statement that appeared on Jonathan Coulton's blog. The entry that started the thread is titled "Please Please Cancel My Account" and is dated June 13, 2006:

> Here's a recording (if that link's swamped, here's a mirror) of a guy trying to cancel his AOL account. Now THAT is funny. Thanks Dr. Smith . . .

Among the next statements some suggest familiarity with the contexts indexed in the post ("if *that* link's swamped . . ."):

> Glenn
>
> June 13, 2006 at 3:24 pm
>
> Tried the mirror first, got bandwidth exceeded. Sigh. First link seems to work, although slow.
>
> [Comment #2]

Other comments expand on the first post in the same spirit:

> Carol
>
> June 14, 2006 at 4:44 pm
>
> I attempted twice to cancel AOL on speakerphone at work, just so my co-workers could laugh at their ridiculous antics with me. It was fun and annoying at the same time.
>
> [Comment #5]

Then the stream went quiet, but after a few months other comments appeared. They were of a different kind:

Zach

October 17, 2006 at 12:58 am

i wnt my aol account cancelled completely

[Comment #15]

Zach repeated his request six minutes later. This was followed within the hour by

Diana

November 7, 2006 at 1:26 am

I need to put my account on hold. I am moving but not into my new address until mid December. What do I do?

[Comment #15]

Fourteen other people made similar requests over the months that followed. In other words some, and eventually quite a lot of, people appeared to believe that they could cancel their AOL account by posting a request to Coulton's blog. Coulton himself eventually assessed these requests as being wrong:

Jonathan Coulton » Blog Archive » Funny Google Thing

May 11, 2007 at 5:55 am

. . . I have been watching with some amusement the growing number of comments at this old post of mine (about the recording of that guy trying to cancel his AOL account) from people who are actually trying to cancel some kind of account. I guess I can see how you could make that mistake if you were really not an internet person, but I really couldn't figure out how everyone was finding their way to that post. But this morning I googled "cancel my account" and guess what's the number one result? Thanks Google. . . .

[Comment #32]

This last comment is written as if addressed to a generalized audience. It could be either "you who are really an internet person" or, ironically, "Google" (although Coulton, as an "internet person," would know that Google does not attend to such comments). This particular comment did not stop the stream of requests, but it did start a new stream affirming, developing, and playing with the making of these requests. For example, the next comment, made two hours after Coulton's, reads thus:

Brett

May 11, 2007 at 7:35 am

Hey JC, looks like you might have the making of a new internet business on your hands here. Global Account Cancellation Services. So when you're not busy writing new songs and performing all over the country, you can hang around on the phone cancelling accounts for other people.

[Comment #33]

The last comment in the thread dates from July 2010—three years later—when Domingo requests, "please cancel my playboy account thanks [Comment #80]."[18]

The eighty comments as read in summer 2011 make quite an interesting (postmodern?) text. It looks like a transcript of a strange conversation. But it is of course not a single conversation but a partial record of multiple conversations that interfere with each other. We have evidence of the way Coulton and his ostensible polity noticed the interference and played with it. We have little evidence of the conversations that led Zach, Diana, and Domingo to post their requests on Coulton's blog. We have no direct evidence of their assessment of the (lack of) response by Coulton, or whoever they imagined they were addressing. We do have some textual evidence that request comments were part of complex sequences. For example, these three statements were posted within three minutes of each other (with no other comment interfering) on the same day:[19]

dr.smith

December 1, 2007 at 11:17 am

sorry but i am really really a girl i am 14 years old it was a mistake that i signed male instead of female please delete my hi5 account.my name is raniquw deadra carroll. it will be very helpfull if you delete my account off hi5.thank you very much.sir/madam.

[Comment #53]

ranique

December 1, 2007 at 11:18 am

my name is ranique

[Comment #54]

ranique

December 1, 2007 at 11:20 am

sorry about puttin your name there.

[Comment #55]

That it was wrong to post these comments on *this* blog is not exactly a problem for the writers—except to the extent that it will not achieve what they wish to accomplish. We have evidence that some felt that something was wrong. As one commenter shouted:

cjohnson

November 14, 2007 at 12:43 am

OH GOD HOW DID I GET HERE I AM NOT GOOD WITH THE COMPUTER

[Comment # 51]

In another paper on this and other such threads, Andrews and Varenne (2011) pointed that such practical mistakes, when they are sequenced within an overall search, can also be seen as evidence for everyday ongoing education about one's actual world. Here we want only to emphasize the vagueness of the markers that indicate to which polity a blog belongs, the complicity of search engines amplifying this vagueness, and the vagaries of the actual design of the visual interfaces provided by the blogging software. As is true of video games, the crowd of engineers and programmers that produce all this—whether or not they are aware of the difficulties they are making for expert users as well as newbies—are themselves limited by their own position and the affordances of their materials.[20] And yet, in this complex network, in Latour's sense, *this* is "it" for some purpose: a place to laugh at AOL making it difficult to cancel an account, a place to cancel the account, or a place where one is judged to be ignorant—but perhaps without serious consequences.

In, Temporary, Conclusion

The attention we gave to people trying to cancel their AOL account may seem to have taken us far from our starting point—playing with the other traditions in which the term "assessment" has currency. Assessments of being "wrong," or "in error," or "ignorant" in the worlds of video gaming or blogging may be embarrassing, but they generally do not threaten one's career. This is quite different from what can happen at the end of a testing sequence for certain high-stakes assessments. In those cases one's life can radically change in the course of the behavioral event; although making a pencil mark on a piece of paper may not be much different from pushing a button on a controller, or posting a brief request on a blog, or twitching. But we are concerned with tracing the differences in the consequentialities of assessments produced by complex polities for political purposes. Assessments do not constitute simply what is happening in the present. They also produce a new future in terms of the polities that make this or that event and its assessment politically consequential—and to what extent. The original act, be it a twitch of the muscles around the eyes, a squeeze of the fingers, or a mark on a test, may be long over when the assessment is made—and the consequences may be even farther reaching.

Many have looked retrospectively at historical conditions and noted that the meting of such consequences does happen and it can be unfair and hurtful. But we are not interested in retrospective explanation or archeologies of the past. Our call is for a recentering of social analyses from a concern with deconstruction to a concern with the ongoing production of emergent futures. Tracing the history of any assessment can be interesting, but that alone is not sufficient. Geertz led the way when he talked about thick descriptions but gave little guidance on how to do this, and his conclusion about the usefulness of such descriptions introduced what became his pessimism about anthropology. "The vocation of anthropology" cannot, in his words, simply be "making available to us answers that others, guarding other sheep in other valleys, have given, and thus to include them in the consultable record of what man has said" (1973, 30). It has to be the identification of what is involved in the giving of answers.

More precisely, the vocation of anthropology, we dare say, is carefully investigating temporal sequences to figure out what happens between the earlier and later parts of the sequence as they concern the placement of the participants and what they will be known for having done. In schools, doctors' offices, and psychological clinics, we know that ultimately winks are winks and twitches are twitches whose intents and purposes can have long-lasting consequences. When a polity plays deeply (to expand on Geertz), the rewards can be great, but the risks are just as great. High-stakes assessments thus cannot fail to become the focus of political activity, and not only at the national level. At the most local of levels, where anthropologists are best at the work of discovery, the politics are just as intense—yet they operate in ways that cannot quite be imagined. As an assessment approaches, and then recedes, a polity gets established; in the world of schooling, for example, parents, children, teachers, and administrators find themselves struggling with inescapable regulations and tools created by people far away. Their world is not quite a stage; and they play what is, after all, not a game. And yet, as Shakespeare intuited, examining stages and games can illuminate when people are assessed and some are found to be experts, whereas others are told they cannot play anymore.

We are starting to get research reports that give us a sense of what can be gained by pursuing this route (Eyal et al. 2010; Koyama 2010). We need more.

:-)

Epilogue

In September 1982, people at the Carnegie Mellon School of Computer Science found themselves faced with a problem of their own making when some of them sent a message about a fire in the elevator. The authors wrote it as a joke. Some of the recipients took it literally. Scott Fahlman suggested a solution that made history:

19-Sep-82 11:44   Scott E Fahlman   :-)

From: Scott E Fahlman <Fahlman at Cmu-20c>

I propose that [*sic*] the following character sequence for joke markers:

:-)

Read it sideways. Actually, it is probably more economical to mark things that are NOT jokes, given current trends. For this, use

:-(

(Fahlman 1982)

This was posted as a comment on a thread after a joking comment had been interpreted as a threat. This was a problem that had to be resolved given the affordances of early versions of software that would become current blogging software. Then, as always, one had to be able to distinguish between messages to be taken at face value and messages to be taken as joking commentary that might have been accompanied with a wink had the statement been made face to face. For there are times when winks *must* be taken as just that. Either there is a fire in the elevator or there is not. On the anniversary of Fahlman's history-making suggestion, commentator Garrison Keillor summarized the thread as follows:

> The following day, after the rumor had finally been put to rest, someone wrote, "Maybe we should adopt a convention of putting a star (*) in the subject field of any notice that is to be taken as a joke." It is, of course, impossible to know whether the writer intended this post as a legitimate course of action or as a joke. Regardless, numerous people chimed in with various suggestions, the earnestness of which was, again, difficult to determine. Was the poster who recommended using the percent sign instead of the asterisk sincere? Possibly. The one who proclaimed that the ampersand looks "like a jolly fat man in convulsions of laughter"? Probably not. The one who developed a complete taxonomy and scale of joke types and values, complete with a coding schema? These were computer scientists, after all. (Keillor 2011)

We should certainly celebrate the power of social processes to give us occasions to laugh.

ACKNOWLEDGMENTS

We wish to thank the people who let us observe them. We are also indebted to the students and colleagues who participated in the seminars of the Study Group on Everyday Education at Teachers College, Columbia University, from 2007 to 2010.

NOTES

1. This chapter is part of a sequence of essays on education and the politics of productive ignorance (Varenne 2007a, 2007b, 2008, 2009, 2011).
2. Note that this is true of any technology that is new to a population. See research on the introduction of snowmobiles and GPS navigation among the Inuit (Aporta and Higgs 2005; Pelto 1973).
3. Foucault, of course, developed this much further into a political critique of our dominant polities as the classify to discipline and punish (1970, 1979).
4. We will not discuss the complex debate between structuralists and symbolists on the matter of the relationship of classifications to meaning or the mind. Our work suggests that this debate was off target and confused the fundamental issues.
5. This description is commonly used in the industry. How the underlying classificatory scheme has been produced is a matter for historical investigation and is a matter of ongoing discussion (Juul 2005; Newman and Oram 2006).
6. They could do that from their own terminals elsewhere in the room.
7. As we did elsewhere (Varenne and McDermott 1998), we capitalize School and Teacher when indexing institutions and roles rather than particular schools or individual teachers.
8. Others, inspired by Rancière (1999), might see here the glory of the ignorant schoolmaster letting their pupils discover for themselves what they are interested in learning, including who can best help them (and who cannot).
9. The situation is comparable but radically different from the moments when a teacher, following the kind of assessment current school reformers advocate, is to be fired for not being able to improve student scores.
10. All participants could handle either language well enough for strictly game-related moves. The boys did a lot of code switching, but mostly about metacommunicational matters. Sometimes they made fun of Li's speech, or shifted into Cantonese when they discussed her moves or planned further play.
11. The quotations included in this chapter are a summary of the published analysis. There the transcript is done according to the usual conversational analysis (CA) strictures and includes the original Cantonese or Mandarin.

12. One of the players considered briefly whether to make up an alternate version of the game in which the point would be to increase the number: How high would it go? What would have to be done in order to increase it? Two of the boys later played yet another alternate version of the game.

13. In this game, the problem is actually quite complex since none of the numbers are scores in the naïve sense. They are stated as percentages and are supposed to give the player information about his state and his progress towards death. This ambiguity was actually built into this particular game by its designers.

14. Adding to the confusion is the fact that half the buttons on the controller do nothing and must be actively ignored.

15. Various message boards provide forums in which users vent their frustrations. Whether these comments affect designers, or how designers filter these comments, is something that remains to be investigated.

16. The classic text should be Robert Redfield's altogether forgotten *The Little Community* (1960), which summarized a quarter century of work struggling with the issues surrounding whether and how a community is a community, to whom, and for what purposes. As the currency of the word "community" has been reconstituted in such phrases as "communities of practice" or "participatory structures," the issues remain.

17. All statements are from a stream of eighty comments to the initial one (Coulton 2006). Note that we are treating Jonathan Coulton as a published author, not as an informant.

18. We do not have evidence that this was indeed the last comment, since Coulton may have decided to delete further comments.

19. The name above the time stamp on the comments should, in the blog designer's view, be the name of the comment writer. The blog designer expects the commenter to see the field labeled "name" on the comment submission form and enter his or her own name. The blog software then posts this data to indicate authorship of the comment. It appears that this writer constructed this box as a place for the name of the addressee, which she took to be "dr.smith"—the only person named in the original post (see fig. 2.4). Within a minute the writer noticed the error and, two minutes later, apologized for what was actually the wrong error.

20. Newbies, in netspeak, are referred to as "n00bs."

REFERENCES

Andrews, Gillian. 2010. "This is Elsewhere.org": Users and machines making literacy work on blogs. PhD diss., Teachers College, Columbia University.

Andrews, Gillian, and Hervé Varenne. 2011. Education into the online world: On the appropriation of online text and the production of everyday knowledge. *Global Media Journal* 11, no. 18, article 1. lass.purduecal.edu/cca/gmj/sp11/gmj-sp11-article1.htm.

Aporta, Claudio, and Eric Higgs. 2005. Satellite culture. *Current Anthropology* 46:729–53.

Bourdieu, Pierre. 1990. *The logic of practice.* Trans. R. Nice. Stanford, CA: Stanford University Press.

Bourdieu, Pierre, and Jean-Claude Passeron. 1977. *Reproduction in education, society and culture.* Trans. R. Nice. Beverly Hills, CA: Sage.

Coulton, Jonathan. 2006. Please please cancel my account. *Jonathan Coulton,* June 13.www.jonathan coulton.com/2006/06/13/please-please-cancel-my-account/.

Dewey, John. 1959. My pedagogic creed. In *Dewey on education: Selections,* ed. M. Dworkin, 19–32. New York: Teachers College Press.

Eyal, Gil, Brendan Hart, Emine Onculer, Neta Oren, and Natasha Rossi. 2010. *The autism matrix: The social origins of the autism epidemic.* Malden, MA: Polity Press.

Fahlman, Scott. 1982. Original Bboard thread in which :-) was proposed. www-2.cs.cmu.edu/~sef/Orig-Smiley.htm.

Foucault, Michel. 1970. *The order of things: An archeology of the human sciences.* New York: Random House.

———. 1979. *Discipline and punish.* Trans. A. Sheridan. New York: Penguin Books.

Garfinkel, Harold. 1956. Conditions of successful degradation ceremonies. *American Journal of Sociology* 61:420–24.

———. 1967. *Studies in ethnomethodology.* Englewood Cliffs, NJ: Prentice Hall.

———. 2002. *Ethnomethodology's program: Working out Durkheim's aphorism.* Lanham, MD: Rowman and Littlefield.

Geertz, Clifford. 1973. Thick description: Toward an interpretive theory of culture. In *The interpretation of cultures,* 3–30. New York: Basic Books.

Gellner, Ernest. 1975. Ethnomethodology: The re-enchantment industry of the Californian way of subjectivity. *Philosophy of the Social Sciences* 5, no. 3:431–50.

Goodwin, Charles, and Marjorie Goodwin. 1987. Concurrent operations on talk: Notes on the interactive organization of assessments. *Papers in Pragmatics* 1:1–54.

———. 1992. Assessments and the construction of context. In *Rethinking context,* ed. A. Duranti and C. Goodwin, 147–90. New York: Cambridge University Press.

Hanks, William. 1996. Exorcism and the description of participant roles. In *Natural histories of discourse,* ed. M. Silverstein and G. Urban, 160–200. Chicago: University of Chicago Press.

Hung, Aaron. 2011. *The work of play: Meaning-making in videogames.* New York: Peter Lang.

Juul, Jesper. 2005. *Half-real: Video games between real rules and fictional worlds.* Cambridge, MA: MIT Press.

Keillor, Garrison. 2011. Nonsense by Matt Cook. *The writer's almanac,* September 19. www.elabs7.com/ functions/message_view.html?mid=1329699andmlid=499andsiteid=20130anduid =09280b15c4.

Koyama, Jill. 2010. *Making failure pay: For-profit tutoring, high-stake testing, and public schools.* Chicago: University of Chicago Press.

Latour, Bruno. 2005. *Reassembling the social: An introduction to actor-network theory.* New York: Oxford University Press.

Lévi-Strauss, Claude. 1966. *Totemism.* Trans. R. Needham. Boston: Beacon Press.

Mauss, Marcel. 1979. *Sociology and psychology: Essays.* Trans. B. Brewster. London: Routledge and Kegan Paul.

McDermott, Ray. 1993. The acquisition of a child by a learning disability. In *Understanding practice,* ed. M. Silverstein and G. Urban, 269–305. New York: Cambridge University Press.

Mehan, Hugh. 1979. *Learning lessons: Social organization in the classroom.* Cambridge, MA: Harvard University Press.

———. 1996. The construction of an LD student: A case study in the politics of representation. In *Natural histories of discourse,* ed. M. Silverstein and G. Urban, 253–76. Chicago: University of Chicago Press.

Mehan, Hugh, A. Hertwerk, and J. Meihls. 1986. *Handicapping the handicapped.* Stanford, CA: Stanford University Press.

Newman, James, and Barney Oram. 2006. *Teaching videogames.* London: British Film Institute.

Pelto, Perti. 1973. *The snowmobile revolution: Technology and social change in the Arctic.* Menlo Park, CA: Cummings.

Pomerantz, Anita. 1984. Agreeing and disagreeing with assessments: Some feature of preferred/dispreferred turn shapes. In *Structures of social action,* ed. J. M. Atkinson and J. Heritage, 57–101. New York: Cambridge University Press.

Rancière, Jacques. 1999. *The ignorant schoolmaster: Five lessons in intellectual emancipation.* Trans. K. Ross. Stanford, CA: Stanford University Press.

Redfield, Robert. 1960. *The little community.* Chicago: University of Chicago Press.

Sacks, Harvey. 1972. Notes on police assessment of moral character. In *Studies in social interaction,* ed. D. Sudnow, 280–93. New York: Free Press.

———.1974. An analysis of the course of a joke's telling in conversation. In *Explorations in the ethnography of speaking,* ed. R. Bauman and J. Sherzer, 337–53. New York: Cambridge University Press.

Suchman, Lucy. 2007. *Human-machine reconfigurations: Plans and situated actions.* 2nd ed. Cambridge: Cambridge University Press.

Varenne, Hervé. 2007a. The production of difference in interaction: On culturing conversation through play. In *Theoretical approaches to dialogue analysis,* ed. L. Berlin, 177–97. Tübingen, Germany: Max Niemeyer Verlag.

———. 2007b. Difficult collective deliberations: Anthropological notes toward a theory of education. *Teachers College Record* 109, no. 7:1559–87.

———. 2008. Culture, education, anthropology. *Anthropology and Education Quarterly* 39, no. 4:356–68.

———. 2009. The powers of ignorance: On finding out what to do next. *Critical Studies in Education* 50, no. 3:337–43.

———. 2011. Education, cultural production, and figuring out what to do next. In *Companion to the anthropology of education,* ed. B. Levinson and M. Pollock, 50–64. Malden, MA: Wiley-Blackwell.

Varenne, Hervé, and May McDermott. 1998. *Successful failure: The school America builds.* Boulder, CO: Westview.

Wikipedia. 2010. Gamecube-controller-breakdown. commons.wikimedia.org/wiki/File:Gamecube -controller-breakdown.jpg.

3

Participatory Culture and Metalinguistic Discourse: Performing and Negotiating German Dialects on YouTube

JANNIS ANDROUTSOPOULOS
University of Hamburg

Introduction

DRAWING ON DISCOURSE THEORY, sociolinguistics and social semiotics, this chapter uses the notion of discourse as social practice for the study of metalinguistic discourse online. Based on two years of ethnographic observation and a mixed-methods approach, it explores the representation of German dialects on YouTube, thereby examining the multimodal performance of dialect in videos and the negotiation of these performances in audience comments. The discussion starts by introducing the notion of discourse as social practice and YouTube as a site of online participatory culture. It then introduces the concept of "participatory spectacle," which focuses on the relation between a video and its audience responses, thereby emphasizing the collaborative character of discourse on YouTube. The representation of German dialects in the mass media and on the internet is then briefly reviewed. An analytic framework that draws on performance, stylization, and multimodality is outlined, and the data is presented. The findings are divided into a discussion of video genres and audience responses across dialect regions, and a contrastive analysis of two vernacular spectacles that engage with the Berlin city dialect. The chapter concludes with a discussion of the ways in which dialect-tagged videos and their comments diversify and destabilize the public representation of dialects in the German-speaking context.

Reframing Discourse in the Study of Computer-Mediated Discourse

Most research on language on the internet proceeds from a concept of discourse that originates in pragmatics and the study of spoken language. Discourse is defined as language in use or naturally occurring spoken language in social context, and juxtaposed either to text or to a structuralist approach to language that stops at the sentence level. In this vein, computer-mediated discourse (CMD) refers to naturally occurring written language in human-to-human communication via computer networks (Herring 2001, 2004). I focus on a second understanding of discourse in linguistics, that of discourse as social practice. A well-known juxtaposition between the two can be found in Gee (2005), who distinguishes between "(lower case) discourse," meaning "language-in-use or stretches of language," and what he terms "capital D discourse," which he defines as "ways of doing and being an X" (Gee 2005, 26–27). According to Gee, discourses are "ways of combining and integrating language, actions, interactions, ways of thinking, believing, valuing and using various symbols, tools, and objects to enact a particular sort of socially recognizable identity" (2005, 21).

Gee's notion of ("capital D") Discourse is inspired by the work of French philosopher Michel Foucault, whose ideas have had tremendous influence across humanities and social sciences since the 1980s (Mills 2004). Following up on Foucault, researchers in fields such as critical linguistics and critical discourse analysis defined discourse as socially situated and institutionally regulated language practice with a reality-constructing capacity (Fairclough and Wodak 1997; van Dijk 2008). This understanding of discourse is captured in Foucault's seminal definition of discourse as "practices that systematically form the objects of which they speak" (Mills 2004, 17). Critical discourse scholars posit that discourse produces social knowledge, and they study how linguistic and semiotic choices contribute to representations and interactions within discourse. To that end, toolkits of analysis are developed, which include categories such as conceptual metaphor, syntactic constructions, lexical choice, rhetorical figures, argumentation patterns, and text-image relationships.

To date, this approach to discourse has been peripheral in CMD studies, just as critical discourse analysis has focused on mass media rather than new media. But intersections do exist—especially in European research, which includes work on public participation in political or therapeutic discourse (Wodak and Wright 2007; Stommel 2009); power relations in the editing of Wikipedia entries (Fraas and Pentzold 2008); the multimodal discourse analysis of websites (Meier 2008); and not least on metalinguistic discourse, notably the construction of new media language itself (Thurlow 2006; see also Squires 2010; Thurlow and Mroczek 2011a). Looking at CMD from a discourse-as-social-practice perspective entails a shift of focus: rather than language in the new media as such, a key question is how discourse in the new media shapes the production of knowledge and the negotiations of power relations among participants in public online encounters.

In this chapter I argue that discourse as social practice offers a window to the linguistic study of online participatory culture. Focusing on discourses on dialect, I ask how people use the opportunities offered by participatory digital media in order to engage with representations of dialect. I examine how YouTube becomes a stage for metalinguistic discourse jointly constructed by videos and audience responses, which negotiate their understandings of German dialects by drawing on various genres, remix techniques, and language styles.

YouTube: Participatory Culture and Participatory Spectacles

Henry Jenkins (2009a) outlines five defining features of online participatory culture: relatively low barriers to artistic expression and civic engagement; support for creating and sharing one's projects; informal mentorship; a belief that contributions matter; and a sense of social connection. Of these the most relevant to my argument is accessibility. Participatory culture is collectively and individually premised on low entry requirements, or accessible means of participation, and YouTube is a prime example for this. Its low barriers and the user support it provides in terms of its interface design facilitate "easy entry into the community and legitimate engagement even at the periphery" (Chau 2010, 68). Depending on individual engagement, participation can then become more regular, and leadership roles with regard to contributing to a YouTube community can emerge.

Also relevant to my argument is the contrast between YouTube's low entry requirements and the conditions of access to mainstream media discourse. In critical discourse analysis, restricted access to the production of media discourse is fundamental to the theorization of discourse and power relationships (such as van Dijk 2008; Fairclough 1995). Media corporations and public broadcast organizations control public discourse in terms of both the selection and presentation of discourse objects; therefore they have a crucial influence on its effects on audiences. Against this backdrop, online participatory culture increases the chance that within a specific (say, political) discourse, contributions from below will be heard and potentially play a role in the unfolding of discourse. YouTube in particular emerged as "a key site for the production and distribution of grassroots media" (Jenkins 2006, 274). YouTube and other social media are global resources for civic engagement, protest, and activism. Recent examples include the role of social media in the "Arab Spring" (Hofheinz 2011) and the uncovering of a former German minister's plagiarism of research for his doctoral dissertation through evidence that was collaboratively documented on a wiki.[1]

In these and other cases, online participatory culture weakens the power of mass media in defining social reality and truth. Although alternative and countercultural publics with their own niche media existed well before YouTube (Jenkins 2006, 2009b), contemporary spaces of online participation offer a much broader reach and interfaces to mainstream mass media, which facilitate reciprocal appropriations of content. Social media activities are regularly quoted and referenced by mass media, just as mass media information is subjected to critique and scrutiny by bloggers and other members of online participatory culture. Fringe media activities are gradually being normalized (Jenkins 2006, 274–76), and patterns of circulation between mainstream media and online participatory practices are becoming denser.

This political (in the broadest sense of the term) dimension of digital participatory culture is one aspect of YouTube theorization in cultural and media studies. Another relevant aspect is its aesthetics, again in the broadest sense of the term. YouTube is celebrated as a site of vernacular creativity in the digital age, characterized by practices of appropriation and remix (Burgess and Green 2009; Lovink and Niederer 2008; Snickars and Vonderau 2009). Lankshear and Knobel (2008) define remix as the practice of taking cultural artifacts and combining and manipulating them into a new kind of creative blend (see also Burgess and Green 2009, 25–26). YouTube users can be viewed as intertextual operators at the interface of global and local cultures, and remix can be used as a resource for engaging with and resisting dominant discourses (Androutsopoulos 2010a).

From a language-centered perspective, remix is one aspect of the new discourse practices that digital media and participatory platforms such as YouTube make possible. Computer-mediated communication (CMC) has evolved from a predominance of written language to a wealth of semiotic resources, and YouTube epitomizes the complexity of modes and media that has by now become the new standard on the participatory web. Although interactive written language remains part of that complexity, such as in the form of audience comments (Jones and Schieffelin 2009; Chun and Walters 2011), the combinations of modes and media enabled by YouTube go beyond the traditional classificatory categories of CMD scholarship—that is to say, modes of communication defined by their degree of synchronicity and publicness. I therefore focus on intertextuality (textual interconnectedness), multimodality (combinations of semiotic modes), and heteroglossia (deployment of sociolinguistic difference) as defining characteristics of online participatory environments (Androutsopoulos 2010a).

Every YouTube page consists of a video, its audience responses (comments and video responses), and a hosting environment that includes a list of related videos and other peripheral elements.[2] Although each textual bit on a YouTube page can be viewed as a distinct textual unit, videos and comments co-occur in a patterned way and are interrelated in meaning making. I use the term "participatory spectacle" to refer to this patterned co-occurrence (Androutsopoulos 2010a), thereby emphasizing the collaborative production and visual character of YouTube content. Viewed as an organic whole, participatory spectacles are multiauthored, multimodal, multimedia, inherently dialogic, dynamically expanding, and open ended. They are multiauthored in the sense that videos, comments, and surrounding elements come from different actors; they are multimodal in that they consist of a variety of semiotic modes; and they are multimedia in terms of their audiovisual structure, which brings film and written language together. YouTube pages are dialogic not only in the obvious sense of comments made in response to videos, but also in terms of relations among comments and the intertextual qualities of many videos. And they are expanding and open ended in that comments and video responses may be added at any time, while their surrounding textual bits—such as lists of related videos—are ever changing, depending on the site's algorithms. All of the above are relevant in terms of how people read and interact with YouTube—whether by visiting a page, playing and replaying a video, commenting, browsing through and rating others' comments, forwarding and sharing, or downloading and remixing.

Before YouTube: Dialect Discourses and Representations in the Media

Dialect—that is, linguistic difference related to space—is a fundamental dimension of linguistic differentiation, and discourse on dialect is nothing new.[3] From a discourse-as-social-practice perspective, dialect discourses are not just reports or discussions about language in relation to local space, but rather practices that contribute to shaping the meaning of the language they discuss.[4] In CMD research, dialect metalanguage has enjoyed little attention. Work on the discursive construction of internet language examines the metalinguistic representation of stereotypical netspeak features such as acronyms, emoticons, brevity, or nonstandard orthography, whereas work on sociolinguistic variation online has examined dialect use rather than dialect discourse. But dialect use can be a part of dialect discourse, and this is particularly obvious with performative uses of language in the media and popular culture.

German is a pluricentric language (Clyne 1992), in which decentralized language norms persist and local varieties of language are not generally stigmatized. Despite ongoing dialect leveling, dialects are very much present in the sociolinguistics of German-speaking countries, with north-south differences in terms of usage and prestige (Barbour and Stevenson 1990). Popular and fictional representations of German dialects look back to a century-old tradition in art, culture, stage, and fiction (Niebaum and Macha 2006). Before the emergence of standard German, dialects were used in early-modern newspapers or manuscript writing as defaults. The restructuring of sociolinguistic space that followed up on standardization positioned dialect in public usage as a secondary choice, by which dialect is inserted into texts or performances that are predominantly in the standard language. In the mass media era, German dialects are a resource for various patterns of contrastive usage, thereby evoking interrelated indexical meaning (Androutsopoulos 2010b). Dialect is used primarily to create localized meaning, or to index a speaker's local origin or affiliation. Dialect is also a resource for signifying social stratification, being relegated to less-educated or less-mobile speakers and indexing lower status than that of other speakers in the same text or performance. Dialect has also been used to index private, familiar, and intimate domains of social life as opposed to public, institutional, or official settings. These indexical and symbolic meanings of dialect are interrelated and co-occur across various media, genres, and topics. For instance, German political caricature often draws on dialect in order to stylize local, working-class voices that are staged as frank, but provincial and narrow minded.

Such representations, in which dialect is not talked about but used in purposeful, reflexive ways, contribute to shaping the social meaning of particular dialects (such as Bavarian or Swabian) as much as dialect as an abstract entity juxtaposed with an equally abstract standard language. There is change in these representations, and new media are part of this change. Recent years have witnessed more media spaces and niches in which local speech can be used as stylistic resource and staged as a positively valued element of institutional identity (Birkner and Gilles 2008; Coupland 2009; Androutsopoulos 2010b). However, dialect use in the mass media is still subject to the normative authority of media institutions and therefore to policing practices which restrict its currency and value. Differences of media, genre, and topic aside, dialect speakers in broadcasts are lay people more often than presenters or hosts, or low-status or minor characters rather than protagonists. The occasional use of dialect by an authority figure such as a reporter or show host will often be double voiced, jocular, or part of reported speech (Androutsopoulos 2010b, 753).

Practices of mediated dialect use are part of dialect discourse to the extent that they rely on and reproduce sociolinguistic knowledge, which ascribes particular values and social positions to local speech. However, due to the historical depth of German dialects, contemporary media discourse perpetuates and reproduces the social place of dialect rather than constructing it anew. An illuminating case in point is the discursive making of Pittsburghese, as studied by Johnstone (2010). Since the 1960s, a number of discursive practices resulted in the widespread awareness of a Pittsburgh city dialect despite the absence of prior academic description. Its typical features are empirically evidenced in spoken language, but are not restricted to the city area; many features are lexically specific. Pittsburghese is constructed not just by feature selection but by being labeled and thematized in genres such as local radio contests, tourist brochures, lay glossaries, Wikipedia entries, and forum discussions. Such online participatory media as web discussion forums figure large among the stages on which Pittsburghese is constructed.

German Dialects Online: From Internet Relay Chat to YouTube

In the German context, dialect use and dialect discourse have been part of CMC since its earliest days. Anecdotal evidence suggests that people have been using the web since its inception in order to reflexively engage with the representation of dialects, whether by producing unofficial, dialect-written home pages for their towns or by setting up glossaries and digital archives of dialect words and phrases (Reershemius 2010). The (now-defunct) "Schwobifying Proxy," a website that was active from 1998 to 2004, produced jocular dialect translations of other websites into mock Swabian dialect.[5] This tradition continues in the Web 2.0 era and benefits from its additional opportunities. In Germany, anyone interested in dialect can access a Google map annotated with audio samples from various dialects (such as dialektkarte.de) or join a variety of Facebook groups dedicated to dialects. Marketing campaigns reproduce traditional representations of (male, middle-aged, working-class) dialect speakers in viral videos (see selection 7, below) or invest in positive, youthful, dynamic representations of dialect speakers. One example is a 2009 German-language campaign by Microsoft's email brand, Hotmail, featuring the slogan *Sag's besser per hotmail* ("Better say it with Hotmail"). These observations set a background against which to assess dialect representations on YouTube.

On YouTube, dialect discourses emerge by virtue of video titles and tags. Giving a video a title or tag that denotes a local dialect—say, *Bairisch* ("Bavarian") or *Sächsisch* ("Saxonian")—makes that video retrievable through a keyword search.[6] A repeated examination of approximately twenty German dialect tags suggests that in June 2011, their hits ranged from 6,870 for *Schwäbisch* (Swabian) to just 1 for Ripuarisch (Ripuarian).[7] Taken together, these dialect tags provide a YouTube dialect map, a folksonomy of German dialects that is accessible to users and researchers. Southern German dialects (such as Alemannisch, Fränkisch, or Pfälzisch) are featured more frequently than northern and eastern ones (such as Sächsisch, Berlinerisch, or Thüringisch), a distribution that reflects the higher vitality of southern German dialects and their more frequent presence in entertainment and popular culture. Some dialect-tagged videos are highly popular, having received more than 2 million views and a few thousand comments. These figures clearly suggest that there is an interest in the representation and discussion of German dialects on YouTube.

The Social Semiotics of Participatory Spectacles: A Toolkit for Analysis

My approach to this material integrates CMD studies, post-variationist sociolinguistics, and social semiotics. In this section I introduce the concepts of performance and stylization and discuss how they can be applied to the YouTube data. I also draw on the framework of social semiotics to address the multimodal nature of participatory spectacles.

Looking at dialect as performance or stylization establishes a theoretical perspective that is juxtaposed to a structuralist understanding of language as "speaker behavior" (Coupland 2001). Performance is understood here to be a mode of speaking characterized by orientation to an audience, attention to the form and materiality of speaking, and reflexivity (see Bauman 1992; Coupland 2001; Bell and Gibson 2011; Pennycook 2007; Scharloth 2009). Richard Bauman points out that in performance "the act of communication is put on display, objectified, lifted to a degree from its contextual surroundings, and opened up to scrutiny by an audience. Performance thus calls forth attention to and heightened awareness of the act of communication" (1992, 44). Stylization, however, focuses more specifically on the representation of speaker personae (Coupland 2001). In stylization, performers bring up images of so-called typical dialect speakers, thereby relying on the cultural and sociolinguistic knowledge they assume sharing with their audiences.

Dialect-tagged videos and their comments generally share characteristics of staged performance: they are publicly available, bounded in space and time (rather short films that are played in a video window on a web page), oriented to an audience, and reflexive of their own communicative properties. The very practice of dialect-tagging a video is reflexive insofar as users decide to associate their video material with a regional dialect. Even if the subject matter of a video is in itself not explicitly performative (as in the case of, say, a dialect speaker who is unaware he or she is being recorded), its display on YouTube frames it as staged performance. Moreover, communicative reflexivity is a feature of most dialect-tagged videos: YouTube videos and their comments do not just happen to use dialect. They explicitly orient to dialect and showcase it for an imagined or assumed audience.

Dialect-tagged videos, then, in principle constitute dialect performances. Dialect stylization, on the other hand, establishes indexical links between dialect performance and aspects of the speaker's social identity, which are more or less explicitly evoked. For instance, one of the videos discussed below (see example 6 in the appendix) shows a working-class Berliner, a tour bus driver, talking about Berlin while driving his bus by some of Berlin's iconic monuments. Here the performance of Berlin dialect is part of the stylization of a typical Berlin dialect speaker, and stylization is achieved through coordinated deployment of dialect use, visual setting, and social activity. The pair of examples examined in section 8 provides two more stylizations of Berlin dialect speakers: a nightclub girl and a computer tutor. In all these cases, dialect stylization is carried out in a fictional mode. However, in the YouTube recitations of a traditional Berlin rhyme (see examples 9–10 in the appendix), the social identity of a typical dialect speaker is not made relevant: these videos focus on voice and content rather than social features of the speaker.

A sociolinguistic study of YouTube dialect spectacles must take into account their visual dimension and the ways in which remix practices create new conditions for dialect performance and stylization, as I will now illustrate. In engaging with dialect, YouTube users appropriate semiotic resources and assemble them anew using media techniques such as separating and recombining video and audio tracks or layering footage with new audio tracks. Dialect performances often draw on different materials and remix them, thereby creating dissonance or incongruence that in turn may generate humor or challenge dialect stereotypes. In order to account for the multimodal and multimedia nature of this material, I draw on the four levels of analysis in the social semiotics framework proposed by van Leeuwen (2005)—discourse, genre, style, and modality—adapting them to the purposes of this research. I briefly outline them here, indicating how they shape the following sections:

- With regard to *discourse,* we focus on the metalinguistic knowledge with which producers and audiences of a participatory spectacle engage. Here we may ask the following: What are the topics of these videos in word and image? How do videos and comments orient to metalinguistic discourse? What semiotic resources do they use in order to thematize dialect? What attitudes towards dialect and its speakers do they communicate? What other discourses are evoked through intertextual and intermedia relations in a spectacle?

- In considering *genre,* the focus shifts to the social activities in dialect-tagged videos and their comments. What genres do dialect-tagged videos draw on, and how do these genres frame various representations of dialect? What genres do comments draw on in engaging with a reference video?

- The dimension of *style* turns to the social identities that participants link to dialect and the linguistic and visual resources that videos and comments draw on in order to index these identities. We may ask how the actors or (fictional) characters in a video are stylized, and what dialect features are used to that end. We may also ask how commenters engage with dialect identities, for example, by identifying themselves as speakers of particular dialects or by expressing stances towards a video's dialect performance.

- In my treatment of *mode* I depart from van Leeuwen's focus on modality and turn to the semiotic modes and technological resources that are part of the production of a video and therefore shape its representation of dialect. Aspects of mode in this sense are the division of labor between language and moving image in a video or the use of remix techniques such as dubbing or collage. However, modality can also be brought to bear on the analysis as regards the epistemic and interactional modalities that videos and comments express with regard to dialect.

This Study
The remainder of this chapter is in two parts. The first discusses dialect discourse in participatory spectacles based on analysis of 310 dialect-tagged videos from six regions (from south to north, these are Bavarian, Swabian, Badenese, Palatinate, Berlin city dialect, and Low German) and comments on selected videos from these regions. All videos were initially coded for five features: (a) their production modes and (b) genres (discussed below); (c) their dialect use (that is, whether the dialect indicated in a video's title or tag is indeed used in the video); (d) the occurrence of dialect metalanguage; and (e) their orientation to localness (whether the area related to a partic-

ular dialect is thematized). This allowed me to filter out videos that engage with dialect only peripherally, and to select focus items for the subsequent qualitative part of the analysis. A selection of 19 items is provided in the appendix. This part of the analysis focuses on the genre orientations of the videos and common patterns of engagement with dialect in the comments to these videos. The second part is a contrastive microanalysis of two videos tagged with *Berlinerisch* (Berlin city dialect). I discuss first how the characters of these two videos perform the Berlin dialect and stylize Berliner identities, focusing on six dialect features. All comments to these videos were coded for their use of dialect features, their overt reference to Berlin dialect, cognitive and affective attitudes to dialect, and reference to commenters' own dialect usage. Qualitative analysis then identified their common and differing themes of dialect discourse.

Performing and Negotiating German Dialects on YouTube
Drawing on the sample of dialect videos listed in the appendix, I examine how participatory videos and audience comments engage in dialect discourse. Information on video producers, audiences, and commenters was not collected systematically; this is difficult to accomplish without a questionnaire. However, the findings suggest distinctions between various types of dialect-tagged content and their producers. Some dialect-tagged videos are extracts of mass media content. Example 16 is a television report on a rock band that uses Low German in their lyrics. Example 13 is a piece of professionally filmed standup comedy, of the kind that is broadcast on late-night German television shows. Example 6 is an instance of viral marketing—a covert commercial that disguises its purpose until the relevant product is shown. The uploaders of such videos may or may not be their actual producers and copyright owners. Other dialect-tagged videos are outcomes of remix practices, by which users appropriate and digitally modify mass media footage. Still other dialect-tagged videos are clearly private material. Example 14 was shot at a family gathering and features a birthday toast performed in the Palatinate dialect by the two sons of the woman celebrating her birthday. Example 8 offers a sequence of dialect jokes, which are illustrated with a variety of still and moving images. The sheer diversity of dialect-tagged videos confirms the suggestion by Burgess and Green that assuming a rigid boundary between "mass media" and "user-created videos" is less useful than a continuum of various hybridization practices. In any case, dialect-tagged videos are not just produced by "ordinary" users (2009, 41–42). A distinct type of producer might be termed the "dialect activist," by which I mean (nonacademic) individuals who contribute to the representation of dialect on YouTube from a fact-oriented, documentary perspective. An example is a series of more than twenty so-called dialect atlases produced and uploaded by one person, including examples 1 and 7. Another type of producer is the media professional specializing in dialect redubs. Perhaps the best-known case is that of "Dodokay," an entertainer who started out by uploading his remixes on YouTube and now runs a dedicated broadcast show. Example 18 is one of his remixes. Concerning their audiences, dialect-tagged videos are overwhelmingly viewed within the German-speaking area, a finding supported both by the language choice of commenters and the statistics that YouTube provides for each video.

In light of the diverse origins and production modes of this material, I find it useful to think of these videos not as having or belonging to a genre with rigid boundaries, but as orienting to particular—sometimes multiple—genre conventions, which may be remixed or parodied. Genre is a useful analytic category in that it enables us to link the social activities staged in a video to traditions of public representation of dialects. Common genre orientations of German dialect-tagged videos include music, theater and comedy, poetry, sermons, story- and joke-telling, media reports on dialect, documenting dialect, learning dialect, and dialect dubbing.

Music, theater, and comedy represent traditional stages of dialect performance in Germany. Folk music with dialect lyrics is at home in many German regions, and the YouTube hits for some dialect tags are replete with folk music performances. Example 5, tagged as *Boarisch* ("Bavarian"), features a folk song by a Bavarian band that a fan visually remixed using photos of Bavarian landscapes. Standup comedy regularly exploits dialect stylizations, in which the link between language and localness is explicitly raised. Example 14 is a comedy excerpt on Palatinate for outsiders. Examples 9 and 10 feature a traditional Berlin rhyme, "Ick sitze da und esse klops," which is offered in several versions on YouTube. Example 10 is recited by an older man in front of the camera and example 9 features an animated line drawing. Vernacular sermons such as example 15, an amateur video recording in a church, are specific to the Low German region. They are an obvious case of online participatory culture documenting local traditions that are inextricably linked to local speech.

Storytelling and joke-telling videos are characteristic to the lay digital literacies enabled by the participatory web. They include amateur footage shot at people's homes or at family gatherings, featuring people giving toasts (see example 13) or telling stories in their local dialect. In example 8, the visual illustration of the dialect jokes includes material that references Berlin, such as a front page of a local newspaper.

Learning and documenting dialect are two popular motives of YouTube dialect performance across regions. Videos that may be termed dialect documentaries present facts and figures about a particular dialect. The two dialect atlas videos in the sample list, one Alemannic (example 1) and one on the Berlin city dialect (example 7), feature a compilation of narrative commentary, dialect speech samples, and expert opinion illustrated by a dialect map. Example 4 presents the Bavarian version of Wikipedia, thereby mixing documentation and comedy. All dialect documentaries in my data voice a positive attitude toward dialect, but some also express concern about maintenance and loss. Example 1 presents the unique vocabulary of the Alemannic dialect, discusses its nonintelligibility to outsiders, then points out that this lexis might be in a process of loss.

Dialect learning is more often than not a source of comedy and humor. Since institutional dialect learning does not exist, participatory videos draw on the idea of learning a vernacular variety of language and translate it into a range of social situations, creating humor out of its incongruence with institutional language learning. Example 12 stages dialect learning in a Berlin nightclub. Example 17 features two girls who deliver a mock dialect lesson. They translate standard German sentences in Low German, and at one point devise a mock translation of a slang expression, commenting on the fact that youth slang has no counterpart in Low German. Such videos draw on the motif of learning in order to raise awareness of issues of inter-generational transmission and dialect loss as well as mobility and migration. In example 12 the Berlin dialect is construed as a boundary between residents and newcomers, its knowledge positioned as a requirement in order to participate efficiently in the capital's youth culture. Both learning and documenting are motives for participatory dialect performance that can be used in order to voice social tensions around the ownership of local space.

Dialect-dubbing videos, called *synchros* by German users (from *Synchronisation,* the German term for dubbing), take dialect performance into remix culture. They appropriate excerpts of television broadcast, popular movies, or pop music and substitute their audio track through a dialect voice, which may or may not be semantically equivalent to the original. The examples that follow illustrate a range of remix approaches and techniques. Hollywood movie excerpts are particularly popular targets (examples 2, 19)—followed by American pop music (example 3), German broadcast content (example 18), or corporate content (example 11). Hollywood movies are by default dubbed in standard German, and YouTubers redub them in dialect. *Star Wars* (example 19) is a movie that is redubbed across dialects, taking the form of a viral series (Shifman 2012). The propositional content of *synchros* is sometimes nonsensical or takes up local issues, whose contrast to the original content generates humor or parody. In the dialect redub of the movie *Full Metal Jacket* (example 2), the redubbed movie dialogue voices the longstanding conflict between the neighboring regions of Baden and Swabia. Example 18 is a highly popular dialect dub of the primetime news show, *Tagesschau,* in which German and foreign politicians are made to declare absurdities in dialect; the newsreaders' voices are cast in dialect as well. Example 3 is a parody of the pop hit "Umbrella" by Rihanna. The song's melody is combined with new audio and a visual collage, both of which celebrate local practices of binge drinking (Androutsopoulos 2010a). Remixes that appropriate global material in order to comment on local practices are celebrated by commenters. Beyond their propositional content, dialect redubs have an additional layer of meaning that emerges through code choice. Giving a dialect voice to media genres that are by default produced in standard German can be read as an implicit critique on the predominance of standard language in the media, and as a hint to the suitability of vernaculars for broadcasting.

Dialect discourse in participatory spectacles is an outcome of the interaction between videos and audience responses—particularly comments. Dialect-tagged videos receive varying numbers of comments ranging from zero to a few thousand. On the whole, videos clearly prompt dialect discourse among commenters. This is not trivial or self-explanatory. In a largely unregulated discursive space such as YouTube, one might have expected comments to be haphazard and incoherent, but this does not apply to the majority of comments. Instead, there are thematically coherent threads of comments and even some sustained interactions among commenters. Comments on (and often in) dialect are not posted simply because of dialect use in the videos referenced. Rather, dialect discourse among commenters is prompted by a video's reflexive orientation to dialect. An example is the video *Zu Hause* ("At home"), a viral video tagged as *Berlinerisch,* whose character speaks in the Berlin dialect. The speaker, story, and setting do not orient to dialect in any way—nor do any of its thirty-three comments.

Commenters have different ways of engaging in dialect discourse. Some focus on dialect performance in the reference video, others use that video as a mere occasion to discuss a dialect. In the two Berlin videos analyzed below, comments on the dialect itself outnumber those on its performance in the video.[8] Some comments share knowledge, others voice feelings about a dialect. Depending on region and video genre, comments may discuss the reach of a dialect (such as where is it spoken or what are the neighboring dialects), its distinctive features, and aspects of its history or status; others debate the authenticity of dialect use in the reference video or take up issues of dialect decline and dialect maintenance. Although negative and stigmatizing voices are not absent, an emphasis on the cultural value and community importance of dialects prevails.

Comments may also use features of the dialect made relevant in the reference video. In the analysis of two Berlin videos below, Berlin dialect features occur in 40 percent of comments on the dialect lesson (example 12) and 63 percent of comments on the dialect tutorial (example 11). Commenters may use dialect features in their own voice or as a voice quoted from the video, and dialect may predominate in a comment or alternate with standard German. Dialect use in comments is clearly a choice. As there is no dialect literacy instruction in Germany, dialect writing is always mediated through standard German orthography. Dialect writing in the comments often does performative labor and identity work. Commenters may use dialect in order to authenticate their own local or regional origin in the process of discussing the performance of dialect in a video. Whenever commenters self-identify with a particular region, they do so by drawing on dialect, however few and emblematic the dialect features they draw on may be.

These general patterns of doing dialect in comments on dialect-tagged YouTube videos are valid across regions and genres; however, differences with regard to regions, genres, and themes exist as well. For example, comments that debate dialect boundaries or emphasize the superiority of one's own dialect to neighboring dialects occur in some regions (such as Bavarian, Franconian, Alemannic, and Badian) but not in others (notably Berlin), for reasons that are historical in nature. Discourses of dialect maintenance and decline are characteristic of Low German in terms of region, and for dialect documenting and learning videos in terms of genres. Comments that voice tensions between newcomers and residents occur in response to videos from Berlin, but not, for example, from Swabia. In addition to their commonalities across regions, comments to dialect videos reproduce social, cultural, and political differences that historically shaped dialect discourse in the German-speaking area.

Stylizing and Negotiating Berlinerisch: *A Comparison of Two Participatory Spectacles*

The second part of the analysis focuses on two participatory spectacles that engage with the Berlin city dialect. Being well studied and recognizable by virtue of numerous popular representations, the Berlin urban vernacular offers a useful descriptive backdrop (Dittmar and Schlobinski 1988; Schlobinski 1987). It has a number of distinctive and fairly stereotyped phonological, grammatical, and lexical features and is associated with a distinctive speech style, the *Berliner Schnauze*—a loudmouth way of talking deemed characteristic of the authentic Berliner. Video tags for the Berlin city dialect include *Berlinerisch, Berliner Schnauze,* and *Berlinisch* (its academic label), and the videos thus tagged present a range of genres and topics.

The two videos analyzed in this section were selected based on popularity (number of views) and genre orientation. The first video (example 12 in the appendix) is called "*Rinjehaun—Berlinerisch für Anfänger*" (See ya—*Berlinerisch* for beginners). Although it has been removed from YouTube, it was part of a series of dialect-lesson videos produced by a now-defunct, Berlin-based online magazine. The video stages a three-minute fictional encounter between two girls, a local and a newcomer, in the bathroom of a Berlin nightclub. We see the girls sitting in adjacent toilet stalls and chatting across the partition. The local girl is a street-style, rough-speaking type. Her narrative is interrupted by the posh and preppy newcomer girl, who does not understand the local's distinctive slang. This leads to a discussion of Berlin slang lexis and its standard German equivalents, during which six word pairs are flashed on the screen. The first few turns of this dialogue are shown in excerpt 1.

Excerpt 1. *Rinjehaun—Berlinerisch für Anfänger* ("See ya—*Berlinerisch* for beginners"), 0:14–0:47

1 A *Ey, Puppe! Wat jeht'n, Alter?*
      Hey doll! What's up, mate?

2 B *Hallo!*
      Hello!

3 A *Ey, hast mal fünf Minuten Zeit, ick muss dir mal wat erzählen.*
      Hey, have you got five minutes? I've got to tell you something.

4 B *Ja?*
      Yeah?

5 A *Cool. Naja, jedenfalls war ick ja am Wochenende mit meen Atzen aus*
        der Hood erstmal im Freibad.
      Cool. Well, over the weekend I went with my *Atzen* (mates) from the
        hood to the open-air pool.

6 B *Du warst mit deinen Eltern im Freibad?*
      You went with your parents to the pool?

7 A *Oh man, man, doch nicht mit meinen Eltern. Mit meinen Atzen. Wo*
        kommst du denn her dass du det nicht kennst?
      Oh, man. Not with my parents, with my *Atzen.* Where do you come
        from if you don't know that?

8 B *Also ich komm aus der Lünebürger Heide, falls es dich interessiert.*
        Sonst noch Fragen?
      Well, I come from Luneburg Heath if that is of any interest to you.
        Any further questions?

9   A   *Nee. Na det merkt man, wer Atze nicht kennt, kann nicht aus Berlin*
          sein.

          Nope. You can tell that if people don't know *Atze,* they can't be from
          Berlin.

10   B   *Naja, kann ich ja nicht wissen. gibt ja genügend Zugezogene in Berlin.*

          Well, how should I know that? There are a lot of newcomers in Berlin.

11   A   *Zujezogen bin ick höchstens.*

          A newcomer. Maybe that's me.

The second video (example 11 in the appendix) is called *MacBookAir auf
Berlinerisch* ("MacBookAir in *Berlinerisch*"). This is a remix that uses an original
video tutorial for that product and substitutes its audio track with semantically equivalent German copy, delivered in Berlin dialect. The video starts by displaying its own
artificiality and reflexively locating its wit in dialect choice. The producer introduces
this video by saying, "Here it comes in *Berlinerisch*," and comments on the time-
consuming labor of lip synchronzation. An excerpt is shown in excerpt 2. In the remainder of this chapter I use the terms "nightclub video" (excerpt 1) and "MacBook
video" (excerpt 2) for ease of reference.

Excerpt 2. *MacBook Air auf Berlinerisch* ("MacBookAir in *Berlinerisch*"), 2.0–2.27

1. *Det Trackpad ist nicht nur besonders groß, sondern bietet ooch einije*

2. *Innovationen der Multitouchoberfläche des iPhone, die wir für det*

3. *MacBook Air anjepasst haben. Sie kennen sicher det Tippen mit zwee Fingern*

4. *fürn Sekundärklick und det Blättern mit zwee Fingern uff'm MacBook und*

5. *MacBook Pro. Uff dem MacBook Air können Sie mit einfachen*

6. *Fingerbewegungen noch effizienter im Programm navigieren.*

7. *Ick zeig Ihnen det mal.*

1. The trackpad is not just quite large, it also offers some

2. innovations of the multi-touch surface of iPhone, which we

3. adapted for MacBook Air. You probably know the two-finger tap

4. for a secondary click and the two-finger scroll on MacBook and

5. MacBook Pro. On MacBook Air you can use simple

6. finger movements to navigate even more efficiently in the program.

7. I'll show you that.

Dialect Features and Dialect Stylization in the Videos   Berlin dialect features abound in both videos.
A variation analysis of six phonological features suggests that dialect variants occur
either categorically or with some frequency. All six features are considered in the tran-
scripts above. The features and findings are as follows (see Barbour and Stevenson
1990, 112–25 for a full description of these features):

1. (g) spirantization: A voiced velar plosive, /g/, is realized as glide or palatal approximant, [j], with variable distribution by phonological environment. Examples in the nightclub video include the verb forms *jeht* for *geht* (line 1) and *zujezogen* for *zugezogen* (line 11), and an example in the MacBook video is the adjective *einije* for *einige* (line 1). Analysis of one environment, the word-initial syllable /gə/, shows that the Berlin variant occurs categorically in both videos (total N=20).

2. (ai) monophthongization: The /ai/ diphthong is realized as long, close, mid-front unrounded vowel [e:], as in *eene* for *eine* ("one"). Examples include *meen* for *mein* (nightclub video, line 5) and *zwee* for *zwei* (MacBook video, line 3). This dialect variant occurs categorically in the nightclub video and in 89 percent of tokens in the MacBook video (total N=12).

3. (au) monophthongization: The /au/ diphthong is realized as a long [o:], a common lexical item being *ooch* for *auch* ("also"). A token occurs in line 1 of the MacBook video. This feature occurs categorically in the nightclub video and in 86 percent of realizations in the MacBook video (total N=9).

4. (au) monophthongization: The preposition *auf* (on) is realized as *uff* with a short [u] in Berlin dialect. This item occurs frequently in the tutorial, as the tutor discusses things to do *on* the computer. This dialect variant scores 50 percent in the nightclub, 88 percent in the MacBook video (total N=26).

5. Word-final /s/ is realized as [t] in a closed set of articles and pronouns, including *wat* for *was* ("what") and *dat* or *det* for *das* ("the, this"). Examples are in lines 3, 7, 9 of the nightclub video and lines 2, 3, 4, 7 of the MacBook video. Focusing on two common items, the dialect variant *et* for *es* is categorical in both videos (N=12) and the variant *dat* or *det* for *das* is categorical in the nightclub and occurs at 70 percent in the MacBook video (N=49).

6. *Ick* or *icke* is the Berlin variant of the personal pronoun *I,* which is *ich* /iç/ in standard German, with the palatal fricative /ç/ replaced by a velar plosive. Examples occur in lines 3 and 5 of the nightclub video, and line 7 of the MacBook video. This feature occurs categorically in the first and in 80 percent in the second video (total N=29).

These six features are "well-established and well-known markers of Berlin speech" (Barbour and Stevenson 1990, 115), and their high frequencies clearly mark the two speakers as Berliners. However, this does not make their dialect performances authentic in the eyes of some commenters, who assess authenticity based on the entire performance rather than isolated dialect features. Moreover, the two videos link dialect to different social domains and institutional discourses, and thereby offer two strikingly different stylizations of Berlin speakers. They do so in terms of additional aspects of dialect performance, notably lexis, and in terms of aspects of performance that do not rely on dialect.

Although the delivery of the Berlin club girl evokes—at least in my reading—working-class associations with her rough timbre and slang lexis, the dialect tutorial is striking for its complex syntax, technical vocabulary, and fluent delivery in a smooth instructional style. These features suggest that the tutorial was scripted, rehearsed, and then read aloud. The two videos appropriate different institutional discourses and stylize Berlin identities in relation to these discourses. The club girl's Berlin dialect is positioned as unmarked, or even desirable, in the nightclubbing context. The MacBook video alludes to the possibility of expert professional advice being delivered in dialect. Both videos represent dialect usage in prestigious domains, be it overt (digital technologies) or covert (nightclub) prestige, and their empowering metamessage about dialect contrasts with, and implicitly challenges, traditional stereotypes of Berlin dialect speakers who are popularly imagined as middle-aged, working class, and unrelated to either youth culture or digital technologies. These stylizations can therefore be viewed as constructing new types of Berlin dialect speakers.

In sum, the two videos are highly similar with regard to typical features of Berlin dialect, but highly different in their sociolinguistic styling. Their lexical choices and prosodic patterns index differing social styles and genres beyond the speakers' regional origin.

Audience Responses to the Videos   Both videos received relatively few comments during data collection; there were ninety-six comments on the nightclub video and forty-two on the MacBook video. This section discusses four common themes of dialect discourse in these two sets of comments: liking and disliking dialect; debating the authenticity of dialect features and speakers; locating dialect in urban space; and reflecting on the conditions of dialect performance.

Example 1 illustrates a common pattern of affective response in my data: a generic evaluation that is ambiguous in its reference to video, dialect use, or both. Examples 2–6 show a range of affective responses—mostly positive ones (with the exception of example 5), and some cast in a dialect voice throughout. Some of these comments use dialect features discussed above, notably spirantization, the lexical variants *wat, dat,* and the personal pronoun *icke* (see examples 1, 2, and 6, below). Example 2 also uses two Berlin vernacular expressions that are explained in the video: *knorke* ("awesome") and *Broiler* ("roast chicken"). Affective comments are typically short and informal in tone. They often use dialect and features of informal digital writing such as emoticons (see also Chun and Walters 2011 for similar findings in YouTube comments). Similar comments include *Voll jut!* ("Really good!"); *Super besser jeths nich :D* ("Super! It just can't get any better"); and *ick finds knorke* ("I find it awesome"). All include some of the dialect features discussed above—notably features 1 and 6—and Berlin lexis (*knorke*). English, used in example 4, is rare. Example 6 is a declaration of cross-regional attractiveness that indicates the covert prestige attached to the Berlin city vernacular. Although the nightclub video prompts more positive and affective reactions overall, a few comments on the MacBook video point out that the use of dialect in the tutorial makes the product more likeable (German: *sympathisch*) to them.[9]

1. [MacBook video] UdvismH

   dit is jut :D (This is good.)

2. [Nightclub video] Evisu03

   dit video find ick_ knorke, und nen broiler + pommes rot weiß jibs nur hier
   (This video is awesome and you can only have roast chicken with fries here.)

3. [Nightclub video] choclatchip92

   geil ;D berlinersich is so geil :D (Cool. Berlinerisch is so cool.)

4. [MacBook video] MMfanAZ

   I just love that Berlinerisch. Very cool. Weiter machen! (Keep it up!)

5. [Nightclub video] KoRny1996

   berlinerisch klingt doof! (Berlinerisch sounds stupid!)

6. [Nightclub video] xXMissLenaXxo

   ick liebe diesen dialekt. komm zwar us hamburch, aba lern jerade berlina schnauze :D (I love this dialect. I come from Hamburg, but I'm now learning the Berlin lingo.)

Metalinguistic critique takes two paths—one focusing on dialect features, and the other on speaker delivery. The nightclub video presents six words as part of the Berlin vocabulary that are opaque to the incomer. All six are scrutinized by commenters with regard to their regional spread, current usage, and precise meaning, as I will show using comments 7–9, in which three users discuss the lexical meaning of *Atze.*

7. [Nightclub video] bireman

   Atze ist eigentlich Bruder (*Atze* actually means brother.)

8. [Nightclub video] norayati

   nee, is nich bruder, is kumpel. kommste aussa lüneburga heide oda wat?
   (No—it's mate, not brother. Are you from Luneburg Heath or what?)

9. [Nightclub video] stachebln

   Also Atze ist definitiv Bruder, Freunde sind Kumpels. // Atze ist eigentlich sogar der kleinere Bruder, Keule hingegen der große Bruder, und die Schwelle ist die Schwester, also bei uns iss dett so, wa!

   (Well, *Atze* definitely means brother; friends are called mates. // *Atze* is actually the younger brother, and *Keule* the older brother, and the sister is called *Schwelle.* Well, that's the way we do it, right!)

Consider how the author of 8 alludes to the nonlocal girl's place of origin—Luneburg Heath (see excerpt 1, line 8) in order to disqualify the explication proposed by 7: The implication is that comment 7 could only have been offered by someone from the province who is not familiar with the capital's vernacular. The author of 9 provides examples from the lexical field of *Atze* and shifts into a dialect voice in the last clause, thereby referring to the in-group of Berlin dialect speakers: *Also bei uns iss dett so, wa!* ("Well, that's the way we do it, right!"). In addition to the dialect pronoun *dett,* the tag-question *wa* is typical for the Berlin vernacular as well. Here metalinguistic knowledge and dialect use work together in authenticating the speaker's claims (see also Johnstone and Baumgardt 2004).

In the audience responses to the MacBook video, several users call the authenticity of the speaker into doubt. As illustrated by examples 10–12 and 14, the criticism is on his delivery rather than dialect features. Consider how the first two comments below adopt a dialect voice including several features, notably 1 (*jut jemacht*), 4 (*uff*), 5 (*dit*), and 6 (*ick*).

10. [MacBook video] berlinerin09

    na ick find dit nicht so jut jemacht, dit kommt nicht so orjinal rüber, ick finds eher auswendig jelernt und uff gesacht

    (Well, I don't find it that well done; it doesn't come across as original. To me it feels rather learned by heart and delivered.)

11. [MacBook video] prochrisk

    Boah ne, sorry, dit is aber ma so ja nich knorke! Da_ hatt er zwar die Vokabeln jepaukt, aber . . . dit klingt so ja nich Original-Berlinerisch . . . keene Stimmmelodie drin, weißte Keule!

    (Oh, well, sorry, but this isn't my thing at all! He did learn his lessons, but . . . it doesn't sound like original *Berlinerisch,* no vocal melody in there, is there, mate?)

12. [MacBook video] dameisenmann

    video_ is kacke // schlechter dialekt und hochdeutscher satzbau.

    (Video is crap // bad dialect and High German syntax.)

These comments pick out the speaker's prosody ("no vocal melody in there") and syntax ("High German syntax") as not conforming to their notions of the original Berlin dialect. Remarkably, these seem to characterize the instruction genre rather than the Berlin dialect per se, and the scripted background of the delivery alluded to by comment 10 ("rather learned by heart and delivered") is also related to genre. Dialect stylization in the MacBook video clearly challenges dialect stereotypes, but it also includes features that seem to conflict with people's expectations of dialect authenticity because they disrupt the traditional link of authenticity to particular types of verbal performance, to which a computer tutorial clearly does not belong. Therein lies the difference between the responses to the two videos: The Berlin girl's style is despised by some—criticized for being *gekünstelt* ("artificial") or *übertrieben* ("exaggerated")—or deemed typical of East Berlin rather than the capital as a whole. But she is not denied local origin or lack of dialect competence the way the speaker of the MacBook tutorial is.

Instead of equating *Berlinerisch* to Berlin, comments negotiate links between dialect and urban space. Taking their cues from the video, commenters localize dialect in subtle and nuanced ways. Viewers of the nightclub video focus on the tension between East and West Berlin, which originated in Berlin's division after World War II and led to social and cultural differences between the city's two parts (Schlobinski 1987). This issue is not raised in the video itself but projected in the girl's dialect performance and read by commenters. In example 13 comments draw on dialect features to authenticate their own claims of metalinguistic authority. The tension between local Berliners and incomers is staged in the nightclub video and revoiced by commenters who take a local stance and distance themselves from what one commenter calls *möchtegern-szene-berliner* ("Wannabe-scene-Berliners by choice"). The speaker of the MacBook video is repeatedly identified as an incomer who tries to imitate the dialect. In example 14, the commenter supports their claims with a reference to dialect usage in two Berlin districts, and links dialect usage by incomers to the popularity of the Berlin vernacular in television shows.

13. [Nightclub video] isimaus26

Sehr Ostlastig . . . wir im Westbalin reden anders! naja, aber schon janz nett!

(Quite heavy on the East . . . we in West Berlin speak differently! Well, still nice!)

14. [MacBook video] Murkelrabe

Hört sich an, als ob ein sonst nur hochdeutsch sprechender Mensch versucht zu berlinern. Leider verscuehn seit Krömer & Co viel zu viele Zugereiste zu berlinern und das hört sich für Urberliner furchtbar an. In Ost-Berlin und den Randgebieten Westberlins (Spandau und Co) sprach man im Alltag den berliner Dialekt. Das Video ist leider "zugereist" und kein Berlinern.

(Sounds as though somebody who usually speaks High German would try to speak the Berlin dialect. Unfortunately, since Krömer and Co. [broadcast comedy show hosts] far too many incomers try to speak the dialect, which sounds awful for original Berliners. In East Berlin and the outer districts of West Berlin (Spandau and Co.) people used to speak Berlin dialect in everyday life. I'm afraid this video is by an "incomer" and not a Berliner.)

Overall, most comments seem to rely on an assumed shared understanding of a so-called authentic dialect, to which video performances and stylizations are compared. Only a few comments reflect on the conditions of participatory dialect performance, discussing these videos in terms of performance choices rather than their dialect accuracy or speaker competence. Example 15 is characteristic of such a reading, insofar as it explicitly acknowledges the purposeful artificiality of the video performance and explains its stylistic choices as an outcome of its audience design. Remarkably, this comment makes its own style-shifting formally obvious. It starts with a heavily marked dialect voice (including the spirantization feature, and the pronoun variants *dit* and *ick*) and rounds it off by means of the notation *[/berlinerisch]*, which is derived from net usage. Likewise, the author of example (16) explicitly treats the nightclub video as performance and does "dialect identity" by switching to dialect (features 1, 5, and 6) in order to reflect on their dialect usage.

15. [MacBook video] N1trux1de

Also ick muss ma sajen, dit hat ma voll jefallen. [/berlinerisch] Hätte zwar teilweise etwas "doller" ausfallen können, aber dann hätte das kein nicht-Berliner mehr verstanden^^ Super Video!!!

(Well, I must say I did like it a lot. [/berlinerisch] It could have been somewhat "fuller" but then no non-Berliner would probably have understood it^^ Super video!!!)

16. [Nightclub video] GerDrSeltsam

Mädels, geile Show, aber als Ossi respektive Sachse muss ich euch sagen,
Broiler und Semmel sind auch bei uns im Tal der Ahnungslosen (Dresden)
gängige Begriffe. Ick denk ma ihr habt eure Schrippe verjessen, nu?!
Und nich über men Dialektmix wundern, ick bin fufschprozent Berlina und fuf-
schprozent Sachse, det is ne ganz feine Mischung!

(Girls: great show, but as an Easterner and Saxon I must say Broiler and Semmel are also familiar to us in the valley of the ignorant [Dresden]. I guess
you've forgotten your *Schrippe* [bread roll] right? // And don't wonder about
my dialect mix, I'm 50 percent Berliner and 50 percent Saxon; that's quite a
fine mixture!)

Comment 16 resembles 14 in terms of the rich sociolinguistic background it
alludes to. The author refers to *Schrippe,* a typical Berlin word for "bread roll";
she or he comments on the regional spread of two other words from the video; and
uses without further explanation the term *Tal der Ahnungslosen* ("valley of the ignorant"), a label for the area of Dresden that originated in the German Democratic Republic. These and other comments offer fragments of linguistic and
sociolinguistic knowledge, which complement the video performances and enable
spectators to link the elements of a participatory spectacle together in a kind of
jointly produced sociolinguistic panorama. Commenters bring their own dialect
identity into play and underscore their normative claims by using the relevant dialect themselves.

Conclusions

Scollon and LeVine (2004) suggest two reasons to study relations of discourse and
technology: First, discourse is inherently multimodal, and multimodal discourse
analysis depends on technologies. Second, technologies facilitate new forms of discourse, notably on the internet. I suggest that the work presented in this chapter
demonstrates a third tier of relations: new forms of discourse enabled by digital technologies offer people opportunities to participate in ("capital D") discourses—that
is, to contribute to and negotiate the social construction of knowledge. I summarize
the implications of these findings for the discursive construction of dialect in the new
media, and briefly consider how this study ties in with the state of linguistic scholarship on CMD.

To what extent do participatory spectacles make a difference to the public representation of dialects in the German-speaking context? Based on the findings of
this study, their impact seems best captured by the notions of diversification and
destabilization. Specifically, dialect discourses on YouTube destabilize existing
mass-mediated regimes of dialect representation by pluralizing the performance
and stylization of dialects. Participatory dialect spectacles do not entirely break
with the tradition of so-called funny dialects; many dialect performances on
YouTube are still cast in an entertaining, jocular key. But they are diverse enough
to include voices and representations which differ markedly from traditional dialect stereotypes. Destabilization works at different levels. First, there is change

at the level of dialect discourses, concerning the knowledge about dialect in its social context that is negotiated by videos and comments. In part, these are long-standing discourses of animosities between neighboring regions, and merely have been transported to a new environment. But others are products of fairly recent processes of political, economical, and cultural change—such as the tensions surrounding the ownership of the Berlin dialect.

A second level of pluralization has to do with the unprecedented options for audience participation offered by YouTube and other social media. The coexistence of staged performance and audience responses within a participatory spectacle means that every representation of dialect can be ratified or challenged by its viewers, that its readings are visibly diverse, and that the authority to speak about language becomes negotiable rather than being delimited from the outset. Third, participatory dialect spectacles draw on new resources of representation with regard to remix techniques and materials. The analysis of dialect redubs illustrates how dialect discourse meets globally circulating popular culture, and how the intersection of local tradition and cultural globalization may be as much a source of humor as of implicit critique. These findings highlight both the popularity of remix practices in German dialect discourses and the inherently linguistic character of media remixing.

This study ties in with the four principles that Thurlow and Mroczek (2011b) identify as pillars of a sociolinguistic approach to new media discourse: discourse, technology, multimodality, and ideology. The framework outlined here entails a nondeterministic approach to technology and a focus on language ideologies. This study shows that research on participatory spectacles raises new challenges for CMD studies. Having focused predominantly on written language, research now needs to take the multimodal structure of online participatory environments into account and examine the ways language becomes tied into multimodal configurations of user-produced digital content. The concepts of multimodality, intertextuality, and heteroglossia offer an adequate backdrop for the analysis of participatory spectacles. Viewed as complex audiovisual configurations, participatory spectacles incorporate written language and are tied together by intertextual relations among their components as much as to various cultural discourses and representations. Representations of dialect are embedded in heteroglossic contrasts within a spectacle (especially in relations of and shifts between dialect and standard German) and at the interface of dialect spectacles and their wider digital environment. This chapter shows that the visual dimension of participatory spectacles is central to their dialect performances, and suggests ways of dealing with this without losing sight of language as both an object and a backbone of participatory dialect discourse.

ACKNOWLEDGMENTS

The research presented here was initiated in collaboration with Horst Simon (Free University Berlin). I am grateful to my graduate students in Hamburg for their assistance with data collection; audiences in Leipzig, London, Glasgow, Vaasa, and Washington, DC, for feedback; and Deborah Tannen and Anna Marie Trester for their feedback and support. I am, of course, solely responsible for any shortcomings in this chapter.

NOTES

1. See the English-language Wikipedia entry for Karl Theodor zu Guttenberg (Wikipedia n.d.), and the collaborative documentation of plagiarism (GuttenPlag Wiki n.d.).
2. The notion of participatory spectacle is applicable to all web platforms used by people to upload, consume, and discuss user-created content—especially photography and music. YouTube is relevant from a language perspective, because language in its multimodal context is a key resource for participatory videos.
3. I use the term "dialect" as a cover and emic term, the way lay people use it on YouTube. Although German dialectology distinguishes between deep dialects and regional varieties of language, on YouTube dialect is part of a binary distinction and juxtaposed to standard German (*Hochdeutsch*). In this usage, the term "dialect" includes phonological (accent) as well as grammatical and lexical features.
4. Johnstone points out, "Dialect boundaries are not inscribed on the landscape, so the world does not present itself to linguists with dialects waiting to be discovered. Just as languages are created in discourse, so are dialects" (2011, 3). Lay discourses on dialect enjoyed little attention in academic dialectology and social dialectology, which define and classify dialects from an etic rather than emic perspective. The recent interest of perceptual dialectology in lay knowledge about dialect is part of the broader sociolinguistic interest in metalanguage (see Milani and Johnson 2010; Jaworski, Coupland, and Galasinski 2004).
5. Its successor website, *The Burble,* provides mock translation of web content into four German dialects (see www.burble.de). An English-language counterpart that has existed since 1998 is *The Dialectizer,* which offers dialectized versions of web content in popular dialects, including so-called redneck and cockney (see www.rinkworks.com/dialect/).
6. Most designations of regional dialects in German are denominal adjectives, roughly equivalent to English place names such as Bristolian, which can refer to a native of Bristol, England, or its dialect.
7. Here are the hits, as of June 7, 2011, for twenty dialect labels (with translations in English): *Schwäbisch* (Swabian): 6,870; *Kölsch* (Cologne dialect): 6,600; *Bayerisch* (Bavarian): 5,390; *Bayrisch* (Bavarian): 5,310; *Sächsisch* (Saxonian): 1,330; *Boarisch* (Bavarian): 1,100; *Plattdeutsch* (Low German): 1,100; *Alemannisch* (Alemannic): 1,090; *Hessisch* (Hessian): 1,060; *Fränkisch* (Franconian): 698; *Bairisch* (Bavarian): 518; *Badisch* (Badenese): 415; *Pfälzisch* (Palatinate): 214; *Niederdeutsch* (Low German): 177; *Plattdütsch* (Bavarian): 117; *Berlinisch* (Berlin dialect): 96; *Berlinerisch* (Berlin dialect): 96; *Thüringisch* (Thuringian) 18; *Mannheimerisch* (Mannheim dialect) 4; *Ripuarisch* (Ripuarian): 1. Note that Low German is officially a distinct regional language rather than a dialect, and that some dialect labels come in two or more spelling variants, such as *Bayerisch, Bayrisch,* and *Boarisch* for "Bavarian."
8. In t'● nightclub video (example 12), 48 percent of comments discuss dialect use in the video and 74 percent discuss the Berlin city dialect as such. In the MacBook video (example 11), 23 percent of the comments discuss dialect use in the video and 40 percent discuss the Berlin dialect as such. Both topics can coincide in a single comment. (Based on all forty-two comments on example 11 and a sample of fifty comments on example 12.)
9. Original screen names are maintained. A label indicating the reference video has been added. A double slash (i.e., //) indicates a line break in the original. English translations attempt to maintain aspects of the original idiomatic style. Emoticons are not repeated in the translation.

REFERENCES

Androutsopoulos, Jannis. 2010a. Localizing the global on the participatory web. In *The handbook of language and globalization,* ed. Nikolas Coupland, 203–31. Malden, MA: Wiley-Blackwell.
———. 2010b. The study of language and space in media discourse. In *Language and space,* vol. 1, *Theory and methods,* ed. Peter Auer and Jürgen E. Schmidt, 740–58. Berlin and New York: de Gruyter.
Barbour, Stephen, and Patrick Stevenson. 1990. *Variation in German. A critical approach to German sociolinguistics.* Cambridge: Cambridge University Press.
Bauman, Richard, ed. 1992. Performance. In *Folklore, cultural performances, and popular entertainments,* 41–49. New York: Oxford University Press.

Bell, Allan, and Andy Gibson. 2011. Staging language: An introduction to the sociolinguistics of performance. *Journal of Sociolinguistics* 15, no. 5:555–72.

Birkner, Karin, and Peter Gilles. 2008. Dialektstilisierung im Reality-Fernsehen. In *Sprechen, Schreiben, Hören: Zur Produktion und Perzeption von Dialekt und Standardsprache zu Beginn des 21. Jahrhunderts,* eds. Helen Christen and Evelyn Ziegler, 101–30. Vienna: Praesens.

Burgess, Jean, and Joshua Green. 2009. *YouTube: Online video and participatory culture.* Cambridge: Polity.

Chau, Clement. 2010. YouTube as a participatory culture. In *New Directions for Youth Development* 128:65–74.

Chun, Elaine, and Keith Walters. 2011. Orienting to Arab orientalisms: Language, race and humor in a YouTube video. In *Digital discourse: Language in the new media,* eds. Crispin Thurlow and Kristine Mroczek, 251–73. Oxford: Oxford University Press.

Clyne, Michael G., ed. 1992. *Pluricentric languages: Differing norms in different nations.* Berlin: Mouton de Gruyter.

Coupland, Nikolas. 2001. Dialect stylization in radio talk. *Language in Society* 3:345–75.

———. 2009. The mediated performance of vernaculars. *Journal of English Linguistics* 37:284–300.

Dittmar, Norbert, and Peter Schlobinski, eds. 1988. *The sociolinguistics of urban vernaculars.* Berlin and New York: de Gruyter.

Fairclough, Norman. 1995. *Media discourse.* London: Arnold.

Fairclough, Norman, and Ruth Wodak. 1997. Critical discourse analysis. In *Discourse as social interaction,* ed. T. van Dijk, 258–84. London: Sage.

Fraas, Claudia, and Christian Pentzold. 2008. Online-Diskurse: Theoretische Prämissen, methodische Anforderungen und analytische Befunde. In *Diskurslinguistik nach Foucault,* eds. Ingo Warnke and Jürgen Spitzmüller, 287–322. Berlin and New York: de Gruyter.

Gee, James Paul. 2005. *An introduction to discourse analysis: Theory and method.* 2nd ed. London and New York: Routledge.

GuttenPlag Wiki. n.d. Collaborative documentation of plagiarism. de.guttenplag.wikia.com/wiki/GuttenPlag_Wiki/English.

Herring, Susan C. 2001. Computer-mediated discourse. In *The handbook of discourse analysis,* eds. Deborah Schiffrin, Deborah Tannen, and Heidi E. Hamilton, 612–34. Malden, MA: Wiley-Blackwell.

———. 2004. Computer-mediated discourse analysis: An approach to researching online communities. In *Designing for virtual communities in the service of learning,* eds. Sasha A. Barab et al., 338–76. Cambridge and New York: Cambridge University Press.

Hofheinz, Albrecht. 2011. Nextopia? Beyond revolution 2.0. *International Journal of Communication* 5:1417–34. ijoc.org/ojs/index.php/ijoc/article/view/1186.

Jaworski, Adam, Nikolas Coupland, and Dariusz Galasinski, eds. 2004. *Metalanguage: Social and ideological perspectives.* Berlin and New York: de Gruyter.

Jenkins, Henry. 2006. *Convergence culture: Where old and new media collide.* New York: New York University Press.

———. 2009a. Confronting the challenges of participatory culture: Media education for the 21st century. The John D. and Catherine T. MacArthur Foundation. www.macfound.org/press/publications/white-paper-confronting-the-challenges-of-participatory-culture-media-education-for-the-21st-century-by-henry-jenkins/.

———. 2009b. What happened before YouTube. In *YouTube: Online video and participatory culture,* eds. Jean Burgess and Joshua Green, 109–25. Cambridge: Polity.

Johnstone, Barbara. 2010. Locating language in identity. In *Language and identities,* eds. Carmen Llamas and Dominic Watt, 29–36. Edinburgh: Edinburgh University Press.

———. 2011. Making Pittsburghese: Communication technology, expertise, and the discursive construction of a regional dialect. *Language and Communication* 31:3–15.

Johnstone, Barbara, and Dan Baumgardt. 2004. "Pittsburghese" online: Vernacular norming in conversation. *American Speech* 79:115–45.

Jones, Graham M., and Bambi B. Schieffelin. 2009. Talking text and talking back: "My BFF Jill" from boob tube to YouTube. *Journal of Computer-Mediated Communication* 14, no. 4:1050–79.

Lankshear, Colin, and Michele Knobel. 2008. Remix: The art and craft of endless hybridization. *Journal of Adolescent and Adult Literacy* 52, no. 1:22–33.

Lovink, Geert, and Sabine Niederer, eds. 2008. *Video vortex reader: Responses to YouTube.* Amsterdam: Institute of Network Cultures.

Meier, Stefan. 2008. Von der Sichtbarkeit im Diskurs: Zur Methode diskursanalytischer Untersuchung multimodaler Kommunikation. In *Diskurslinguistik nach Foucault,* ed. Ingo Warnke and Jürgen Spitzmüller, 263–86. Berlin and New York: de Gruyter.

Milani, Tommaso M., and Sally Johnson. 2010. Critical intersections: Language ideologies and media discourse. In *Language ideologies and media discourse,* eds. Sally Johnson and Tommaso M. Milani, 3–14. London: Continuum.

Mills, Sara. 2004. *Discourse.* London: Routledge.

Niebaum, Hermann, and Jürgen Macha. 2006. *Einführung in die Dialektologie des Deutschen.* 2nd. revised edition. Tübingen: Niemeyer.

Pennycook, Alastair. 2007. *Global Englishes and transcultural flows.* London: Taylor and Francis.

Reershemius, Gertrud. 2010. Niederdeutsch im Internet. Möglichkeiten und Grenzen computervermittelter Kommunikation für den Spracherhalt. *Zeitschrift für Dialektologie und Linguistik* 77, no. 2:183–206.

Scharloth, Joachim. 2009. Performanz als Modus des Sprechens und Interaktionsmodalität. In *Oberfläche und Performanz,* eds. Angelika Linke and Helmuth Feilke, 233–53. Tübingen: Niemeyer.

Schlobinski, Peter. 1987. *Stadtsprache Berlin. Eine soziolinguistische Untersuchung.* Berlin and New York: de Gruyter.

Scollon, Ron, and Philip LeVine. 2004. Multimodal discourse analysis as the confluence of discourse and technology. In *Discourse and technology: Multimodal discourse analysis,* eds. Philip LeVine and Ron Scollon, 1–6. Washington, DC: Georgetown University Press.

Shifman, Limor. 2012. An anatomy of a YouTube meme. *New Media and Society* 14, no. 2:187–203.

Snickars, Pelle, and Patrick Vonderau, eds. 2009. *The YouTube reader.* Stockholm: National Library of Sweden.

Squires, Lauren. 2010. Enregistering internet language. *Language in Society* 39, no. 4:457–92.

Stommel, Wyke. 2009. *Entering an online support group on eating disorders: A discourse analysis.* Amsterdam: Rodopi.

Thurlow, Crispin. 2006. From statistical panic to moral panic: The metadiscursive construction and popular exaggeration of new media language in the print media. *Journal of Computer-Mediated Communication* 11, no. 3, article 1. jcmc.indiana.edu/vol11/issue3/thurlow.html.

Thurlow, Crispin, and Kristine Mroczek, eds. 2011a. *Digital discourse: Language in the new media.* Oxford: Oxford University Press.

———. 2011b. Introduction: Fresh perspectives on new media sociolinguistics. *Digital discourse: Language in the new media,* xix–xliv. Oxford: Oxford University Press.

van Dijk, Teun A. 2008. *Discourse and power.* Basingstoke, UK: Palgrave Macmillan.

van Leeuwen, Theo. 2005. *Introducing social semiotics.* London: Routledge.

Wikipedia. n.d. Karl Theodor zu Guttenberg. en.wikipedia.org/wiki/Karl-Theodor_zu_Guttenberg.

Wodak, Ruth, and Scott Wright. 2007. The European Union in cyberspace: Democratic participation via online multilingual discussion boards. In *The multilingual internet: Language, culture, and communication online,* eds. Brenda Danet and Susan C. Herring, 385–407. Oxford: Oxford University Press.

Appendix: List of YouTube Videos

(Paste video ID into the YouTube search bar or add to www.youtube.com/watch?v=)

Alemannic

1. Dialektatlas #101—Alemannisch 1/2 ("Dialect atlas #101: Alemannic 1/2")
   Video ID: L_eTpWs-NyY
2. Full Metal Jacket auf Badisch Alemannisch ("*Full Metal Jacket* in Badenese Alemannic"):, currently banned
   Video ID: FXZNVvxxeHQ

Bavarian
    3. Schwappe Productions—An Preller ("Schwappe Productions: A hangover")
       Video ID: icmraBAN4ZE
    4. Wikipedia auf Boarisch 1/3 ("Wikipedia in Bavarian 1/3")
       Video ID: eWiNV_2BFAA
    5. So schee war da somma—Oache Brothers ("Summer was so nice: Oache brothers")
       Video ID: qSAOfSUKkRo
Berlin City Dialect
    6. Berliner-Schnauze . . . Stadtrundfahrten (Kostprobe) ("Berlin loudmouth . . . City Tours [Sample])"
       Video ID: NbgMqW-Qj8s
    7. Dialektatlas #107—Berlinerisch ("Dialect atlas #107: Berlinerisch")
       Video ID: jI8YpXrZog
    8. Geile Witze—mit Berliner Schnauze ("Cool jokes: Berlin loudmouth style")
       Video ID: QzSkJfUAxo
    9. Ick sitze da und esse Klops ("I'm sitting there eating meatballs")
       Video ID: xuSqhddzXl4
   10. Ick sitze hier und esse Klops ("I'm sitting here eating meatballs")
       Video ID: XCGgeVLIJCE
   11. MacBook Air auf Berlinerisch ("MacBookAir in *Berlinerisch*")
       Video ID: jg7L9PX8lrY
   12. Rinjehaun-Berlinerisch für Anfänger ("See ya! *Berlinerisch* for beginners")
       Video ID: UxPSz54l3ps, no longer available.
Palatinate
   13. Christian Chako Habekost: Pfälzisch für Außergewärdische ("Palatinate for outsiders")
       Video ID: Ab_ZAcHJQKE
   14. Marcel und Björn zum 50. von Mama Gisela ("Marcel and Björn on the fiftieth birthday of Mama Gisela")
       Video ID: T0OUmNEH4fo
Low German
   15. Bernhard Busemann: Plattdeutsche Predigt über Lukas 12 ("Bernhard Busemann: Low German sermon on Lukas 12")
       Video ID: ylOUc_OtXnI
   16. De fofftig Penns bi Gooden Abend RTL ("De fofftig Penns on *Good Evening RTL*")
       Video ID: YSOocW73UMk
   17. Learning Plattdeutsch mit uns ! ("Learning Low German with us!")
       Video ID: pS4qN5Zm0KI
Swabian
   18. Die ARD Tagesschau auf Schwäbisch—dodokay SWR ("ARD News of the day in Swabian")
       Video ID: IOXvvnMetII
   19. star-wars-auf-schwaebisch ("Star Wars in Swabian")
       Video ID: UOxY2lRcII4

4

"My English Is So Poor . . . So I Take Photos"
Metalinguistic Discourses about English on FlickR

CARMEN LEE
Chinese University of Hong Kong

FLICKR (www.flickr.com) is a photosharing site that allows people to upload, display, and share photos. Although photographs are often perceived to be the central element of Flickr, members of Flickr also interact in various writing spaces; they provide titles, captions, and tags (or keywords) for their photos as well as comment on one another's photos. These writing spaces form a cross-modal cohesive tie between the posted photos and surrounding text. Each Flickr member also has a profile page, on which many people write short autobiographies detailing where they come from, what

This photo was taken on Novembe Shi, Beijing, CN.

©Yahoo!2010.

296 views   23 commer

This photo belongs to

ShanLuSF's photostream (1,000)

This photo also appears in

▸ Beijing / 北京 (set)
▸ Fall / 秋 (set)
▸ Winter / 冬 (set)

Tags

Beijing · autumn · fall · snow grey · china · 北京 · 中国 · 角楼 · foctooimage · blizzard

License

© All Rights Reserved
Ⓡ Request to license ShanLuSF Images

autumnter 一叶知冬

Autumn, but feels like winter, snow comes so early this year, I haven't got one shot of fall yet! went out shooting for a few hours, cold, tired but had a lot of fun! the nicest snow I have ever seen in Beijing.

Comments and faves

⭐ pop500km, S~y ~O, Wei Zhang@Hudson, orientalimage, and 20 other people added this photo to their favorites.

cyemura **pro** (22 months ago)
Okay, here's your comment.

Figure 4.1 A Flickr photo page with bilingual writing.[1]

cameras and lenses they use, and their passion for photography. Flickr is basically a public and global online platform (although users can control access to their photos), so its users vary geographically, culturally, and linguistically. Users who do not use English as their dominant language in their offline lives may still choose to create written content in English in addition to their native language. Figure 4.1 shows a page by a Chinese-speaking user, with a bilingual title "autumnter 一叶知冬," and tags in Chinese and English, surrounding the uploaded photo.

This chapter draws upon data collected as part of a larger study of the multilingual literacy practices associated with Flickr. The broader study (Lee and Barton 2011) focuses on the ways in which people creatively deploy their language resources in new online spaces and how these practices shed light on current understanding of vernacular literacies (Barton and Lee 2012). Although the study originally sought to observe and describe multilingual activities, the participants often revealed their attitudes toward different languages without prompting. These metalinguistic attitudes about language, collected from people's self-generated contents on Flickr and follow-up email interviews, often centered on Flickr users' perception of the functions of English and their knowledge of the language in relation to their online participation. Many scholars have acknowledged extensive use of languages other than English in web spaces (such as Danet and Herring 2007; Herring et al. 2007), but the initial findings of ongoing research on Flickr show that English is still seen as a common language by international participants (Lee and Barton 2009), which is in line with traditional claims about the dominant role of English online (such as Garland 2006; Luke, Luke, and Graham 2007). The importance of English, especially to those whose primary language is not English, is often reflected in the participants' explicit self-evaluations of their English proficiency level on their Flickr profile page, photo captions, and comments, as shown in the following examples by two users from France and Germany, respectively.

Sorry to write in French but my English is too poor to express my feelings (lefete, French)

My English is limited and not so well as it should be :(. (Berta, German)

It is these self-assessments of English on Flickr that inspired this study. This chapter focuses on the ways in which metalinguistic discourses about English are constructed on Flickr and the social meanings associated with them, through addressing three interrelated questions:

1. How do people who do not use English as their primary language talk about their knowledge of English on Flickr?
2. What are the motivations behind such discourses?
3. What is the relationship between such discourses and participation on Flickr?

Drawing on a textual database of 1,292 statements of self-evaluation of English proficiency and interview data from ten participants, I identify various types of metalinguistic discourse about English on Flickr. In addition, I use data from online interviews to explain why such discourses exist on Flickr. My understanding of the data was mainly informed by the analytical framework of stancetaking (Jaffe 2009), which is a useful approach to understanding how Flickr users' attitudes regarding their own linguistic skills are discursively constructed. Using Gee's (2004) concept of affinity spaces, I also show the ways in which such seemingly self-deprecatory comments serve to encourage social networking, widen participation, and support informal learning.

Metalinguistic Discourse and Folk Linguistic Attitudes Online

Sociolinguists have long been interested in investigating nonlinguists' beliefs, attitudes, and theories of language—an area that is often referred to as folk linguistics (Niedzielski and Preston 2000). Widely adopted in perceptual dialectology and research on spoken language (for example, Preston 1996), folk linguistic attitudes have not been researched extensively in the context of computer-mediated communication (CMC). Among those studies that do deal with the folk linguistics of new media language, many are concerned with the ways in which mass media discursively construct young people and their online language use. A case in point is Thurlow's (2007) analysis of mass media representations of language online in a corpus of news articles, in which moral panics about young people's language standards and other language ideologies are discursively constructed.

From an insider's perspective, a growing amount of research begins to examine media users' self-reflection and comments on their own online language use. Squires's (2010) work presents a comprehensive analysis of the various labels given to internet-based registers on different "sites of metadiscourse" (457), one of which is interactive online discussion, in which commenters express opinions about the register used in their comment threads. Squires convincingly argues that metadiscourse about online registers is largely shaped by standard language ideology and technological determinism. In my ongoing research on Facebook status updates (Lee 2011), I also make explicit reference to my participants' own theories of language in understanding their perceptions of the language used in their status updates. For example, to explain how he wrote his status updates on Facebook, an interviewee frequently referred to grammar items as in "*It depends on the aspect of the verb and the tense.*" A number of new media scholars have given attention to metalinguistic discourses about different languages found in the commenting system of various Web 2.0 or social media such as YouTube (Androutsopoulos 2011; Benson 2010). To date, however, no published work has specifically focused on media users' self-evaluation of their English skills in relation to their internet participation. It is this emerging aspect of metalinguistic discourse online that interests me. In particular, this chapter discusses the ways in which talking about one's own English proficiency can serve meaningful social purposes on one of the most popular Web 2.0 sites, Flickr.

Data and Methods

To understand how Flickr participants construct evaluative comments about their English-language proficiency, a textual database of sentences with explicit remarks about one's knowledge and competence in English was first collected from Flickr, with specific focus on photo descriptions, comments, tags, and user profiles. Although I am aware that Flickr users also express their opinions about other languages they know (for example, "*my Japanese is limited*"), English is perceived to be the common language on Flickr (Lee and Barton 2009), and is more frequently mentioned and evaluated than other languages. Thus, the analysis presented in this chapter focuses on English only.

The initial stage of the research involved keyword searches of six expressions that Flickr users commonly used to evaluate their proficiency in English. These six search phrases derived initially from my active participation in Flickr, as well as observations derived from the data in the broader study of multilingual practices on Flickr. Table 4.1 summarizes the six key phrases and the number of examples collected in the keyword search.

The first five expressions deal with the participant's own evaluation of or reflection on their knowledge of English. The last expression, "Your English is . . ." was added in order to elicit other people's responses to these self-evaluations. In the searches, I focused on user profiles, descriptions (captions), tags, and comments. In the corpus, participants' screen names, current locations, and languages spoken were noted, if such information was available.

This initial stage allowed me to collect a textual database of 1,292 examples of self-evaluation of English and 325 examples of others' responses. For the self-evaluations, I carried out a basic meaning-based content analysis of the attitudes toward one's own English-language proficiency and the stance taken in constructing such discourses, thus addressing the first research question about the types of self-evaluation. The immediate linguistic context of these expressions—that is, what the participant said before and after the sentence collected—as well as other texts appearing on their photo pages, were also taken into account when relevant. To further understand the motivations behind describing one's English proficiency and how such comments affect levels of participation in Flickr, participants were chosen from the pool of writers identified in the keyword searches to participate in interviews conducted via Flickr's private email system. The ten interviewees were selected because (1) they were active members (that is, they posted photos regularly) and (2) English was not their primary language when they were not using Flickr. I also selected people from a range of nationalities and native lan-

■ Table 4.1
Summary of text data

Search phrase	Example	No. of occurrences
"My English is __."	"My English is poor."	730
"I don't know English __."	"I'm from brazil, and *i don't know english* very well . . . lol"	72
"I don't speak English __."	"i don't speak english, i'm speak french."	156
"I don't understand English __."	"I'm sorry I don't understand English well."	64
"English is not my __."	"English is not my first language."	270
"Your English is __."	"Your English is much better than my German."	325

guages: these included two German users from Germany, two Italian speakers from Italy, and two Portuguese speakers from Brazil; the rest were from France, Finland, Korea, and Malaysia. The interview questions were designed to identify the motivations behind the self-evaluation of English proficiency (research question 2) as well as to examine the relationship between such comments and participation in Flickr (research question 3); topics covered included their reasons for discussing their knowledge of English, and how doing so would affect their relationship with other Flickr members.

My analysis of metalinguistic discourse about English was informed by the notion of stancetaking in discourse analysis (Du Bois 2007; Jaffe 2009). Stance is "a public act by a social actor achieved dialogically through overt communicative means" (Du Bois 2007, 163). According to Du Bois, stance is often expressed through positioning, evaluation, and alignment, thus forming what he calls a stance triangle (2007). The two most commonly identified stances are *epistemic* stance, which refers to the claiming of knowledge or belief toward a stance object; and *affective* stance, which is expressed through feelings, mood, and emotion about a stance object (Jaffe 2009). Stancetaking is thus a useful framework for analyzing the ways in which attitudes toward English-language skills are constructed discursively. Understanding the ways writers position themselves by talking about their English-language abilities also reveals how such metalinguistic discourse facilitates social networking and participation in the Flickr community.

Metalinguistic Discourse about English on Flickr

The self-evaluative comments of English collected were first categorized into seven basic types, primarily according to their meaning. In the following, I provide descriptions and examples for these types so as to provide a snapshot of the possible ways of constructing self-evaluative discourses about English by the Flickr users in the present study.

1. *Perceived Knowledge of English:* All of the expressions collected were negative evaluations of the writers' English-language skills, and explicitly tell readers how little English a given writer knows. These expressions convey writers' affective stance toward their own English with some typical adjectives of evaluation such as "good," "bad," "terrible," "poor," or in terms of weakness and incompetence.

- *My English is poor/terrible/horrible*
- *My weakest trait is my english ability . . .*

2. *Apologetic and Forgiveness Seeking:* A great deal of the sentences collected (235 sentences, 18 percent) are accompanied by apologies; users generally ask their target readers to forgive possible grammatical and spelling errors in their English captions or comments. Some even apologize for not speaking English as a first language:

- *my english is not perfect, so excuse my grammar and occasional mistakes in text :)* (JV image, Czech)
- *Well, i'm sorry, my english is so shitty ugh because i'm french so sorry.* (red-dot, French)

3. *Native Speaker Norm as a Model of "Good" English:* In this type of self-evaluative comment, what people say about their English-language proficiency is often juxtaposed with the so-called native speaker norm. Within the corpus, a large number of comments (340 sentences, 26 percent) made reference to native speakers of English; 145 revealed negative attitudes about "not being native English speaker" or being more likely to make mistakes in English.

> ■ *Sorry for the grammar mistakes, english is not my mother language.* (Camilo, Spanish)
> ■ *pity that english is not my mother language . . . otherwise i'd be glad to give my point of view about the question.* (wesley)

4. *External Resources:* Some Flickr members admitted to a limited knowledge of English and explained what was supporting their English writing on Flickr. A small number (31) of the statements collected referred to dictionaries, online translators such as Google Translate, and other people in their lives who could act as literacy brokers in their participation in Flickr.

> ■ *My English is Google translator. . . . Mi español es el traductor de Google. . . . Mon français est traducteur de Google . . .* (Angelo, Italian)
> ■ *I don't understand english but I have got translation through this website, this relpy wrote by my daughter, you can type english* (pklam, Chinese)

5. *Self-improvement:* Although the previous types present quite negative attitudes towards the writers' English proficiency, as many as 104 examples expressed the writer's commitment to learning English and to self-improvement.

> ■ *I'm really glad I found this site cause apart from sharing my pics I get to practice my English a bit.*" (Gabriel, Polish)
> ■ *my English is poor. Therefore I want to make friends with foreigner, so that I can improve my oral English skill.* (Kaki Wong, Chinese)

6. *Humor and Playfulness:* A small number of the examples (23) collected discuss English-language proficiency in a lighthearted, playful, and humorous manner:

> ■ *i don't speak english . . . really . . . all i know how to say is . . .i don't speak english.* (Pam)
> ■ *My English is not perfect, so be kind if you're the Shakespeare's kind of person or try to write like this in Spanish.* (Kris001, Spanish)

7. *Photography as the Lingua Franca:* Although they perceive their English proficiency to be limited, for many language is secondary to photography on Flickr. Thus, a small number of the statements (40) in the corpus more or less reflect people's awareness of the central role of photography on Flickr:

> ■ *I don't understand english very well, but this photo impress me. Sometimes the image is enough.* (Jean, Italian)
> ■ *My English is so . . . poor! so, I take photos . . .*

■ 唉中文都一樣不見得是好 ! (sigh. My Chinese isn't good either!)

■ 都是拍照算了 (I should stick to taking photos.) (Tian, Chinese)

This initial content analysis of the corpus also reveals participant stances regarding the English they use on Flickr and their perceived knowledge of English in general. The construction of these statements conforms to the two most common types of stance mentioned earlier—epistemic and affective stances. These evaluations of English skills are constructed epistemically by expressing knowledge of English (for example, "I don't know English"), or affectively, expressing feelings about their English using adjectives common in evaluations (for example, "My English is bad"). In addition, these types of stances are expressed in similar linguistic structures: extensive use of first-person singular pronouns "I" and "my"; and words that denote possession, such as "my own English," thus claiming ownership of their "poor" English. These linguistic means also serve as means of self-positioning in such stance-taking acts.

Motivations for Claiming Knowledge of English on Flickr

Although it was not my intention to judge a particular participant's English, what struck me in many instances was that a participant's written English on Flickr was indeed highly communicative, despite his or her negative self-evaluations. This was taken up further in the email interviews. When interviewees were asked why they made such explicit comments about their own English skills on Flickr, their responses were quite divided. A number of them worried about possible communication breakdowns if their readers did not understand their English:

I scare I write something funny mistakes or peoples don't understood me. (digikid, Finnish)

By the same token, some considered the image that they might project to their target audience if they did not use correct English. Thus, admitting to limited proficiency in English (which may well be interpreted as being modest) is an act of politeness, a request to others to accept their errors in English. This is illustrated by Amilia's explanation:

I think by telling people that my English is not good, so they can accept that; "Oh, his English isn't good enough, that's why there is some grammar error in his photo's description/title." when there is a grammar error in my photo's description or titles. (Amilia, Malaysian)

A similar idea is expressed by Celia, who pointed out that she could not tolerate errors in her native language:

Warning people not to know English, because in Portuguese bother me much spelling mistakes and grammatical serious!

For some users, by contrast, telling others how much English they know or do not know projects a sense of self, in that knowledge of English is part of the identity that they would like to project on Flickr:

Well, I don't think it's so important to tell people how my english is. . . . my poor english level is a part of me. So I thought it was right to notice this point. (Mika, French)

These interview excerpts show that this self-deprecation is more than simply an act of devaluing oneself or being modest. Telling others how much English one knows or does not know serves a meaningful purpose on Flickr. From the limited set of interview data collected, it is apparent at least that talking about their English-language skills allows Flickr users to build rapport, to ensure mutual intelligibility, and to negotiate identity in the Flickr world.

Competence, Participation, and Learning in Affinity Spaces

These seemingly negative comments about English-language skills are indeed taken by participants quite positively—and even playfully as demonstrated by type 6 of the content analysis. For one thing, switching languages is certainly an indication of a person's readiness to communicate. Flickr members speaking different languages are willing to write captions and comments in English because they view English as a language common to all Flickr members, even though many participants said they do not use English outside Flickr (Lee and Barton 2009).

The data are also evidence of people's strong desire to participate and display competence on Flickr. Competence broadly refers to expert skills and the knowledge one needs in order to become a legitimate member of a given community (Lave and Wenger 1991). For many Flickr participants, being competent in English is indeed central to Flickr membership. They are also aware that linguistic competence can be constantly negotiated. This is often achieved through the act of self-evaluation, as presented in this chapter. Evaluation is an act of alignment and positioning in discourse (Du Bois 2007). Again using the concept of stance-taking, I argue that by repositioning themselves as less-than-competent English speakers by making self-deprecatory comments such as "My English is so poor," people are negotiating their identities so that they will be accepted by others as legitimate participants on Flickr. And these negative self-evaluations are indeed a central discourse type in such negotiations.

In addition to negotiating membership, a great deal of social networking is also initiated by explicitly declaring one's own English-language abilities. A case in point is a photo page that belongs to CB, a German speaker, that displays a picture of her Japanese-style bento lunch. Underneath the photo, CB wrote her photo title and caption in English:

Bentolunch for tomorrow (Friday)

Today my new bentobox arrived! It's a pretty bentobox with a little bunny on the top.

Of course I had to use it, so I prepared my bento for tomorrow quickly ^.^

(Sorry, I know my English is so so bad! I definitely have to learn it better .. T.T

This photo description, although written in quite good English, contains what I have called apologetic evaluation (type 2), written in parentheses: "Sorry, I know my English is so so so bad!!" This, however, brings CB a great deal of encouraging and supportive comments from other Flickr users, who even praise her English. Here are three of the six comments posted originally below the photo caption:

COMMENTER A: Pretty bento. And I think your English is good!

COMMENTER B: Trust me, your English is a lot better than the English of many native speakers. ^_~

CB: thank you so much, [commenter A]. . . . I learned english for 5 years at school, but I think it isn't good enough for that ><" Hehe, nice to meet you, [commenter B]!! Your comment is so nice ^.^

All of the comments (including the one written by CB herself) interestingly point to CB's remark about her English being "so so so bad," instead of the actual content of the image, or the description of the bento lunch underneath. In response to such encouraging comments, CB, while expressing her gratitude, stresses again that her English "isn't good enough." What seems to be a traditional compliment-giving-and-response sequence serves to build solidarity between CB and her Flickr friends. This short exchange clearly demonstrates how such seemingly negative metalinguistic discourse about English can shape social networks and widen participation on Flickr.

Apart from the standard apologetic type of discourse about her own English, my attention was also drawn to CB's commitment to learning. She says in the photo caption, "*I definitely have to learn it better . . . T.T* (crying emoticon)." Her commitment to learning and self-improvement allows her to reposition herself as an active language learner with a positive attitude. It seems that her perceived poor English is actually one of the strongest motivations behind her participation on Flickr. This kind of self-improvement and learning discourse (type 5) is indeed very prominent in my data; users often follow laments about their "poor English" with declarations of their commitment to learning better English through active participation on Flickr. This commitment to self-improvement is common discourse throughout Flickr (Barton 2012). Positive comments and feedback from other members also provide a friendly, supportive, and relatively safe environment in which informal learning can take place (see also Davies and Merchant 2009). This resonates with Gee's (2004) notion of affinity spaces, which helps to explain the presence of discourse about "learning better English" on Flickr. Affinities are Gee's response to the traditional notion of communities of practice (Lave and Wenger 1991). Unlike communities of practice, affinities do not assume static group membership, but bring people of all backgrounds together in pursuit of common interests and goals. Most importantly, in an affinity space, all kinds of knowledge are welcomed and valued. Flickr is certainly one such space. Even though Flickr users see English as the dominant language of interaction, English, non-English, and even "poor English" are acknowledged and valued. After all, this learning space is defined by the common endeavor of photography, and to a lesser extent, social networking.

Conclusions: Talking about Language on Web 2.0

This chapter reveals the ways in which English is discussed on one popular Web 2.0 site, and provides an overview of the possible types of discourse about English and language learning on Flickr. A microexample of a photo page from one user (CB) has been used to demonstrate how these discourses are embedded and situated in the context of a Flickr photo page. My findings show that on Flickr, people, especially those who do not speak English as their native language, often talk about English and learning it; evaluate their own and others' knowledge of English; are motivated English learners; and regularly reflect upon their folk linguistic theories (Niedzielski and Preston 2000). Whereas my focus herein is English on Flickr, future research may look into how online participants talk about other languages used in social media such as YouTube (Androutsopoulos 2011; Benson 2010).

I also specifically demonstrate that seemingly negative evaluations of one's own English-language proficiency are not simply born of modesty or self-abasement; explicitly acknowledging one's limited knowledge of English is indeed a powerful tool on Flickr—it encourages social networking, widens participation, and supports informal learning. The study also reveals the ways in which Flickr provides unique opportunities to create a collaborative, supportive environment for ordinary people to express their vernacular and nonlinguistic theories of language through self-generated multimodal content, including images and the written word.

ACKNOWLEDGMENTS

I would like to thank Deborah Tannen and Anna Marie Trester for their insightful comments and editorial suggestions. I thank David Barton for commenting on an earlier draft of this paper. I am also grateful to participants at GURT 2011 who provided useful feedback on my presentation.

NOTE

1. Permissions have been sought from Flickr users to reproduce the screenshot (fig. 4.1) and the text from CB's photo page. All Flickr usernames in this chapter are pseudonyms.

REFERENCES

Androutsopoulos, Jannis. 2011. Dialects on display: performance and negotiation of linguistic localness in the participatory web. Keynote speech, Georgetown University Round Table on Languages and Linguistics, Washington, DC, March 12.

Barton, David. 2012. Participation, deliberate learning and discourses of learning online. *Language and Education* 26, no. 2:139–50.

Barton, David, and Carmen Lee. 2012. Redefining vernacular literacies in the age of Web 2.0. *Applied Linguistics* 33, no. 3:282–98.

Benson, Philip. 2010. Funny teacher saying foul language: New literacies in a second language. Paper presented at the 17th International Conference on Learning, Hong Kong, July 8.

Danet, Brenda, and Susan C. Herring, eds. 2007. *The multilingual internet.* New York: Oxford University Press.

Davies, Julia, and Guy Merchant. 2009. *Web 2.0 for schools.* New York: Peter Lang.

Du Bois, John W. 2007. The stance triangle. In *Stancetaking in discourse: Subjectivity, evaluation, interaction,* ed. Robert Englebretson, 139–82. Amsterdam: John Benjamins.

Garland, Eric. 2006. Can minority languages be saved? Globalization vs. culture. *The Futurist* 40, no. 4. www.omniglot.com/language/articles/minority_languages.php.

Gee, James Paul. 2004. *Situated language and learning.* London: Routledge.

Herring, Susan C., John C. Paolillo, Irene Ramos-Vielba, Inna Kouper, Elijah Wright, Sharon Stoerger, Lois Ann Scheidt, and Benjamin Clark. 2007. Language networks on LiveJournal. *Proceedings of the 40th Hawaii International Conference on System Sciences,* ed. Ralph Sprague. Los Alamitos, CA: IEEE Press.

Jaffe, Alexandra. 2009. *Stance: Sociolinguistic perspectives.* Oxford: Oxford University Press.

Lave, Jean, and Etienne Wenger. 1991. *Situated learning: Legitimate peripheral participation.* Cambridge: Cambridge University Press.

Lee, Carmen. 2011. Texts and practices of micro-blogging: Status updates on Facebook. In *Digital discourse: Language in new media,* eds. Crispin Thurlow and Kristine Mroczek, 110–28. New York: Oxford University Press.

Lee, Carmen, and David Barton. 2009. English and glocal identities on Web 2.0: The case of Flickr.com. In *Englishization in Asia,* ed. Kwok-kan Tam, 1–20. Hong Kong: Open University of Hong Kong Press.

———. 2011. Constructing glocal identities through multilingual writing practices on Flickr.com. *International Multilingual Research Journal* 5, no. 1:39–59.

Luke, Allen, Carmen Luke, and Philip Graham. 2007. Globalization, corporatism, and critical language education. *International Multilingual Research Journal* 1, no. 1:1–13.

Niedzielski, Nancy, and Dennis Preston. 2000. *Folk linguistics.* Berlin: Mouton de Gruyter.

Preston, Dennis. 1996. Whaddayaknow? The modes of folk linguistic awareness. *Linguistic Awareness* 5:40–74.

Squires, Lauren. 2010. Enregistering internet language. *Language in Society* 39, no. 4:457–92.

Thurlow, Crispin. 2007. Fabricating youth: New media discourse and the technologization of young people. In *Language in the media,* eds. Sally Johnson and Astrid Ensslin, 213–33. London: Continuum.

5

"Their Lives Are So Much Better Than Ours!"

The Ritual (Re)construction of Social Identity in Holiday Cards

JENNA MAHAY
Concordia University Chicago

Introduction

TWO YEARS AGO I received one of those professionally printed holiday photo cards from some close friends who had recently moved to France. It was a particularly nice one. It was printed on heavy cardstock and opened up like a card you might buy at the store—except that it had their own pictures on it. On the front were two photos of their family of four, accompanied by the words "Joyeux Noel" and an elegant design. It opened up to four more photos on the left-hand side of their two children having fun in various leisure time activities, with a preprinted narrative of the highlights of the past year on the right-hand side. My four-year old daughter looked at it, and upon seeing the photos of her friends, asked me to read it to her. I had a feeling that somehow this was not going to go well. I read to her about their wonderful new life in France, the castles they had visited, how the kids loved their private school, and how quickly they were picking up French. Their dog, Jack, was having a fine time chasing birds in the vineyard behind their house. Sure enough, as soon as I finished reading, my daughter burst into tears. "Their lives are so much better than ours!" And then came, "I want to move somewhere. I feel like I've been here for a hundred years!" While contemplating whether I should remind her that she had not yet been on this earth even five years, I was struck by the clarity with which she recognized, and the directness with which she articulated, the aspects of both status and elite mobility being conveyed in this card. Out of the mouths of babes . . .

The seeds of this analysis were actually planted quite a few years ago, when I first started receiving holiday cards that had been created using the (then-new) digital technology in which the individual uploads his or her own photos to a website and designs one's own holiday card with them, selecting various designs and greetings provided by the website. The card is then professionally printed by an internet-based company and shipped back to the individual, who then sends them to everyone on his or her list. I remember being somewhat surprised to see pictures of our friends on top of Mount Kilimanjaro, on the beach, and in Sicily on their honeymoon printed on the holiday cards they sent us. While dutifully hanging them on the wall, I wondered to myself, "What does this have to do with Christmas?" As I watched the holiday photo card technology develop, it seemed that these cards became less about wishing someone happy holidays, and more about something else. To be sure, holiday cards have always communicated something about the sender's social identity and status. But the introduction of the technology to create one's own customized professional-quality holiday photo cards online has turned them into something more.

This study analyzes holiday photo cards on two of the leading high-end photo card retail websites from a sociological perspective. The study systemically examines the images, text, and design of these cards, as well as how they are described on the retail websites. I first briefly review the relevant literature on the performance and construction of social identity, and then describe the data and methods, findings, and conclusions of this study. My analysis shows that the availability of the digital technology that allows one to create one's own customized holiday photo cards has turned the holiday card tradition into a powerful medium for constructing and displaying one's own social identity in terms of class and status, but also in terms of membership within the hegemonic family ideal. Further, this analysis finds that a powerful part of what is ultimately communicated and reinforced through these holiday photo cards is a normative ideal of happiness itself. And finally, the ability to create one's own professional quality holiday photo cards adds legitimacy and authority to one's constructed social identity and the ideals portrayed.

The (Re)construction of Social Identity

Holiday photo cards can be seen as an important aspect of one's "performance" of social identity from an interactionist perspective (Goffman 1959). Previous research has examined other forms of sent communication, such as greeting cards and vacation postcards, as a performance of social identity (West 2010; Thurlow and Jaworski 2010), but holiday cards are somewhat different in that they are sent on an annual basis to a wider social network and are infused and legitimated by the wider social meanings of the holidays. For many, the holiday card is the only communication they have with much of their extended social network, and is thus a primary means of performing the family's social identity for a number of people. Even for those with whom one does have regular contact, holiday photo cards are powerful symbolic expressions, in crystallized form, of the sender's self, sent on an annual basis.

Goffman (1959) has noted that in American culture, status is one of the primary things being communicated in any performance. The holiday photo card can signify status in a number of ways, primarily through the cultural and economic capital represented in an elite holiday photo card. Bourdieu (1986) has theorized several different aspects of cultural capital, the most relevant being *embodied cultural capital,* which he defines as "long-lasting dispositions of the mind and body" to understand and appreciate cultural goods, tastes, and styles that are validated and defined as prestigious. Bourdieu also defines *objectified cultural capital* as the objects that require this special knowledge to understand, use, and appreciate (Bourdieu 1986; see also Mohr and DiMaggio 1995). To create elite holiday photo cards, one must have the cultural knowledge of what constitutes prestigious design, quality materials, and aesthetically pleasing photos. Additionally, one must possess all of the technical apparatus and expertise to take the digital photo (or have it professionally taken), upload it to the computer, then upload it to one of the more prestigious online retailers (one must know which website to go to), and from there create one's own distinctive card.

The holiday photo card also indexes the leisure time available to construct this rather elaborate and time-consuming performance. Thus, in the making of holiday photo cards, an objectified form of cultural capital, one demonstrates embodied cultural capital. Because cultural capital is perceived as a combination of an "innate property and the merits of acquisition," it thus functions as symbolic capital—unrecognized as capital and seen as "legitimate competence," thereby translated into respectability and honorability (Bourdieu 1984).

Cultural objects also gain meaning in their movement through social space. As Jaffe remarks about greeting cards, although they are private, their journey from the store to the purchaser's home to being signed, addressed, stamped, mailed, and delivered adds a "layer of public declaration" to its meaning (1999, 137). Thus, Jaffe finds that an anniversary card invokes not just the private details of the couple's relationship, but the public nature and meaning of marriage. Similarly, a holiday card can invoke not just good wishes from one particular family to another, but the public meaning of family, happiness, and holidays.

Data and Methods

This study is based on qualitative analysis of holiday photo cards shown on two of the leading high-end holiday photo card retail websites, Shutterfly and Tiny Prints. I also conducted a quantitative analysis of the family forms represented on the 644 holiday cards displayed on the larger of these websites, Shutterfly. The sample cards shown on the websites can be seen as reflecting consumer behavior (demonstrating who is likely to purchase the product and why); the websites themselves are a place where interested individuals learn how these cards are supposed to look and who is meant to put their photos on holiday cards.

Representations of Class and Status

Qualitative analysis reveals a number of ways in which holiday photo cards can communicate status. First, the aesthetics of the card signify elite status. Indeed, this is the way cards are sold on the higher-end websites; leading retailers emphasize the style that is being sent rather than the message:

- Send a touch of the French countryside with this charming red and green holiday card. Personalize it with three favorite photos and a unique message. (shutterfly.com, fig. 5.1)
- Vintage elegance. Ornate flourishes in a sage-green hue and a cocoa-brown border frames a favorite photo in this holiday card. Add your family's name to traditional season's greetings. (shutterfly.com)
- Simplify your holiday style in a refined and elegant way with this luxe monogrammed holiday photo card from Picturebook. This sophisticated design is sure to impress with its sleek and timeless look. (tinyprints.com)

Figure 5.1 Figure captured from the Shutterfly website.

In all of these examples, it is the style that is foregrounded and most important, rather than the message. In the first example, clearly what is being sent here is the elite status signified by the "French countryside," with the holiday wishes as an afterthought. In the second example, words such as "vintage," "sage-green hue," and "cocoa-brown border" require a certain embodied cultural capital to identify it as signifying an elite aesthetic. In this example, the photos of one's family are literally placed inside the frame of one's cultural capital and sent to everyone in one's social network. The third example, from Tiny Prints, uses words such as "refined," "elegant," "sleek," and "timeless" to signify the aesthetic of those with high cultural capital. In this example, the card is also monogrammed with the family's initial, another sign of distinction. Both of the leading high-end websites allow consumers to choose from a variety of different design collections by different named designers, much as one would purchase couture clothing.

Similarly, West (2010) found that for those with higher cultural capital (measured by occupation and educational attainment), greeting cards are more an expression of taste than of sentiment. The style of representation takes priority, reflecting those in the middle and upper classes who are divorced from the necessities and practicalities of everyday life. They do not focus on the usefulness of objects so much as the form of objects and what they represent. West (2010) has also found that in the selection of greeting cards, consumers with relatively high cultural capital prioritize card design over written sentiment, and thereby perform exclusivity through taste—even in the form of mass culture. The focus on the aesthetics of the card over the message indexes the "leisure and education that result in the appreciation of objects and activities with complex codes" (365). Thus, the creation of these holiday photo cards are a performance of embodied cultural capital—knowledge, taste, and competence.

Interestingly, the cards displayed on the retail websites also highlight the fact that consumers can add their own unique message, reflecting the idea that those with high cultural capital also typically seek greeting cards that "announce their separateness from an industrialized mode of production" (West 2010, 368). They look for cards that show uniqueness, individuality, and creativity so as to distinguish themselves from the mass market. Thus, the ability to customize holiday photo cards online also provides a prime tool for the performance of cultural capital, and the retailers have clearly tapped into this.

In addition to the ability to add one's own unique message, another way of distinguishing oneself from the mass market is the complex, foldout designs of the cards themselves. On their website, Tiny Prints writes, "*Showcase* your family's sweet style this season with a *truly unique* Tri-Fold Accordion Card from Petite Alma featuring an eclectic design of inviting hues and a checkered format that will make your moments even more delightful!" (emphasis mine). The "family's sweet style" here is signified by the unique *form* of the card itself, not just the message. Clearly, the consumer's desire for differentiation is reflected, and in the text quoted above, the retailer emphasizes that this is how a family's style is showcased in its performance for others.

One distinguishing feature of Tiny Prints that is informative for the cultural capital argument here is that Tiny Prints advertises that their "skilled designers" review each holiday card that is created on their website to ensure the card makes the correct impression: "Skilled designers will review your tri-fold holiday card orders for layout, spelling and etiquette to ensure that all of your tri-fold holiday cards are exceptional. Trust us with your photo holiday cards and you'll be sure to excite everyone on your photo holiday card list" (Tiny Prints n.d.). This highlights the fact that these cards are intended to index cultural capital in terms of design and cultural knowledge. Those who can afford to purchase their holiday cards on Tiny Prints are assured that their card will achieve the desired effect. Yet because it is designed by the consumer, the role of economic capital is hidden, and converted into a more legitimate, seemingly meritocratic competency, or cultural capital.

As is true of all cards, the *quality* of materials signifies not only cultural capital but also the price of the card, and therefore the economic capital of the sender. Cards are advertised as being printed on "premium cardstock" (Shutterfly n.d.), and the websites assume consumers possess sufficient technical knowledge about paper quality to appreciate the cards' "110 lb, 15 pt thickness" (Tiny Prints n.d.).

A new feature that these leading retailers offer is a more professionalized version of the holiday newsletter that is often enclosed in the traditional store-bought holiday card. Shutterfly now offers the "Story Card" (fig. 5.2), about which customers are told: "Decorate their mantle with four lovely ribbon ornaments holding four lovely photos. There's room to tell your Christmas story with updates from several months of the year. A delightfully dotted border frames this Christmas card" (Shutterfly n.d.). The updates on this card feature middle- and upper-class activities such as a piano recital and horseback riding lessons, another way in which the elite "style of life" (Bourdieu 1984) of those with high cultural capital is indexed. The children's photos are literally turned into ornaments on this card. In addition, the website invites customers to consider not only how their recipients will view the card, but

merry christmas

FEBRUARY

Lizzy performed in her
first piano recital and
did great!

MAY

Michael caught his first
fish with Grandpa! He
can't wait to go

JULY

Skyler got first place
at her championship
swim meet!

DECEMBER

Lily enjoyed horseback riding camp
and continues to take horseback
riding lessons.

LOVE, THE THOMSONS

■ Figure 5.2 Figure captured from the Shutterfly website.

also how the card will look showcased in the recipients' home ("Decorate their mantle"), thus expanding the card's visibility to the recipient's social networks.

The professional quality of the story card created on these websites also allows the purported truth of the message on the card to be taken for granted, since the author's hand becomes invisible. As Jaffe notes, there is a "kind of certainty embedded in the card as commodity: freedom from the requirement to grapple with the contingent, socially constructed nature of meaning" (1999, 133). The writer's hand is backgrounded, made invisible in these professionally printed photo holiday story cards. The story is somehow legitimated and the meaning is in a sense publically declared.

Finally, let us consider what is actually shown in the photos themselves. Many photos on the holiday cards analyzed herein show the family in various acts of conspicuous leisure, most commonly on the beach or at a ski resort (fig. 5.3). Holiday cards featuring vacation photos reflect what Bauman (1998, 2000) and others have described as the social inequality in spatial mobility. Holiday cards of the elite typically include images and narratives highlighting travel for tourism and leisure. As noted by Thurlow and Jaworski (2010), being a global traveler is recognized as an elite status and is aspired to in today's world. Even more so is the global traveling *family,* as this is an even more expensive and impressive endeavor. Vacation postcards serve to provide evidence of where the tourist has been and what they have seen, verifying the authenticity of the tourist's experience and thus identity as a tourist (Thurlow and Jaworski 2010), but the holiday card goes one step further—showing the family itself on the beach or other exotic location (rather than a generic card of the

Figure 5.3 Figure captured from the Shutterfly website.

landscape bought off the rack). This unquestionably identifies the entire family as members of the modern elite globalized community. The holiday card may be thought of as a kind of membership card that must be renewed yearly, for this is an identity that must be continually performed in order to maintain its veracity.

Writing travel into the annual holiday card is a way of weaving this elite mobility into their social identity as a family, situating them in a particular socioeconomic strata. Families are no longer just sending vacation postcards or showing pictures to others upon returning from a trip. By printing these vacation photos on their annual holiday cards, tourism is no longer a temporary performance, but literally written into their identity of *who they are as a family* and sent to every person in their social network. Although the discourse of tourist postcards often refers to the transience of the touristic state and demarcations of here (vacation) and there (back home [Thurlow and Jaworski 2010]), printing vacation photos onto holiday cards blurs these boundaries. The extraordinary experiences and alternate state of the touristic period—the *escape* from the daily grind—are (re)constructed to represent the normal, so-called real, everyday life of the family. Vacation photos are no longer relegated to the inside of a photo album, or even to one's social media website where they wait for others to look at them. By putting them on a physical holiday card and sending them to everyone in one's social network, others are obligated not only to view but to display them in their own homes.

Thus, the images printed on holiday photo cards are a powerful way of communicating meaning without having to state it outright. Jaffe argues that greeting cards are socially useful because they "do interactional work that is delicate or difficult" (1999, 125). In this case, the images shown in photos, and the style of the card, communicate meaning that is neither easy—nor socially acceptable—to put in words. Thus, the photo holiday card may be one of the only socially acceptable ways to display status to persons in one's social network with whom one has little other interaction.

Holiday Cards, the Hegemonic Family Ideal, and Happiness

The holiday cards on the leading websites both reflect and reinforce the hegemonic ideal of the first-time married heterosexual nuclear family with young children. The vast majority (82 percent) of holiday cards shown by the online holiday card retailers studied here include two-parent families with children, most with more than one child. According to recent analyses, however, only 17 percent of US households consist of a married couple with any children under the age of eighteen (White et al. 2011). In the holiday cards shown on the online retail websites, if the parents are depicted with only one child, that child is usually young, with the promise or expectation of more to come. Only rarely is a couple shown with only one older child. Only 2 percent of the online retailer cards analyzed show only a mother or father with the child, although this represents 5.6 percent of all US households (White et al. 2011). However, in cards that do show only a mother or father with the child, the other parent is still present in the text. All of the one-parent cards shown on the websites listed the names of the individual people in the family that it was sent from, and in each case the other parent was listed as well (see fig. 5.4).

In cards with only a couple (no children), the couple is almost always young, in love, often at their wedding, and clearly a child is imminent. For example, the couples without children are almost always portrayed in a private moment of romantic tenderness, and in one card featured on the website, the couple is actually pictured lying together on the bed in what one would imagine to be a postcoital moment. What we do not see are pictures of older couples who have clearly chosen not to have children, or older couples whose children have left the household. There were also no same-sex couples or families represented; the cards show an entirely heterosexual world.

■ Figure 5.4 Figure captured from the Shutterfly website.

Cards that feature multiple photos show various different socially valued dimensions of the hegemonic family. One typical card (fig. 5.5) shows a picture of each of the following dimensions of the family: (1) the whole family unit together, including the mother, father, and two children; (2) the two children together in a moment of sibling bonding; (3) each child individually, to celebrate the uniqueness of each; and (4) the husband-and-wife couple bond. The last dimension is sometimes foregone, perhaps again reflecting the primacy of children in the hegemonic family ideal.

In addition, all of the holiday cards shown on the websites depict families in which every family member shares the same last name: for example, "Happy Holidays from the Horton Family." The three words at the end of that sentence are a powerful signifier of both the form of the hegemonic family ideal and the sender's accomplishment of it. Signing the card from the entire family that shares one last name emphasizes the primacy of the family unit and the likelihood that this is a first marriage. In families with children from a previous marriage, the children may have different last names and the family cannot sign the card in this way. In addition, women who kept their own last names after marriage in order to maintain their individual social identities cannot sign the card in this socially approved way. On rare occasions only the first names of those in the family were printed on the cards, with no last names; perhaps this is a way for different families to send holiday photo cards while hiding the fact that they do not meet this hegemonic ideal of the family. This allows families to save face and still represent themselves as part of this ideal even if they have not lived up to it in reality. In *no* cases were different last names printed on a holiday card shown on the retail websites. This implies that only those who have accomplished this hegemonic family ideal (or who [re]construct themselves as having achieved this ideal) should put their photos on holiday cards.

Not only is the hegemonic family ideal communicated in these cards, but also the very definition of happiness. This is accomplished in large part by the relationship between the messages printed on the cards and the images placed next to them. Many

Figure 5.5 Figure captured from the Tiny Prints website.

Figure 5.6 Figure captured from the Shutterfly website.

cards featured images of family togetherness among the sender's family, with the message, "May your holidays be filled with love and laughter." The recipient is in a sense forced not only to define "love and laughter" as shown by the images of joyful family moments with young children behind the words, but also that this is what makes *holidays* happy—that this is what one should wish for around the holidays. It also invites the recipient to make a direct comparison between one's own holiday family experiences and those depicted in the carefully constructed images of the sender's family.

Many cards shown on the websites simply had a picture of a young child or children with the word "Joy" printed over it (figs. 5.6, 5.7). In fact, one common design

Figure 5.7 Figure captured from the Shutterfly website.

Figure 5.8 Figure captured from the Shutterfly website.

features the word "Joy" with a picture of the child(ren) in the middle of the O, literally inserted into the middle of the word (fig. 5.8). Clearly, the child is the very definition of happiness. Another card features a photo of three children together with the words "Happy Everything" (fig. 5.9). According to the calculus of the photo cards featured on the retail websites then, having one child defines joy, while having three children defines *everything* that is happy.

Similarly, although with added moral weight, a card on Tiny Prints features a photo of a young child with "Blessed" printed in large script over the bottom of the image, with the words "so much to be grateful for this holiday season" printed underneath (fig. 5.10). The metamessage is clearly that even being blessed means having young children.

Figure 5.9 Figure captured from the Shutterfly website.

■ Figure 5.10 Figure captured from the Tiny Prints website.

Discussion

The availability of the technology to create one's own professional-quality customized photo card has transformed the annual holiday card ritual into an important project of identity (re)construction. Through the holiday photo card, one displays both cultural and economic capital to everyone in one's extended network. The holiday photo card requires extensive cultural capital in order to understand and use the technology required, as well as to select the prestigious designs, colors, layouts, and paper quality. Images of both conspicuous leisure and elite mobility are also prominently displayed—and now printed within the card itself—giving it a legitimacy and authority never before enjoyed.

In addition to class and status, however, the holiday photo card prominently displays the hegemonic family ideal. Taken together, the cards communicate powerful messages about status, family, and even the definition of happiness (or being blessed) through the combination of the images, text, and the physical qualities of the card. The card's messages are given added weight by the card's construction and movement through social space, as well as the cultural context (the holidays) in which the card is sent. In all, recent advances in digital technology have created a privileged way of displaying social identity in holiday photo cards that both reflects and reinforces economic and social power through this annual ritual.

REFERENCES

Bauman, Zygmunt. 1998. *Globalization: The human consequences.* New York: Columbia University Press.
———. 2000. *Liquid modernity.* Cambridge: Polity.
Bourdieu, Pierre. 1984. *Distinction: A social critique of the judgment of taste.* Cambridge, MA: Harvard University Press.
———. 1986. Forms of capital. In *Handbook of theory and research for the sociology of education,* ed. John G. Richardson, 241–58. New York: Greenwood Press.
Goffman, Erving. 1959. *The presentation of self in everyday life.* New York: Doubleday.

Jaffe, Alexandra. 1999. Packaged sentiments: The social meanings of greeting cards. *Journal of Material Culture* 4:115–41.

Mohr, John, and Paul DiMaggio. 1995. The intergenerational transmission of cultural capital. *Research in Social Stratification and Mobility* 14:167–99.

Shutterfly. n.d. shutterfly.com.

Thurlow, Crispin, and Adam Jaworski. 2010. *Tourism discourse: Language and global mobility.* London: Palgrave Macmillan.

Tiny Prints. n.d. tinyprints.com.

West, Emily. 2010. A taste for greeting cards: Distinction within a denigrated cultural form. *Journal of Consumer Culture* 10:362–82.

White, Jeremy, Ford Fessenden, Sergio Pecanha, and Matthew Ericson. 2011. How many households are like yours? *New York Times,* June 17. www.nytimes.com/interactive/2011/06/19/nyregion/how-many-households-are-like-yours.html.

6

The Medium Is the Metamessage
Conversational Style in New Media Interaction

DEBORAH TANNEN
Georgetown University

Introduction

IN 1981 I ORGANIZED the Georgetown University Round Table on Languages and Linguistics "Analyzing Discourse: Text and Talk." In my introduction to that volume (Tannen 1982a, ix) I explain that I regard "text" and "talk" not as two separate entities—text as written language and talk as spoken—but rather as "overlapping aspects of a single entity": discourse. I suggested, moreover, that the word "discourse" is invaluable as a corrective to the tendency to think of spoken and written language as separate and fundamentally different. Research by many of the participants in that meeting supported this view. Bright (1982) showed that spoken discourse exhibits verse markers like those associated with written poetry, and Chafe (1982) demonstrated that spoken Seneca rituals contain many features of written language. In my own research (for example, Tannen 1982b), while ostensibly focusing on spoken and written discourse as well as on orality and literacy, I emphasize that the division is illusory. I suggest that we think instead of oral and literate strategies that are found in speaking or writing.

Another major thread of my research has been analyzing everyday conversation. Early on I developed the notion of "conversational style," whereby speakers think they are simply saying what they mean and accomplishing interactional goals, but in doing so they necessarily choose among many options for each of the full range of linguistic phenomena such as pitch, amplitude, length of pauses, rate of speech, intonational contours, relative directness versus indirectness, discourse structure, and humor. These relatively automatic choices differ according to numerous cultural influences. I have tended to emphasize five primary influences: ethnicity, geographical background, age, class, and gender, while noting that there are innumerable other influences on style, such as sexual orientation and profession. I have shown, furthermore, that features of conversational style function to communicate not only messages—the meaning of words—but also *metamessages*—indications of how speakers intend what they say and what they are trying to do by saying those words in that way in that context.

These two research threads—on one hand, examining spoken and written language, and on the other, analyzing everyday conversation—converge in the discourse of new media.[1] Email, texting, Gchat, IM, SMS, Facebook, and other types of digital media discourse are widely understood to be written conversation. (For support of this point see Herring 2010.) In this chapter I build on and reinforce this view by demonstrating that the discourse of digital media interaction is characterized by written linguistic phenomena analogous to those I have identified as constituting conversational style in spoken interaction. I show, furthermore, that metamessages are conveyed in electronic interaction not only through the forms of discourse used but also through the choice of medium itself. I hope thus to contribute to an understanding of how new media interaction works, and how it affects interpersonal relationships.

A subtext of my argument is a response to the widespread the-sky-is-falling alarm with which many older Americans have responded to young people's use of social media. I join Thurlow (2006) and Crystal (2008), among others, in pointing out that much of what is being done by young people using new media is not, as their elders often perceive and fear, fundamentally different from what has always been done with language in social interaction. But doing the same old thing in new ways can also present new challenges. One such challenge posed by new media is that the potential metamessages one must take into account increase as the number and type of media platforms among which one must choose proliferate. Moreover, interpreting new media metamessages is especially challenging because media ideologies, as Gershon (2010) demonstrates, are emergent and continually evolving, and they tend to vary greatly not only from one user group to another but also among users in ostensibly the same social groups.

Overview

In what follows I begin by defining the term "metamessage" and explaining how I use it. I then explain and illustrate the linguistic phenomena that constitute conversational style in spoken interaction, with emphasis on the contrast between what I have dubbed "high-involvement" and "high-considerateness" styles. Next I explain how I first came to see parallels between regional differences in spoken conversational style and generational differences in digital discourse style, leading to the metaphoric characterization of cross-generational new media interaction as a kind of cross-cultural communication. With this as background, I introduce and illustrate social media analogs to conversational style, showing that differences tend to pattern not only by generation but also by gender. I then describe an "enthusiasm constraint" characteristic of cross-cultural and cross-regional spoken style. Examples of analogous phenomena in text messages exchanged by women college students include exclamatory punctuation, repetition, capitalization, and greater message length as unmarked displays of enthusiasm. The notion that these discursive practices are unmarked is crucial: their use by young women in the examples presented does not signal literal enthusiasm, but rather is necessary to avoid the impression of apathy or negativity. I go on to present other digital analogs to metamessages in conversation. Indirectness is seen in the brevity of text messages and in a link to a YouTube video. Next I consider digital analogs to the pacing and pausing of turn exchange in spoken conversation. Following that I present examples of metamessages communicated by the choice of medium, including the use of multiple media to send the same message. I next consider medium-related challenges posed by the proliferation of media options. My last example is of a miscommunication that resulted from the mechanics built into the digital platform used when sending text messages. In conclusion I suggest that the alarm with which older adults have greeted young people's new media practices resembles not only the negativity that commonly accompanies cross-cultural differences in conversational style but also the alarm that accompanied the introduction of a communication technology that we now accept without question: the printing press.

All the examples I present and discuss are of naturally occurring electronic discourse exchanged among friends and family. They were provided by students in my classes who gave permission for their use and who, along with the interlocutors in their examples, are identified (or not) according to their preferences.

Metamessages

The concept of metamessages traces to Gregory Bateson's essay "A Theory of Play and Fantasy." Bateson explains that "human verbal communication can operate and always does at many contrasting levels of abstraction" (1972, 177–78). He illustrates "the seemingly simple denotative level" with the sentence, "The cat is on the mat." He illustrates what he calls "the metacommunicative level" with the sentence, "My telling you where to find the cat was friendly."[2] Bateson's notion of metacommunication is key to his seminal concept of framing. He explains that during a visit to the Fleishhacker Zoo in San Francisco, he observed monkeys at play and wondered how a monkey knew that an obviously hostile move, such as a bite, should be interpreted as play. He concluded that monkeys have a way of communicating the metamessage "This is play," thus allowing another monkey to correctly interpret the spirit in which a bite was intended. In other words, the metamessage signaled the activity the monkeys were engaged in. Applying the concept of metamessage to human interaction, Bateson further explains, "In these, the subject of discourse is the relationship between the speakers." He notes that "the vast majority" of metacommunicative messages are implicit rather than explicit.

When I refer to messages and metamessages in spoken interaction, I am adapting Bateson's framework to distinguish meaning at two levels of abstraction. I use the term "messages" to refer to what Bateson described as the "seemingly simple denotative level," that is, the meaning of the words as they would be decoded by a dictionary and a grammar. My use of the term "metamessages" derives from his concept of metacommunication, in which "the subject of discourse is the relationship between the speakers" and is overwhelmingly implicit. That is, metamessages communicate how a speaker intends a message, or how a hearer interprets a message—what it says about the relationship that one utters these words in this way in this context.

Conversational Style in New Media Discourse

When the topic of conversation among my peers turns to new media use, especially texting, I frequently hear comments expressing alarm, disapproval, and scorn toward young people's tendency to send and receive text messages while engaging in face-to-face interaction. Most of my peers consider it self-evident that an individual's attention is owed to the people present, and diverting attention to a handheld device is self-evidently rude. I also frequently hear the parents of teenagers or young adults express disapproval, incredulity, and distress because their children often fail to return phone calls promptly—or at all. Although I tend to be relatively neutral on these topics, I understand, in an automatic, gut-level way, why parents and other older adults respond as they do. I was surprised, however, to learn from the students in my class that they and many of their peers react with incredulity to the suggestion that exchanging text messages while in company might be rude—and further, that they regard telephone calls as rude and intrusive, a notion that sparks parallel incredulity among older adults. These contrasting views, and their association with older and younger generations, respectively, are reflected in an article in *The Washington Post* (Shapira 2010) that quotes a mother's complaint about her teenage children: "None of the kids call us back! They will not call you back." The same article quotes a thirty-year-old as saying, "There's something confrontational about someone calling you."

These mutual accusations and the mutual incredulity they evoke remind me of a pattern at the heart of my research on cross-cultural differences in conversational style: the tendency to view one's own sense of what is rude and what is polite as self-evident, while regarding differing views as illogical if not disingenuous. A paradigmatic case of contrasting conversational styles that I have observed, and demonstrate at length elsewhere (Tannen 2005), is the use of and attitudes toward interruption and overlap in conversation. Those whose style I identified and described as "high-involvement" often talk along with others as a display of enthusiastic listenership, whereas those whose style I characterized as "high-considerateness" regard it as self-evident that only one voice should be heard at a time, so anyone who begins speaking before another has stopped is obviously—and rudely—interrupting. These contrasting conversational styles can be understood as reflecting Robin Lakoff's (1973, 1975) and Brown and Levinson's (1987) politeness schemas. The notion that it is rude to vocalize while another holds the floor corresponds to Brown and Levinson's negative politeness and Lakoff's first rule of politeness, "Don't impose." The assumption that an attentive listener should vocalize to show involvement corresponds to Brown and Levinson's positive politeness and Lakoff's third rule of politeness, "Maintain camaraderie." Everyone easily understands why people regard as rude what they perceive to be interruptions. It may be somewhat less obvious to some that not talking along can be equally unacceptable to high-involvement-style speakers. This perspective was articulated by one such speaker to whom I was explaining that high-considerateness style follows Lakoff's "Don't impose" rule of politeness. She responded, "But the not imposing is so offensive!"

Conversational style differences thus result in mutual accusations of rudeness regarding overlapping speech: for one group of speakers it is rude to talk along, whereas to another group it is rude for a listener to just sit there like a bump on a log. These respective accusations are parallel to cross-generational attitudes toward use of communication technology: for many members of one generation it is rude not to return phone calls, whereas for many members of the other, it is rude to make phone calls in the first place. Similarly, whereas members of one group find it rude to use a handheld device to text while in face-to-face interaction, members of the other may not—and may, in fact, deem it rude to fail to respond immediately to a text message, regardless of where they are and what they are doing when it arrives. Moreover, members of each group regard their own assumptions about what is rude as self-evident while reacting with disbelief—or worse—to the other group's contrasting assumptions.

I will present one more new media example that struck me, early on, as similar to patterns I had observed and characterized as cross-cultural differences in conversational style. My student Maddie Howard reported to our class that her brother and her boyfriend, in explaining why it is not rude to send or receive text messages while engaged in face-to-face interaction, commented, "But it takes so little time." This exact explanation reminded me of high-involvement-style speakers' reactions to the judgment of high-considerateness-style speakers about a particular interactional practice. I experienced the practice I have in mind, and its geographic distribution, as a native of Brooklyn, New York, living in California. Based on my experience growing up and living as an adult in New York City, I took for granted the appropriateness of the following scenario: A customer in a department store wishes to ask a quick question, such as "Where is the ladies' room?" There is no unoccupied salesperson in sight, so the customer approaches a salesperson who is serving another customer, and hovers in a conventionalized way. The salesperson glances up, the customer quickly posits the question, and the salesperson utters a cryptic reply, such as "second floor." The customer says, "Thank you," and heads to the second floor while the salesperson returns to the sales encounter. The kinesics of such an exchange are eloquent: by hovering at a short distance, the inquirer signals a respect for the primacy of the ongoing sales encounter; the occupied salesperson maintains a physical orientation to the customer being served, similarly signaling that their encounter is ongoing. The exchange takes only a few seconds and is not perceived by anyone to be an interruption. When I attempted to initiate an encounter of this type in California, however, I was stunned to be reprimanded by the salesperson: "I'm serving this customer now. I'll help you when I'm finished with her." My reaction was exactly that expressed by Maddie Howard's brother and boyfriend: How could anyone mistake this for an interruption? It takes so little time. In fact, isn't it self-evidently rude to expect someone to wait a significant period of time—especially someone in need of a ladies' room—to ask a question so fleeting that the answer could have been delivered in far fewer words than the salesperson used to articulate the reprimand? I suspect that this is the logic behind young people's conviction that it is appropriate to send a brief text message while in face-to-face interaction: not only does the exchange of text messages take too little time to constitute an interruption, but it would furthermore be rude to keep the sender waiting for needed information when providing that information takes so little time.

As a native of New York City and a high-involvement-style speaker, I continue to see self-evident logic and advantage to the conversational routine I have just described. As an analyst of conversational interaction, I can see the logic of both perspectives, and can understand why the same behavior can be seen as polite in one part of the country but rude in another. In the following sections I show that parallel processes of contrasting interactional routines can characterize gender- and generation-related differences in new media discursive practices.

Markers of Enthusiasm and Intensity

Many aspects of social media discourse that tend to differ from one group to another can be understood as associated with high-involvement as contrasted with high-considerateness conversational style. In my previous work (Tannen 1986, 2005), I describe these different conversational styles with reference to geographic region and ethnicity. Among users of new media, the differing uses—and contrasting interpretations of those uses—tend to pattern by age and gender. I begin by exploring in more depth the expression of enthusiasm and its relation to gender.

An element of high-involvement style in spoken conversation is what I call an "enthusiasm constraint." An example I examine elsewhere (Tannen 1986) was provided by a Greek woman. She recalled that when she was a young girl, if she asked her father whether she could go somewhere, and he answered, *"An thes, pas"* ("If you want, you can go"), she knew that she should not go, because his approval had been unenthusiastic. If he had really approved, he would have said something more like *"Nai, na pas"* ("Yes, you should go"). I also describe a cross-cultural difference with regard to the enthusiasm constraint within an American family. A mother who had been raised in New York City was raising her own children in Vermont. When they told her of some event in their lives, she frequently responded with expressive lexical and paralinguistic features such as, "Wow! Oh my god!" In her high-involvement style, her word choice and emphatic voice quality showed enthusiastic interest and attention. Her children, however, who had learned a relatively high-considerateness style, would look around to see what had frightened their mother. When they realized she was responding to them, they'd groan, "Oh, Mom! It's not THAT big a deal!" They were certain that her overreaction was a personality quirk unique to their mother.

These expectations with regard to the expression of enthusiasm vary by cultural or regional background: Greek in my first example, and New York City compared with New England in the second. Parallel patterns have been described by Baron (2004) and Herring (2003) as characterizing gender-related expectations of expressiveness in electronic exchanges, such as in young women's greater use of emoticons. The students in my classes have found similar patterns. Examples of text message and email exchanges that they have gathered demonstrate that gender differences in the use of new media conventions for the expression of emotion constitute a kind of cross-cultural communication and potential miscommunication.

Example 1: Contrasting Expectations of Enthusiasm Markers

A student in my class found evidence of a kind of cross-cultural miscommunication in an instant message (IM) exchange she had with her younger brother, who was attending a college situated midway between their hometown and Washington, DC, where Georgetown University is located. The exchange began when she sent her brother the following IM:

Hey! So, I have an idea for President's Day Weekend!

Her brother responded,

Oh God, you and your ideas . . . what is it?

The student did not react explicitly to her brother's use of sarcasm, a rhetorical device identified by Herring (1995, 2003) as more common in men's computer-mediated communication than in women's. She simply went on to explain her idea: to visit him on her way home. (Her meaning was unambiguous, although she miswrote "on the way back"):

I'm gonna go home from Saturday to Monday, but what do you think of me coming to visit you on the way back? I can take the train and stay over Thursday and Friday night. We can do something fun during the day on Friday, it's supposed to be really nice out!

Her brother replied,

Okay cool. Thursday is fine, but I have a club baseball tournament I'm leaving for Friday.

Her next message said,

Oh . . . okay. Well we can get dinner and go out on Thursday then??

Her brother responded,

Dinner sounds good. I'll pick you up at the station.

Her next response showed how she had been interpreting her brother's messages thus far. She, too, used sarcasm:

Wow . . . good thing you sound excited . . .

Her brother denied that he had intended to communicate indifference:

What? Sorry, sorry, I am. I am.

The sister reported that she had truly suspected that her brother was not thrilled with the prospect of her visit, but she later encountered independent evidence that he was. Not only had he repeated "sorry" and "I am" in his reassurances, but, more important, his actions communicated enthusiasm, as he called her repeatedly on the phone and talked about wanting her to meet his friends. Note the significance—the metamessage of enthusiasm—communicated by his choice of technology: the telephone rather than email.

This example shows that the siblings shared certain assumptions about new media use, such as the enthusiasm entailed by making telephone calls, but they differed in expectations of how enthusiasm should be communicated in digital discourse. The sister, along with other class members, believed that differences regarding the display of enthusiasm patterned by gender. This observation is supported by Herring and Zelenkauskaite (2009), who found that women tend to use more nonstandard typography, including repeated letters and punctuation, and by Waseleski (2006), who found a similar gender pattern in the use of exclamation points. In order to see what made this young woman suspect that her brother was not enthusiastic about her proposed visit, we can compare his responses to those of the young woman in the next example.

Example 2: Enthusiasm Markers as Shared Conventions

Example 1 illustrated cross-gender miscommunication due to stylistic differences regarding the display of enthusiasm in digital interaction. Example 2, provided by Kimberly Garity, demonstrates how an enthusiasm constraint operates in digital media discourse among young women. It is a text message exchange between Kimberly and her friend Jillian, who had previously lived in the same dormitory. Jillian wrote,

> Hey so I haven't seen you the ENTIRE week and I reeeally miss you!
> What are you doing tonight/tomorrow for meals?
> Sorry I had to miss lunch yesterday!
> But really, this needs to change because I miss McCarthy 8
> only because I can't just stop by your room to chat!

Here is Kimberly's response:

> I miss you too!!!!!!!!
> R you going to Justin and Lance's tonight??
> Slash wanna do din tomorrow??
> I can't wait to catch up on life!!

In analyzing this exchange, Kimberly noted a range of enthusiasm markers, including multiple exclamation points ("I miss you too!!!!!!!!" and "I can't wait to catch up on life!!"). Even question marks were reduplicated ("R you going to Justin and Lance's tonight??" and "Slash wanna do din tomorrow??"). (The word "slash," which refers to the typed symbol [/], designates an option or a topic switch—a fascinating example of how digital discourse represents spoken discourse, even if it means more keystrokes.) Kimberly observed, however, that these markers of enthusiasm were not meant literally. Rather, they are expected—unmarked in the linguistic sense. Had she not used them, it would have been marked; that is, their absence would have carried special meaning, and her friend might well have concluded that Kimberly was unenthusiastic about getting together.

When we discussed this example in class, several women commented that they regularly repeat the final vowel in the salutation "Hi," so it reads, for example, "Hiiii." A single-i "Hi," they explained, comes across as cold, even sullen. One student reported that she had to tell her mother to please add "i's" to her salutation to avoid this impression—even though she knew that her mother did not intend it. Because reduplicating word-final vowels is unmarked, single vowels in that position take on negative metamessages for those who have become accustomed to letter repetition as an enthusiasm constraint. As with all elements of conversational style, our reactions to unexpected style features are emotional and automatic. In that sense, the impression of coolness conveyed by her mother's single-i salutation could be seen as the result of cross-cultural miscommunication. Telling her mother to please add "i's" is thus parallel to correcting the grammar or pronunciation of a nonnative language speaker: the corrector knows what the speaker means, but the utterance doesn't sound right.[3]

A similar example in Arabic was provided by a student from Oman. She received an email message from a friend with the subject line "Salaaaaaaaaaaaaaaaaaaaaaaaam sooha," where "sooha" is a diminutive form of the recipient's (pseudonymous) name, and *salam,* the Arabic equivalent of "hi" rendered in English letters, is emphasized by repetition—for a total of 23—of the vowel "a."

Example 3: Volubility versus Taciturnity

If a young man's omission of conventionalized enthusiasm markers could result in the mistaken interpretation of negativity by his sister, in other cases the impression of negativity can be intended. In the following example, which was provided by Lauren Murray, a student ("Mary"—a pseudonym) initiated an IM exchange with a friend with whom she had had an argument in order to see whether the friend was ready to put the fight behind them. Here is how the exchange went:

MARY: Hey.

FRIEND: Hi.

MARY: Hey what's going on? I haven't talked to you in forever.

FRIEND: Nothing much.

MARY: Cool. How's work going?

FRIEND: Good. Busy.

MARY: That sucks. Is it fun at all?

FRIEND: Not really.

MARY: Sweet. Have you met any new guys in the office?

FRIEND: Not really.

MARY: Oh, that sucks. Well, I'm sure you will. Ha.

FRIEND: Ha.

MARY: Omg. The other day I heard Pat dropped out of school and is definitely not going back. I can't believe it. It's so terrible. You know?

FRIEND: Cool.

MARY: Oh, yeah. Did you find an apartment yet?

FRIEND: Nope.

MARY: Alrighty then. I guess I'm gonna go now.

FRIEND: Bye.

As this exchange unfolded, it became clear to Mary that her friend was still angry at her, because all Mary's attempts to get a conversation going were met with cryptic, usually monosyllabic responses. Perhaps most striking is the reply "Cool" following Mary's observation that a mutual acquaintance "dropped out of school" and her evaluation of this news as both surprising ("I can't believe it") and regrettable ("It's so terrible").

To test whether this expectation of enthusiasm was gender related, Lauren Murray showed the exchange to seven women and five men and asked for their interpretations. All five men attributed the friend's short responses to her being busy or indifferent but not angry. Six of the seven women said that the friend was angry. For the women, at least, the enthusiasm constraint was at work: terse replies communicated coolness.

Example 4: Repetition and Capitalization
In the next example, as in the preceding one, taciturnity is used to send a negative metamessage. In addition, this example demonstrates a use of intensity markers that is parallel to their use in service of the enthusiasm constraint. Example 4, provided by Jacqueline Fogarty, illustrates the use of enthusiasm markers in the issuing of an apology.

Jackie and a number of friends had gathered in order to go somewhere together. As everyone in the group piled into taxis, only Jackie was left awaiting a last member of the group, who had been delayed. Finding herself alone, Jackie sent the following (sarcastic) text message to a friend who was among the group:

Thanks for waiting for Melissa with me thats cool

The friend responded,

JACKIE I AM SO SO SO SORRY! I thought you were behind us in the cab and then I saw you weren't!!!!! I feel soooooooo bad! Catch another cab and ill pay for it for youuuuu

The friend conveyed the sincerity and depth of her apology (either actual or represented—it is neither possible nor necessary to distinguish) by capitalization ("JACKIE I AM SO SO SO SORRY!"), multiple exclamation points ("I saw you weren't!!!!!"), word repetition ("SO SO SO SORRY"), reduplication of word-final vowels (at the end of "so" in "I feel soooooooo bad!" and at the end of "you" in "ill pay for it for youuuuu").

The repetition of the final vowel in "youuuuu" is particularly interesting, since its impact is solely visual. When reading "soooooooo," one can hear the word "so" with the vowel sound elongated, as one imagines someone saying, "I feel soooooooo bad!" But repeating the final "u" in "you" doesn't work the same way. For one thing, the vowel sound doesn't reside in the letter "u" but in the double-digit "ou." More important, "hearing" the sentence in one's mind with that sound elongated ("I'll pay for it for yoooooooo") doesn't sound like anything anyone would say for emphasis. It seems instead that the reduplication of the word-final letter is a visual means to provide emphasis and communicate sincerity and depth of emotion, much like the previously discussed repetition of the final letter in the salutation "Hiiii."

In reply to her friend's message, Jackie texted,

no its fine we are walking

In this message, the lack of expressive markers, and the resultant impression of taciturnity, indicated how less than fine it really was. Jackie's friend then wrote, seriously Jackie please, get a cab, I feel so bad!!!

Here the friend's repeated final exclamation points indicate the depth of her feelings and hence the sincerity of her apology. But Jackie was not to be mollified. She replied,

we are walking there its fine.

Throughout this example, the friend uses expressive spelling, capitalization, repetition, and reduplicated punctuation to send a metamessage of intensity along with her message of apology. And Jackie's omission of these features indicates her continuing displeasure and reluctance to let her friend off the hook.

Indirectness and Its Discontents

As far back as Lakoff's (1973) early work on communicative style, linguists have focused a great deal of analysis on indirectness in conversation, with its powerful potential to communicate as well as its risk of misinterpretation. Lakoff made clear that indirectness is fundamental and pervasive in conversational interaction; it is simply impossible for speakers to make explicit in every utterance all the assumptions, implications, and metamessages intended or, in Goffman's sense, "given off"—that is, communicated unintentionally. Indirectness is pervasive in new media interaction as well; indeed, the opportunities and the liabilities of indirectness are enhanced by the constraints of the media themselves.

Example 5: Brevity as Indirectness

The word "cryptic" suggests that brevity can be associated with unstated, even hidden, meaning. Thus brevity, which is commonly regarded as characteristic of text messages, frequently entails ambiguity. Example 5 shows the potential ambiguity inherent in a one-word text message. Fiona Hanly wrote the following description of the complex potential metamessages that she and her friends took into account when considering how to interpret a missive composed of a single word:

> On Thursday evening, out to dinner with several friends, one of my friends, Lauren, received a text from a boy she was interested in that read simply: "Hey." To which she wondered: what did he mean with "hey?" Did he really mean just hey? Was he checking to see if she was busy? Was he actually interested in her like she was interested in him? Was he bored? How should she respond—should she assume that there was something implied by his text, address the frame of the conversation, or just respond on the message level he had set up?

Brevity is a common motivation for texting rather than telephoning: one does not have to say, "Hello, how are you? Did I call at a bad time?" before getting to the content of a message. Neither does one have to signal the end or take leave: no "Okay, I'll talk to you later" is required, nor even a fleeting "Take care." This example demonstrates, however, that the brevity of the text message "Hey" means that the text message could be interpreted in many different ways, each possible interpretation entailing indirect meanings that could plausibly have been implied—and equally plausibly denied.

Example 6: An Electronic Link as Indirectness

Greg Bennett provided another example of indirect meaning interpreted, and possibly implied, by a common new media discursive practice: providing a link in the form of a URL to be clicked on. The participants in this exchange, a young woman and young man, were friends, but the woman was beginning to develop a romantic interest in the man. One day, he posted a link on her Facebook wall to a YouTube video that featured a song with rather romantic lyrics. Pleased that the video seemed to imply that his interest in her was also becoming romantic, she sent him an SMS message saying, "Saw the video. Were you trying to say something?" He replied, "ummmm . . . i just thought it was a cool video. why?" This reply brought her back down to earth with a thud. She concluded that she had misread his intent: he was not romantically interested in her after all.

This example illustrates both the communicative potential and the inherent ambiguity of posting a link to another medium or message, such as a YouTube video—a form of indirect meaning that is particular to electronic interaction. The example also parallels gender patterns in conversational style with respect to directness versus indirectness. In a discussion of conversational style differences regarding indirectness (Tannen 1986, 79), I give the example of a man who had repeatedly asked a woman coworker to join him for lunch, and was uncertain how literally to interpret her repeated refusals, which were always accompanied by plausible explanations for why she was unable rather than unwilling to accept. He tried to clear things up by asking a direct question: "Do you really mean you can't, or are you trying to tell me you don't want to have lunch with me so I shouldn't ask again?" Even though the latter assumption was accurate, the woman could not bring herself to say, "I don't want to have lunch with you—ever," so she said something like, "Oh, well, sure, you know, it's a really busy time for me." His attempt to force her to be direct failed, because indirectness was the only way she could refuse an invitation.

Looked at from the perspective of conversational style differences with regard to indirectness, it is possible that the young man who posted the link to a YouTube video really was developing a romantic interest in the young woman. However, by posting a link, he was expressing it indirectly. By asking, "Were you trying to say something?" the young woman was asking him to shift from indirect to direct communication. His seemingly clueless "ummmm . . . i just thought it was a cool video" might reflect, as she concluded, that she had been wrong to interpret the link as an indirect expression of romantic interest. However, she might also have been wrong in drawing this conclusion. It is possible that his response indicated his discomfort with direct expression of romantic interest rather than a lack of such interest.

Electronic links, then, can be seen as a form of indirectness that is particular to and pervasive in electronic interaction.

Pacing and Pausing in Turn-Taking

A final linguistic feature of new media discourse that parallels conversational style in spoken interaction is relative pacing in the exchange of turns. In spoken conversation, everyone has a sense of how long a pause is normal within a turn before listeners get the impression that a current speaker is finished so another is free—or obligated—to take the floor. Elsewhere I demonstrate at length (Tannen 2005) that there are cross-cultural and cross-subcultural differences in pacing and pausing, and that these differences lead to mutual negative evaluations and frequent misinterpretations. When interlocutors have differing expectations regarding the length of interturn pauses, the one who expects a shorter pause will get the impression that the other has finished when that other is simply waiting for the length of pause that signals an open floor. The latter feels that the former is interrupting and hogging the floor, while the former feels forced to do all the interactional work with someone who either has nothing to say or is unwilling to say anything. In both cases, the speed of response has led to interpretations—sometimes valid, sometimes not—about interlocutors' intentions and abilities.

In the exchange of electronic messages, it is clear when a sender's turn has ended, but interactants must still decide how quickly to respond to messages they receive, and speed of response carries metamessages with regard to intentions. My students tell me that they frequently confer on the appropriate way to respond to electronic messages, and have advised friends, "Don't respond right away; you don't want to seem desperate." This advice is predicated on the assumption that a speedy reply indicates enthusiasm, and that when it comes to the delicate negotiations of romantic interest, too much enthusiasm equates with desperation. In the same spirit, a lengthy response time could indicate a lack of enthusiasm. Furthermore, as with spoken conversational style, interpretations can turn out to be mistaken. A student reported that when her boyfriend did not respond quickly to a text message she sent, she concluded that he was angry at her. It turned out that the reason was merely technological: his cell phone battery had run out. The interference of such purely technical phenomena—all electronic equipment can malfunction, break, or run out of battery power—introduces the risk of unintended meaning that may be seen as a kind of indirectness particular to electronic interaction.

The examples thus far have illustrated digital discourse analogs to elements of conversational style in spoken discourse. I first showed that volubility versus taciturnity, capitalization, repetition, and emphatic punctuation can be requisite, unmarked markers of enthusiasm in digital discourse, particularly among young women. I then suggested that brevity of text messages, the provision of electronic links, and the pacing of turn exchange all constitute kinds of indirectness that are particular to digital interaction. Like indirectness in conversation, these aspects of computer-mediated interaction entail the sending and interpreting of unstated meaning, or metamessages. In the next and final section, I turn to a phenomenon that is particular to new media interaction: the metamessages communicated by the choice of medium.

The Medium Is the Metamessage

In the multiplatform environment of electronic discourse, the choice of medium itself sends metamessages. My use of the term "metamessage" in this context is parallel to Gershon's (2010) notion of "second-order information."

The mere use of a medium communicates meaning. For example, when Greg Bennett told of a blog post he had written that was related to the topic of our course, I asked him if he had received any responses, and he said, "It got thirty hits." The literal answer to my question would have been, "No, the blog hasn't received any responses." But that would have indicated a lack of interest on the part of readers, or even a lack of readers, which would have been misleading. The level of reader interest was better communicated by reporting the number of "hits": on thirty separate occasions, a reader had engaged with the blog. (We don't know whether this was thirty separate readers; a "hit" could represent a new reader or a return reader.) Enthusiasm or interest among readers was a metamessage indicated by their use of the medium.

Example 7: Communicating Intensity by Using Multiple Media

In example 4 Jacqueline Fogarty's friend emphasized the sincerity of her apology by repeating words and word-final vowels in text messages. In example 7 a college student sends a metamessage of sincerity in an apology by a different sort of repetition: using two different media to send the same message. Maddie Howard had been busy studying when a friend interrupted to ask her a question. Soon after, the friend apologized for the interruption by sending both a text message and email. Here, first, is the email message. (The phrase "app rising" refers to "Appalachia Rising," a conference held at Georgetown to oppose mountaintop removal mining.)

> great :) oh and sorry for barging into your study sesh last night! there were some stranded app 2 rising folks and i was gonna see if i could drive them. :/

Maddie also received the following text message the same day:

> Apologies for intruding on your homework time last night!

Each missive alone communicated the apology; sending two separate messages, each by a different medium, added emphasis. It is worthy of note that the gravity of the offense that instigated this apology is less than that in the previous example. Perhaps that is why this email message includes only a single exclamation point ("last night!"), although it does include two emoticons (the opening ":)" and the closing ":/"). This seems fitting, as the inconvenience visited upon Maddie, having her homework session briefly interrupted, is less than that experienced by Jackie, who was left stranded by her friends. The emphasis by multiple media as compared with emphasis by capitalization and repetition seems, respectively, perfectly suited to the seriousness of the respective offenses.

Metamessages in Medium Choice

Another example of a metamessage communicated by the choice of medium was recounted by Caitlin Sudman. Caitlin noticed that the Facebook status of a friend, Sue, had changed from "in a relationship" to "single." This status change alerted her Facebook friends that Sue and her boyfriend had broken up. Predictably, many of those friends posted messages of support and sympathy on Sue's Facebook wall. Caitlin noticed, however, that none of those messages were sent by Sue's close friends. Caitlin was certain that this did not mean that her close friends cared less about Sue than did her Facebook friends. She surmised that Sue would have contacted her close friends by another medium—a private one, such as email or telephone—before making the information about her breakup available on the public medium of Facebook. Learning an important development in a close friend's life on Facebook would be distancing, even rejecting—a sign that one was not, in fact, a close friend.

Awareness that choice of medium sends metamessages is not a new phenomenon. Older adults can recall when we had to choose among several media to convey information: face-to-face conversation, telephone, or letter. A letter, furthermore, could be handwritten or typed. Today those same options are available, but so are many electronic options as well. The dilemma posed by sorting through the potential metamessages associated with each medium was described by a student in my class:

> I recently had to contact someone for the potentially awkward purpose of asking him to be my partner for an upcoming ballroom dancing competition. The message I had to convey to him was to let me know ASAP because registration had to be in, ideally at the end of the same day. He had earlier told me he would let me know well ahead of time, but he didn't. I had several steps to take and decisions to make along the way in contacting him and they were all tied to issues of which medium to use. The first step was to decide which medium to use to contact him. The message needed to be prompt, but I also wanted to avoid the face threatening act of contacting him by phone or in person because that would make it harder for him to say no. I wanted to give him an out if he wanted to decline. I rejected email as too formal. Such a tone would have seemed odd and possibly demanding, even desperate. My remaining choices were texting or Facebook. While texting would have been ideal in terms of time and tone, I didn't have his phone number. So, I turned to Facebook. The first thing was to check whether he was on Facebook Chat. Unfortunately, he wasn't. I had to then decide whether I wanted to post my question or subtle reminder about the deadline on his wall or in a private message. A wall post would have better conveyed the idea that I was not being pushy and was simply reminding him that he agreed to give me an answer before the deadline. A private message would make it less awkward for both parties involved if he preferred to dance with someone else. However, while nowhere near the level of email, a private Facebook message is formal in the context of the three, well four if you count the Status message pings, ways of contacting someone by Facebook. I went to his profile page and saw a recent exchange he had with someone else about how he and his actual partner, who later told him she couldn't go to the competition, were dancing together. But I thought my message would look strange right above that one. So, I picked the private message. But I had one final choice: what to fill in as the subject. Now, this just may be me being weird, but I wasn't sure where to proceed from there because the subject is what introduces the reader to the message. It's the first thing he sees. It sets the tone. I solved the dilemma by getting right to the point and asking about the competition in the title and adding the point about the deadline in the body of the message. Since I was at my computer for a long time after, I did check for a reply, but more than that, I checked to see if he was on Facebook to see whether he had gotten the message.

This eloquent articulation of the factors the writer had to take into account in choosing a medium for her brief query dramatizes how each new medium entails both new opportunities and new liabilities with regard to potential metamessages entailed in the choice of medium.

Example 8: Pitfalls Built into the Technology

Sometimes miscommunication can result not from the choice of a medium but from the mechanics built into it. My final example demonstrates such a liability. Example 8, provided by James Boyman, is a text exchange between James's thirteen-year-old sister Laura and his cousin Nick, who was also thirteen. Nick told James that it is common practice among his peers to put a tagline on text messages as a personal signature, much like the signature that routinely appears at the bottom of many people's email messages. There is a difference, however: whereas the signature appended automatically to the end of an email message is visible to both sender and receiver, a text message tagline automatically appended to every text message sent does not show up on the screen of the sender's handheld device. (In the following example, Nick's tagline, "saints suck," refers to a football team, the New Orleans Saints.)

The exchange began when Laura initiated a text message to Nick:

hi wats up?

Nick's reply appeared on Laura's cell phone screen:

nothing much. Wats up with u?
saints suck

Responding to the second line of Nick's text message, Laura wrote,

oh, ur upset about the football game

To this, Nick replied,

yeah I am
saints suck

Noticing the repetition of the final line, Laura replied to this by sending the message,

u already said that

Seemingly puzzled by this remark, Nick wrote,

wat do u mean?
saints suck

Laura, puzzled in turn, replied,

u said it again

Nick then wrote,

wat are u talking about?
saints suck

At this point, Laura figured it out:

> oh its ur signature

Nick, however, was still clueless:

> wats my signature?
> saints suck

At that point, Laura had to end the exchange. (Note that "g2g" is an abbreviation for "got to go"):

> nev mind. g2g moms here

Nick then took his leave as well—none the wiser about the role played by his tagline in creating confusion:

> bye
> saints suck

The potential ambiguity of Nick's signature, "saints suck," is built into the medium. For the receiver of the text messages, it is not immediately apparent—as it would be with an email signature—what is preprogrammed and what is part of the specific message. For the sender it is easy to forget about the signature, which is not visible on his screen. If Laura does not know how the words "saints suck" were intended, Nick is not aware that those words are there at all. The misunderstanding thus results from a liability built into the medium.

Conclusion

The preceding example is a microcosm of a theme I mention at the outset: although new media interaction poses new challenges, much of what happens in digital conversation is similar to what has always happened in spoken conversation. Implicit in my illustrating a range of new media analogs to conversational style in spoken interaction is the *plus ça change* claim that new media interaction is not an entirely new world, but a world in which many familiar interactional activities are being accomplished in new ways. In this spirit, it may be helpful to remember that what Crispin Thurlow (2006) dubs "moral panic" has accompanied the introduction of all new media. Historian Elizabeth Eisenstein reminds us of Plato's fear that the invention of writing would destroy memory. She further documents the mixed reaction sparked by the invention of the printing press, as reflected in her title, *Divine Art, Infernal Machine.* Reminiscent of ambivalent reactions to digital media, the printing press was hailed as a potential solution to a vast array of problems but also railed against as the source of an equally broad range of devastation, including the risk of political chaos resulting from widespread pamphleteering and information overload. Eisenstein provides this example of such ambivalence:

> Leibniz, when addressing Louis XIV in 1680, paid tribute to the way printing duplicated books and thus made it possible "to preserve the greater part of our knowledge." But he also expressed alarm about the "horrible mass of books"

that kept on growing. Unless contained and restrained, he advised, the increase in output would result in intolerable disorder, and it would become "a disgrace rather than an honor to be an author." (2011, 87)

Contemporary readers are unlikely to have feared that the printing press risks rendering it a disgrace to write a book, yet Leibniz's tone resembles the scorn often heard today toward those who profligately disseminate their words in blogs and twitter feeds.

This spirit of scorn and moral panic with which members of older generations have greeted younger generations' uses of new media has led me to think of new media interaction as a kind of cross-cultural communication. The present study represents my elaboration of this metaphoric premise. In interpersonal interaction taking place over new media, as in interpersonal conversation, meaning is communicated on two levels of abstraction: message and metamessage. Whereas messages can be understood by reference to the meaning of words and grammatical usage, metamessages are communicated by aspects of conversational style found in electronic discourse that resemble those in spoken interaction. The examples in this chapter include the use of emphatic punctuation; capitalization; and repetition of words, letters, or punctuation marks. These are parallel to the use of amplitude, intonation, and elongation of sounds to create emphasis and emotional valence in speaking. I also suggest that the brevity of text messages and the posting of electronic links as well as metamessages communicated by the choice of medium are all forms of indirectness, with corresponding potential for communication of unstated meaning as well as for ambiguity and misinterpretation. Furthermore, metamessages communicated by the speed of response are parallel to interpretations (and potential misinterpretations) of pacing and pausing in spoken conversational turn exchange.

New media discourse, however, also entails unique vehicles for positive or negative and intended or unintended metamessages. Sending a message via two different media is a way of communicating emphasis or intensity, and the choice of medium itself sends metamessages—and such potential metamessages must be taken into account in making that choice. There are also liabilities built into the technology of electronic media, such as the potential for technological breakdowns and the automaticity of a signature tagline that is visible to the recipient but not the sender. In sum, I have identified some of the ways that new media discourse parallels phenomena in spoken interaction, as well as some ways that it differs, in order to shed light on the discourse of digital social media and how the use of such media affects interpersonal interaction.

ACKNOWLEDGEMENTS

I am grateful to all the students in my classes who helped me understand their own and their peers' uses of digital media in their personal interactions, especially those whose examples are cited herein. In addition to those named in connection with specific examples, I would also like to thank Isabella Janusz and Sarah Mirabile. Finally, I am grateful to Susan Herring and Anna Marie Trester for helpful comments on an earlier draft.

NOTES

1. Finding a term to refer to the topic of this chapter is problematic. As Susan Herring points out in her chapter, "new media," which is used here and in the title of the volume, "is lacking in historical per-

spective"; the term "digital media" is too broad, as it includes video games; and computer-mediated communication (CMC) is no longer descriptive, since handheld devices, for example, are not computers. In this chapter I use "new media," "social media," "digital discourse," "electronic communication," and other related terms interchangeably, in order to refer collectively to the use in interpersonal interaction of email, Gchat, IM, SMS, text messages, and Facebook.

2. Bateson also identifies a second type of meaning that operates on the same level of abstraction as metacommunication: "metalinguistic," in which "the subject of discourse is the language." He illustrates that level with the example sentence, "The verbal sound 'cat' stands for any member of such and such class of objects."

3. Anna Marie Trester reminds me that the metaphoric parallel between native and nonnative speaker is not entirely arbitrary but rather reminiscent of the common observation that young people are "native speakers" of new media discourse, whereas for older people it is a second language.

REFERENCES

Baron, Naomi. 2004. See you online: Gender issues in college student use of instant messaging. *Journal of Language and Social Psychology* 23, no. 4:397–423.

Bateson, Gregory. 1972. A theory of play and fantasy. In *Steps to an ecology of mind,* 177–93. New York: Ballantine.

Bright, William. 1982. Literature: Written and oral. In *Analyzing discourse: Text and talk,* ed. Deborah Tannen, 271–83. Washington, DC: Georgetown University Press.

Brown, Penelope, and Stephen Levinson. 1987. *Politeness: Some universals in language usage.* Cambridge: Cambridge University Press.

Chafe, Wallace. 1982. Integration and involvement in speaking, writing, and oral literature. In *Spoken and written language: Exploring orality and literacy,* ed. Deborah Tannen, 35–53. Norwood, NJ: Ablex.

Crystal, David. 2008. *Txtng: The gr8 db8.* Oxford: Oxford University Press.

Eisenstein, Elizabeth. 2011. *Divine art, infernal machine: The reception of printing in the West from first impressions to the sense of an ending.* Philadelphia: University of Pennsylvania Press.

Gershon, Ilana. 2010. *The breakup 2.0: Disconnecting over new media.* Ithaca, NY: Cornell University Press.

Herring, Susan C. 1995. Men's language on the internet. *Nordlyd* 23:1–20.

———. 2003. Gender and power in on-line communication. In *The handbook of language and gender,* eds. Janet Holmes and Miriam Meyerhoff, 202–28. Malden, MA, and Oxford: Basil Blackwell.

———. 2010. Computer-mediated conversation: Introduction and overview. *Language@Internet* 7, article 2. www.languageatinternet.org/articles/2010/2801.

Herring, Susan C., and Asta Zelenkauskaite. 2009. Symbolic capital in a virtual heterosexual market: Abbreviations and insertion in Italian iTV SMS. *Written Communication* 26, no. 1:5–31.

Lakoff, Robin. 1973. The logic of politeness, or minding your p's and q's. In *Papers from the Ninth Regional Meeting of the Chicago Linguistics Society,* eds. Claudia Corum, T. Cedric Smith-Stark, and Ann Weiser, 292–305. Chicago: University of Chicago Department of Linguistics.

———. 1975. *Language and woman's place.* New York: Harper and Row.

Shapira, Ian. 2010. Texting generation doesn't share boomers' taste for talk. *Washington Post,* August 8. www.washingtonpost.com/wp-dyn/content/article/2010/08/07/AR2010080702848.html.

Tannen, Deborah. 1982a. Introduction. In *Analyzing discourse: Text and talk,* ed. Deborah Tannen, ix–xii. Washington, DC: Georgetown University Press.

———. 1982b. Oral and literate strategies in spoken and written narratives. *Language* 58, no. 1:1–21.

———. 1986. *That's not what I meant!: How conversational style makes or breaks your relations with others.* New York: William Morrow.

———. 2005. *Conversational style: Analyzing talk among friends.* Rev. ed. New York and Oxford: Oxford University Press.

Thurlow, Crispin. 2006. From statistical panic to moral panic: The metadiscursive construction and popular exaggeration of new media language in the print media. *Journal of Computer-Mediated Communication* 11, no. 3, article 1.

Waseleski, Carol. 2006. Gender and the use of exclamation points in computer-mediated communication: An analysis of exclamations posted to two electronic discussion lists. *Journal of Computer-Mediated Communication* 11, no. 4, article 6.

7

Bringing Mobiles into the Conversation
Applying a Conversation Analytic Approach to the Study of Mobiles in
Co-present Interaction

STEPHEN M. DIDOMENICO
Rutgers University

JEFFREY BOASE
Ryerson University

IN FOCUSING ON THE MUNDANE conduct of everyday life, Erving Goffman's work drew attention to the fundamental practices that define mutual co-presence. Now, in the so-called digital age, we increasingly find ourselves having to reconcile new forms of communication with Goffman's chief domain of face-to-face interaction. Although scholarly interest in new forms of mediated interaction has grown steadily, only recently have scholars begun to consider how communication technologies—particularly mobile devices—are woven into co-present interaction. It is the intersection of these two domains, specifically co-present interaction and mobile usage, that is the focus of this chapter.

This chapter summarizes a study involving a single instance of conversation taken from a larger collection of videotaped naturally occurring interactions involving mobile phones. Using a conversation analytic approach, we draw on the concept of technological affordance and Goffman's distinction between primary and secondary involvement to provide a nuanced look at how mobiles become integrated into co-present interaction. Three themes emerge from our data when mobiles are used during co-present interaction: shifting between primary and secondary involvement is highly dynamic, the shift to mobile use as a secondary involvement depends on the speaking role that is being enacted during the co-present involvement, and the distinction between primary and secondary involvement is blurred when reference to mobile interactions is made during co-present interaction. In each case we argue that these occurrences can be explained with reference to the time and space transcending affordances of mobiles.

Mobile Communication Studies and the Study of Co-present Interaction
Although a substantial and growing body of research has focused on the implications of mobile use for a variety of outcomes (see Campbell and Park 2008; Katz 2006, 2008,

2011), only a handful of studies have directly examined mobiles in everyday social encounters. Ling (2008), for example, draws upon the ritual-centered theorizing of Durkheim, Goffman, and Collins to discuss what he calls "mediated ritual interaction," interactions afforded by new communication technologies.[1] Ling describes a "social limbo" surrounding these mediated forms of talk, in which participants must balance competing lines of activity while dealing with "the pressure to either be clearly in or clearly outside a social interaction" (2008, 173). Humphreys (2005) offers a related account of how participants in public spaces respond to their interlocutors' incoming mobile calls. Using observations of public places and in-depth interviews, she identifies a range of general themes. One theme, referred to as "dual front interaction," occurs when participants on the phone were observed to engage in various nonverbal behaviors to maintain interaction with their co-present interlocutor (such as iconic illustrators or the rolling of the eyes), unknown to the caller. This shows how mobile use may create situations in which participants must simultaneously manage their relations across multiple distinct speech events.[2] One limitation to Humphreys's study, however, is the exclusive focus on mobile use to make voice calls as opposed to other functions such as sending and receiving text messages. In this chapter we focus specifically on the occurrence of mobile texting during co-present interaction.

To frame our understanding of how mobiles are used in co-present interaction, we draw on the concept of technological affordance. The concept originated from the work of Gibson (1977), who posited that animals and humans have an innate ability to recognize the opportunities that objects in their environments afford for particular actions. The concept has been adopted more loosely by computer and social scientists to refer to the idea that technology provides opportunities and constraints on human action, without the assumption that these opportunities and constraints are innately known by individuals (see Norman 1999). The concept has been used to strike a theoretical middle ground between technologically deterministic approaches that downplay the role of human agency, and social constructionist approaches that ignore the physical properties of technology (see Hutchby 2001). The concept is particularly well suited to our purposes because we wish to acknowledge the opportunities that mobile devices provide, while examining autonomous behavior of our participants outside of their use of this technology. As is discussed in our analysis, the affordances of mobile devices to transcend time—that is, asynchronous communication—and space, by permitting communication with distant others, are particularly relevant to understanding the behavior that emerges in our data.

To frame our understanding of the interactional dynamics of co-present conversation, we draw on Goffman's (1963) distinction between primary involvements and secondary involvements: "Men as animals have a capacity to divide their attention into main and side involvement. A main involvement is one that absorbs the major part of an individual's attention and interest, visibly forming the principal current determinant of his actions. A side involvement is an activity that an individual can carry on in an abstracted fashion without threatening or confusing simultaneous maintenance of main involvement" (43).

Contemporary scholarship in the disciplines of linguistics and anthropology has extended Goffman's theorizing by examining the inherently multimodal nature of human interaction (LeBaron and Streeck 1997; Norris 2004, 2011; Schegloff 1984; Stivers and Sidnell 2005). Kendon (2004) and Goodwin (1986, 2000, 2003) have explored the semiotic dimensions of face-to-face encounters, including the array of linguistic, material, and embodied aspects participants draw upon within the interactional situation. Recent work has focused on the emergent negotiation of social action in such diverse contexts and environments as a subway control room (Heath and Luff 2000), cars (Haddington and Keisanen 2009), airplane cockpits (Nevile 2005), and beauty salons (Toerien and Kitzinger 2007). This chapter extends this work by examining the interactional resources used when negotiating mobile involvements during ordinary conversation.

Data and Methods

We draw on the inductive methods of conversation analysis (for example, Atkinson and Heritage 1984), where video or audio recordings of episodes of naturally occurring interaction are reviewed closely in order to generate rich, detailed descriptions of the interactional practices through which participants co-construct and interpret social actions. In collecting the data, participants signed informed consent forms and were asked to use a video camera to record a time when they would ordinarily be together. They were not explicitly told to use their mobiles during the interaction. The recordings were then transcribed using a modified version of the standard Jeffersonian transcription conventions (see appendix) and analyzed to examine participants' mobile-related actions.

We focus on a single instance of interaction to illustrate some of the trends that emerge from our larger collection. This particular episode of interaction consists of three female college students hanging out in the kitchen of one of their homes (see fig. 7.1 below to better understand their initial body positions, which remain generally constant). As the conversation progresses we discover that one of the women is

■ Figure 7.1 The participants (from left to right): Amy, Brianne, and Caitlyn (Amy and Brianne's phones are circled in white).

waiting for a male friend to join them. One of the women completed the video recording with her two friends using a small digital video camera for the purposes of extra credit in an undergraduate course on research methods. Her only instructions were to capture a social activity that would have occurred regardless of whether it was being recorded. None of the women were encouraged to use mobile phones at any point during the data collection process.

Analysis and Discussion

A consistent finding from our exploration was that participants continuously oscillate between attending to the co-present interaction as their primary involvement and their mobiles as their secondary involvement. Although we do not have data on the specific activity that occurred on the mobile devices—the video camera did not capture the screens of the devices—the mobile activity followed a consistent pattern that is most clearly recognized as an exchange of text messages.

One way these back-and-forth shifts in involvement were prompted is through the chimes that are emitted from mobile phones. Most mobile models today give users the option of having the device produce a chime to indicate that a new text message has been received. This feature is strikingly similar to Schegloff and Sacks's (1973) notion of the summons-answer adjacency pair, a pair of social actions in which a participant may be called (or summoned) by a ringing phone so that he or she may engage in opening a conversation with the caller. The subsequent response from the individual answering the phone (for example, "Hello?") can be understood to be a responding action to the opening summons initiated by the caller (Schegloff 2007). However, unlike a voice call summons, a text message summons affords the possibility of establishing mobile side involvements *without* suspending the co-present interaction. This is of great significance since participants' monitoring of the turn-by-turn details of interaction (including syntactic and gestural relevancies) is crucial for projecting and negotiating the availability of speaking turns (Sacks, Schegloff, and Jefferson, 1974; see also Bolden 2003). The following case illustrates how this affordance allows for dynamic switching between primary and secondary involvements, and how this switching is dependent on the situated organization of turn taking.

Case 1

In the following excerpt Amy and Caitlyn are discussing therapists while Brianne is outside talking to a friend. Just prior to this excerpt, Amy has been telling a lengthy story about her reasons for considering therapy:

Excerpt 1 [MIC1:314–321]

```
01 AMY:   With my parents splitting
02        up and my mom staying no-
03        like yester- the other
04        day [she's like            ]
05            [((phone chimes))      ]
```

Figure 7.2 "She's like. . ." (line 04).

```
06        sh- like I heard it from
07        my family that they've
08        been talking about it
09        but from hearing it from
10        my mom like really like killed
11        me she was like it's
12        your fault me and daddy
13        got split up. And I was
14        like What? And my mom
15        blames me for everything
16        because it's just easier
17        to blame somebody el[se]
18 CAT:                      [ye]ah
19        of course.=
20 AMY:   =for something. So it was
21        just like always me like
```

At the beginning of this exchange (lines 01–04), Amy continues to hold the floor as she reports further details about her family circumstances. Just as she is producing the utterance "she's like" (line 04, see fig. 7.2), her mobile chimes to indicate the receipt of a new text message. However, Amy does not shift her gaze toward the mobile and maintains her primary involvement with Caitlyn as she continues with her multiunit turn (lines 06–17, 20–21).

As we will see below in a segment occurring nearly four minutes later, Amy finally shifts her gaze to her mediated secondary involvement while Brianne reenters the room:

Excerpt 2 [MIC1:094–127]

094 AMY: I have- I don't
095   think I have <u>any</u>
096   memories of my parents
097   being af<u>fec</u>tionate towards
098   each other,
099   (0.2)
100 AMY: That's why I don't understand
101   why I'm such like a m<u>u</u>sh.
102   I don't know if it's cause like=
103 CAT: =You y<u>ea</u>rn for it.
104 AMY: Yeah.
105   (0.3)
106 AMY: Cause like <u>u</u>sually like
107   they say like if a kid is
108   like br<u>ou</u>ght up into like,=
109 CAT: =Is he c<u>o</u>ming? ((to BRI))
110 BRI: He didn't want to come in.
111 CAT: Why,
112 BRI: I don't know. I told him about
113   the video and he didn't <u>wa</u>nt to.
114 AMY: ehh <u>he</u>h heh
115 BRI: <u>You</u> can put your <u>foot</u> there.

■ Figure 7.3 "<u>You</u> can put your <u>foot</u> there" (line 115).

Figure 7.4 "seen them being affectionate" (lines 121–22).

116 CAT: O:h that's okay.

117   (0.2)

118 CAT: So what were you saying Amy,

119   cause your parents aren't

120   like (.) affectionate?

121 AMY: <u>Yea</u>h like I've never seen

122   them being affectionate

123   so I I'd thought that

124   I would like <u>not</u>

125   want affection? But

126   I feel like (.) I'm

127   the complete opposite.

Just after Caitlyn offers an assessment of Amy's account making clear her need for affection (lines 106–8; "you yearn for it"), Amy begins a new turn at talk. Next, before Amy can come to a point of possible completion, Caitlyn interrupts her (with "Is he coming?") in order to address Brianne, who just has just reentered the room. Brianne provides a brief answer ("He didn't want to come in"), followed by Caitlyn's pursuit of an account ("Why") as to why the friend Brianne was visiting with outside the house did not join the three of them inside. Brianne then provides a brief answer ("He didn't want to come in"; line 110) and account explaining why he did not join them ("I told him about the video and he didn't <u>wa</u>nt to"; lines 112–13), which elicits laughter from Amy (line 114).

Immediately after the floor is taken from her, Amy shifts and holds her gaze on her mobile and proceeds to type into it with both hands. This lack of gaze and mutual orientation with Brianne and Caitlyn's actions displays Amy's lack of interactional availability to take the speaking floor. Caitlyn produces a question ("So what were you saying Amy, cause your parents aren't like (.) affectionate?" lines 118–19) that is addressed to Amy and designed as an attempt to return to the topic they had been discussing before it was interrupted by Brianne's entrance into the room. It is worth noting that her question is designed with an address term ("Amy"), presumably as a means to explicitly select Amy to take the floor. This reliance on explicit address (as opposed to pursuing mutual gaze) demonstrates Caitlyn's orientation to Amy's lack of involvement with their co-present conversation and her privileging of her secondary involvement with her mobile. Immediately following, in line 121, Amy places her phone back on the table (see fig. 7.3) and takes the floor to respond to Caitlyn's request for topic resumption ("Yeah like I've never seen them being affectionate"; lines 121–27).

This case illustrates the importance of the time-transcending affordance of mobile texting. The asynchronous nature of mobile texting allows Amy to make her secondary mobile involvement dependent on the dynamics of her role in the local turn taking organization of the primary co-present involvement. If the summons had occurred through a synchronous voice call, Amy would have been forced to choose between suspending her co-present interaction as a primary involvement and switching to the voice call, or ignoring the voice call completely and rejecting the summons altogether.

This tolerance for response delay may also be explained through reference to the space-transcending nature of mobile devices. A lack of shared place means that nonpresent individuals are unaware of the extent to which the individual that they texted is available for interaction. For these reasons, mobiles afford a less constrained set of expectations regarding the response time between the initiating chime and the responding action. This allows Amy to carry on her co-present interaction as a primary involvement, while meeting her obligation to respond to the mobile summons when the time is right. Finally, one can also observe that Amy's opportunity to shift her gaze toward her phone is occasioned by Brianne's reentering into the room where she and Caitlyn were conversing. Such a shift in participant structure—where Amy now has two interlocutors in the immediate, local context—provides an opportunity for Amy to redistribute her attention between the co-present and mobile involvements.

Case 2
This case shows how participants may attempt to blur the boundaries that exist between their secondary mobile and primary co-present involvements. In the following excerpt the women are just coming to the end of a series of tellings related to substance addiction:

Excerpt 3 [MIC1:790–828]

42 CAT: =Like his friend that
43   just got out of rehab
44   three months ago, he's

45	in law school.
46 AMY:	((drops her mouth))
47 CAT:	Like (.) how
48	[does that like (.)
49	that's crazy.]
50	[((Amy picks up phone))]
51	(0.5)
52 CAT:	°Like° I
53	[dunno it's
54	just (.) nuts.]
55	[((Amy begins
56	typing into phone))]
57	(1.2)
58 BRI:	[((yawns))]
59	[(0.9)]
60 AMY:	Trish says she thinks
61	Tom just read my text
62	message.
63	(0.2)
64 AMY:	Cause I was like (.) she
65	was like (.) um (0.3) she
66	was like um (.) she was
67	like (dislike) Tom question
68	mark? and I was like no

Figure 7.5 Bri yawns during silence (line 58).

■ Figure 7.6 "Tom just read my text message" (lines 61–62).

69   just up<u>set</u> with him and
70   I was like that wouldn't
71   have been <u>n</u>ice of him I
72   was like he's <u>hurt</u>ing my
73   <u>baby</u> and she was like
74   (0.2) she was like I
75   think he just read your
76   message and I was li:ke
77   (0.2) I was like why do
78   you say that and she goes
79   because he opened my
80   phone saying <u>oh</u> you have
81   three messages like with
82   an attitude? and I was
83   like <u>s:o</u>? I didn't say
84   anything w<u>ro</u>ng I'm just
85   stating the <u>truth</u>,
86   (2.0)
87 CAT: <u>Drama drama drama</u>
88   <u>drama drama</u> hhhheh-heh

Starting in lines 42–45, Caitlyn produces a multiunit turn built upon their prior discussion of substance addiction ("Like his friend that <u>just</u> got out of rehab three months ago, he's in law school."). Amy then produces an embodied assessment by dropping her jaw as a display of disbelief in response to Caitlyn's telling. Possibly as an attempt to elicit a proper response from Brianne, Caitlyn recompletes her telling and provides her own assessment ("that's <u>crazy</u>"; lines 47–48). Simultaneous with Caitlyn's recompletion, Amy picks up her mobile (line 50), directs her gaze toward it, and begins typing into it (lines 55–56). No visible or aural sign of uptake to Caitlyn's concurrent actions is displayed. Thus, up to this point, Amy has managed both the co-present and mediated involvements as distinct from one another.

Next, after a noticeable silence (and yawn from Brianne) where a story response was still relevant (lines 57–59), Amy takes the floor to present a summative report ("Trish says she thinks Tom just read my text message"; lines 60–62), presumably related to her current text message exchange (see figs. 7.5 and 7.6). Following this, Amy goes on to produce a story about her text exchange ("Cause I was like . . ."; lines 64–85), complete with several uses of the English quotative "like" (Dailey-O'Cain 2000; see also Golato 2000) presumably to mark the reporting of the individual text messages that made up the exchange (see related work on reported speech in conversation, such as Tannen 1995; Holt and Clift 2007). It is unclear what Amy refers to when she says, "he's <u>hurt</u>ing my <u>baby</u> . . ." (lines 72–73) or "I'm just stating the <u>truth</u>" (lines 84–85), but for our purposes understanding the meaning of these remarks is secondary to our analysis. As a result of Amy's actions, what may have previously been considered a secondary involvement through the mobile phone has now been explicitly acknowledged in the co-present interaction and made into a legitimate topic of conversation (essentially spoken into the here-and-now context of the encounter). Furthermore, Brianne and Caitlyn are both granted greater epistemic access to Amy's mobile-bound communicative activities (via her report that "Trish says she thinks . . ."), thus reconfiguring the previously independent nature of the two interactions.

In this case, the affordance of the mobile device to transcend space is particularly relevant to explaining this behavior. Here the interlocutors have only visual or aural access, effectively positioning them as a type of bystander (or unratified participant) in the participation structure of the mobile-related side involvement (Goodwin and Goodwin 2004). Because of this constraint on Brianne and Caitlyn's involvement in the mobile exchange, Amy was afforded the opportunity to refer to the text exchange in the co-present conversation, thereby blurring the boundary between her secondary and primary involvement. If the individual with whom Amy had the text exchange was co-present, such a blurring would have been unlikely, if not impossible, since any interaction between Amy and the individual would have been a primary rather than secondary involvement.

Conclusion

Our study has at least two implications for the study of discourse and new media technologies. First, at the theoretical level, we show how the concept of primary and secondary involvement is relevant to understanding the dynamic switching and blurring that takes place when mobile texting occurs during co-present interaction. We further show the relationship between this switching and the local management of conversational turn-taking. This may point to emerging social norms regarding mobile usage among friends or peers, but further research is necessary to support this possibility. Second, we show how a conversation analytic approach can be used to understand the increasingly technologically rich nature of social encounters. Using such an approach we demonstrate how mobiles are woven into the various linguistic and embodied resources that participants draw upon to produce social actions.

This study points to at least two areas of future work. This study is exploratory in nature and would benefit from the use of a larger collection of instances of interactions to enhance the rigor of our findings. Our analysis does not incorporate the actual content of the text messages that were sent and received during the conversation. Researchers would do well to consider how the study of everyday discourse can be extended to examine both of these mediums as they unfold concurrently in situated context.

APPENDIX: TRANSCRIPTION KEY

.	indicates falling intonation (not necessarily end of sentence)
(0.5)	indicates amount of silence, in tenths of seconds
__	underlining shows a sound that is stressed
:	indicates that the preceding sound is extended or stretched
(h)	indicates laughter incorporated into a word
?	indicates rising intonation (not necessarily a question)
[ ]	marks the beginning and ending of overlap
hhh	marks an audible outbreath
°	encloses speech that is produced quietly
-	indicates a cutoff in the course of production
=	indicates no interval between two utterances (that is, they are latched together)

NOTES

Special thanks go to Galina Bolden, Jenny Mandelbaum, Cynthia Gordon, and Deborah Tannen for their helpful suggestions and comments.

1. Ling ultimately argues that these forms of interaction should not be excluded from having the potential to create and maintain the social solidarity often associated exclusively with co-present rituals. Collins (2004) takes the opposing position. Although he acknowledges the possibility of mediated rituals, Collins concludes that such forms of interaction are incapable of generating the type of emotional energy characteristic of co-present ritual interaction.

2. Humphreys further acknowledges cases where the participants across both interactions converge to create "three-way interactions," or when the participant on the phone serves as a type of mediator between the co-present and nonpresent interlocutors (2005, 821–22). Although we hope to explore this type of interactional event in future research, we do not pursue it in this chapter.

REFERENCES

Atkinson, John M., and John Heritage. 1984. *Structures of social action: Studies in conversation analysis.* Cambridge: Cambridge University Press.

Bolden, Galina B. 2003. Multiple modalities in collaborative turn sequences. *Gesture* 3:187–212.

Campbell, Scott W., and Yon Jin Park. 2008. Social implications of mobile telephony: The rise of personal communication society. *Sociology Compass* 2:371–87.

Collins, Randall. 2004. *Interaction ritual chains.* Princeton, NJ: Princeton University Press.

Dailey-O'Cain, Jennifer. 2000. The sociolinguistic distribution of and attitudes toward focuser *like* and quotative *like*. *Journal of Sociolinguistics* 4:60–80.

Gibson, James J. 1977. The theory of affordances. In *Perceiving, acting, and knowing: Toward an ecological psychology,* eds. R. E. Shaw and J. Bransford, 67–82. Hillsdale, NJ: Lawrence Erlbaum.

Goffman, Erving. 1963. *Behavior in public places.* New York: Free Press.

Golato, Andrea. 2000. An innovative German quotative for reporting on embodied actions: *Und ich so/und er so* "and I'm like/and he's like." *Journal of Pragmatics* 32:29–54.

Goodwin, Charles. 1986. Gestures as a resource for the organization of mutual orientation. *Semiotica* 62:29–49.

———. 2000. Action and embodiment within situated human interaction. *Journal of Pragmatics* 32:1489–522.

———. 2003. The body in action. In *Discourse, the body and identity,* eds. Justine Coupland and Richard Gwyn, 9–42. New York: Palgrave Macmillan.

Goodwin, Charles, and Marjorie H. Goodwin, 2004. Participation. In *A companion to linguistic anthropology,* ed. Alessandro Duranti, 222–44. Oxford: Blackwell.

Haddington, Pentti, and Tiina Keisanen. 2009. Location, mobility and the body as resources in selecting a route. *Journal of Pragmatics* 41, no. 10:1938–61.

Heath, Christian, and Paul Luff. 2000. *Technology in action.* Cambridge: Cambridge University Press.

Holt, Elizabeth, and Rebecca Clift, eds. 2007. *Reporting talk: Reported speech in interaction.* Cambridge: Cambridge University Press.

Humphreys, Lee. 2005. Cell phones in public: Social interaction in a wireless era. *New Media and Society* 7:813–36.

Hutchby, Ian. 2001. *Conversation and technology: From the telephone to the internet.* Cambridge: Polity Press.

Katz, James E. 2006. *Magic in the air: Mobile communication and the transformation of social life.* New Brunswick, NJ: Transaction.

———. ed. 2008. *Handbook of mobile communication studies.* Cambridge, MA: MIT Press.

———. 2011. *Mobile communication: Dimensions of social policy.* New Brunswick, NJ: Transaction.

Kendon, Adam. 2004. *Gesture: Visible action as utterance.* Cambridge: Cambridge University Press.

LeBaron, Curtis, and Jürgen Streeck. 1997. Built space and the interactional framing of experience during a murder interrogation. *Human Studies* 20:1–25.

Ling, Richard S. 2008. *New tech, new ties: How mobile communication is reshaping social cohesion.* Cambridge, MA: MIT Press.

Nevile, Maurice. 2005. You always have to land: Accomplishing the sequential organization of actions to land an airliner. In *Discourse in action: Introducing mediated discourse analysis,* eds. Sigrid Norris and Rodney H. Jones, 32–44. London: Routledge.

Norman, Donald. 1999. Affordance, conventions, and design. *Interactions* 6:38–43.

Norris, Sigrid. 2004. *Analyzing multimodal interaction: A methodological framework.* London: Routledge.

———. 2011. *Identity in (inter)action: Introducing multimodal interaction analysis.* Berlin and New York: Mouton de Gruyter.

Sacks, Harvey, Emanuel. A. Schegloff, and Gail Jefferson. 1974. A simplest systematics for the organization of turn-taking for conversation. *Language* 50:696–735.

Schegloff, Emanuel A. 1984. On some gestures' relation to talk. In *Structures of social action,* eds. Maxwell J. Atkinson and John Heritage, 266–96. Cambridge: Cambridge University Press.

———. 2007. *Sequence organization in interaction. A primer in conversation analysis.* Cambridge: Cambridge University Press.

Schegloff, Emanuel A., and Harvey Sacks. 1973. Opening up closings. *Semiotica* 8:289–327.

Stivers, Tanya, and Jack Sidnell. 2005. Multi-modal interaction. *Semiotica* 156:1–20.

Tannen, Deborah. 1995. Waiting for the mouse: Constructed dialogue in conversation. In *The dialogic emergence of culture,* eds. Dennis Tedlock and Bruce Mannheim, 198–219. Chicago: University of Illinois Press.

Toerien, Merran, and Celia Kitzinger. 2007. Emotional labour in action: Navigating multiple involvements in the beauty salon. *Sociology* 41:645–62.

8

Facework on Facebook
Conversations on Social Media

LAURA WEST AND ANNA MARIE TRESTER
Georgetown University

Introduction

AS ERVING GOFFMAN TELLS US, there is no such thing as faceless communication. This observation—no less true in the world of social media than it is in the world of so-called face-to-face interaction—is palpably present in Facebook. Face, in this sense, is the part of us that both requires and is vulnerable in social interaction. On Facebook, social interaction takes place when members provide other members with something they can respond to, comment on, and approve of, and in turn when they acknowledge other members through updates and posts. In this investigation we focus on the back-and-forths this creates on users' walls with an eye to identifying norms about politeness that these reveal and the linguistic strategies used to accomplish such moves.

When linguists first entered computer-mediated communication (CMC) research, they adopted the foci that researchers from other fields had outlined: characterizing online language as being more like written or spoken communication, and describing the various features and genres present in texts on the web. But in a special issue of the *Journal of Sociolinguistics,* Jannis Androutsopoulos (2006) called for researchers to shift to more ethnographically grounded user-related approaches to social media. In the same issue, Georgakopoulou writes, "it is pleasing to see how ethnography, the champion of the irreducibility of lived experience and of situated understandings, is finding its way into CMC" (2006, 551). Finally, she challenges these ethnographies of CMC spaces, more specifically, to capture the way participation takes place on particular sites and "the expectations and norms about what is licensed, encouraged or prohibited" there (552).

This investigation heeds this call, as well as that issued by Herring (in the present volume), by considering the expectations and norms surrounding facework on the social networking site Facebook, drawing from an ongoing ethnography involving sixty Facebook users as participants. Our analysis makes use of interactional sociolinguistics "combining wider contextual knowledge with linguistic and conversational analysis to illuminate the interpretive processes of interaction" (Sarangi and Roberts 1999, 13), and intertextuality, the process of referring to, drawing upon, or reshaping earlier texts within the context of a later one, to consider the basic social moves of the site (post-ing, "friending," liking, commenting, and tagging). We explore how face-threatening acts (FTAs) are avoided and how facework is accomplished through intertextual links that allow conversations to take place online. Our contextualized understanding of the interactional norms surrounding intertextuality on this social networking site is grounded in observations of our participants' linguistic practices as well as in semistruc-tured individual and group interviews and discussions including those conducted as part of a workshop we held on this topic at the Georgetown University Round Table on Lan-guages and Linguistics (GURT) in March 2011. Additionally, we draw insight (specif-ically about norms violations) from jokes about Facebook created on the site fakebook.com and recently published in a *Washington Post* blog entry (Petri 2011).

Overview

We begin by providing three types of background to the investigation: an overview of the theoretical concepts of face and intertextuality and how they work in the context of our analysis; a brief review of the literature done by linguists on online social interac-tion generally and on Facebook in particular; and a description of the study and review some of the key Facebook practices and terminology. We then explore how the need to present something for others to acknowledge seems to be the driving impulse behind many posts on the site (as evidenced both in the content of the posts and in voiced frus-tration with friends who fail to give this acknowledgment), and that both the poster and the potential respondents seem to be expected to do some intertextual work to tie texts together on the site. Thus we show how the concepts of face and intertextuality are built into the norms shaping main activities of the site: (1) friending, (2) self-presentation, (3) replying and responding, and (4) issuing birthday wishes and event invitations.

Regarding friending, we find that the act of requesting and accepting friends on the site requires maintenance of the relationship in the form of noticing friends' self-presentation (performing positive facework toward the hearer). We then demonstrate how self presentation, or accomplishing positive facework toward the self, can be tricky in that it must avoid appearing overly self-congratulatory. Next we explore some of the meanings signaled by liking something, and some of the expectations about responding, beginning and ending our investigation with the navigation of norms sur-rounding the new feature of tagging.

Observing that only friends can perform face threats toward one another and be perceived as joking, and that awareness of facework norms can be manipulated by members to playfully tease one another to signal friendship, we consider how inter-textuality becomes implicated in facework on this site. Being a friend on Facebook may involve doing a significant amount of intertextual work when commenting, by responding to the post in a similar tone (often playful or casual), and sometimes re-peating language and building on the original text and sometimes driving the inter-action forward by drawing on outside cultural texts.

Background

Facework and intertextuality are two analytical concepts borrowed from sociology and literary theory, respectively, that have proved invaluable to the study of social interactions. Here we provide readers with a brief overview of the concepts and demonstrate how combining them can create an analytical framework for understanding the communicative norms of an online network.

Facework and Intertextuality

Erving Goffman proposed the notion of face as a theoretical concept informed by the Chinese idea of saving face. He defines the concept as "an image of self delineated in terms of approved social attributes." This, he explains, is constructed through "the pattern of verbal and nonverbal acts by which [the speaker] expresses his view of the situation and . . . his evaluation of the participants, especially himself" (1955, 213).

Lakoff (1973) treated politeness in terms of pragmatics, building on Grice's (1967) rules of conversation to create rules of politeness: "1) don't impose; 2) give options; and 3) make addressee feel good—be friendly" (298). The first two rules address what Brown and Levinson, drawing from Goffman's concept, later refer to as negative face, which they define as a "basic want to maintain claims of territory and self-determination"—put more simply, the desire to be free from social obligations (1987, 70). Lakoff's third rule is similar to what Brown and Levinson define as positive face, or a "desire to be ratified, understood, approved of, liked or admired" (Brown and Levinson 1987, 62).

The basic premise of Brown and Levinson's politeness theory is that everyone has two faces that become vulnerable in interactions: a positive face and a negative face. They claim that face is what drives peoples' decisions during interactions, guarding against what Brown and Levinson (1987) later termed FTAs, which can threaten either a person's positive or negative face. Actions that threaten the negative face of the hearer, for example, are those that indicate that the speaker does not intend to respect the hearer's desire to remain unimpeded, and instead, intends to impose by pressuring the hearer to do a certain task or respond or react a certain way.

The way to avoid these face threats is to anoint the face of another, highlighting the speaker's awareness of the hearer's face needs and indicating a certain respect for these. For instance, a speaker may perform positive facework toward the hearer (also referred to as "positive politeness") by suggesting that they like the hearer as a person or share the same likes and desires, or by indicating that they view the hearer as part of an in-group with the speaker. Facework toward the hearer's negative face occurs when social actions, which might otherwise be face threatening, are done with hedging, being indirect or giving the hearer an out. In short, face and politeness theory concern how social interactants relate to one another.

Intertextuality, on the other hand, deals with relationships among texts. Kristeva (1980) first introduced the term, drawing from scholarship of the literary theorist M. M. Bakhtin (1981, 1984, 1986) on dialogism. Through the work of Becker (1994) and Bauman and Briggs (1990), we adopt a process orientation to intertextuality, viewing it as a process of referring to, drawing upon, or reshaping earlier texts within the context of a later one. Linguists have long used the concept of intertextuality to make sense of relationships among texts and, more recently, to understand the web of social texts created online. For example, Baym (2006) draws from a two-year ethnographic study of an online discussion group centered around soap operas to demonstrate that the "solidarity of computer-mediated groups can be enhanced through references to common knowledge," in the form of well-known cultural texts and to "the group's previous discourse" (2006, under "Humor and the Establishment of Group Solidarity and Identity in CMC").

Researchers have shown that one of the key ways in which members of any group use intertextuality to accomplish facework is by creating common ground through jokes and a "self-deprecating style of humor" (Bury 2005, 157). Norrick, in his writing on intertextuality and humor, asserts that "joke telling counts as positive politeness (Lakoff 1973; Brown and Levinson, 1978, 1987), as an invitation to demonstrate membership and solidarity" (1989, 118). Although ours is the first study of which we are aware to consider facework-oriented intertextuality on Facebook (considering the social meaning of responding to and anticipating posts, texts, and images), it is certainly not the first study to consider norms regarding face online generally or within the Facebook community in particular, as we will now review.

Previous Research on Politeness in Online Interaction

In one of the earliest studies that examined how politeness and FTAs were affected by lack of verbal context, Simmons (1994) looked at postings to an online bulletin board system, revealing that because replies and responses were occurring in a public space, this upped the degree of threat to members' faces. Several participants in the study noted that face threats, such as ridicule, that took place in a public setting tended to create much more impassioned responses than those made in private messages (20). He predicts that over time, CMC discourse will show a greater use of positive face strategies as people adjust to their "faceless voices" (45)—a prediction that was borne out in studies such as Morand and Ocker (2002), which showed that interactants in CMC often adorn messages with indices of positive politeness, such as emoticons and acronyms such as "jk" (for "just kidding").

Similarly, Graham's (2007) ethnography of a group called ChurchList looked at expectations about politeness in an online community of practice, finding that a successful member of an online group must be aware of politeness norms and be convincing in their knowledge of and respect for the community's expectations. Graham found that something is more likely to be interpreted as impolite by a hearer when the speaker is perceived to have *intended* to attack the face of the hearer. For instance, Graham describes a woman who criticized a message in the LISTSERV, addressing the original poster using the distancing referent "the gentleman who posted earlier" and then referring to "people" who think the same way. The community interpreted her comments as being very inappropriate, which Graham claims is due to their interpretation of this act as "the equivalent of talking about someone in his/her presence as if s/he were not there," which would be considered a face threat in most circumstances (750). The woman claimed that she did not know that the original poster would read her comment, but this ignorance about the medium was not deemed acceptable by the other members. In Graham's words, "If one is not proficient in meeting the demands of the computer medium . . . then one may be more likely to be interpreted as having attacked another's face with intent" (756). Our exploration of Facebook norms involving face reveals a high degree of positive facework and Facebook-specific communication practices, which speaks to users' awareness of their posts' vulnerability to interpretations of impoliteness.

On the other side of the coin, in a study that looked at how successful Facebook users were at projecting the positive image of themselves that they thought they were projecting, Barash, Ducheneaut, Isaacs, and Bellotti (2010) found that although many times members succeeded in conveying a sense of themselves as "cool" and "entertaining" (two of the most desired qualities of the young Facebook community), some posts were rated (by one hundred Facebook users) as going "too far" and projecting "a self-aggrandizing image that clashes with the light-hearted tone" expected of most social networking posts (210). In other words, doing positive facework in posts is a bit of a balancing act; it can easily tip into a threat to a member's positive face—painting them as a braggart—if done incorrectly.

In another study of Facebook, Viswanath et al. (2009) used a specific network on the New Orleans regional network site to observe over 60,000 members and 800,000 interactions and how their activity on the social site evolved. The study found that interactions among users who interacted infrequently were often in response to prompts by Facebook, such as birthday reminders. They also found that interactions between users decrease over time, "implying that most activity links die out" (37), although some relationships demonstrated this trend to a lesser degree. These activity links are created by acknowledging one another's texts. This study reveals that it requires effort to perform positive facework toward so many friends (users have an average of 120 friends on the site), so they either stop doing so in many cases or take the easy way out (responding only to Facebook reminders).

Finally, the architecture of the space in which online communication occurs is also important to understand as influencing the social behaviors that occur there. Papacharissi explored three social networks and compared various aspects of the online social spaces that might be influencing the interactions taking place therein. She claims that social networks are "fostering interaction that is primarily interpersonal and founded upon norms of everyday interaction adapted to the online setting" (2009, 202). Specifically, she concludes that Facebook members may "project more carefully crafted presentations of the self" (215) mostly due to the informal nature of the site, which Papacharissi terms a "loose" community, based on Goffman's notion. She explains that a loose community or network is one in which a wider variety of behaviors might be observed due to fewer restrictions on the type of interactions that can occur. She claims, again following Goffman, that these loose networks "require users to be more mindful of interaction, looking for cues to adjust their behavior and providing cues for others to adapt theirs" (214). Such careful creations of show and tell and mindfulness of others' signals create a large amount of work for members trying to respect both their own positive and negative face wants and those of other members.

Data and Description of Facebook Practices and Terminology

Since 2009 we have been conducting an ethnography—or netnography—of the Facebook community, a study that now includes sixty participants. Following

Kozinets in remembering that we are studying "not texts online, but people's interactions through various technologically-mediated means" (2009, 113), our netnography involves reflective field notes, in which we record "observations regarding
subtexts, pretexts, contingencies, conditions, and personal emotions" during our
time online in order to "decipher the reasons behind cultural actions" (114). Re-
cruitment for the present study was done via Facebook by creating an events page
that explained the project and asked people to respond if they agreed to allow the
researchers to collect data from their walls. We also asked that friends invite more
friends to participate so that we could capture interactions featuring back-and-forth
conversation between two or more project participants. Although we have changed
the names and removed the photos, all of the verbatim posts and comments that we
present here involve people who have consented to participate in research. If an interaction includes a participant from whom we did not have explicit permission to
collect data, we do not include their actual words and instead provide a summary
of their part in the interaction.

For ease of reference, the important Facebook terms relevant to this discussion are defined and summarized in table 8.1, below, and will be contextualized
in the discussion to follow. On Facebook, every member has a profile page on
which their wall appears. Posts, in addition to appearing on walls, are blasted to
friends via the newsfeed, which automatically distributes news among users' networks, choosing which data to feed each member's homepage according to an al-
gorithm based on that member's traffic patterns on the site. In this way, when a
user logs onto Facebook, they immediately see a list of friends' recent activity without having to visit each of their walls to see what has been posted since their last
visit to the site. Members then interact with each other by liking or commenting
on these texts, which our investigation will consider as a form of intertextuality
implicated in facework.

■ Table 8.1
A summary of Facebook practices and terminology

Facebook term	Description
Profile	The Facebook page that is unique to each member where they enter identifying information.
Friend	A member who is connected with another member on the site through either requesting or accepting the connection.
Wall	A member's profile space where he or she can post updates and where friends can type messages.
Update	A semipublic text placed on a member's wall and to the newsfeed. It may take the form of bits of news, hyperlinks, videos, or photos. These can be typed and posted from a member's phone in addition to his or her computer.
Comment	A reply to a post made by the original poster or by another member.
Like	A clickable response device located under a post signaling acknowledgment and approval of the content.

Data Analysis

Thus far we have discussed the analytical terms and described the basics of the Facebook communicative context. We now turn to the data to demonstrate how the above concepts shed light on particular Facebook practices and the discursive expectations of the site. The data come from two separate sources: actual interactions we observed on Facebook, and joke interactions from the *Washington Post* blog entry about Facebook interactions. We argue that these jokes ring true precisely because they identify expectations about norms of interaction. By matching up joke examples with collected examples from our participants, we point out the potential face-threatening events highlighted in the jokes about Facebook, which are often deftly avoided in real Facebook interactions.

Tagging on Facebook: An Example

To illustrate how face and intertextuality are mutually implicated in Facebook interactions, we will begin with an example drawn from our GURT workshop. When we opened the floor for discussion of face in Facebook, the conversation turned immediately to an FTA involving peoples' literal faces: the process of tagging photos. Using the tag feature, people can put up photographs of themselves and others, and by labeling them with a member's name, link them to a profile page, such that they appear in a running border across the top of the named member's homepage. Because tagging in Facebook is a relatively recent (within the past few years) intertextual development, users are still figuring out what all of its implications are. Group discussion about this practice veered immediately to the pitfalls, and included comments such as this:

> What if someone puts a picture that is unflattering of me because I don't look particularly good on that particular day or because they have captured me doing something that I would not necessarily want to show the world that I do?

Fears such as these speak to perceived threats to the tagged member's positive face. That person's desire to be ratified, understood, approved of, liked, or admired is in danger if someone else—who is not as protective of these face wants—is the one responsible for establishing textual links, in this case photos, on Facebook. Because people are most sensitive to their own face wants, it is possible that a picture of someone else might appear fine to the poster, but that the person in the photo may feel they look fat or tired, or that they are engaged in activities that might detract from the positive image of themselves that they have been carefully crafting on Facebook thus far (by posting photos that make them look thin, attractive, or fun).

But then the workshop discussion turned to the threats to both speaker and hearer's positive face if the tagged member removed the tag. If they choose to undo the intertextuality by removing the link to their profile, essentially disowning the image in the photo, they run the risk of damaging the friendship because the owner of the photograph may think the objections to the image are different than they actually are. Participants imagined their friends wondering,

> Did my friend object to being pictured with me?

> Why did they not accept my overture of friendship?

YourFriendWithACamera I just posted a huge album that contains no flattering pictures of anyone. I have spent the past three hours tagging them so that you can spend the next six hours untagging them.

5 hours ago · Comment · Like

 You Thanks, Carl! Glad you're putting in the effort.
5 hours ago

Figure 8.1 Tagging photos (joke data).

We then introduced an intertextual reference to face threats in tagging from some joke examples we took from Petri's *Washington Post* blog entry. Laughter from the audience cued us to the recognition of the flouting of Facebook norms in the interaction presented as figure 8.1, which humorously explores the practice of photo tagging of YourFriendWithACamera (aka Carl). The creator of this joke has chosen to highlight one of the potential face threats of photo tagging; by posting these unflattering photos, Carl gives the appearance of someone who does not care about maintaining his friends' positive faces or protecting their negative faces. By linking unflattering photos to their profiles, he is harming the desirable image that they wish to present on Facebook. Further, by constraining their future actions for approximately six hours (the exaggerated time that they will have to spend untagging these photos to repair and satisfy their positive face wants), he threatens their negative faces and does damage to the presentation of his own positive face, for which "you" sanction him by sarcastically observing, "glad you're putting in the effort." In referencing the widely recognized, ongoing navigation of norms surrounding the practice of tagging, humor comes from the fact that real interactants on Facebook largely *avoid* these face-threatening acts. Thus, the joke sets the stage for exploring the ways that users actually navigate these face threats linguistically.

Being a Friend on Facebook

When friendliness is emphasized, as is the case on this social networking site, "the reflex of social closeness is, generally, the reciprocal giving and receiving of positive face" (Brown and Levinson 1987, 77). "S (speaker) should take notice of aspects of H's (hearer) condition (noticeable changes, remarkable possessions, anything which looks as though H would want S to notice and approve of it)" (103). And, of course, whenever someone posts something on his or her wall, it is precisely so that others will notice it. This, then, creates texts that form the foundation of social interaction on the site.

The creators of Facebook have structured the social site to facilitate intertextuality, encouraging members to acknowledge and respond to texts that have been presented by other members: each post has a clickable like feature below it, a commenting option allowing others to react to and remark on a post, and a share option for reposting the message on their own wall. Figure 8.2 is what appears at the top of every user's home, or profile, page, where they create communicative content.

Thus, when someone creates a profile and relays messages in the world of this social networking site, a version of him- or herself is presented that becomes imme-

Figure 8.2 Facebook text box.

diately vulnerable to social interaction, and the myriad motivations and possible pit-falls therein. In short, the stage is set for the social act of facework. One of the primary means of engaging in such facework on Facebook is posting, which we characterize as an intertextual practice because fundamentally it involves the act of sharing texts in the form of short messages (or status updates), photos, links, or videos.

Again, the structure of the site itself contributes to intertextuality. Because Facebook stacks the replies and responses in chronological order underneath the initial post, a sort of heading is made which gives comments context and keeps the initial post in the consciousness of participants, allowing future readers to have what Chafe calls the same "activation states" of information in their minds while interpreting the conversation (1994, 54). Months later someone can read the comments and look back at what the starting topic was and how the conversation progressed. This format often prompts people to make use of explicit intertextuality, reusing and recycling wording and framing from previous statements or texts. Facebook users are, in fact, expected to interact regularly with the space and with other members (their friends) in this way.

A source of insight into the expectations concerning such practices may be found in the groups that members form on Facebook, for example, the open group "If you don't write on my wall then WHY did you friend request me?" that was created in late December 2010, and which members of the public can join, like, and comment on. Discussion on the group's wall speaks to the "unspoken oddities about the rule of friendship on Facebook" including, as one member described it, "when someone who never spoke to me in HS (high school) friend requests me." The very creation of the group and the conversational activity on it highlight the importance of paying attention to members' positive faces, as does its self-description:

> This [group] is for the people who get random friend requests by others who apparently add them for the sole purpose of raising their "friend" quotient. They never write on your wall, comment on your post/pics, "like" anything, message you OR respond to you when you do any of the above for them.

Owing to the strong desire that members have for attention from others in the community, a member who friends someone for their own positive face gains (to increase their number of friends) without further acknowledging that friend is seen to be neglecting their facework obligations toward that friend. The act of friending, according to this group, should be to show a genuine interest and recognition of aspects of another person (positive facework) in the form of posting, commenting, liking, or sending and responding to messages. But when someone does not explicitly notice the other member by engaging in these intertextual linguistic practices, this is felt by some to be disregarding a norm to perform positive facework toward one's Facebook friends. And this lack of approval by those who can see a member's updates is seen as a positive face threat.

The rule is to engage with the community by noticing the positive self-image members present and make one's awareness and appreciation of them known, or suffer the social consequences, such as "the FB boot." As the creator of the group described above posts, "I just deleted 88 people and feel so much better after doing so! How many people can you find who need the FB boot?" As these comments speaking to the violations of the norms suggest, this "bald-on-record face threatening act" (Brown and Levinson 1987, 95)—deleting people from a member's list of friends— seems to be a just reaction to the friends' prior face threat to them (not acknowledging their self-presentation texts). As we see then, the practices of introducing and responding to texts as a means for avoiding face threats and demonstrating facework are central to Facebook. Intertextuality is thus implicated in many of the other core organizing activities central to the site and built in to accomplishing facework in the practice of friending, maintaining friendships, and in a variety of other contexts.

Self-Presentation on Facebook

Evidence of the dangers inherent in sharing about oneself on Facebook can be found in our joke examples. Figure 8.3 highlights the type of post that attempts, unsuccessfully, to accomplish positive facework toward the poster, provoking instead an undesirable and disapproving reaction. Rather than impressing others and having them admire her, "I am achieving considerable professional success" causes readers to respond negatively, expressing dislike and even hatred toward their friend (wanting to "suffocate" her). The claim to success prompted by her positive face need to be admired is perhaps too blatant in that it makes others reexamine their own worth, threatening both the positive face of the poster and the positive and negative faces of the readers, who are forced to compare their own professional status with the poster's ideal position. This is why actual Facebook members don't usually post in this way (and why

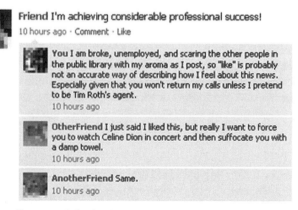

Figure 8.3 The dangers of bragging (joke data).

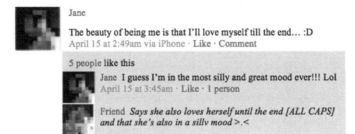

Jane

The beauty of being me is that I'll love myself till the end... :D
April 15 at 2:49am via iPhone · Like · Comment

5 people like this

Jane I guess I'm in the most silly and great mood ever!!! Lol
April 15 at 3:45am · Like · 1 person

Friend *Says she also loves herself until the end [ALL CAPS] and that she's also in a silly mood >.<*

Figure 8.4 Positive face mitigated (ethnographic data).

the joke is funny); instead, people are more careful about performing positive facework toward themselves through posts, mitigating their claims with emoticons, punctuation, etc. as demonstrated in the next example of an actual Facebook interaction.

Figure 8.4 is an excerpt from our Facebook ethnography data, and reveals how users present their positive faces while playing down or padding their claims. When Jane explicitly performs positive facework by talking about "the beauty of being me" and loving herself, we refer to her implied self-confidence and suggested love-of-life personality as the post's metamessage—a term first used in discourse analysis by Tannen (2005). Jane doesn't explicitly make these claims. Instead, she doctors the text so that readers won't picture her typing or saying this with a haughty sincerity. The emoticon :D represents an open-mouthed smile and gives a contextualization cue (Gumperz 1982) for readers to interpret Jane as expressing, "I don't take myself too seriously." Dresner and Herring (2010) have observed in a detailed analysis of emoticons that they may be used to "downgrade the utterance to a less face-threatening speech act" (9).

The time stamps are also illuminating here in drawing informed conclusions about the intentions of the poster. Observe that an hour later, Jane intertextually engages with her own post, perhaps feeling upon rereading her original statement that it might be misinterpreted, so she does another downgrade by explicitly claiming to be feeling "silly" and using another popular online tactic to signal a good sense of humor: "lol." The "laughing out loud" abbreviation paints another picture for readers of how Jane might be saying this; it makes up for the lack of paralinguistic context cues. She might have successfully performed a self-confident air and avoided the potential face threat of misinterpretation by hearers by laughing or smiling a certain way in a face-to-face interaction, but uses the keyboard to save face in an online interaction.

Figure 8.5 presents another interaction, which begins with a potentially face-threatening brag downgraded with "lol," which prompts potential face-threatening back-and-forths consistently padded with "lol" and typed laughter. Nina shares the fact that she does not have to go to school. The punctuation and "lol" mark this as a happy bit of news, rather than what might be read as a brag (by friends who still have to go to school that day—including those who may live at a distance from Nina in

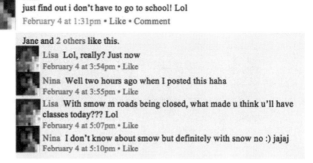

Nina
just find out i don't have to go to school! Lol
February 4 at 1:31pm • Like • Comment

Jane and 2 others like this.

Lisa Lol, really? Just now
February 4 at 3:54pm • Like

Nina Well two hours ago when I posted this haha
February 4 at 3:55pm • Like

Lisa With smow m roads being closed, what made u think u'll have classes today??? Lol
February 4 at 5:07pm • Like

Nina I don't know about smow but definitely with snow no :) jajaj
February 4 at 5:10pm • Like

▨ Figure 8.5 No school today! (ethnographic data).

geographic locations that do not share the same weather conditions and as such do not get the day off due to snow). Lisa responds by teasing Nina for not realizing until "just now" that she did not have to go to school, implying that she should have known earlier because of the "smow and roads being closed." The play frame is cued again by Lisa's use of "lol," which is familiar to social media users and, perhaps, an intertextual reference to Nina's original post. Had Lisa not conveyed a sense of joking, it could have been a serious threat to Nina's positive face, since it implies that Nina is slow to comprehend the obvious. However, since it was done so blatantly and with laughter, seen in the informal context of Facebook it is most easily interpreted as friendly banter. Such moves are read in the context of Facebook as being playful. Only friends can perform face threats toward one another and be perceived as joking, and such palling around online requires experience in the specific community to learn how to properly employ intertextual practices to create these friendly interactions on the site.

Nina then threatens Lisa's positive face right back, but also pads it with typed laugher ("haha"), by pointing out that Lisa's "just now" is not correct in the context, since the original post was created "two hours ago." Lisa responds by continuing the conversation along the lines of padded face threats and ignoring the previous one to her own positive face; she asks Nina how she could doubt school being canceled given the weather (again, suggesting that Lisa did not see the obvious, although the "lol" cues the joking frame and serves to diminish this implied face threat as friendly teasing). Nina continues to poke fun at Lisa's lack of proficiency with the medium, first her apparent unawareness of time stamps, and second her disfluency in her typing ("smow" for "snow"), which is also padded with laughter ("jajaj"). Responding to Lisa's unmeant gesture (the misspelling of a word) with laughter is a polite move, as pointed out by Goffman who claims that "one way of handling inadvertent disruptions is for the interactants to laugh at them" (1959, 53).

Using previous posts as subject matter for new posts and for creating jokes and a self- or, in this case, other-deprecating style of humor, friends stay connected as Facebook friends through these short exchanges. Lisa continues to respond to the "just" plus the content of the first post; Nina replies by teasing Lisa about the form of her responses. Both participants use intertextuality, recycling ideas and linguistic tactics, and referring back to previous texts to create new ones—exemplifying one way that conversations are created, and friendships maintained, on the social site.

In capturing some playful teasing around how posts and comments should go, this example now moves our discussion from posts to reactions to posts. All potential Facebook interactions begin with a post. We have already considered the potential face threat that a post may never be responded to or expanded upon (a threat so severe it merits giving the boot), but when someone does respond, the coveted response is one that accomplishes positive facework, showing involvement in the life of the poster by demonstrating that the hearer is also interested in things that are interesting to the speaker, whether in a play frame and teasingly or in other keys, negotiated by the participants.

Responding to Facebook Posts: Liking and Commenting
Facebook provides two options for demonstrating interest (responding to posts) to intertextually perform positive facework. Rather than writing a comment that engages with the post in some meaningful way, users may simply click the like button to indicate having noticed and appreciated a friend's post, and in so doing accomplish facework for both parties' positive faces. In addition, by clicking like neither interactant (poster or responder) is committed to any future action, thus protecting both participants' negative faces. However, if clicking the like button is a way to demonstrate interest without making a huge effort, it might also carry the metamessage of being a minimal effort response.

The following joke exploits such a metamessage for the purposes of humor. In this interaction "Somebody" has posted a link to an article, demonstrating mild enthusiasm for it and leaving "You" to decide how to respond.

The creators of Facebook have given members an easy way to meet this need of the poster, and the name of the feature is loaded with intertextual ties to the familiar social act of expressing approval toward something presented by a speaker. However, does simply clicking like fully combat the possible face threats noted above? It seems to constitute going on record with positive politeness, but does it "[assure] the addressee that the Speaker considers himself to be 'of the same kind,'" that he "wants his wants?" (Brown and Levinson, 1987, 71–72). Can it really assure the hearer that the speaker likes him? After all, since a choice to like can be a choice not to say anything more about it, like can embed the very choice of having chosen not to comment.

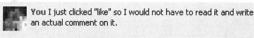

Somebody This is a link to an article that is only mildly interesting.
6 hours ago · Comment · Like

    You I just clicked "like" so I would not have to read it and write an actual comment on it.

    5 hours ago

▥ Figure 8.6 What like really means on Facebook (joke data).

As the joke points out, responding presupposes that the hearer has cared enough about the speaker to read what he or she posted, but simply clicking like can actually hide whether or not this was indeed done. Interactional research into the process of intertextuality can help us understand how this works. By posting an article that he is not particularly excited about, "Somebody" may be understood to have failed to adhere to the interactional norms surrounding intertextuality in this context, because "You" are not brought into engagement with this text either. It is precisely through communicating, negotiating, and coming to share such orientations that participants do facework through intertextuality in this online context; thus, it is not sufficient simply to acknowledge THAT you engage with a text—to bring your fellow interactants into the process, you must also share HOW you engage with it and WHY. Such negotiation of shared orientations to prior texts is, as Trester (2012) claims, one of the primary functions, the *why* of intertextuality. Because as Becker has observed, "social groups seem to be bound primarily by a shared repertoire of prior texts" (1994, 165), texts provide opportunities to do "being a community" by negotiating shared orientations to texts and to each other. Thus, in the joke example, if "Somebody" does not demonstrate having made the effort to do the interactional work, clicking like may be one way of responding that takes the same half-hearted tone.

Of course, in the joke example, the respondent is relaying his thoughts about clicking like (ironically, by commenting), and it is the fact that he has admittedly only liked the post to avoid any real engagement with the text that is the source of the humor. Whereas liking can be a sort of back channeling, and a quick way to save the poster from the face threat of having an unacknowledged post existing publicly for a stretch of time, commenting can involve intertextual engagement with the other through the text.

Figure 8.7, taken from an actual interaction we captured on Facebook, exemplifies the more frequently observed pattern: interactions begin with one or two interactants liking a post, after which the interaction is typically moved forward by comments. Meredith posts a description of a bird that has been tapping on her windowsill. Several of her friends (Amy, Lauren, and Jane) join in on the conversation by means of comments that offer playful explanations for the bird's sudden appearance. Later, when Meredith appears to be annoyed at his continued presence, observing "oh my gosh . . . he's tapping again," her friends begin offering tongue-in-cheek solutions for solving the perceived problem, displaying orientation to the now entextualized bird text in a variety of ways.

As the conversation unfolds over the course of the day (as indicated by the timestamps), we may observe that Meredith's friends find a variety of ways to intertextually engage with her original post, and their comments on her post flatter Meredith's positive face by showing involvement in her life. By bringing in other texts that the bird text reminds them of, they demonstrate HOW they are interested in things that are interesting to her (in this case, the sudden appearance and erratic behavior of birds). For example, Jane's comment "All MY cats are present and accounted for" at the sudden disappearance of the bird can of course only be interpreted by reference back to her earlier playful offer "Want me to send you a kitty?" as a means of remov-

Figure 8.7 A bird tapping at the window (ethnographic data).

ing the source of perceived annoyance. This local text of the proffered cat then becomes a resource with which to create shared experiences and accessible cultural referents for playful exchanges; when the bird finally disappears, Jane jokingly asserts that all her cats are accounted for, continuing the conversation by both responding to Meredith's update about the bird being gone and creating textual coherence by linking her current response to her earlier offer to send a kitty.

Intertextuality allows us to systematically unpack how facework is being done when we consider Jane's humorous intertextual reference to the film *Failure to Launch*. By saying, "There's a hilarious scene about a girl & a bird who is driving her crazy. Better than the main story line in fact," she invites her friends to share in her repertoire of prior texts (providing context for those who may not recognize the name of the film alone). Moreover, by showing her orientation to the text she invites Meredith into her view of the text and to draw a parallel to the current context (and thus her choice to recontextualize it) to convey that she finds Meredith fun and funny as well. Thus, she has used intertextuality two ways here—to index a shared repertoire of texts, then using these texts to accomplish positive facework toward Meredith by finding parallels in her orientation to the text to admirable characteristics in her friend. It is the latter piece of intertextual engagement that is necessarily absent when like is used. Thus, to like is to make intertextual reference both to the now widely recognized practice of providing quick online positive feedback and the familiar social act of expressing approval, but liking may carry the interactional risk of being a missed opportunity for intertextually accomplishing facework. Another practice that also offers a potentially low facework return is the act of being one of dozens of friends wishing someone a simple "Happy Birthday" on Facebook.

What "Happy Birthday" Means on Facebook

As users of the site well know, Facebook sends reminders when a friend is celebrating his or her birthday, thus potentially diminishing the significance of the act of remembering friends' birthdays. The act of remembering is an act of friendship because it is an opportunity to anoint positive face, but also because it requires an effort on a friend's part (precisely because it presents a negative face threat when the friend whose birthday it is expects this effort). We begin by considering one of the joke examples.

Presented as figure 8.8, a joke interaction from Petri's blog entry presents "You" wishing your friend Carl a happy birthday by means of a Facebook post. Like our other joke examples, this example carries the face-threatening possibility to the extreme, demonstrated through such sarcastic comments as "We must be really close friends." However, a recent study found that "over 54% of the interactions between the infrequently interacting user pairs [in their data] can be directly attributed to Facebook's birthday reminder feature" (Viswanath et al. 2009, 1), so it seems possible that this act may be becoming cliché and devoid of much potential for positive facework.

In fact, even as she was writing this section, Trester took a quick break to dip into her email only to find herself being reminded by Facebook that today is the birthday of one of her friends. She dutifully jumped over to that person's wall to come up with some interesting and unique way to say "Happy Birthday," as birthday facework on Facebook seems to now be more about crafting text that includes more than the simple phrase, adorned with expressive punctuation or textual reference to knowledge shared with that member. It is nigh impossible to be the first birthday wisher nowadays and given that each message is sandwiched in between dozens of other "Happy Birthdays," the only way to do positive politeness here indeed seems to involve coming up with an entirely novel or uniquely personal way of issuing this wish.

 You Hey, Carl! Facebook told me it was your birthday! As I was writing, "Happy Birthday!" I looked over our past wall conversations. It turns out that the last time we communicated was last year, when Facebook also told me it was your birthday. We must be really close friends! Happy Birthday, I guess.

9 hours ago · Comment · Like

Carl Who are you?
8 hours ago

 Figure 8.8 Happy Birthday (joke data).

Figure 8.9 Happy Birthday (ethnographic data).

Our next example is taken from a Facebook interaction collected as part of our ethnography focusing on new members to Facebook of the Baby Boomer generation, which considers how they learned to manage their membership on the social networking site. Jill, a Facebook user over the age of fifty, who had been a member less than two years at the time of the data collection, responds to birthday wishes. Although younger users who have been members longer often do something along the lines of a single post on their wall at the end of the day saying simply, "Thank you everyone for the well wishes," Jane responds individually to each poster, a considerable threat to her negative face in being a huge investment of time.

This data highlights a gap between new members' assumptions or impulses as compared to the more frequently observed established norms. Offline a person is usually expected to acknowledge a verbal birthday greeting or a written card individually, but the Facebook community seems to have adopted a norm to lessen the negative face threat that receiving dozens (or even hundreds) of birthday wishes would otherwise cause. Such false expectations about what being a Facebook member requires of someone is one of the reasons older generations may be reluctant to join the site.

Defining and Reacting to FTAs: Returning to Tagging

The seeds of this project were sown when a colleague of ours told us about her mother's tearful reaction to being invited to Facebook. When we tried to understand this emotional response by asking her daughter why her mother felt such a strong reaction, our colleague told us that her mother felt overwhelmed by the perceived demands of having to keep up with so many friends, and her expectations about how this would be accomplished in this context. Moreover, the invitation itself was another threat to her face, since she now felt that she was obligated to respond in some way, and did not want to appear rude by declining the invitation.

Although tears seem an extreme reaction to an invitation to join Facebook, this reaction pointed to something essential about the importance of facework in this context and led us to realize we did not always share an opinion about the realities of navigating the face rituals within the site. As users of Facebook ourselves, we found that one determining factor in how we each oriented to face rituals on the site was owing in large part to when in our lives we began to engage with the site. Trester shared a higher level of awareness of the FTAs inherent to Facebook, which also seemed to be supported in discussion playback sessions that we used to explore some of the thinking about the site's social and interactional norms. These discussions revealed a divide in practices falling along the line of those who used Facebook as part of their high school and college experience and those who did not. Those who are currently twenty-eight to thirty-two years of age now seem to serve as the boundary between two ways of using new media, although a great deal more research must be done to support an age-based explanation of perception of face threats.

To illuminate the room for interpretation that exists, figure 8.10 is a Facebook interaction that we collected that illustrates a negotiation involving a newer practice on the site resulting from the addition of the tagging feature. Mark uses a wall post to announce that he is going to New York and invite his friends there to hang out. In issuing this invitation, he tags the addressees such that not only are these friends directly addressed, but everyone can see everyone else who was included in the message.

Both authors reacted differently to this data. Although Trester found this to be a blatant negative face threat to the tagged parties (in constraining their future courses of action by saddling them with the work of organizing his social plans), not to mention the positive face threat involved for both speaker and hearer for any friends who were not included, West thought this to be an efficient and low-stakes way for Mark to contact friends and inform them of his visit—one that somewhat elegantly minimally threatened negative face for not constraining future courses of action by not obligating anyone to respond.

Mark
Attention NYCple: please kindly consider hanging out with me next weekend. Then do it. [List of tagged names] [List of non-tagged names]
February 12 at 9:59pm • Like • Comment

> Friend 1 *Asks when Mark will be there, and says he has "dibs" on [List of names] but tells Mark he can hang out with them too.*
> February 12 at 10:05pm • Like

> Mark Hey no dibsies! I'll get there Friday evening and leave earlyish Monday. Maybe we should find somewhere easy to get to Friday night and try to make everyone come to us.
> February 12 at 10:09pm • Like

> Friend 2 Word
> February 12 at 10:12pm • Like

> Friend 3 Yes.
> February 13 at 12:02am • Like

> Friend 4 Mark number number number number # # number # ##
> February 13 at 4:45am • Like

> Friend 5 im in, anytime anywhere
> February 13 at 1:28pm • Like

■ Figure 8.10 Coming to New York (ethnographic data).

We may begin by considering how Mark's invitation is different from an invitation issued in another medium, such as a mass email message. Using a Facebook post reflects a choice on his part to issue his invitation in a more public way, which some may perceive as entailing less of an obligation to respond (as opposed to being invited by email, phone, or text, which might make one feel more directly put on the spot), thus possibly mitigating the negative FTA toward the invitees. Conversely, issuing the invitation in this way might be perceived as more public than an email message. And by employing the tagging feature rather than using a message or simply posting this on his wall, Mark may be perceived as inviting a degree of public scrutiny on this invitation, including who was invited and how those who have been invited choose to respond or whether they respond at all.

Mark pads the FTA by his linguistic choices, for example using "NYCple" as a playful term for people living in New York, and its creative and colloquial sense makes the request informal. Moreover, he also plays with mixing registers in his post, using "Attention," which is a more formal and even institutional lexical choice, with "NYCple," and then returning to formal register with "please, kindly consider," thus framing the post as a request. Humor is suggested in the command that immediately follows the formal, hyper-polite language: "then do it." Given that Mark is in his mid-twenties and a longtime user of Facebook, the creativity of the language and the odd appearance of a formal register on Facebook suggests a casualness about the invitation. He has framed his post as a lighthearted request, padding both the threat to his positive face (and the tagged friends' negative faces) in case no one accepted.

Mark's initial request to hang out is (on the surface quite face threateningly) immediately countered by Friend 1, who reveals that he is also going to New York then and calls dibs on the right to hang out with several of the friends that Mark had listed. To further his prior claim, Friend 1 gives Mark permission "to join," usurping the position of being the inviter and the reason for the gathering—which, if communicated with malice, would be a definite face threat to Mark, who has been publicly put in a less important position. However, Mark playfully negates the face threat by denying Friend 1's right to make such a conversational move ("no dibsies!") and counters with a more specific plan for the event he is proposing: "Maybe we should find somewhere easy to get to on Friday night and make everyone come to us." He playfully indexes his shared rights to claims on his friends by casting them as audience to his conversation with Friend 1 about what they can make them do, thus putting them on equal footing and creating a we—accomplishing positive facework to them as a pair and building solidarity through intertextuality and humor.

Although Mark's response has upped the ante in terms of face threats (from a request or invitation to hang out to talk of "making" the friends come), several friends in succession show an affirmative response, signaling that they have likely interpreted this in jest. Interestingly, each friend finds a unique way to express that they are amenable, as was observed in the variant happy birthday wishes: Friend 2 writes "word" (a very colloquial way of signaling agreement), Friend 3 writes, "yes," Friend 4 gives his phone number (in a way that will presumably not be recognized by a computer spammer), and Friend 5 says, "im in."

The invitation may be said to have been ultimately successful because several friends do respond in the affirmative about hanging out with Mark but the exact details of where and when and who are not present, so they must have been negotiated in another medium (if at all). We may also observe that not everyone who was invited was tagged, nor did all of those who were tagged respond. It may be argued that Mark's invitation does not seem to have been read as a negative face threat to those invited, since they did not feel obligated to respond. Or it is possible that those who could hang out with Mark wanted to say so publicly to do positive facework toward Mark, but those who would not be able to chose to respond in a more private way to avoid a possible threat to Mark's positive face.

Beginning and ending our discussion with the negotiation of norms surrounding this newer feature, we wish to show how Facebook provides a new terrain for mapping media ideologies, "beliefs about how a medium communicates and structures communication," paying attention to what Gershon calls the second-order information that tells us how this message should be interpreted, what a user interprets this message to mean because of how it was communicated (2010, 19). Every interaction on Facebook can itself be a seen as a site of ongoing negotiation, because the creation of these norms and practices is ongoing and emergent.

Conclusions

We draw from an ethnographic exploration of how members of this online space linguistically accomplish facework through practices of friending, posting, and replying, as well as rituals such as issuing invitations and wishing happy birthday, which we characterize as intertextual. Thus, linking intertextuality to the concept of face can provide a new means for understanding some of the site's central organizing practices.

Although there are recognizable norms and expectations on Facebook—revealed by the fact that we can laugh at situations that overtly violate them—members may differ in their understanding of what is actually face threatening and are creative in how they linguistically navigate the possible FTAs that they do recognize. By looking first at purposely constructed humorous interactions flouting the expectations surrounding face, and then at actual interactions driven by these expectations, we hope to have shown how speakers maneuver social demands in these media and how users' linguistic behaviors reflect their awareness of the obligations surrounding face in this context. We have suggested that the need to present something for others to acknowledge seems to be the driving impulse for many posts on the site (as evidenced both in the content of the posts and in the Facebook group discussed earlier that voices frustration with friends who fail to give this acknowledgment), and that both the poster and the potential respondents seem to be expected to do some intertextual work to tie texts together on the site.

The social practices that occur on Facebook, and indeed in any online medium, according to Baym (2006) are more complicated than nonmediated interactions, since they lack facial, body, and prosodic cues; thus we have followed the advice and example of Baym, Androutsopoulous, Georgakopoulou, some of the major figures in CMC research, and grounded our study and explanation of the data in an ethnographic study of the site. This has enabled us to bolster our claims about Facebook exchanges in evidence outside the individual excerpts we present above.

ACKNOWLEDGMENTS
We thank the participants in our study and audience members of our workshop at GURT 2011 for their input and feedback. In addition, we greatly appreciate the careful reading of our chapter and comments and suggestions that we received from Deborah Tannen.

REFERENCES

Androutsopoulos, Jannis. 2006. Introduction: Sociolinguistics and computer-mediated communication. Special issue, *Journal of Sociolinguistics* 10, no. 4:419–38.

Bakhtin, Mikhail. 1981. *The dialogic imagination: Four essays.* eds. Michael Holquist and Caryl Emerson. Trans. Michael Holquist. Austin: University of Texas Press.

———. 1984. *Problems of Dostoevsky's poetics.* Ed. and trans. Caryl Emerson. Minneapolis: University of Minnesota Press.

———. 1986. The problem of speech genres. In *Speech genres and other late essays,* eds. Caryl Emerson and Michael Holquist, trans. Vern W. McGee, 60–102. Austin: University of Texas Press.

Barash, Vladimir, Nicolas Ducheneaut, Ellen Isaacs, and Victoria Bellotti. 2010. Faceplant: Impression (mis)management in Facebook status updates. In *Proceedings of the Fourth International AAAI Conference on Weblogs and Social Media,* 207–10. Menlo Park, CA: AAAI. www.aaai.org/ocs/index .php/ICWSM/ICWSM10/paper/view/1465.

Bauman, Richard, and Charles L. Briggs. 1990. Poetics and performance as critical perspectives on language and social life. *Annual Review of Anthropology* 19:59–88.

Baym, Nancy K. 2006. The performance of humor in computer-mediated communication. *Journal of Computer-Mediated Communication* 1, no. 2, article 5. jcmc.indiana.edu/vol1/issue2/baym.html.

Becker, A. L. 1994. Repetition and otherness: An essay. In *Repetition in discourse,* vol. 2, ed. Barbara Johnstone, 162–75. Norwood, NJ: Ablex.

Brown, Penelope, and Stephen Levinson. [1978] 1987. *Politeness: Some universals in language usage.* Cambridge: Cambridge University Press.

Bury, Rhiannon. 2005. *Cyberspaces of their own: Female fandoms online.* New York: Peter Lang.

Chafe, Wallace. 1994. *Discourse, consciousness and time: The flow and displacement of conscious experience in speaking and writing.* Chicago: University of Chicago Press.

Dresner, Eli, and Susan Herring. 2010. Functions of the non-verbal in CMC: Emoticons and illocutionary force. *Communication Theory* 20:249–69.

Georgakopoulou, Alexandra. 2006. Postscript: Computer-mediated communication in sociolinguistics. *Journal of Sociolinguistics* 10, no. 4:548–57.

Gershon, Ilana. 2010. *The breakup 2.0: Disconnecting over new media.* Ithaca, NY: Cornell University Press.

Goffman, Erving. 1955. On face-work: An analysis of ritual elements in social interaction. *Psychiatry: Journal of Interpersonal Relations* 18, no. 3:213–31.

———. 1959. *The presentation of self in everyday life.* New York: Anchor Books.

Graham, Sage. 2007. Disagreeing to agree: Conflict, (im)politeness and identity in a computer-mediated community. *Journal of Pragmatics* 39:742–59.

Gumperz, John J. 1982. *Discourse strategies.* New York: Cambridge University Press.

Kozinets, Robert V. 2009. *Netnography: Doing ethnographic research online.* Los Angeles and London: Sage.

Kristeva, Julia. 1980. *Desire in language: A semiotic approach to literature and art.* Ed. Léon Roudiez. Trans. Thomas Gora, Alice Jardine, and Léon Roudiez. New York: Columbia University Press.

Lakoff, Robin. 1973. The logic of politeness; or, minding your p's and q's. In *Papers from the Ninth Regional Meeting of the Chicago Linguistics Society,* eds. Claudia Corum, T. Cedric Smith-Stark, and Ann Weiser, 292–305. Chicago: Chicago Linguistics Society.

Morand, David A., and Rosalie J. Ocker. 2002. Politeness theory and computer-mediated communication: A sociolinguistic approach to analyzing relational messages. *Proceedings of the 36th Hawaii International Conference on System Sciences,* ed. Ralph Sprague. doi:10.1109/HICSS.2003.1173660.

Norrick, Neal R. 1989. Intertextuality in humor. *Humor* 2, no. 2:117–39.

Papacharissi, Zizi. 2009. The virtual geographies of social networks: A comparative analysis of Facebook, LinkedIn and ASmallWorld. *New Media and Society* 11, nos. 1 and 2:199–220.

Petri, Alexandra. 2011. What we really mean when we post on Facebook. *Washington Post,* January 31. voices.washingtonpost.com/compost/2011/01/what_we_really_mean_when_we_po.html.

Sarangi, Srikant, and Celia Roberts, eds. 1999. *Talk, work, and institutional order: Discourse in medical, mediation and management settings.* Berlin: Mouton de Gruyter.

Simmons, Timmothy. 1994. Politeness theory in computer mediated communication: Face threatening acts in a "faceless" medium. MA thesis, Aston University.

Tannen, Deborah. 2005. *Conversational style: Analyzing talk among friends.* Rev. ed. New York: Oxford University Press.

Trester, Anna Marie. 2012. Framing entextualization: Intertextuality as an interactional (improvisational) resource. *Language in Society.* 41, no. 2:237–58.

Viswanath, Bimal, Alan Mislove, Cha Meeyong, and Krishna P. Gummadi. 2009. On the evolution of user interaction on Facebook. In *Proceedings of the 2nd ACM SIGCOMM Workshop on Social Networks,* eds. John Crowcroft and Balachander Krishnamurthy. New York: ACM Press.

9

Mock Performatives in Online Discussion Boards
Toward a Discourse-Pragmatic Model of Computer-Mediated Communication

TUIJA VIRTANEN
Åbo Akademi University

Introduction

PERFORMATIVES (Austin 1962) have received little attention in online environments. Yet the formal performative marker "hereby" appears on personal websites, discussion boards, and, to some extent, blogs—in contexts of informal computer-mediated communication (CMC). This chapter accounts for the motivations and communicative success of explicit performatives including the formal marker, by investigating their forms and discourse-pragmatic functions in data from discussion boards on beauty and fashion. For example, a user expressing regret over the sums of money that she has recently spent on makeup gets the response "I hereby grant you permission to blow cash on how you look." More specifically, this chapter contributes to the study of text-based CMC by proposing two terms, "mock performative" and "discourse transformer," and devising a discourse-pragmatic model for the analysis of online performativity.

Unlike performativity, the notion of performance—users performing social action through discourse—has been the subject of several studies, concerning, for instance, "cyberplay" (Danet 2001), the social processes of "doing genre" online (Giltrow in press), online narrativity (Georgakopoulou in press), and performance through the enactment of stereotyped offline scripts (Herring 2000). Rather than performance at large—the making of the action performed through discourse—this chapter deals with the phenomenon of performativity in text-based CMC—the doing of an action by typing it in, its self-referential enactment in a virtual reality (for a discussion of the making and doing of personal narrative, see Peterson and Langellier 2006).

Overview
The chapter explores explicit performatives incorporating the marker "hereby" in text-based CMC, using data from US-based discussion boards on beauty and fashion. These performatives have their roots in institutional discourse but are put to use in informal conversations between interlocutors of equal status who participate in the interaction of their own free will. I propose the term "mock performative" for such instances as

that described above. Although mock performatives may appear both offline and on-line, their use in text-based CMC is of particular interest to linguists because (1) they allow users to "do things with words," in the Austinian sense, solely by typing in the performative; (2) they are noncancelable; and (3) they bring change to a virtual reality under construction. Mock performatives evoke Austin's notion of etiolation, a shifting or weakening of one or more aspects of the performative speech act (such as authority or address) without turning the speech act into a nonact. CMC-sensitive approaches to performatives grapple with the construction of multiple worlds, real and virtual, and thus adapt to an open-ended pluralism of what there may be.

Another important impetus for the study of mock performatives in CMC is pro-vided by their ability to initiate joint play sequences in the discussion thread. I pro-pose the term "discourse transformer" to characterize the work that mock performatives do in signaling a shift to a play mode. Because of their status as dis-course transformers, the dispreferred response to mock performatives is textual si-lence. In these forums users generally express alignment to license the play mode. They do so by juggling institutional scripts that are to be shared. Furthermore, the playfulness of mock performatives allows users to assume authority over other par-ticipants. Mock performatives usually appear as responses to previous contributions.

A discourse-pragmatic model is devised to capture the effects of the mock per-formatives in the forums. The model draws parallels between the linguistic domains of (1) form, content, and style; (2) discourse functions; (3) the situated micromprag-matics; and (4) the sociocultural macropragmatics. The impact of mock performa-tives on each of them is examined through the lenses of five major discourse-pragmatic phenomena: (1) structuring; (2) highlighting; (3) constructing; (4) linking; and (5) authenticating. The model is proposed as a point of departure for the study of performativity in text-based CMC.

After the literature review, I present the methods and materials of the study. When mock performatives are introduced, the concern is with their form, content, and stylistic fit in the online discussions. Joint juggling of scripts originating in court-room discourse and awards ceremonies, focusing on the participant roles involved in their playful use; the function of mock performatives as discourse transformers; and mock performatives in terms of five discourse-pragmatic phenomena, resulting in a model of computer-mediated discourse, complete the chapter.

Literature Review

Searle defines performative utterances as follows:

> [S]ome illocutionary acts can be performed by uttering a sentence containing an expression that names the type of speech act, as in for example, "I order you to leave the room." These utterances, and only these, are correctly described as performative utterances. On my usage, the only performatives are what Austin called "explicit performatives." Thus, though every utterance is indeed a *performance,* only a very restricted class are *performatives.* (1989, 536)

Explicit performatives can incorporate the formal marker "hereby,"—for example, the meeting is (hereby) adjourned, and I (hereby) apologize. Searle paraphrases the performative marker as "by-this-here-very-utterance," "here" being the self-referential part and "by" the executive part (1989, 552). The verb is in the dramatic present: its utterance is simultaneous with the act being performed. The source of authority is typically institutionalized, as in the first example, creating the extralinguistic fact of an adjournment. But language itself is an institution that empowers people to perform linguistic declarations, such as the apology of the second example, creating a linguistic fact (Searle 1989).

The explicit performatives under investigation forcefully evoke Austin's (1962) notion of etiolation as a fundamental dimension of language use, albeit not in focus in his own work. Etiolation refers to the shifting or weakening of one or several aspects of individual speech acts without turning the speech act into a nonact. Austin's examples include the shifting of speech-act authority in quotation, that of address in soliloquy, and both of them in acting; further, in joking, etiolation affects sense, and in fiction, reference (Austin 1962, 22; Sbisà 2007, 469). It is important to note that the speech act thus etiolated will still be a speech act in its own right. The use of performatives in computer-mediated discourse (CMD) strongly suggests a need for developing performative theory to incorporate fully "the doctrine of the *etiolations* of language" (Austin 1962, 22)—or, in Sbisà's terms, "ontological pluralism" (put simply, the open-ended pluralism of what there may be [2007, 471])—in order to come to grips with the existence of several different (virtual) realities to which users adapt and which they help construct and alter through CMC. Such virtual realities are reminiscent of text worlds and universes of discourse, which are regularly construed by interlocutors for the purposes of textual interpretability (for these notions, see Enkvist 1989). The two main characteristics of performativity in text-based CMC—doing things by typing them in, and constructing virtual realities through them—warrant investigations of this classic pragmatic phenomenon in a new light. Online performatives, too, are noncancelable, and they bring change to the virtual world under construction (and sometimes also to participants' so-called real worlds).

Studies of online performativity include investigations of particular speech acts, such as apologies in email (Harrison and Allton in press), which have real-life force. Further, the CMC-specific phenomenon of emoting has been subject to early study (on emotes, see Cherny 1995; Kolko 1995; Werry 1996; on the differences between emotes and an expanding category of performative predications, see Herring in press). Actions in a virtual world can be performed by typing in constructions that refer to the user's online character in the third person, such as "*wipes away a tear*" in example 2, below. The increasing popularity of such typographically marked constructions across modes of text-based CMC, including texting in mobile phones, raises the issue of the limits of the traditional concept of performative utterance. Although they are beyond the scope of this chapter, emotes are touched upon when they accompany explicit performatives, which appear in the messages as "said," not as "emoted" (for further discussion, see Virtanen in press).

The inferencing work that is necessary for interlocutors to be able to communicate has been approached, for instance, through reference to concepts such as "frames" (Minsky 1975) and "scripts" (Schank and Abelson 1977). Although these and related terms have many uses in the literature, a simple example might be the kinds of entities and steps that can be taken for granted in a given cultural context by mentioning the word "bus." Buses are expected to have drivers and passengers, a large number of seats, timetables, and many other characteristics that can be subsumed under the umbrella of a "bus frame." Scripts are dynamic and involve temporal succession, so a "bus script" could include the culture-specific steps of, say, consulting the timetable, waiting for the bus at a bus stop, getting on the bus when it arrives, paying the fare, finding a seat, and getting off at another stop—perhaps through the back door. When a particular frame or script is activated in discourse, it will not be necessary to explain the commonplaces related to them. Shared frames and scripts thus function as shorthand in communication. But when interlocutors' tacit assumptions do not conform with particular stereotyped frames and scripts, there is the risk of misunderstanding. Tannen (1979) defines frames and scripts as "structures of expectation." In the analysis that follows, the term "script" is used to refer to the dynamic, stereotyped sequences of actions and events that are activated through performatives.

Also of interest is Goffman's (1974) notion of framing, referring to interlocutors signaling what they do in conversation, such as joking. This, in turn, invites expressions of alignment, by which interlocutors negotiate situated interpersonal relationships (Goffman 1981). Tannen (1993a) views this kind of interaction-oriented framing in terms of people's metamessages about what is going on in the talk. Exploring interactive frames of interpretation in the activities that interlocutors think they are engaged in, Tannen and Wallat (1987) devise an analytic framework for integrating this sense of the notion with an understanding of frames as structures of expectation (these latter being concomitant, for instance, with Minskyan knowledge frames). The performatives under investigation serve as discourse transformers by signaling shifts to a play mode (play frame) in the interaction. In so doing, they trigger responses of resistance to or acceptance of the act, which manifest same-script or other-script discourse. In her analysis of cyberplay, Danet (2001) makes a distinction between play and playfulness: whereas users occasionally engage in virtual play (such as a virtual performance of a birthday party, or of *Hamlet*), playfulness is an inherent characteristic of CMC of many kinds. The performatives index playfulness, and they succeed in initiating play sequences in the interaction when other users align with the activated play mode.

Methods and Materials

To detect explicit performatives in informal text-based CMC, in September 2006 searches were conducted for the keyword "hereby" in all messages across the publicly available English-language discussion boards on a US-based website, on which participants review beauty products and discuss makeup and fashion. The members were predominantly females of all ages, and mainly located in the United States, Canada, United Kingdom, and Australia. Instances of the word "hereby" were found in twenty-nine asynchronous threads in five different discussion boards. The data were not collected for quantitative purposes; instead, the threads were studied using discourse-analytic methods.

The examples are anonymized as concerns (1) product placement, (2) temporal pointers, and (3) nicknames. The temporal distance between the actual times of the posts has been kept intact to show their chronology in a threading system that occasionally deviates from temporal sequentiality. Nicknames are replaced by common female first names and numbered consecutively for ease of reference. The pace of communication is at times very rapid, and users type their messages directly on the subject line rather than in the message box provided; hence, the abbreviation "r/o" in example 4, below, is an instruction to read on in the message box.

Mock Performatives

The explicit hereby performatives in the corpus can be labeled mock performatives. Users playfully adopt the role of a powerful figure in religious, royal, judicial, or managerial scripts, which are expected to be familiar to the members of the virtual community. In other instances mock performatives carry allusions to institutional authorities in stereotyped situations such as awarding prizes and certificates, crowning beauty queens, giving permission, or making declarations of consequence. Consider the following examples:

I hereby	sentence you to . . .
	arrest you for . . .
	recruit you to . . .
	appoint you to . . .
	crown you . . .
	award you . . .
	grant you permission to . . .
	declare you . . .
I hereby	declare that . . .
You are hereby	excommunicated
	sentenced to a lifetime of . . .
	banished from this kingdom

The mock performatives are anchored to identifiable stereotyped scripts with the formal beginning "I hereby," followed by a verb in the dramatic present naming the action that is thus performed. The passive is less usual. The verb can be institutionalized or an ordinary, everyday verb. Adverbials such as "officially" or "solemnly" are sometimes used to reinforce the mock performative when the verb is not part of the stereotype, as in "I hereby and officially transfer my ice cream and hot fudge allowance to you." Users react to off-topic discussion (conveniently abbreviated OT), and this example, from a fragrance board, is a playful response to someone who cheekily suggests ice cream and hot fudge as discussion topics.

The conspicuous style shift from informal to formal at the outset of the explicit performative is immediately followed by another style shift in the verb phrase, or in the subsequent cotext, of the performative construction. This second shift from formal to informal serves to adjust the mock performative to the style of the discussion in order to give it an optimal stylistic fit.

Users occasionally extend authority over themselves, as in "I am hereby banned from purchasing any more of the following: r/o" (see Virtanen in press). However, most of the mock performatives in the forums involve authority over other interlocutors.

Mock performatives can be directed to a particular interlocutor ("you"), in the presence of a secondary audience, as in examples 1, 2, and 3, below, or jointly to all users of the virtual community at hand, as in example 4. Let us explore in more detail some of the scripts mediated by mock performatives.

Juggling Scripts

Many of the mock performatives found in the data are grounded in a courtroom script. Example 1 illustrates the activation of such scripts in a makeup board. In line 3, the user Mary1 first assumes the role of the accused ("guilty as charged"), only to turn into a judge after another participant, Linda3, appears on the scene to plead guilty through alignment: "me tooo." The discourse marker "well" (see, for example, Jucker 1993) signals disruption in the construction of the appropriate virtual felicity conditions, while the contingency of the courtroom script being enacted is assured by another explicit performative: "you are hereby sentenced to . . ." The hierarchy of roles is thereafter maintained, even as the user sentenced to "a lifetime of addiction, plus time already served," Linda3, is transformed into a negotiator successfully striking a deal with Mary1.

Example 1

Couldn't you use the [Brand] lip stains on your cheeks as well? Mary1 1:44 PM
- ohh it's your blush addiction!! Patricia2 1:45 PM
- guilty as charged Mary1 1:51 PM
   o me tooo. Linda3 1:52 PM
      ▪ well, you are **hereby** sentenced to a lifetime of addiction, plus time already served Mary1 1:53 PM
         ▪ I'll take it . . . as long as I get my blush too! heh. Linda3 1:56 PM
            • deal Mary1 1:57 PM

The juggling of scripts indexes playfulness and creativity; yet the scripts activated cannot be considered brand new. The institutional or official character of the performative is crucial, its recognition thus demanding some degree of stereotyping. The roles adopted involve absolute or great power, and high agentivity. But this example shows that the opposite can sometimes be true: witness the affected role of the accused pleading guilty, which imbues other users with authority. Authority is crucial, irrespective of whether it is overt, covert, assumed, or assigned to another user. Apart from the primary roles of the agent and the affected, there are also audience responses to the explicit performatives such as applause, laughter, expressions of agreement, and seconding of motions. Moreover, there are some signs of conventionalization in audience response, including "ita" ("I totally agree"); "2nd" ("I second the motion").

Another popular script that is associated on these discussion boards with mock performatives is an award-ceremony script. Hence, in line 3 in example 2, below, Elizabeth5 assumes the authority of awarding Barbara4 the "Master Makeup Artist's certificate" through a mock performative, motivating the decision by a brief evaluation of Barbara4's "smokey eye tutorial" including the picture that she has posted in the forum. Three responses appear immediately. Jennifer6 types in "agreed!" and Maria7 emotes applause (as shown in the last line). The receiver of the certificate, Barbara4, reacts twice, first with a textual display of great emotion and gratefulness ("awww. that is soooo sweeeet!"), reinforced by the stereotyped wiping away of a tear—enacted by typing what looks like an emote, but would, in Herring's (in press) terms, be a performative predication—a smiley, and another emote (or performative predication), this time an expository noun: "*tears of joy*." Barbara4 adopts another voice in a parody of award winners' speeches in a televised gala for her second response, made two minutes later. The bestower of the award, Elizabeth5, types in laughter, in capital letters for high intensity.

Example 2

Alright . . . smokey eye tutorial . . . PIC HEAVY!!! Barbara4 12:24 AM
   o [many responses, several with side sequences]
   o I **hereby** award you the *Master MA* certificate! That is excellently done and shown! Elizabeth5 12:30 AM
      ■ agreed! Jennifer6 12:31 AM
      ■ awww. that is soooo sweeeet! *wipes away a tear* :) *tears of joy* Barbara4 12:31 AM
         ■ *Oh my goodness! this is such an honor to recieve this award. I would like to thank all those little people that i had to step on to get to this place . . . .and i would like to thank my producers, and . . . .* Barbara4 12:33 AM
            • LOL Elizabeth5 12:39 AM
               ■ **applauds** Maria7 12:31 AM

Mock performatives allow users to assume authority playfully. Responses vary from acceptance to resistance. The activated script can be negotiated, and users tend to engage in joint play by producing same-script or other-script discourse. A discussion of the ability of mock performatives to initiate play sequences in the interaction is thus in order.

Mock Performatives as Discourse Transformers

The mock performatives under investigation predominantly function as discourse transformers, switching the generally playful discussion of topics related to beauty and fashion into an explicit play mode (play frame). Interlocutors readily engage in the mediated script by making (1) a verbal acknowledgment, (2) another same-script or other-script performative, (3) an emote (or performative predication), or (4) a combination of an emote or performative predication and another explicit performative. The dispreferred response is silence, as in example 3 from the middle of a long discussion of fashion products that users find (un)attractive. By pursuing the discussion along previous lines, the interlocutors textually ignore the discourse transformer typed in by Carol9. Textual silence, too, may be revelatory of the effects of a particular performative on a virtual world under construction. Yet its dispreferred nature at this point lies in the fact that other users do not explicitly opt for a joint play sequence at the invitation conveyed by the mock performative. This particular mock performative may, however, still function in the interaction as a playful expression of disagreement. Moreover, this example illustrates the use of emoting to construct virtual felicity conditions: the user adopting the role of a king chooses to reinforce the activated script by waving the scepter.

Example 3

I love my [Brand] Donna8 9:30 PM
  • I **hereby** banish you from this kingdom!!!!!!!!!!! *waves septer* Carol9 9:31 PM

Even when met with textual silence, performative acts are noncancelable once they have been typed in, except perhaps by the same user repairing the contribution (see the discussions in Cherny 1995; Kolko 1995; see also Herring 2001). Yet in these forums the play mode triggered by the mock performative needs to be licensed by the virtual community for joint construction of the virtual world thus created or altered. Otherwise the mock performative remains an act of byplay, in a similar fashion as that of much of the inherently playful discourse emerging in CMC contexts, including emoting.

Example 4 illustrates a play sequence culminating the discussion. The discourse transforming mock performative, starting from line five, is prefaced by "ok," which indicates an attempt to conclude the discussion. The wide repertoire of scripts manifest in the series of responses to this mock performative might be hypothesized to be evoked by the ritual underspecification of a mere declaration (as compared to the ritualistically richer acts of sentencing users to a particular punishment, bestowing awards on them, and banishing them from a virtual kingdom). Two abbreviations appear in the example: "SO," on the first line, refers to "significant other"; "r/o" is discussed above.

Example 4

On a break with SO—I deserve a mini-haul . . . . right?? ;-) Margaret10 9:43 PM
  • [a series of short responses expressing empathy, between 9:43–9:49 PM]
  • The very best medicine there is! Who needs men when there's makeup? :P Dorothy11 9:47 PM
    o Ok. I, Lisa12, **hereby** do declare that any and all problems, breakups, breaks, r/o arguments, or any other "situations" with any SO be it man or woman, totally warrant, deserve, and indeed require splurges, hauls and indulgences of any kind. Lisa12 9:51 PM
      ▪ You are CORRECT! :) Nancy13 10:21 PM
      ▪ SO HELP ME GOD. Karen14 10:07 PM
      ▪ here, here! :D Betty15 9:53 PM
      ▪ I second the motion! Helen16 9:52 PM
        ▪ thirded. Motion passes. Sandra17 9:55 PM

To sum up, mock performatives serve to transform the discourse into a play mode, inviting user alignments. Play sequences manifest same-script or other-script discourse. When met with textual silence, mock performatives still contribute to the playfulness of the interaction as instances of byplay. Their effects can be negotiated, discussed, or textually ignored, but the performative act itself cannot be denied: the change that mock performatives bring to virtual reality takes place simply when users type them in.

Exploring Mock Performatives across Linguistic Domains toward a Discourse-Pragmatic Model

To devise a CMC-sensitive model of performativity, this section explores the impact of mock performatives across linguistic domains by investigating their contributions to five different discourse-pragmatic phenomena: (1) structuring, (2) highlighting, (3) constructing, (4) linking, and (5) authenticating. The linguistic domains considered relate to (1) the form, content, and style of the mock performatives; (2) their discourse functions; contributions to (3) the situational micropragmatics; and to (4) the sociocultural macropragmatics of the interaction.

Mock performatives adopt a particular shape and predominantly appear in the active voice. They contribute to topic management, and discourse *structuring* at large, by providing playful responses to previous contributions. Most importantly, however, the mock performatives under attention function as discourse transformers: they indicate a shift into a play mode, which may be sustained by other users over a sequence of contributions (see examples 2 and 4). One instance of the performative marker "hereby" suffices per play sequence. Frequent audience responses to mock performatives may turn into abbreviations (ita; 2nd). In terms of micropragmatics, mock performatives serve mitigation and thus help realize the conventionalized politeness structure of the interaction (see examples 1 and 3). As concerns macropragmatics, mock performatives may contribute to ritualization within a particular virtual community.

Mock performatives function in the service of *highlighting*. The formal performative construction deviates from the structural iconicity of the default informal interaction, even though a sequence of performatives may bring local parallelism into the text. Moreover, mock performatives can initiate the culmination of the discussion, thus also contributing to the creation of a "peak profile" in the discourse through the play sequence (Longacre 1983). This is the case in example 4. In pragmatic terms, mock performatives add to the expression of involvement and affect, and ultimately contribute to bonding within the virtual community. Switching into a play mode allows users to take time off from their main concerns, the discussion of beauty and fashion, without abandoning them altogether (there is a separate forum for OT discussions). Like the rest of the interaction included in the data, the play sequences appear to be socially gratifying as they display feelings and attitudes in the text (see the discussion of female CMC in Herring 2003). However, these mock performatives allow for a shared sense of unpredictability concerning the effects of play on the virtual reality at hand. The negotiation of this reality through interlocutors' responses serves to join them into what Beeman calls "the performance loop," joint participation in "reinforced feedback," whereby also "the actions of the performer are . . . affected and changed" (2010, 121).

Mock performatives contribute to the task of *constructing* entities and states of affairs for virtual worlds. They allow for high agentivity in the semantic roles adopted by users. The text worlds built by interlocutors contribute to the creation and alteration, through discourse, of shared virtual realities. Mock performatives are also partial to identity construction through the projection of user personae, as well as the construction of group identity for the virtual community.

The ritualistic beginning of mock performatives—generally consisting of a first-person reference, the performative marker, and possibly an institutional verb or adverb—*links* it to a recognizable prototype. And the playful intertextuality invokes stereotyped scripts. In micropragmatic terms, mock performatives constitute the main means for participants to adopt roles of great authority in the interaction, and imbue others with concomitant roles through their audience design (usually roles of less power than themselves). In macropragmatic terms, mock performatives serve as metapragmatic links, facilitating mock institutionalization through the (inter)mediation of stereotyped scripts. The juggling of scripts manifests users' metapragmatic awareness of linguistic variation, their assumptions about what is shared by interlocutors in terms of cultural knowledge, and a tolerance for flexibility in the interpretation of the participant roles involved, resulting in same-script and other-script responses within play sequences.

Finally, mock performatives contribute to the *authentication* work that interlocutors engage in through the recontextualization process. The stylistic fit of the construction is assured through style shifting: first a switch from informal to formal style and then back again to informal discourse, which is the default in the forums. Mock performatives involve authentication in discourse, allowing interlocutors to recognize the mediated institutionalized stereotype. But they also involve de-authentication, signaling detachment from such a context and freeing the users from the full implications of the official or institutionalized discourse. This process, in turn, constitutes an avenue to authenticity of a new kind, creating CMD that is situated, unique, personal and in some sense "genuine" for the interlocutors (Gill 2008, in press). Thus, a balance between the stereotype and its de-authentication is critical to a successful recontextualization.

Conclusion

This chapter explores explicit performatives incorporating the marker "hereby" in informal CMD by investigating their forms and discourse-pragmatic functions in data from online discussion boards on beauty and fashion. Two terms are coined to explain their use in text-based CMC: the performative constructions under investigation were labeled mock performatives, and their function of shifting the discourse into a play mode motivated their characterization as discourse transformers. Although uptake can be assumed to be regular due to the persistence of the written record (unlike in the Austinian example, in which a warning shouted to others in a gale may not be heard), responses to mock performatives are investigated to understand their preferred and dispreferred nature and the character of the play sequence thus created. The effects of mock performatives are analyzed in terms of a discourse-pragmatic model. The model is based on the identification of five discourse-pragmatic phenomena which run across the linguistic domains of (1) form, content, and style; (2) discourse; (3) micropragmatics; and (4) macropragmatics. These five discourse-pragmatic phenomena are (1) structuring, (2) highlighting, (3) constructing, (4) linking, and (5) authenticating. In order to come to grips with multiple realities, performative theory needs to incorporate the kinds of discourse-pragmatic work that users do by typing mock performatives into their texts. The two concepts this chapter proposes, mock performative and discourse transformer, as well as the discourse-pragmatic model, may contribute to this end.

ACKNOWLEDGMENTS

I am grateful to Loukia Lindholm for collecting the data for this study. Due thanks also go to the editors of the volume for constructive and insightful comments, as well as to participants of the GURT 2011 conference. I am especially indebted to Susan Herring for useful suggestions and rewarding discussions of performativity in CMC. I have also benefited from personal communication with Martin Gill on authenticity and Yrsa Neuman on ontological pluralism. Needless to say, all errors and shortcomings are my responsibility.

REFERENCES

Austin, John L. 1962. *How to do things with words.* Cambridge, MA: Harvard University Press.

Beeman, William O. 2010. Performance pragmatics, neuroscience and evolution. *Pragmatics and Society* 1, no. 1:118–37.

Cherny, Lynn. 1995. The modal complexity of speech events in a social mud. *Electronic Journal of Communication 5.* www.cios.org.

Danet, Brenda. 2001. *Cyberpl@y: Communicating online.* Oxford: Berg.

Enkvist, Nils Erik. 1989. Connexity, interpretability, universes of discourse, and text worlds. In *Possible worlds in humanities, arts and sciences,* ed. Sture Allén, 162–86. Berlin: de Gruyter.

Georgakopoulou, Alexandra. In press. Narrative analysis and computer-mediated communication. In *Pragmatics of computer-mediated communication,* eds. Susan C. Herring, Dieter Stein, and Tuija Virtanen. Berlin and New York: Mouton de Gruyter.

Gill, Martin. 2008. Authenticity. In *Handbook of pragmatics online,* eds. Jef Verschueren and Jan-Ola Östman. Amsterdam and Philadelphia: John Benjamins. www.benjamins.com/online/hop.

———. In press. Authentication in computer-mediated communication. In *Pragmatics of computer-mediated communication,* eds. Susan C. Herring, Dieter Stein, and Tuija Virtanen. Berlin and New York: Mouton de Gruyter.

Giltrow, Janet. In press. Genre and computer-mediated communication. In *Pragmatics of computer-mediated communication,* eds. Susan C. Herring, Dieter Stein, and Tuija Virtanen. Berlin and New York: Mouton de Gruyter.

Goffman, Erving. 1974. *Frame analysis: An essay on the organization of experience.* New York: Harper and Row.

———. 1981. *Forms of talk.* Philadelphia: University of Pennsylvania Press.

Harrison, Sandra, and Diane Allton. In press. Apologies in email discussions. In *Pragmatics of computer-mediated communication,* eds. Susan C. Herring, Dieter Stein, and Tuija Virtanen. Berlin and New York: Mouton de Gruyter.

Herring, Susan C. 2000. "Doing gender" in the internet. Guest lecture, Växjö University, Sweden, April 10.

———. 2001. Computer-mediated discourse. In *The handbook of discourse analysis,* eds. Deborah Schiffrin, Deborah Tannen, and Heidi Hamilton, 612–34. Oxford: Blackwell.

———. 2003. Gender and power in on-line communication. In *The handbook of language and gender,* eds. Janet Holmes and Miriam Meyerhoff, 222–28. Oxford: Blackwell.

————. In press. Grammar and electronic communication. In *The encyclopedia of applied linguistics,* ed. Carol A. Chapelle. Malden, MA, Oxford, and Chichester: Wiley-Blackwell.

Jucker, Andreas H. 1993. The discourse marker *well:* A relevance-theoretical account. *Journal of Pragmatics* 19, no. 5:435–52.

Kolko, Beth. 1995. Building a world with words: The narrative reality of virtual communities. *Works and Days* 13, nos. 1 and 2:105–26. acorn.grove.iup.edu/en/workdays/toc.html.

Longacre, Robert E. 1983. *The grammar of discourse.* New York: Plenum Press.

Minsky, Marvin. 1975. A framework for representing knowledge. In *The psychology of computer vision,* ed. Patrick Henry Winston, 211–77. New York: McGraw-Hill.

Peterson, Eric E., and Kristin M. Langellier. 2006. The performance turn in narrative studies. *Narrative Inquiry* 16, no. 1:173–80.

Sbisà, Marina. 2007. How to read Austin. *Pragmatics* 17:461–73.

Schank, Roger C., and Robert P. Abelson. 1977. *Scripts, plans, goals, and understanding: An inquiry into human knowledge structures.* Hillsdale, NJ: Lawrence Erlbaum.

Searle, John R. 1989. How performatives work. *Linguistics and Philosophy* 12:535–58.

Tannen, Deborah. 1979. What's in a frame? Surface evidence for underlying expectations. In *New directions in discourse processing,* ed. Roy O. Freedle, 137–81. Norwood, NJ: Ablex. Reprinted in *Framing in discourse,* 14–56. New York and Oxford: Oxford University Press.

————. 1993a. Introduction. In *Framing in discourse,* 3–13. New York and Oxford: Oxford University Press.

————. ed. 1993b. *Framing in discourse.* New York and Oxford: Oxford University Press.

Tannen, Deborah, and Cynthia Wallat. 1987. Interactive frames and knowledge schemas in interaction: Examples from a medical examination/interview. *Social Psychology Quarterly* 50, no. 2:205–16. Reprinted in *Framing in discourse,* 57–76. New York and Oxford: Oxford University Press.

Virtanen, Tuija. In press. Performativity in computer-mediated communication. In *Pragmatics of computer-mediated communication,* eds. Susan C. Herring, Dieter Stein, and Tuija Virtanen. Berlin and New York: Mouton de Gruyter.

Werry, Christopher C. 1996. Linguistic and interactional features of Internet Relay Chat. In *Computer-mediated communication: Linguistic, social and cross-cultural perspectives,* ed. Susan C. Herring, 47–63. Amsterdam and Philadelphia: John Benjamins.

10

Re- and Pre-authoring Experiences in Email Supervision
Creating and Revising Professional Meanings in an Asynchronous Medium

CYNTHIA GORDON AND MELISSA LUKE
Syracuse University

Introduction

THIS ANALYSIS RESULTS from a collaborative, interdisciplinary research project undertaken by a communication scholar (Gordon) and a scholar in counselor education (Luke) to investigate the discourse of email supervisory communication in the context of student internships required as part of counselor education and training. Master's-level students enrolled in counseling programs complete internships at varying sites according to academic program (for instance, school counseling students intern in local schools, whereas mental health counseling students intern in community agencies, hospitals, or residential organizations). In addition to participating in onsite and in-class group experiences, interns also communicate with a supervising professor via a weekly email exchange. In these emails, interns describe their internship experiences, and share and reflect upon their thoughts and feelings regarding these experiences. The purpose of the supervisory exchanges is to track the internship activities and interns' development as counselors, and to facilitate interns' reflectivity, or their ability to critically analyze and consider their own professional performance. In responding to interns' emails, then, supervisors aim to provide opportunities for them to explore and expand their knowledge and skills so that they are better able to meet their professional responsibilities. Email supervision is thus a means of helping supervisees through their internships, but also a way of socializing them into professional identities and practices.

Our interest in email supervision is motivated broadly by two general issues. First, although supervision is a discursive phenomenon and a fundamental part of professional development, there is only a relatively small body of discourse analytic research examining this communication, especially in the context of counseling supervision. Second, although supervision via email is now a common practice, it remains understudied.

Our analysis is specifically motivated by our interest in a phenomenon related to the concept of "authorship," previously identified by Vásquez (2007) in her analysis of face-to-face supervision of language teachers. Analyzing narratives that novice teachers told to their supervisors following a teaching observation, Vásquez found that supervisors at times "destabilized" and "reformulated"—or re-authored—novices' accounts as a means of facilitating development of professional competence and identities. For example, one supervisor reevaluates a novice teacher's perspective on events, likely to facilitate the apprentice's creation of a positive self-image (Vásquez 2007, 664). We found a similar phenomenon in our data.

We develop the concept of re-authorship by drawing on Bakhtin's (1981, 1986) notion of dialogue, and by examining different forms of re-authorship in the asynchronous context of email. We also extend the concept of re-authorship beyond revising narrative discourse, and beyond communication about actual internship behaviors. Our analysis identifies two primary forms of re-authorship—reinforcement and reframing—and one related form, advice giving, which we understand to be pre-authorship, stemming from Bakhtin's perspective on utterances as oriented to both past discourse and anticipated future discourse. Key linguistic devices in these collective processes of co-authorship include uses of adjectives and adverbs, professional jargon, first-person-plural pronouns, repetition, discourse markers, and speech acts, especially praising, agreeing, and encouraging or suggesting. We suggest that re- and pre-authorship together serve as productive means of accomplishing widely recognized supervision goals in the context of email. These goals pertain to socializing internship (counseling) behaviors, professional thought processes, and appropriate supervisory communication behaviors (in this case, email communication behaviors).

In what follows we review previous research in two areas: the discourse analysis of expert-novice interaction and Bakhtinian understandings of authorship. We then introduce our dataset and analytic methods and we turn to our analysis, wherein we delineate and give examples of the three forms of co-authorship we identified, demonstrating how each one functions in the context of supervisory communication, in particular regarding socialization. We show how supervisors *reinforce* (and thereby re- or co-author) supervisees' email communication behaviors (such as their selection of message topic), professional counseling behaviors (such as how they interact with clients), and emotional responses to their internship experiences. We demonstrate how, through reframing, supervisors attempt to reshape and adjust, and in particular expand, interns' understandings of their professional experiences and practices. We suggest that supervisors' advice giving is usefully conceptualized as *pre-authorship,* and serves as a means of directing interns' future professional discourse and behaviors. We conclude by summarizing our findings regarding co-authorship in the context of supervisory email discourse, and discuss their implications in relation to the fields of counseling and supervision, and the discourse analysis of computer-mediated communication (CMC).

Background
Our analysis is grounded in previous discourse analytic work on expert-novice communication and in theorizing related to the notion of authorship. There is a small but rich body of research in discourse analysis examining the details of expert-novice communication in what can be described as supervisory contexts. These include in-

teractions between experienced and novice medical practitioners (Atkinson 1999; Erickson 1999); MA and PhD students and their thesis and research advisors (Chiang 2009; Goodwin 1994; Vehviläinen 2009); and expert and novice teachers, including teaching assistants (Burdelski 2004; Vásquez 2004, 2007; Vásquez and Urzúa 2009; Waite 1992, 1993). These studies focus on a variety of issues, most notably how the asymmetry inherent in such encounters affects the production of speech acts such as assessments and directives by experts and how expert-novice socialization occurs. They collectively take the broad perspective we do—that supervision cannot productively be analyzed as a "one-way phenomenon" because both parties are responsible for co-constructing the encounter (Waite 1993, 697).

Two studies are especially relevant for our research. First, Burdelski's (2004) analysis of supervisor-teaching assistant weekly meetings examines narratives that teaching assistants wrote in their teaching journals and how supervisors responded in face-to-face meetings. He observes that teaching assistants wrote open-ended narratives; supervisors used closed-ended narratives to assign meanings to assistants' stories, advise them as to future courses of action, and justify their own positions. Supervisors thus contributed substantially to assigning meanings to teaching assistants' experiences. Second, Vásquez (2007) analyzes novice teachers' oral narratives that were recorded in nineteen post-teaching observation meetings. She finds that novice teachers tell two primary types of narratives—"reflective" narratives, which focus on internal states (thoughts and feelings) of the teacher, and "relational" narratives, which concentrate on interaction between individuals in the story. In both narrative types the novice teachers tended to formulate their "moral stance" (Ochs and Capps 2001) in uncertain terms. Most important for our purposes, Vásquez (2007) demonstrates that the supervisors play a pivotal role in shaping novices' accounts, sometimes challenging and re-authoring novices' narratives. For example, one teacher, in telling a narrative about an in-class activity she conducted, evaluates her own performance negatively throughout, including in her coda: "So at that point in time I finally—I realized this [the activity] isn't—this isn't gonna wrap up that well, I don't think." Her supervisor disagrees: "No it did," and explains why, reconstructing the story's resolution in a way that affirms the teacher's competence. As Vásquez explains, the teacher's "perspective on and evaluation of the same events are revised, or 're-authored'" by the supervisor (2007, 664).

Although neither Burdelski nor Vásquez explicitly draws on Mikhail Bakhtin's theories in their work, they are fundamental to our analysis. Bakhtin's (1981, 1986) dialogic view of language highlights the "already-spoken-about" quality of utterances (Morson and Emerson 1990, 136–39); this means, as Morson and Emerson explain, "Every time we speak, we respond to something spoken before and we take a stand in relation to earlier utterances about that topic" (137). O'Connor and Michaels's (1993, 1996) analysis of "revoicing" in teacher-student classroom interactions draws on this perspective: teachers reformulate what students say to accomplish tasks such as clarifying and explicating students' contributions, crediting students with ideas, and advancing class discussion. Applying Bakhtin's thinking to Vásquez's findings on re-authorship would yield a related understanding: When supervisors revisit novice teachers' prior discourse, they "take a stand" toward this discourse; in other words, they lend their voices to—and re-author—its content and meaning while also accomplishing the supervisory task of socialization.

Re-authorship is closely related to Tannen's (2007) analysis of repetition in discourse and her reconceptualization of reported speech as "constructed dialogue": speakers draw on others' words for their own purposes, and in recreating and recontextualizing them, construct new meanings (they do not merely report). Our understanding of re-authorship is also connected to Duranti's (1986) broader understanding of co-authorship in interaction and in particular to the notion of audience as co-author. (Both Tannen and Duranti explicitly draw on Bakhtin in their theorization.) We adopt the overarching idea that revisiting a topic is a kind of repetition that enables participants to share authorship of others' words and actions, and to reshape them retrospectively (see also Erickson's 1986 discussion of retrospective and prospective recipient design). As Tannen (2007) explains, repetition fundamentally alters the meaning of the "original," and "old" language thus becomes something new, and multivoiced.

We likewise build on Bakhtin's observation that utterances not only always respond to prior utterances, but also metaphorically "look forward" to others. As Bakhtin (1986, 94) explains, a speaker constructs an utterance "while taking into account possible responsive actions, for whose sake, in essence, it is actually created." Thus, we also consider how the email messages anticipate future messages and other actions; each email can be thought of as a "link" in "the chain of speech communication" (Bakhtin 1986, 94). A similar understanding of supervisor-supervisee face-to-face interaction has been proposed: Oliver, Nelson, and Ybañez conceptualize it as a dialogic co-construction, noting that "interaction among supervisor and supervisees impacts each of the people in the room, which then impacts the next interaction, which then impacts each of the people in the room and so on" (2010, 61).

Oliver, Nelson, and Ybañez's (2010) research also points to a wider phenomenon in the research on expert supervision of novices: it examines face-to-face encounters. However, email is increasingly used for supervisory communication; it remains understudied generally, but especially within discourse analysis. Recent exceptions are Crossouard and Pryor (2008, 2009) and a pilot study we conducted (Gordon and Luke 2012; Luke and Gordon 2011). Crossouard and Pryor (2008, 2009) use discourse analysis to examine email messages exchanged between a cohort of first-year professional doctorate students and their supervisor (a "doctoral tutor" who provided them assessment and feedback). Their 2008 study emphasizes how students are encouraged to conceptualize learning as entailing the development of researcher identities; the 2009 analysis focuses on how the tutor's feedback moves between different levels of authority (such as directly criticizing versus making suggestions), and between addressing program requirements and students' priorities.

Our previous research (Gordon and Luke 2012; Luke and Gordon 2011) investigates email messages exchanged between eight school counseling interns and their supervising professor (these data have been integrated into the current study's larger database). An assumption within the counseling and supervision literature is that supervision works to develop professional identities of interns (Auxier, Hughes, and Kline 2003); Luke and Gordon (2011) show how this identity development is facilitated linguistically through supervisors' and interns' uses of repetition, pronouns, and labeling. Gordon and Luke (2012) expand these findings by conceptualizing professional identity development as mutual negotiation of interns' "face" (Goffman 1967): We explore the construction of interns' knowledge and competence, as well as the establishment of their connections to and autonomy from others in their "community of practice" (Lave and Wenger 1991). In so doing, we highlight how uses of repetition, pronouns, discourse markers, and "constructed dialogue" (Tannen 2007) accomplish the facework that we suggest underlies professional identity development.

We build on this previous research while addressing re-authorship in email supervision. In the spirit of Herring's (2004) computer-mediated discourse analysis (CMDA), we consider the asynchronous, text-based context of email in our investigation, while also viewing "online behavior through the lens of language" (339).

Data

Our data were collected from students enrolled in their capstone internship of a master of science counseling program at a university in the northeastern United States. Students were informed that the parameters of the internship course required email supervision, but participation in our study was optional. Twenty-three students enrolled in five different internship classes over three semesters agreed to participate. They were supervised by one of three supervisors: a professor (Luke), or one of two advanced PhD students who also agreed to participate in our study.

Of the twenty-three participating students, eighteen were women and five were men. Ages of interns ranged between twenty-four and fifty-two years old; nineteen interns identified as Caucasian domestic students, and four identified as international students of color. The first supervisor (Supervisor A) self-identifies as an African American, female, PhD student with two years of experience. Supervisor B self-identifies as a white, female professor; at the time of the study she had eight years of supervisory experience. Supervisor C self-identifies as a gay, white, male PhD student with four years of supervisory experience.

Students received the following instructions regarding communication with their supervisor:

> You are required to send one email per week to your email supervisor. Your email can address any part of your school counseling internship experience. The message need not be more than a few lines in length. The purpose of the email communication is for you to reflect on the aspects of your school counseling internship that had your attention during the past week.

Email exchanges, transferred to Word documents, ranged in length from five to thirty-eight single-spaced pages per student.

The supervisor answered each student email within forty-eight hours, which is standard protocol (see Clingerman and Bernard 2004). The supervisors were directed to respond to the core theme of each email, and to complete the communication cycle in their emails (rather than initiating new topics).[1] The goals of supervision, as outlined by Bernard (1979, 1997) and Lanning (1986), include developing interns' skill behaviors (intervention); encouraging reflection on case progression and their own decision making (conceptualization); facilitating self-reflection on emotion, culture, and related issues (personalization); and teaching appropriate record-keeping and collegial engagement (professional behavior). These goals, we find, are accomplished in part thorough supervisors' re-authoring and pre-authoring practices.

Analysis

Our analysis is data driven: We repeatedly read the data to identify patterns, and drew on the discourse analytic and counselor education and supervision literatures to collaboratively make sense of emerging patterns. Our previous pilot study also sensitized us to the presence of re-authorship (see Gordon and Luke 2012; Luke and Gordon 2011). We used NVivo 9, a qualitative data analysis software program, to assist us in data management and organization—including both the storage of the emails by intern, supervisor, semester, and area of counseling, and the coding of textual material into categories that we developed. Intercoder agreement was achieved by collaboratively coding a subset of the emails, then coding the remainder independently and cross-checking our coding of each passage, as suggested by Creswell (2009). In line with many previous CMDA studies, we couple "counting and coding" with qualitative consideration of individual examples (see Herring 2004). We identify two broad ways that the supervisors re-authored interns' experiences: we call these reinforcing and reframing. We discuss each in turn, with examples. This is followed by our discussion of the related phenomenon of pre-authoring.

Re-authoring through Reinforcing

The first strategy we discuss is supervisors' re-authoring through reinforcing. Supervisors reinforce by revisiting a topic or theme introduced by the intern and supporting the intern's reported behaviors, experiences, or understandings. Repeating—whether on the lexical, syntactic, thematic, or other level—fundamentally alters the meaning of what is repeated, blending voices together in a new context, following Bakhtin (1981, 1986) and Tannen (2007). This achieves what we understand to be co-authorship of interns' discursive understandings of their experiences. In 260 examples of reinforcing we note three types: supervisor reinforcement of interns' email communication behavior (such as their selection of topics to discuss), reinforcement of professional internship-site behavior (such as how they reportedly interacted with clients), and reinforcement of interns' emotional responses to their experiences.

Reinforcing Email Behavior   Supervisors reinforce interns' supervisory email behavior, including what they chose to report and reflect upon in their messages, as well as how. They thereby reinforce the interns' professional behavior (here, how, and what to communicate to the supervisor) as well as the personalization (or emotional reflection) element of supervision.

Supervisors often use the speech act of thanking to reinforce interns' communicative choice to send the messages, as well as to confirm interns' appropriate provision of information. For example, Supervisor C begins a message to Jaime with "Thank you for your email," and Supervisor A responds to Dwayne's first message with "Thank you for your first email of the course." In this way they affirm the students' supervisory communication behavior of having sent a message.

Praising is also used to reinforce interns' supervisory communication choices, including what information to share in the messages and how to reflect appropriately upon internship experiences. For example, in response to a message sent by Mei Li, Supervisor B begins by remarking, "WOW Mei Li, what a powerful reflection," thus bolstering the intern's abilities to identify, discuss, and reflect upon meaningful issues in in-depth, productive ways. Similarly, Supervisor C responds to a message from Xao by indicating, "You raise some interesting issues," and to a message from Christine with "The issue you raise around power is an important one." Adjectives such as "powerful," "interesting," and "important," coupled with thanking and praising, retrospectively reflect upon and positively reinforce interns' email communication in the context of supervision.

Reinforcing Professional Counseling Behavior   Supervisors also reinforce behaviors interns describe as having exhibited at their internship sites, thus accomplishing the intervention (or skill behavior socialization) aspect of supervision.

The speech act of praising plays a role in this reinforcement. For example, in response to Belinda's description of how she handled a panicked teenage client at her internship site, a drug treatment center, Supervisor A writes, "I think all in all Belinda you did a good job with this client." In response to Paula's description of how she gives her clients tasks to accomplish prior to their meetings with her, Supervisor A remarks, "Love the homework piece that you are giving to your clients." Supervisor B responds to Danielle's email describing how she used group interactions with students at her school to encourage students to see her individually by stating, "It is clear that your work was successful in generating individual appointments with students, which it sounds like was one aim."

In these examples, supervisors use positive assessments, including adjectives such as "good" and "successful," to affirm behaviors interns reportedly exhibited vis-à-vis clients. They thus co-author interns' understandings of their counseling behaviors.

Reinforcing Emotional Responses   As is relevant to the goals of supervision, supervisors reinforce interns' reported thoughts and feelings. Within the culture of counseling, thoughts and feelings are considered to be of great value; counselors need to deal with their own "stuff" (or issues) in order to be good counselors. In this spirit interns frequently express their emotions, and supervisors frequently reinforce them.

When Alyssa expresses feelings of guilt and concern after withdrawing from the internship class (and therefore having to leave her internship site), Supervisor A reassures her: "With any major transition, it is normal to feel out of sorts." Similarly, when Noreen describes her feelings about leaving her internship site at the end of the semester, Supervisor B responds, "It makes sense that you're working through a very mixed reaction to the endings with your clients." When Rachael expresses her worry about the fact that multiple client cancelations reduced the amount of practice hours she was able to gain, Supervisor B remarks, "Of course, you're concerned about getting your direct client hours when you have 4 no shows in one day." Supervisor C reinforces Adrian's description of feeling exhausted in a different way, stating, "Having been a part-time student for my first few years in the doc program, I can very much identify with the weariness you have noted in this week's email."

Supervisors normalize interns' described emotions through various strategies, including through adjectives such as "normal" and adverbs such as "of course"; by suggesting that interns' responses are appropriate or "make sense"; and even by creating parallels between interns' experiences and their own. Supervisors thus revisit and validate, and thereby re-author, interns' described emotions.

In summary, in reinforcing interns' email communication behaviors, their counseling behaviors, and their emotional reactions, supervisors do not blatantly "change" intern conceptualizations, instead they "repeat" or "reiterate" them. Nevertheless, we suggest reinforcing is usefully conceptualized as a kind of re-authorship, through a Bakhtinian lens. Supervisors take what an intern composed in a previous email and recontextualize it in their own email in agreement and support, lending their perspective and voice to the discourse on the topic.

Re-authoring through Reframing

The second kind of re-authoring we identify can be described as "reframing," following Tannen and Wallat's (1993, 59) understandings of framing as related to "structures of expectation," and of "interactive frame" as referring to "frames of interpretation" that participants use to understand situations, events, and utterances. What Vásquez (2007) conceptualizes as re-authoring in her study of face-to-face expert-novice discourse is akin to our description of reframing, which we suggest is one particular kind of re-authoring. When reframing occurs, supervisors invoke new understandings of interns' experiences. They do this by labeling interns' behaviors and experiences using professional jargon and concepts from professional practice, and by encouraging different interpretations of emotions and events. Thus, reframing often encourages interns to view their experiences not only through the lens of the profession, but also from multiple perspectives. Considering multiple perspectives and understandings, sometimes referred to as "both-and" (an in-group term), is an especially important part of reflection; it thus works toward interns' professional development in terms of conceptualization (reflection on case development) and personalization (self-reflection and awareness). (The "both-and" notion is reminiscent of discourse analytic understandings of linguistic strategies as potentially having multiple simultaneous meanings; see Tannen 1996.) In reframing, supervisors offer alternative "definition[s] of what is going on [or what went on] in interaction" (Tannen and Wallat 1993, 59).

In our first example of reframing, Christine emails her supervisor at the end of week 4 of her internship about her feelings about missing some internship hours for personal reasons earlier in the semester. (The extracts we present in what follows appear in their original forms; spelling, grammar, capitalization, etc., are not changed. We use [sic] to acknowledge spelling and other errors in the messages. Such errors seem to reflect a level of relative informality in the messages. They could also reflect comfort between interns and supervisors.)

(1a) Christine $\rightarrow$ Supervisor C

Due to some events that occured [*sic*] unexpectedly in my life, I had to take a few hours out of interning a couple weeks ago. I feel now that I am behind (and I am, if you consider my overall hours), and all I feel like I do is intern! Overall, I am not concerned I will not get my hours, but I have to make sure I definitely stay on top of them. Also, I have to be careful of missing time unless I really need to.

In response to this message, the supervisor offers an adjusted understanding of Christine's situation:

(1b) Supervisor C $\rightarrow$ Christine

It sounds like the stress of the semester and your many requirements are beginning to get to you! Having spoken to you earlier, I do understand some of those unexpected and traumatic events that you are referring to (i.e. car break-in, deaths, etc.). I think for me it raises the issues that we aren't counselors in a vacuum, but also have our own life's situations and expectations to handle. For me, I think this email raises the importance of counselor self-care, as well as thinking about priorities.

While reinforcing Christine's emotions through showing understanding ("I do understand"), Supervisor C also subtly reinterprets Christine's unexpected life events, loss of hours, and feelings of being "behind" as the result of "stress of the semester and your many requirements"; Christine herself did not use the word "stress" or the phrase "many requirements," instead referring to "some events" and "hours." The supervisor also normalizes her experiences, creating a shared perspective using "we" and "our": he remarks, "We aren't counselors in a vacuum, but also have our own life's situations and expectations to handle." This situates Christine's described experiences within the broader professional field, as something presumably all counselors must manage as part of their professional role. Thus her worries are reframed from individualized to an integral counseling issue. Supervisor C also offers a new overarching meaning to her email message: Her described experiences are understandable and addressable through two professional activities—prioritizing tasks to address conflicting demands, and taking care of oneself (which is referred to in the profession using the term "self-care").

In offering these different and multiple understandings, the supervisor opens up new ways of thinking for Christine. He segments these alternate conceptualizations using "for me" and "I think," both of which can be understood as discourse markers (following Scheibman 2009 regarding "for me," and Kärkkäinen 2003 regarding "I think"); discourse markers frequently play a role in transitioning between alternative reframings in our data.

In the next example Tamara describes her surprise regarding her clinical site director's attention to case notes (written records of a counselor's work with an individual client), and the supervisor offers an even more complex reframing. Tamara frames case notes as being unsatisfying because they are too vague; she attributes this vagueness to "CYA" ("cover your ass"), which refers to the idea that documentation protects providers of counseling services.

(2a) Tamara → Supervisor B

All interns were asked to bring casenotes [*sic*] to supervision this week by our
clinical director here. We reviewed these in individual supervision. I was
surprised by the extent to which there is concern about CYA. Every word
seems to matter. I tend to choose my words carefully anyway, and did not feel
overly criticized. I found the review helpful, but the emphasis on writing notes
at this agency seems to be about avoiding opinion and being vague. I tend to
include too much detail. It is a fine line between writing the kind of note that
the agency expects and actually writing something that will be useful to myself
or another therapist in the future. I certainly don't remember the details from
one session to the next. I feel that we can be so concerned with CYA and
vagueness that we might fail to write anything substantial.

In her response, the supervisor reconceptualizes the intern's experiences with case
notes (bolded font has been added to draw attention to phrases of particular analytic
importance):

(2b): Supervisor B → Tamara

You seem to have encountered some of **the tensions that can exist between
individual attempts at being therapeutic and the beauracratic [*sic*]
attempts to minimize liability.** Of course, you address how counterintuitive
this is, because like yourself, detailed records would seem to provide better
quality and continuity of care. I sense some disappointment about how much
**agency effort and resources are being expended regarding the exact word
selections** used in notes, when in your opinion there might be far better uses of
this collective energy, including your own. Lastly, it seems like part of **your
surprise might result from a lack of communication** as to why this focus or
the rationale for the vagueness and omission of any clinical judgment in case
notes.

The supervisor's response reframes the intern's description of her experiences. The supervisor does not address what might be Tamara's underlying concern about avoiding
words that might get a counselor in trouble (this could be owed to supervisors' general reluctance to be too critical of site-specific practices). She does, however, suggest
multiple understandings of the phenomenon, and in so doing, accomplishes reframing. First, she suggests that what Tamara described can be conceptualized as "tensions"
that exist between an individual therapist's efforts at effective therapy and a bureaucratic interest in liability. Second, she focuses on what she perceives to be the intern's
concern about seemingly excessive attention to word choice by reconceptualizing it
as the more technical and encompassing issue of expenditure of "agency effort and
resources." Third, using the discourse marker "lastly," she suggests that the intern's reaction can be understood as related to a "lack of communication" around the whole
issue of case notes. In these ways, Supervisor B reframes the intern's complaints and
concerns about case notes within the field of professional practice, where individual
therapists must work within bureaucratic requirements and with limited resources, and

where communication is a pivotal issue. (It is possible that in doing so she has over-looked Tamara's actual concern, although we cannot be certain.)

These examples are 2 of the 279 instances of reframing we identified. Although some of the "shifts" in frame are more extreme than others, in all, supervisors attempt to portray a different understanding—and often multiple possible understandings—of an internship site or emotional experience. The use of discourse markers like "lastly" and "for me" play a role in this; other examples of reframing involve prefacing by discourse markers such as "however," "in addition," "moreover," and "that being said" (see Gordon and Luke 2012 for a discussion of "that being said" in supervisory communication). Supervisors also use professional names and categories to socialize interns into shared professional—rather than idiosyncratic—conceptualizations of certain kinds of situations. Thus, concern about lack of internship hours due to personal life events is reconceptualized as a normal professional matter that causes stress and brings to mind the importance of self-care. Likewise, concern about vagueness in case notes is re-authored by the supervisor, becoming the broader professional issues of therapeutic/bureaucratic tensions and worksite communication.

Pre-authoring

Finally, we examine a phenomenon that we suggest is closely related to re-authoring: pre-authoring, or advice giving by the supervisors, which occurred frequently (we identify 342 examples). Although previous research on re-authorship in supervisory contexts does not encompass this concept, we suggest that pre-authoring is a closely related interactional pattern when considered within Bakhtin's dialogic understanding of social interaction.

Prior research finds advice giving to be a careful process in expert-novice interactions (Vásquez 2004). We similarly find that advice is typically provided indirectly and with attention to social face, occurring through speech acts such as encouraging and suggesting (rather than ordering). However, more interesting for our purposes is the larger idea that supervisors' email messages not only "look back" to interns' past messages, but also "look forward" to the future. Example 3 is a case of pre-authoring; the supervisor attempts to affect the intern's thinking about two topics—her understanding of her client's progress, and of the intern's own "self-efficacy" (a professional term which refers to belief in one's own capabilities).

(3) Supervisor B → Linda

> I encourage you to consider the meaning you attribute to your clients'
> development or lack thereof, as well as how/where/when/why your self-
> efficacy increases/decreases related to your work.

Supervisor B advises Linda to consider certain issues; she also can be viewed as even more indirectly advising her to think (and communicate) using such terms as "self-efficacy."

In the next example, the supervisor advises that the intern proactively learn about and test out new counseling techniques (interventions):

(4) Supervisor A → Martin

We can never have too many interventions under our belt so I definately [*sic*] encourage you to research and read more and don't be afraid to practice new interventions once you believe that it will fit the client(s) you are seeing.

Supervisor A encourages the intern as well as attempts to shape his future counseling behaviors. As in the previous extract, the supervisor may also be indirectly promoting (advising) the intern's use of professionally relevant terminology ("interventions," "clients").

In the next example, Supervisor C gives advice on internship emails; by socializing the intern into the expectations and norms of supervisory communication, he pre-authors the intern's future messages while also contributing to her professional development.

(5) Supervisor C → Belinda

Hi Belinda,

Seems like you have had a lot going on with different sessions. What would help me is if you focused on one client . . . discussed what the issues are for that client and then what awareness you are having of yourself. Also presenting reflection for me with that client.

In this example, the supervisor asks for a focus on one client (instead of a general discussion of many). He does not demand such behavior, but rather hints that that is what he wants ("What would help me is"). As part of this, he asks the intern to demonstrate self-reflection in the emails (conceptualization), an important component of counseling experience and practice and also a goal of supervisory communication.

Examples such as these capture how supervisors offer forms of advice to interns—they typically encourage, suggest, and recommend. This echoes prior research findings on the somewhat mitigated nature of expert-novice communication. Most importantly, they show how supervisors attempt to shape—to "pre-author"—interns' future thoughts and behaviors by advising, thus shaping future reflection and skill behaviors. In using professional jargon, they could be understood to be modeling proper understandings and uses of discipline-relevant terminology for the future. In their email messages, the supervisors both re-author and pre-author; they co-author interns' discourse, experiences, interpretations, and behaviors.

Conclusion

We suggest that re- and pre-authorship, together constituting co-authorship, are useful in considering supervisory email communication. Although the concept of co-authorship resonates easily with face-to-face encounters (where a co-present "audience" [Duranti 1986] shapes the discourse), we find that it is relevant to email as well, especially when considered in the context of the supervisor's role: in a Bakhtinian spirit, we suggest that supervisors' messages respond to interns' emails and the past experiences described therein through reframing and reinforcing; they anticipate interns' to-be-experienced events (including future emails) as well through pre-authoring. In using various linguistic strategies in re- and pre-authoring, experts attempt to socialize novices through affecting their interpretations of past experiences, feelings, and professional behaviors, and through potentially affecting future behaviors—they become co-authors.

Our analysis represents an initial interdisciplinary exploration of email supervision as co-authorship; there remains much to be learned, for instance, about interns' uptake of supervisors' re- and pre-authoring. However, we believe our research at this stage contributes to three areas: the discourse of email supervision, co-authorship and supervision goals, and email as a co-constructed discursive phenomenon.

Our analysis identifies co-authorship patterns of email supervisory communication, outlining forms and functions of what we have called reframing, reinforcing (collectively, re-authoring), and pre-authoring. This deepens our understanding of the nature of supervisors' contributions to the authorship of interns' discourse and experiences, while also uncovering a range of discursive strategies that are used, including adjectives and adverbs, professional vocabulary items, repetition, and discourse markers, as well as speech acts, in particular praising, agreeing, and encouraging or recommending.

We identify re- and pre-authoring as means of pursuing goals of supervision (as presented by Bernard 1979, 1997; Lanning 1986): intervention, conceptualization, personalization, and professional behavior. By reinforcing interns' skills, behaviors, and internship activities, reframing their conceptualization of these within professional understandings, and advising future behaviors, supervisors accomplish the goals of intervention and professional behavior, encouraging appropriate counselor-client and collegial engagement. Reframing, reinforcing, and pre-authoring are also all used to facilitate self-reflection on emotion, culture, and related issues, which helps accomplish the personalization goal, by encouraging interns to become aware of their own experiences and viewpoints. Reframing and pre-authoring in particular are used to encourage reflection on case progression and decision making from professionally relevant perspectives (conceptualization). Thus, our research demonstrates how supervisors' discursive revision of interns' described experiences, as well as their anticipation of interns' future experiences, functions in pursuit of the professional socialization of novice counselors.

Finally, this study contributes in a small way to the development of a computer-mediated discourse analysis that is "informed by a linguistic perspective," making interpretations that are "grounded in observations about language and language use" (Herring 2004, 339). Specifically, it demonstrates the utility of applying interactive concepts such as co-authorship and a Bakhtinian perspective to asynchronous CMC. Doing so lends insight not only into how socialization occurs in this medium, but also into how seemingly "individually composed" email messages can be usefully conceptualized as being jointly constructed, and how various kinds of "co-authorship" phenomena occur in expert-novice discourse online.

ACKNOWLEDGMENTS

We thank the student interns and supervisors who generously allowed us to collect and analyze their email messages. We also thank students in Cynthia Gordon's Spring 2011 Applied Discourse Analysis course and audience members at GURT 2011 for their feedback on earlier versions of this chapter. In addition, we greatly appreciate the comments and suggestions that we received from Deborah Tannen.

NOTE

1. The supervision response protocol consisted of the following: (1) if there were multiple themes within a student email, the supervisor attempted to identify and respond to the core theme; (2) the supervisor responded in a manner that completed the communication cycle; (3) the supervisor refrained from asking questions or opening up a new line of communication that could prompt a subsequent student response; and (4) as appropriate, the supervisor encouraged the student to raise certain topics in internship class or with their site supervisor. When the supervisor responses were sent to the students, the respective internship instructor was copied and she or he chose whether and how to address supervisory content within the class.

REFERENCES

Atkinson, Paul. 1999. Medical discourse, evidentiality and the construction of professional responsibility. In *Talk, work and institutional order: Discourse in medical, mediation and management settings,* eds. Srikant Sarangi and Celia Roberts, 75–107. New York: Mouton de Gruyter.

Auxier, C. R., Frances R. Hughes, and William B. Kline. 2003. Identity development in counselors-in-training. *Counselor Education and Supervision* 43:25–38.

Bakhtin, M. M. 1981. *The dialogic imagination: Four essays.* Eds. Michael Holquist and Caryl Emerson. Trans. Michael Holquist. Austin: The University of Texas Press.

———. 1986. The problem of speech genres. In *Speech genres and other late essays,* eds. Caryl Emerson and Michael Holquist, trans. Vern W. McGee, 60–102. Austin: The University of Texas Press.

Bernard, Janine M. 1979. Supervisor training: A discrimination model. *Counselor Education and Supervision* 19:60–68.

———. 1997. The discrimination model. In *Handbook of psychotherapy supervision,* ed. C. Edward Watkins Jr., 310–27. New York: John Wiley and Sons.

Burdelski, Matthew. 2004. Close- and open-ended narratives of personal experience: Weekly meetings among a supervisor and teaching assistants of a "Japanese language education practicum." *Linguistics and Education* 15:3–32.

Chiang, Shiao-Yun. 2009. Personal power in a power-full "I": A discourse analysis of doctoral dissertation supervision. *Discourse and Communication* 3:255–71.

Clingerman, Tamara L., and Janine M. Bernard. 2004. An investigation of the use of e-mail as a supplemental modality for clinical supervision. *Counselor Education and Supervision* 44:82–95.

Creswell, John W. 2009. *Research design: Qualitative, quantitative, and mixed methods approaches.* Thousand Oaks, CA: Sage.

Crossouard, Barbara, and John Pryor. 2008. Becoming researchers: A sociocultural perspective on assessment, learning and the construction of identity in a professional doctorate. *Pedagogy, Culture and Society* 16:221–37.

———. 2009. Using email for formative assessment with professional doctorate students. *Assessment and Evaluation in Higher Education* 34, no. 4:377–88.

Duranti, Alessandro. 1986. The audience as co-author: An introduction. *Text* 6:239–47.

Erickson, Frederick. 1986. Listening and speaking. In *Languages and linguistics: The interdependence of theory, data, and application,* eds. Deborah Tannen, 294–319. Washington, DC: Georgetown University Press.

———. 1999. Appropriation of voice and presentation of self as a fellow physician: Aspects of a discourse of apprenticeship in medicine. In *Talk, work and institutional order: Discourse in medical, mediation and management settings,* eds. Srikant Sarangi and Celia Roberts, 109–43. New York: Mouton de Gruyter.

Goffman, Erving. 1967. *Interaction ritual: Essays on face-to-face behavior.* New York and Toronto: Pantheon.

Goodwin, Charles. 1994. Professional vision. *American Anthropologist* 96:606–33.

Gordon, Cynthia, and Melissa Luke. 2012. Discursive negotiation of face via email: Professional identity development in school counseling supervision. *Linguistics and Education* 23:112–22.

Herring, Susan C. 2004. Computer-mediated discourse analysis: An approach to researching online behavior. In *Designing for virtual communities in the service of learning,* eds. Sasha A. Barab, Rob Kling, and James H. Gray, 338–76. New York: Cambridge University Press.

Kärkkäinen, Elise. 2003. *Epistemic stance in English conversation: A description of its interactional functions, with a focus on "I think."* Amsterdam: John Benjamins.

Lanning, Wayne. 1986. Development of the supervisor emphasis rating form. *Counselor Education and Supervision* 25:191–96.

Lave, Jean, and Etienne Wenger. 1991. *Situated learning: Legitimate peripheral participation.* Cambridge: Cambridge University Press.

Luke, Melissa, and Cynthia Gordon. 2011. A discourse analysis of school counseling supervisory e-mail. *Counselor Education and Supervision* 50:274–91.

Morson, Gary Saul, and Caryl Emerson. 1990. *Mikhail Bakhtin: Creation of a prosaics.* Stanford, CA: Stanford University Press.

O'Connor, Mary Catherine, and Sarah Michaels. 1993. Aligning academic task and participation status through revoicing: Analysis of a classroom discourse strategy. *Anthropology and Education Quarterly* 24:318–35.

———. 1996. Shifting participant frameworks: Orchestrating thinking practices in group discussion. In *Discourse, learning, and schooling,* ed. Deborah Hicks. New York: Cambridge University Press.

Ochs, Elinor, and Lisa Capps. 2001. *Living narrative.* Cambridge, MA: Harvard University Press.

Oliver, Marvarene, Kaye Nelson, and Kathy Ybañez. 2010. Systemic processes in triadic supervision. *The Clinical Supervisor* 29:51–67.

Scheibman, Joanne. 2009. Routinized uses of the first person expression *for me* in conversational discourse. In *Formulaic language (volume two): Acquisition, loss, psychological reality, and functional explanations,* eds. Roberta Corrigan, Edith A. Moravcsik, Hamid Ouali and Kathleen M. Wheatley, 615–38. Amsterdam: John Benjamins.

Tannen, Deborah. 1996. *Gender and discourse.* New York: Oxford University Press.

———. 2007. *Talking voices: Repetition, dialogue, and imagery in conversational discourse.* 2nd ed. Cambridge: Cambridge University Press.

Tannen, Deborah, and Cynthia Wallat. 1993. Interactive frames and knowledge schemas in interaction: Examples from a medical examination/interview. In *Framing in discourse,* ed. Deborah Tannen, 57–76. New York: Oxford University Press.

Vásquez, Camilla. 2004. "Very carefully managed": Advice and suggestions in post-observation meetings. *Linguistics and Education* 15:33–58.

———. 2007. Moral stance in the workplace narratives of novices. *Discourse Studies* 9:653–75.

Vásquez, Camilla, and Alfredo Urzúa. 2009. Reported speech and reported mental states in mentoring meetings: Exploring novice teacher identities. *Research on Language and Social Interaction* 42:1–19.

Vehviläinen, Sanna. 2009. Student-initiated advice in academic supervision. *Research on Language and Social Interaction* 42:163–90.

Waite, Duncan. 1992. Supervisors' talk: Making sense of conferences from an anthropological linguistic perspective. *Journal of Curriculum and Supervision* 7:349–71.

———. 1993. Teachers in conference: A qualitative study of teacher-supervisor face-to-face interaction. *American Educational Research Journal* 30:675–702.

11

▦ Blogs
A Medium for Intellectual Engagement with Course Readings and Participants

MARIANNA RYSHINA-PANKOVA AND JENS KUGELE
Georgetown University

Introduction

▦ IN THE AGE OF WEB 2.0 TECHNOLOGIES and computer-mediated communication (CMC) that give access to a sea of information and offer various opportunities for responding and co-constructing it in chats, online forums, wikis, or blogs, a gruff traditional humanities professor questions skeptically whether blogs used in educational settings are just a new format for what one has been doing all along or a new form with yet-unexplored potential for fostering learning, reflection, and academically argumentative writing. Practitioners have reflected on the positive effects of using blogs in education (Ferdig and Trammell 2004; Lowe and Williams 2004; Oravec 2002; Walker 2005; Williams and Jacobs 2004). Researchers have tried to prove their effectiveness in learning in various disciplinary domains: teaching methods (Al-Fadda and Al-Yahya 2010; Hernández-Ramos 2004), information technology (Cuhadar and Kuzu 2010), political science (Lawrence and Dion 2010), business administration (Williams and Jacobs 2004), English (Richardson 2003), and composition and academic writing classes (Kelley 2008; Wang and Fang 2005). Most of the evidence, however, comes from quantitative results (number and frequency of blogs produced) and overwhelmingly from learner questionnaires and surveys in which students give feedback on what they perceive to be the advantages of blog writing in academic courses.

Changing the focus on what instructors or students think about blogs to what they in fact do when they create this new discourse form, we propose to investigate the blog entries themselves. Given that course-related blogging has been associated with fostering engagement in content learning and an academic exchange about it, as one of its most beneficial aspects, we examine blog entries with the help of discourse analytical tools that help us demonstrate that

1. Learners do, indeed, engage in content learning as they interact with their peers through blogs;
2. this engagement is evident from the use of particular linguistic strategies employed; and
3. this engagement enables us to make a strong statement about blogs as an instrument for promoting learning and academic argumentation.

Data for our study comprise blog entries written for a course on the representation of witches in history, literature, and film. This course (taught in English) has been offered by the Department of German and serves as one of the courses that can be taken to fulfill the second of the two required humanities and writing classes at Georgetown University. In the particular context of this study, blogs are chronologically organized, and entries are published online with the goal of discussing class readings and responding to other students' entries on these readings.

Recognizing the critical role of language in knowledge construction, this study defines learning in connection to its realization though particular linguistic means. Specifically, it looks for evidence of learning in the linguistic strategies that students use in their blogs to express their perspectives on the course content and relate their views to the opinions and interpretations of other blog writers. To identify these strategies, a systemic-functional framework of appraisal and specifically ENGAGE-MENT (written in all caps when referring to the term in its systemic-functional technical sense [Martin and White 2005]) is used. In line with this framework, the study analyzes markers of dialogic engagement as being significant to the genre of blog writing, reveals to what extent they are used by the learners, and discusses their function as instruments for academically accepted discursive knowledge construction and knowledge sharing.

We begin the discussion with an overview of studies that support the claim about the conduciveness of blog writing for content learning. We then describe the institutional and instructional context of the study, its participants, and the function blogs served in the course. In the next section we explain the methodology behind the study. This is followed by reports on the quantitative results and qualitative discussion with regard to three aspects: engagement with content, engagement with course participants, and engagement as expression of one's own opinion. We conclude with a summary of the results and their implications for viewing blogs as a useful tool for learning disciplinary content and improving academic writing skills.

Content Learning through Blog Writing: Theoretical Assumptions and Research Evidence

From a theoretical perspective, what makes one presume that interaction through blog writing can promote learning? The belief can be grounded in the framework of the sociocultural theory of learning that demonstrates the central role of interaction through language or languaging (see Swain 2006) for knowledge construction. According to the sociocultural theory developed by the Russian psychologist Vygotsky (1978, 1987) and used by American researchers for theorizing about educational practices (Wells 1999; Wertsch 1985, 1991), learning occurs in the process of participation in a goal-oriented activity through interaction with others and by means of symbolic tools developed by a culture, language being the most critical of them. Learning to perform mental tasks through language use in a dialogue with an expert and peers leads learners to acquire new knowledge. Beyond that, such engagement results in developing mental capabilities that allow learners to augment this knowledge by recontextualizing it in line with their own previous experiences, other learning, and under the pressure of new tasks.

With regard to this ability to participate in collaborative meaning-making crucial for learning, if we follow the sociocultural theorists, blogs seem to offer a unique space for students to contribute to the knowledge construction process in an academic setting with their own voice. This is so partly due to the affordances blogs offer for out-of-class asynchronous discussion, in terms of both time for turn-taking and time for reflection that is not always possible in high-enrollment courses or for more reticent or shy learners. Bloch and Crosby (2008), noting the distinguishing features of blogs, point to two other qualities that potentially make them effective tools for fostering academic engagement: the nature of authorship and their textuality. Authoring public pieces of writing through blogs assumes a dialogue with an audience that includes other well-informed knowers: classmates, instructors, and often those in a larger blogosphere outside the class community. In Bakhtin's (1981, 1986) view, any verbal communication, whether oral or written, is always dialogic: it responds to the previous utterances and anticipates the subsequent ones. This aspect of language use becomes especially urgent in blogs in view of their openness to a larger audience and the possibility of immediate feedback from it.

This interactional essence of the blog medium makes blog authors engage with their subjects in more intense and critical ways, as observed both by blog writers (for example, Blood, Lingerfelt, and Johnson [cited in Walker 2005]) and by practitioners in education (Ferdig and Trammell 2004; Lowe and Williams 2004; Oravec 2002; Walker 2005) who use blogs in their courses. They note that offering new perspectives requires that blog writers actively engage with the ideas of other knowledgeable participants of interaction and resolves the tension between accounting for their positions and establishing one's own authority. To overcome this challenge, blog writers need to process information from various sources and propose new interpretations by taking an explicitly intersubjective stance and acknowledging the ideas of others either endorsing or challenging their own positions, a task at the essence of academic learning and knowledge construction.

The textual nature of blogs is the second crucial feature that can be conducive for engagement with content learning in an academically appropriate way. Unlike class conversations that are oral and in contrast to other forms of CMC such as chats—which are mostly of sentence length—blog entries are often longer and are more or less coherent entities. Even if not all blogs (see a discussion in Myers 2010) display coherence and textuality as a genre, they are conducive for containing texts that are organized rhetorically, and in educational settings students can be asked to purposefully shape their entries as short argumentative wholes. Given their public nature and textuality, blogs can become a space for engaging with other participants about course content in academically valued ways: through the use of a public voice that reasons by constructing textually well organized and logically written academic arguments.

These combinations of interactivity and textuality, on the one hand, and of strong authorial voice and intersubjectivity, on the other hand—unique for the genre of blog writing—have been utilized by practitioners to foster learning in various disciplines. For example, in a teacher preparation course (Hernández-Ramos 2004), blogs were used with the goal of developing a professional voice among teachers as active creators of knowledge and for promoting reflection about readings and teaching practice.

The study reported that students wrote actively in their blogs and found the experience gratifying. Quotations from their blog entries illustrate well their reflection about theory and pedagogical practice. The researcher concluded, however, that to identify the specific ways in which blogs engage learners and determine what blogs can tell instructors about the learning needs of students a detailed qualitative analysis of blog entries would need to be conducted.

In an MBA course unit on macroeconomics and international political economy, blogs were used to support learning through improving the quantity and quality of discussions of the course materials among the students (Williams and Jacobs 2004). The results of the student questionnaires about the use of blogs demonstrated the value of blogs in at least three areas. First of all, they were perceived to be a good way of sharing one's own ideas and considering other students' comments in a way that would inspire further debate of the issues. Furthermore, blogs were praised for the opportunities they offered to increase participation and interaction among students beyond the limits of classroom time. Finally, learners pointed out that their active involvement in blogging was not for the sake of getting a grade but to satisfy a desire to shape the discussion by expressing their thoughts. All that made the authors conclude that blogs not only contributed to more intensive and collaborative content exploration, but as "distinctly open environment for topic advancement allowed students to direct their own learning in a manner that transcended the existing curriculum" (Williams and Jacobs 2004, "The BGSB MBA Blog") a desirable result in any subject learning that is resonant with the sociocultural idea of active knowledge building and reconstruction enabled through content-based interaction.

This deeper engagement with content that involves reflection on readings and their recontextualization is also reported by graduate student learners in Xie and Sharma's study (2005), which unfortunately does not give any information about what courses students writing the blogs were enrolled in. Nevertheless, the research shows that having to respond to the readings by blogging made students take an active stance toward course materials, pose questions, and connect the readings to their life experiences. These students also noted another important aspect of blogs and knowledge construction. Blogging allowed them not only to engage in reflection about content but also to observe changes in their learning; blogs are permanent texts revealing a "history of . . . thoughts," "a roadmap of . . . [one's] development in an area" (842).

Use of blogs for engagement and reflective response to readings was also advocated for literature and political science classes. Richardson reported that blog writing in his modern American literature class could "stimulate debate and motivate students to do close reading of the text" (2003, 40). Lawrence and Dion (2010) noted the value of blogs in a political science classroom for engagement in the most current political events and development of critical reading and thinking abilities. They see similarities between the strategies the best political bloggers take as they closely follow political news and evaluate statements and actions of politicians and the requirements of a political science class in which students need to critically discuss primary and secondary sources to support their own line of argument.

Similar to the instructional uses in the research discussed above, the rationale for assigning blogs in the course in which our study takes place was to tap into their potential for fostering content learning through the interactive negotiation of issues with other participants in the context of the course.

Context of the Study

This section focuses on the instructional context from which the study originates. It describes the institutional context, course content, writing assignments, and use of the blogs in the course, and gives information about the blogs selected for the analysis.

Institutional Context

Blog entries were collected from a course titled "Witchcraft in History, Literature, and Film." This course is taught in English and comprises two seventy-five-minute class meetings per week. The students in the course are mostly freshmen and sophomores. The overall course goals are to learn about the phenomenon of witch hunting as one of the most disturbing and inexplicable occurrences in human history and to further improve and refine one's writing abilities—with particular emphasis on writing within an academic context.

Course Content

Through analysis of various historical documents, literary and filmic adaptations, and selected academic publications, the course investigates and traces the construction of notions of the witch and of witchcraft throughout the centuries in the German-speaking world and beyond. The first part of the semester focuses on historical and trial records in early modern Europe, with an emphasis on the German situation and the Salem witch trials in seventeenth-century New England. Later the course explores literary works and films with a particular focus on fairy tales from the Brothers Grimm to Disney, dramas from Shakespeare to the twentieth century, and contemporary filmic depictions of the witch theme. In addition to interpreting primary sources from the fields of history and literature and film, students are exposed to secondary literature on the course topic.

Writing Assignments

Representing the breadth of academic genres, writing assignments in the course include an introduction to a scholarly book, an abstract, a book review, an annotated bibliography, and a research paper. Blog writing was introduced (originally in 2008, by Professor Astrid Weigert) in the first unit of the course, "Historical and Trial Records," as an instrument for fostering more engaged reading prior to class meetings. The expectation was that if students wrote for a larger audience that included their classmates, the quality of their writing and their level of involvement would improve and contribute to a stimulating intellectual atmosphere of the class.

Blog Use

In light of the very loose genre boundaries of blogs, the assignment sheet characterized the blog entries for this class as well-informed expert contributions that stimulate nuanced responses and therefore require formal academic language. The blog task functioned in the following way: For each set of texts, four experts (students who needed to become particularly well informed about the texts under consideration) were assigned in advance. These experts were to start off the blog discussion by presenting the current readings and by pointing to thematic, argumentative, and genre-specific similarities or differences between them. Two days after the experts' postings, the rest of the class was to assume the role of respondents and post their comments online. Their blog entries were to comment on arguments presented by the expert discussants and to add a new dimension to the readings not mentioned by the discussants. Students were to post their blog entries once a week for six weeks, the duration of the first unit. They received a holistic grade for all their blog entries and an individual grade for their expert entries.

Student involvement in blog writing was relatively high. All twenty-one students submitted discussion blog entries; fifteen students submitted an entry for each theme throughout the first unit, and only two people wrote one or two blog entries, respectively, during the semester. An average number of respondent blogs per theme was 8.6; one theme elicited 13 responses and two themes elicited 5 responses.

Data: Blogs Selected for the Study

The blog entries chosen for this analysis were written by five respondents and came from the second part of the first unit, which explored the active role of preachers in the discursive construction of the notion of "the diabolical witch." The average length of the entries was 86 T-Units, which are defined as independent clauses with all their subordinate clauses; the total number of words was 1,737; and the average number of words per text was 347.4.

Methodology

Following research in the sociocultural and systemic-functional linguistics frameworks that demonstrates the critical role of language and verbal interaction in learning (Halliday 1993; Halliday and Matthiessen 1999; Christie and Martin 1997; Painter 1996, 2007; Lemke 1988, 1990; Vygotsky 1987) we search for evidence of engagement with content in linguistic resources blog writers used to explicitly address various perspectives on content and to weave them into expressions of their own understandings and interpretations.

To identify these resources the systemic-functional framework of appraisal (Martin and White 2005), we specifically used the concept of ENGAGEMENT. ENGAGEMENT is a system of semantic choices and the range of their likely linguistic realizations available to the writers for expressing perspectives on an issue in relation to other positions. ENGAGEMENT resources enable writers to construct an intersubjective stance both with regard to the issues under discussion and in relation to the other readers involved in the negotiation of content as in the context of course-related blog writing. Oriented toward rhetorical effects as opposed to specific wordings, the ENGAGEMENT system encompasses resources that have traditionally been discussed under such categories as modality (Palmer 1986), evidentiality (Chafe and Nichols 1986), projection (Halliday and Matthiessen 2004), or metadiscourse (Hyland 2005).

The framework distinguishes between monoglossic and heteroglossic statements. The monoglossic statements are called "bare assertions" (Martin and White 2005, 28) and present propositions as facts without recognizing any dialogistic alternatives:

Excerpt 1

Throughout history, the church has had a tenuous relationship with sexual behavior.

By contrast, heteroglossic statements recognize the voices of others and are characterized by engagement strategies, as in the following example, where elements in bold represent (also in the examples below) a particular type of engagement identified using the taxonomy by Martin and White (2005):

Excerpt 2

As other course participants noted, throughout history, the church has had a tenuous relationship with sexual behavior.

Within the heteroglossic category, four major strategies of positioning oneself with respect to other alternative positions are singled out by Martin and White (2005):

Disclaim as *deny* or *counter:* the textual voice positions itself in opposition to the ideas of others
Proclaim as *concur, pronounce,* or *endorse:* the textual voice represents a position as compelling and well-founded
Entertain: the textual voice represents a position as explicitly subjective and thus one possibility among many
Attribute as *acknowledge* or *distance:* the textual voice refers to the opinions of others.

These strategies have their likely linguistic realizations. For example, proclaim or endorse, a common strategy for arguing for one's own position by means of supporting it through reference to another source that is presented as valid and undeniable, is often construed through such quoting verbs (or their nominalized equivalents) as *show, point out, demonstrate,* or *emphasize.*

Excerpt 3

As discussants **correctly pointed out,** Bernardino of Siena, Martin Le Franc, and the anonymous author of the Errores Gazariorum all have an even more aggressive campaign against witches than did the authors of our previous readings.

In this excerpt the writer evaluates the proposition put forth by other classmates positively and uses it as a starting point for his own argumentation. Other illustrations of each type of engagement strategy from student blogs are given in appendix A. Because there is no direct match between a type of engagement strategy and its linguistic form, the data are coded in line with the discussion on lexicogrammatical construals of ENGAGEMENT in Martin and White (2005) by Ryshina-Pankova and later triangulated with the coding by another coder. Monoglossic statements were coded in line with the same procedure. The inter-rater reliability was 90 percent and all disagreements were resolved through discussion.

The following sections demonstrate what tracking of the rhetorical strategies of engagement through their lexicogrammatical construals could reveal about students' negotiation of content and academic argumentation about it with other blog writers.

Results

Tables 11.1–11.4 present the blog writers' use of various engagement strategies in terms of four categories: (1) engagement clauses versus bare assertions; (2) engagement with the authors of the readings; (3) engagement with the opinions of other class participants; (4) and engagement as expression of one's own opinions on the readings. The quantitative results can be summarized in the following ways:

1. Strategies of dialogic engagement, either with the opinions of other course participants or with the positions of the authors of the readings, comprise 79.06 percent of all T-Units (as independent clauses with all their subordinate clauses) in the blogs.

2. With respect to the engagement with the positions of the original authors on the issue of witch hunting, the authors' communicative intents are acknowledged in 31.39 percent of clauses and used as endorsement for one's own argument in 10.46 percent of clauses. Engagement with the authors of the readings comprises 44.44 percent of all engagement instances.

Table 11.1
Engagement clauses versus assertions

Engagement clauses	68	79.06%
Assertions	18	20.93%

Table 11.2
Engagement with the authors of the readings[a]

Engagement resources	No. of instances	Reference to the no. of T-Units (%)
Attribute: acknowledge	**27**	**31.39**
Attribute: distance	0	0
Proclaim: endorse	**9**	**10.46**
Total:	**36**	

36/81 (total number of engagement instances): **44.44%**

[a]The numbers in all tables do not add up to 100% because different engagement resources could appear in one and the same clause. If the same type of engagement resource appeared in a T-Unit twice, it was counted only once.

▦ Table 11.3
Engagement with the opinions of other class participants about the readings

Engagement resources	No. of instances	Reference to the no. of T-Units (%)
Attribute/acknowledge	**11**	**12.79**
Proclaim/endorse	**3**	**3.48**
Disclaim/counter	**2**	**2.32**
Total:	**16**	**18.60**

16/81 (total number of engagement instances): **19.75%**

▦ Table 11.4
Engagement as expression of one's own opinion on the readings

Engagement resources	No. of instances	Reference to the no. of T-Units (%)
Proclaim: pronounce	4	4.65
Proclaim: concur	1	1.16
Entertain: probability	**9**	**10.46**
Disclaim: counter	**15**	**17.44**
Disclaim: deny	0	0
Total:	**29**	

29/81 (total number of engagement instances): **35.8%**

3. With regard to the engagement with the opinions of other course participants on the readings, table 11.3 demonstrates that 12.79 percent of all
clauses display references to the opinions of other blog writers through acknowledgment, and in 3.48 percent of clauses an endorsement strategy is
used. Disalignment through disclaim or counter occurs in only 2.32
percent of clauses. All together references to the opinions of other
blog writers comprise 19.75 percent of the total number of engagement
instances.

4. In connection to the blog writers' expression of one's own perspectives on
content, the disclaim or counter reference strategy stands out, with 17.44
percent of clauses containing this resource. Entertain or probability that
helps construe one's own view as possible against the backdrop of other alternative positions is used in 10.46 percent of clauses. Finally, proclaim or
concur and proclaim/pronounce strategies that explicitly present one's subjective position as compelling and well founded are least preferred—
comprising only 4.65 percent and 1.16 percent of clauses, respectively.
Overall, expression of one's own opinion comprises 35.8 percent of all engagement instances.

Discussion

The results demonstrate that explicit engagement with the ideas of others, which we propose to be indicative of content learning, is present in almost four-fifths of the clauses (79.06 percent) and is thus a dominant feature of blog writing in this course. Moreover, the results show that blog writers use a wide gamut of such strategies. They engage in the negotiation of content by constantly alluding to the discursive practices of the authors of course readings, aligning or disaligning themselves with the opinions of other blog writers, and considering or declaring various possible interpretations.

Engagement with Course Content

A frequent strategy (44.44 percent of all engagement instances) for engagement with course content is through references to the authors of the readings. Although this is an expected result that follows from the nature of the assignment, the analysis confirms that the students do, indeed, fulfill the requirements of the task. The strategy of attribution enables blog writers to engage with content issues and themes on the meta-level, employing the so-called distancing helicopter approach, as metaphorically defined by the course instructor. Learners elevate their discussion from the recitation of what happened to the witches to engagement with how the authors of original documents about witches discursively constructed the happenings, a strategy evident in the following:

Excerpt 4

While **two of the authors focused on describing,** in full detail, the shocking and disturbing practices that witches partook of, **the others tried to prove** that the witch threat was real.

Attribution used in this example, realized through various linguistic means (for example, through such verbs as "describe," "point out," "demonstrate," or "account"—and their nominalized forms) enables learners to go beyond a simple summary of the content of the readings, a goal indicated by the blog writing task sheet (see appendix B). Establishing the role of this strategy for an interpretative stance on readings is important. If the use of attribution seems to be a given in a class made up of highly literate Georgetown students, it is something that needs to be taught explicitly in other contexts, such as that of second- or foreign-language learners.

Engagement with Course Participants

Weaving the voices of other course participants into one's own reflection on the issues is an important aspect of student blogs. Most often this allusion takes the form of acknowledging the ideas of others (used in 12.79 percent of clauses), as in the example below:

Excerpt 5

As the discussant post *Witchcraft and Sexual Deviance* mentioned, the church and the public believed that if witches were willing to so publicly flout the word of the Lord, they must also disobey other societal conventions.

In some cases, reference to the blogs of other class participants endorses the author's own line of reasoning (used in 3.48 percent of clauses), as in the following example:

Excerpt 6

The hating increases

As the centuries passed, accounts of witchcraft became more and more specific; details of witches' ceremonies and oaths became more concrete and whatever the condemned humans confessed to was treated as fact. **As discussants correctly pointed out,** Bernardino of Siena, Martin Le Franc, and the anonymous author of the *Errores Gazariorum* all have an even more aggressive campaign against witches than did the authors of our previous readings. By depicting their rituals and customs, they look to paint the most grotesque picture of witches possible. Their frenzied accusations were some of the main catalysts of the subsequent witch hunts.

Here the attribution strategy helps the author to argue, as also manifested in the title of this blog entry, that accounts of witchcraft became increasingly accusatory towards the witches and thus justified subsequent witch hunts.

Note that in these two excerpts, references are made to a general group of discussants as well as to particular posts by course participants, illustrating a relatively high level of explicit engagement with the ideas of other blog writers in the class (allusion to other students' ideas comprised 19.75 percent of all engagement instances). Although this engagement is mostly realized in terms of aligning oneself with the ideas of other class participants (87.5 percent of all instances in the category of engagement with the opinions of classmates), there are two instances in which students overtly argue with their classmates. In this case the disclaim or counter strategy is used, as may be seen in the examples to follow.

Excerpt 7

Although the religion motif was not commonly discussed among the discussants, the relevance of this theme to these various texts needs to be brought to attention.

Excerpt 8

Multiple discussants identified child murders as a common motif. **While the child murders occur frequently throughout the passages,** they seem to be only a piece of the motif.

This strategy helps students to juxtapose different ideas in a clear way and establish a new interpretation in a rhetorically explicit manner.

Engagement as Expression of One's Own Opinion on the Readings

Although engagement with other blog writers' opinions by means of directly challenging them is rare, disclaim or counter is a frequent move in the blogs that appears in almost one-fifth (17.44 percent) of the clauses. When not used to explicitly oppose interpretations of other classmates, it is deployed for revealing one's own perspective on the readings in a twofold way. First it is used to demonstrate to the reader new aspects through a comparison of different readings:

Excerpt 9

In comparison to the earlier readings, this week's texts show signs of growing fervor as Europe draws closer and closer to the historic craze of "witch" hunting.

Second, it is employed to point out something new, interesting, surprising, and counter to expectations of the audience and thus worthy of note:

Excerpt 10

Yet it is interesting to note that among all of the fears of society, sexual behavior is the one most associated with witches.

Excerpt 11

Suddenly, with this shocking revelation, the non-'witches' are not quite as blameless as they had been.

The disclaim or counter move is crucial for the dialogic construction of new knowledge: it allows writers to put forward their own original interpretations of the readings by anchoring them in existing interpretations or expectations and then expanding or supplanting them.

A similar purpose of establishing a new view of the readings is also fulfilled by another engagement strategy, proclaim or pronounce:

Excerpt 12

In addition to acknowledging the extraordinary descriptive abilities of the text's authors, **I took particular note** of the new message that quite forcefully takes shape in Bernardino of Siena's passionate sermon, ordinary citizens should be held responsible and should be subsequently disciplined for withholding information that might help locate, apprehend, and punish current witches.

A new aspect singled out by the writer of this excerpt is positioned as a compelling subjective finding that is supplementary to other ideas about the readings. One possible explanation for a rather scarce use of this strategy (used in 4.65 percent of clauses) has to do with the fact that the task sheet required students to use formal academic writing style in their blog entries. The proclaim or pronounce strategy—with its emphasis on the explicitly subjective authorial stance as compelling and well founded—may often be avoided in academic writing, in which objective realizations of stance are preferred (Coffin and Hewings 2004; Hewings 2004; Schleppegrell 2004). A similar explanation seems to be plausible with regard to the infrequent use of proclaim or concur (used in 1.16 percent of clauses). This strategy positions the author and the reader as agreeing with each other and presents this agreement as being taken for granted:

Excerpt 13

The ability of a population to successfully reproduce is **obviously** a crucial aspect of a society's survival.

In academic argumentative writing, however, propositions generally need to be argued for and substantiated with evidence or their force is often modulated by means of the entertain or probability strategy. In the following example the proposition made by the author is presented as one possible alternative, which makes it harder to refute than a proposition with a proclaim or concur move that assumes it is universally true:

Excerpt 14

As the name implies, **it seemed** as if eating children was one of the main focuses of anti-witch writings.

The entertain or probability strategy is often deployed not only to leave dialogic space for other possible interpretations, but also to provide evidence for one's thesis by speculating about the content and making its implications explicit. This function of entertain or probability is illustrated below; the author's main argument is about a new aspect of witch hunting: involvement of ordinary citizens and non-witches who could be accused of being accomplices of witches and thus subject to the same punishments.

Excerpt 15

The passionate "witch" frenzy grows and finds new victims

For example, **let's imagine** that an old woman from a local village is singled out and accused of "witchcraft." A subsequent legal trial takes place to determine the extent of her "evil doings," and the townspeople call for witnesses as well as additional evidence. The trial concludes, the "witch" receives her "due" punishment—burning, drowning, etc.—however the story is far from over. At this point, the townspeople's suspicions mount as they wonder why some of the witnesses had never spoken earlier. Why did the old woman's neighbor remain silent until the last possible minute? How could the old woman's cousin not have noticed her strange behavior? The questions fly and the fingers point. Suddenly, a rash of additional accusations builds as the witnesses themselves are called to trial on charges of "witchcraft."

The author of this excerpt engages the readers by asking them to consider ("entertain") a certain possible scenario, based on the original readings. This scenario works to substantiate her thesis.

Do learners engage in content learning as they interact with their peers through blogs, and how does this engagement take place? We can conclude that, given our assumption that content learning is about engagement with various perspectives on content that can be tracked by means of a functional linguistic analysis, the quantitative results and their qualitative discussion demonstrate a high level of engagement in content learning within the blog-based interaction. The engagement strategies singled out from student blogs provide evidence that the course participants do in fact fulfill the demands of the blogging task as spelled out by the task sheet. The use of various attributive as well as disclaim or counter and entertain or probability strategies speaks to the fact that bloggers do refer to the readings and to the ideas of their peers, and they are able to expand them by pointing out some new dimensions in their understanding of the readings.

In evaluating the level of engagement based on the results, one could note that although students refer to the ideas of other course participants to align themselves with them or endorse their own opinions, they rarely challenge each other by distancing themselves from the views of others (there are no instances of acknowledge or distance strategy) or by countering them (only two instances). This reluctance to question the propositions of other classmates is also reported by Bloch and Crosby (2008) in their analysis of blogs by ESL students and by Coffin and Hewings (2005) in their investigation of entries in asynchronous electronic conferences in a long-distance applied linguistics course. Drawing on the work in the field of argumentation studies (for example, Mitchell and Andrews 2000), Coffin and Hewings point out the importance of argumentation, including refutation strategies for learning disciplinary knowledge, and state that this lack of critique towards other classmates' ideas in their data was "limiting the degree of argumentative interplay between the opinions and views being put forward" and weakened learners' arguments (2005, 41).

To improve engagement with other course participants and content matter through blogs, students could be alerted to the role of argument in academic knowledge construction and instructed to examine their peers' entries more carefully, taking issue with them by means of a disclaim or counter move more frequently. This, however, might continue to be a difficult strategy to adopt, given the unwillingness of students—especially those who are at the beginning of their academic careers, as these students are—to publicly oppose each other. Encouraging an argumentative stance can also become part of class meetings, during which a safe learning environment might be created to explicitly teach students how to engage with their peers' work by means of evaluation and respectful critique. This could be accomplished by presenting a blog model to course participants with the goal of analyzing it with them in terms of salient engagement strategies and their functions. Including some of the most important engagement strategies on the blogs assessment sheet could also raise learners' awareness of academically important argumentative strategies.

Conclusion

This study explores content learning in blogs by tracking their linguistic realizations by means of ENGAGEMENT analysis. The results of the analysis demonstrate that blog writers do engage in academically valued negotiation of content that includes dialogically expanding strategies of attribution and consideration of various alternatives, as well as dialogically contracting strategies of countering other discussants' opinions and proclaiming one's own views (Martin and White 2005, 102–4). Whereas these strategies are present in all blogs in the data, only some of their authors are able to alternate between these resources in a strategic way in order to construct a convincing academic argument in which a new perspective is established and defended against the background of other opinions.

To return to the initial skeptical questions about the significance of blogs as a new instrument for fostering intellectual engagement in discipline-based courses, our results enable us to argue that blogs do, indeed, provide a conducive environment for learning content through interaction with others and through practicing academic argumentation about content. In this respect blogs can be considered a unique medium. On the one hand, they allow learners to engage in academic literacy practices in a way that would not be possible in oral classroom settings. These practices can be further embedded in classroom meetings, potentially contributing to substantive and intellectually rich academic discussions.

On the other hand, blog writing encourages a self-initiated dialogue among class participants about course-related issues that would not be possible in traditional writing assignments, for which the teacher is the only dialogic partner and arbiter. Blog-based interaction can allow students to learn how to engage with a variety of voices and a variety of knowers and construct their own argument by explicitly drawing on them—whether in alignment or disalignment. And this is, in essence, a crucial aspect of intellectual engagement and critical inquiry.

REFERENCES

Al-Fadda, Hind, and Maha Al-Yahya. 2010. Using web blogs as a tool to encourage pre-class reading, post-class reflections and collaboration in higher education. *US-China Education Review* 7, no. 7:100–106.

Bakhtin, M. M. 1981. Discourse in the novel. In *The dialogic imagination: Four essays,* ed. Michael Holquist, trans. Caryl Emerson and Michael Holquist, 259–422. Austin: University of Texas Press.

———. 1986. *Speech genres and other late essays.* Ed. Michael Holquist and Caryl Emerson. Trans. Vern W. McGee. Austin: University of Texas Press.

Bloch, Joel. 2007. Abdullah's blogging: A generation 1.5 student enters the blogosphere. *Language Learning and Technology* 11:128–41.

Bloch, Joel, and Cathryn Crosby. 2008. Blogging and academic writing development. In *Computer-enhanced language acquisition and learning,* ed. Felicia Zhang and Beth Barber, 36–47. Hershey, PA, and New York: Information Science Reference.

Chafe, Wallace, and Johanna Nichols, eds. 1986. *Evidentiality: The linguistic coding of epistemology.* Norwood, NJ: Ablex.

Christie, Frances, and J. R. Martin, eds. 1997. *Genre and institutions. Social processes in the workplace and school.* London: Cassell.

Coffin, Caroline, and Ann Hewings. 2004. IELTS as preparation for tertiary writing: Distinctive interpersonal and textual strategies. In *Analysing academic writing,* ed. Louise J. Ravelli and Robert A. Ellis, 153–71. London: Continuum.

———. 2005. Engaging electronically: Using CMC to develop students' argumentation skills in higher education. *Language and Education* 19:32–49.

Cuhadar, Cem, and Abdullah Kuzu. 2010. Improving interaction through blogs in a constructivist learning environment. *Turkish Online Journal of Distance Education* 11:134–61.

Ferdig, R. E., and K. D. Trammell. 2004. Content delivery in the "blogosphere." *Technological Horizons in Education Journal* 31. thejournal.com/Articles/2004/02/01/Content-Delivery-in-the-Blogo sphere.aspx.

Halliday, M. A. K. 1993. Towards a language-based theory of learning. *Linguistics and Education* 5:93–116.

Halliday, M. A. K., and Christian M. I. M. Matthiessen. 1999. *Construing experience through meaning: A language-based approach to cognition.* London: Cassell.

———. 2004. *An introduction to functional grammar.* 3rd ed. London: Edward Arnold.

Hernández-Ramos, Pedro. 2004. Web logs and online discussions as tools to promote reflective practice. *The Journal of Interactive Online Learning* 3, no. 1. www.ncolr.org/jiol/issues/pdf/3.1.4.pdf.

Hewings, Ann. 2004. Developing discipline-specific writing: An analysis of undergraduate geography essays. In *Analysing academic writing: Contextualized frameworks,* ed. Louise J. Ravelli and Robert A. Ellis, 131–52. London: Continuum.

Hyland, Ken. 2005. *Metadiscourse: Exploring interaction in writing.* London and New York: Continuum.

Kelley, Michael John. 2008. The impact of weblogs on the affective states and academic writing of L2 undergraduates. PhD diss., University of Virginia.

Lawrence, Christopher N., and Michelle L. Dion. 2010. Blogging in the political science classroom. *Political Science and Politics* 43:151–56.

Lemke, J. L. 1988. Genres, semantics, and classroom education. *Linguistics and Education* 1:81–99.

———. 1990. *Talking science: Language, learning, and values.* Norwood, NJ: Ablex.

Lowe, Charles, and Terra Williams. 2004. Moving to the public: Weblogs in the writing classroom. In *Into the blogosphere: Rhetoric, community, and culture of weblogs,* ed. Laura Gurak, Smiljana Antonijevic, Laurie Johnson, Clancy Ratliff, and Jessica Reyman. Minneapolis: University of Minnesota Libraries. blog.lib.umn.edu/blogosphere/moving_to_the_public.html.

Martin, J. R., and P. R. R. White. 2005. *The language of evaluation: Appraisal in English.* New York: Palgrave.

Mitchell, Sally, and Richard Andrews, eds. 2000. *Learning to argue in higher education.* Portsmouth, NH: Boynton Cook.

Myers, Greg. 2010. *The discourse of blogs and wikis.* London and New York: Continuum.

Oravec, Jo Ann. 2002. Bookmarking the world: Weblog applications in education. *Journal of Adolescent and Adult Literacy* 45:616–21.

Painter, Clare. 1996. The development of language as a resource for thinking: A linguistic view of learning. In *Literacy in society,* ed. Ruqaiya Hasan and Geoff Williams, 50–85. London: Longman.

———. 2007. Language for learning in early childhood. In *Language, knowledge and pedagogy,* ed. Frances Christie and J. R. Martin, 131–55. London: Continuum.

Palmer, F. R. 1986. *Mood and modality.* Cambridge: Cambridge University Press.

Richardson, Will. 2003. Web logs in the English classroom: More than just chat. *English Journal* 93:39–43.

Schleppegrell, Mary J. 2004. Technical writing in a second language: the role of grammatical metaphor. In *Analysing academic writing: Contextualized frameworks,* ed. Louise J. Ravelli and Robert A. Ellis, 172–89. London: Continuum.

Swain, Merrill. 2006. Languaging, agency and collaboration in advanced second language proficiency. In *Advanced language learning: The contribution of Halliday and Vygotsky,* ed. Heidi Byrnes, 95–108. London: Continuum.

Vygotsky, L. S. 1978. *Mind in society: The development of higher psychological processes.* Ed. M. Cole, V. John-Steiner, S. Scribner, and E. Souberman. Cambridge, MA: Harvard University Press.

———. 1987. Thinking and speech. In *The collected works of L. S. Vygotsky,* vol. 1, *Problems of general psychology,* ed. Robert W. Rieber and Aaron S. Carton, 239–85. New York: Plenum.

Walker, Jill. 2005. Weblogs: Learning in public. *On the Horizon* 13:112–18.

Wang, Jenny, and Yuenchiu Fang. 2005. Benefits of cooperative learning in weblog networks. *Educational Resources Information Center.* www.eric.ed.gov/PDFS/ED490815.pdf.

Wells, Gordon. 1999. *Dialogic inquiry: Toward a sociocultural practice and theory of education.* Cambridge: Cambridge University Press.

Wertsch, James V. 1985. *Vygotsky and the social formation of mind.* Cambridge, MA: Harvard University Press.

———. 1991. *Voices of the mind: A sociocultural approach to mediated action.* Cambridge, MA: Harvard University Press.

Williams, Jeremy B., and Joanne Jacobs. 2004. Exploring the use of blogs as learning spaces in the higher education sector. *Australasian Journal of Educational Technology* 20:232–47.

Xie, Ying, and Priya Sharma. 2005. Students' lived experience of using weblogs in a class: An exploratory study. *Educational Resources Information Center.* www.eric.ed.gov/PDFS/ED485009.pdf.

APPENDIX A: ENGAGEMENT STRATEGIES

Bare Assertion: presents propositions as facts without any engagement strategies
One of the devil's greatest strengths is tricking those weak of morals into thinking he is something else.

Disclaim: the textual voice positions itself in opposition to the ideas of others

Deny: invokes an alternative position and rejects it

Counter: invokes an alternative position but does not reject it directly. It offers an alternative position instead.

No examples in the data

***Although the religion motif was not commonly discussed** among the discussants, the relevance of this theme to these various texts needs to be*

brought

to attention.

Proclaim: the textual voice represents a position as compelling and well-founded

Concur: announces the addresser as agreeing or having the same knowledge as the putative reader

Endorse: expresses alignments with an attributed position

Pronounce: expresses authorial emphasis or explicit authorial interventions

*The ability of a population to successfully reproduce is **obviously** a crucial aspect of a society's survival.*

*In comparison to the earlier readings, this week's texts **show** signs of growing fervor as Europe draws closer and closer to the historic craze of witch hunting.*

*In addition to acknowledging the extraordinary descriptive abilities of the text's authors, **I took particular note** of the new message that quite forcefully takes shape in Bernardino of Siena's passionate sermon.*

Entertain: the textual voice represents a position as explicitly subjective and thus acknowledges it as one among many
As one might imagine, this latest revelation in the history of "witchcraft" proves to be incredibly important in later years during the peak centuries of witch hunting.

Attribute: the textual voice refers to the opinions of others

Acknowledge: attributes propositions to a source

Distance: attributes proposition to a source but distances itself from it

As the discussant post Witchcraft and Sexual Deviance *mentioned, the church and the public believed that if witches were willing to so publicly flout the word of the Lord, they must also disobey other societal conventions.*

No examples

APPENDIX B: BLOG ENTRIES TASK SHEET

Instructions: Blog entries for Unit I (historical sources)

Blog URL: TBA via email

Blog entries serve as preparation and springboard for classroom discussion of an assigned set of texts. At the same time, they serve as opportunities for academic writing. Blogs for this class require formal academic language. They should be approx. five hundred words in length.

We will have two types of bloggers: (1) discussants and (2) respondents.

For each set of texts, we will have four "experts," i.e., students who will be particularly well informed about the texts under consideration. These experts will start off the class discussion by summarizing the arguments presented in their blog entries.

Discussants:

Blog entries are to focus on drawing connections between the various texts, *not* on summarizing content. Such connections could be similarities or differences in theme, genre, purpose, audience, author background, structure of argument, style, language use, etc. One approach would be to try to see if there is a "red thread" running through the texts and how it plays out individually in each text. Another idea would be to see if, after reading through all assigned texts, you can name one or two key concepts that are evident in all texts.

Respondents:

Blog entries will comment on arguments presented by discussants *and* add a new dimension, such as references to other aspects of a text or references to a text not mentioned by the discussant. It must be clear to the reader that you are writing a response.

Assessment:

Holistic grade for *all* blog entries; individual grade for your "expert" entries as discussant and respondent.

Timeline:

For Tuesday classes:	Discussants post by midnight Saturday
	Respondents post by midnight Monday
For Thursday classes:	Discussants post by noon Wednesday
	Respondents post by 6 a.m. Thursday

12

Reading in Print or Onscreen
Better, Worse, or About the Same?

NAOMI S. BARON
American University

Do Technologies Change Us?

THE YEAR WAS 1968. The United States was finally gaining traction in the space race against the Soviet Union. In December, NASA launched the Apollo 8 mission that circled the moon. For the first time it was possible to see our planet from beyond a low-earth orbit. Photographs taken on that mission profoundly altered millions of people's perceptions in ways unrelated to astronomy. The Soviet Union was no longer an abstraction on a Mercator-projected map but physically viewable as part of a single, contiguous globe. So, too, were China, India, Colombia, and South Africa. Those pictures from space offered a new sense of possibility for global engagement, which mushroomed in the following decades in such diverse forms as an explosion in international commerce, labor outsourcing, and concern about global climate change.

In a similar way, with the development of information and communication technologies (ranging from telephones and artificial intelligence programs to robots and social networking sites), users of these technologies have been exposed to circumstances that may alter our perspectives on such issues as how humans interact with machines, how we relate to one another, and what it means to learn—and to know. To understand the types of potential changes we are talking about, I consider, in turn, four scenarios.

The first is drawn from the work of Sherry Turkle, a psychologist at the Massachusetts Institute of Technology. Turkle has written much on the attitudes of contemporary adults and children regarding relationships between real, animate objects and mechanical counterparts (Turkle 1995). Our example is drawn from her book *Alone Together: Why We Expect More from Technology and Less from Each Other*. In November 2005 Turkle had taken her daughter Rebecca, then aged fourteen, to an exhibit on Charles Darwin at the American Museum of Natural History in New York. For the exhibition the museum had brought two giant tortoises from the Galapagos Islands, where Darwin had done some of his groundbreaking research contributing to the theory of evolution. Turkle writes,

One tortoise was hidden from view; the other rested in its cage, utterly still. Rebecca inspected the visible tortoise thoughtfully for a while and then said matter-of-factly, "They could have used a robot." . . . She said she thought it was a shame to bring a turtle all this way . . . when it was just going to sit there in the museum, doing nothing. Rebecca was both concerned for the imprisoned turtle and unmoved by its authenticity. (2011, 3)

Turkle's story highlights the contemporary question of whether the sophistication (and efficiency) of contemporary robots potentially challenges assumptions about the desirability of interacting with living beings.

The second example comes from the work of media critic Howard Rheingold and involves social concerns that trace back to the late 1800s, when the telephone was introduced into private homes in the United States. Rheingold (1999) focuses his inquiry on the Pennsylvania Amish, who to this day do not allow telephones in their homes (Umble 1996). In an interview with an Amish man from Lancaster, Pennsylvania, Rheingold asked why he did not have a telephone. The man replied,

What would that lead to? We don't want to be the kind of people who will interrupt a conversation at home to answer a telephone. It's not just how you use the technology that concerns us. We're also concerned about what kind of person you become when you use it.

The larger social question, of course, is what about those of us who allow telephones not only into our homes but into our lives at large—talking with or texting someone else while sitting in a café with friends or transacting business at a bank? What kind of people do we become as we continually privilege interaction with an absent third party over conversation (or even shared silence) with the person physically before us?

The third illustration concerns people's personalities, and it comes from the work of Elias Aboujaode, a psychiatrist at the Stanford School of Medicine, specializing in obsessive-compulsive disorders. In *Virtually You: The Dangerous Powers of the E-Personality,* Aboujaoude examines the kind of people we become when we use technology—including the likes of websites, instant messaging (IM), Facebook, and Twitter:

The Internet is . . . fundamentally changing us. . . . [O]ur online traits are unconsciously being imported into our offline life, so that our idea of what a real-life community should be . . . is being reconfigured in the image of a chat room, and our offline persona increasingly resembles that of our avatar. . . . I recognize the good in cyberspace but strive for an assessment of the Internet that is more mindful of our psyche. (2011, 11–12)

The question Aboujaode raises is whether our lives online are reshaping (and not for the better) our perceptions of who we are in our physical, embodied existence.

The last case involves the possible effects of the internet upon cognition. In summer 2008, the journalist Nicholas Carr wrote an article in *Atlantic Monthly* titled "Is Google Making Us Stupid?" He then elaborated upon the question in *The Shallows: What the Internet Is Doing to Our Brains* (2010). Carr argues that the internet is reshaping our brains, making it difficult for us to concentrate on continuous, complex written text:

> Sometime in 2007 . . . I began to notice that the Net was exerting a much
> stronger and broader influence over me than my old stand-alone PC ever
> had. . . . The very way my brain worked seemed to be changing. . . . I began
> worrying about my inability to pay attention to one thing for more than a
> couple of minutes. . . . I missed my old brain. (2010, 16)

In much the same vein, the psychiatrist Edward Hallowell (2006) has suggested that use of new digital media is causing acquired attention deficit disorder. More recently, a team of psychologists (Sparrow, Liu, and Wegner 2011) has explored how availability of the internet may be redefining the extent to which we remember information—or where to find it.

Whether we are convinced by some writers' cautionary arguments (particularly the cognitive one), it is clear that technologies can influence our level of competence in what educated societies have seen as basic skills.[1] Pocket calculators undermined the need to remember how to perform simple addition and subtraction; spellcheck has rendered knowledge of correct orthography less valuable; and in Japan, the availability of word processing on computers is making even teachers of Japanese forget the stroke order in which the kanji (Japanese characters) must be written.

In this chapter I focus on the technology of the written word. More specifically, I look at the conditions under which we decode writing—that is, how we read. I consider two questions:

- Does the medium on which we encounter written words affect how we read?
- Do new reading platforms redefine what we mean by reading in the first place?

Historically, writing has appeared on a vast array of surfaces: clay, wax, stone, tortoise shell, papyrus, parchment, paper, newsprint, and now on various sorts of digital screens. In each instance, the affordances of the medium (including, for example, portability, fragility, cost, and strain on the eyes) might affect the way we read, how much we read, how much we remember of our reading, and the extent to which we value or personalize the medium or the text. For instance, we are far less likely to toss out Shakespeare's First Folio than a copy of yesterday's newspaper. Similarly, we might be more inclined to tackle Kant's *Critique of Pure Reason* in hard copy than on an iPhone.

This chapter contrasts the ways in which we read using two media: print (such as books on library shelves) and digital screens. Reading print entails reading tangible hard copy. Reading onscreen refers to reading done on computers, ebooks, or portable devices such as mobile phones or tablets. My question is whether reading on one platform is better, worse, or about the same as reading on the other.

I begin by looking at the notion of print culture, considering in turn the historical rise of writing and reading, the transition from print to print culture, and some presuppositions of and challenges to print culture. I then turn to data from a pilot study of reading practices by a group of American undergraduate students, and close by discussing the pros and cons of reading in each medium, along with possible consequences for what it means to read.

Print Culture

Contemporary attitudes toward printed text grow out of a long evolutionary process, beginning with the appearance of written language.

The Rise of Writing and Reading

Writing (and hence, reading) began roughly five thousand years ago, having developed independently in several different civilizations (Sumeria: c. 3000 BCE; Egypt: c. 3000 BCE; China: c. 1500 BCE).[2] The emergence of writing allowed for complex administrative organization (Chadwick 1959), and so is often viewed as a prerequisite for the rise of cities, as evidenced in Mesopotamia and Egypt.

However, the availability of writing in a society need not imply that the culture itself can be characterized as a written culture. In classical Greece and Rome, literacy rates across the populations—as well as the need for literacy—were low (Harris 1989). The same situation held true through much of the European Middle Ages (Baron 2000; Clanchy 1993). What is more, knowledge of reading and writing were often asymmetric: In Europe (and then early America), pupils were generally first taught to read. If they progressed further in their education, instruction in writing would follow.

Another historical variable involves writing technologies and techniques. In older civilizations, writing was commonly done on clay tablets (as in Mycenaean Greece or Assyria) or scrolls (as in ancient Israel). The codex (or book) form as we know it did not appear until c. 400 CE (Roberts and Skeat 1983). The custom of leaving spaces between words on the page emerged only later (c. 600–800 CE), first in Latin texts used in western Europe and subsequently in the vernacular languages (Saenger 1997).

The first printed book in the West was Johannes Gutenberg's Bible, produced in Mainz in the mid-1450s. Printing arrived in England in 1476, when William Caxton set up his press at Westminster in London. However, just as the existence of writing in a society hardly guarantees that society at large is literate—or that the society functions as a written culture—availability of print does not ensure that printed works play a central role in the lives of even the educated populace. In the case of England, it would take almost two hundred years before one could accurately speak of a print culture.

From Print to Print Culture

What is print culture?[3] It is a set of attitudes regarding how we read and write, presupposing the availability of print technology. Two simple examples illustrate the point. The first concerns standardization of spelling. Although it is commonly believed that the arrival of print promptly led to the standardization of spelling, concerns for consistency in spelling did not take hold in England until well into the seventeenth and even the early eighteenth centuries (Scragg 1974). Second, multiple printed copies of the same book were often not actually identical until modern times. It has been estimated, for instance, that twenty-four thousand variations of the King James Bible came into being between 1611 and 1830 (Johns 1998, 91).

By the eighteenth century, a print culture had emerged in much of Europe that shaped how the written word was produced and decoded. This culture included not only issues of editorial consistency (such as standardized spelling and exact replication of text), but also attitudes toward readers' interaction with a written work and tools for facilitating this interaction. Some of these methodologies and tools had been available before the proliferation of printed works. However, the spread of print (and with it, literacy) transformed the way that societies writ large interacted with the written word.

Presuppositions of Print Culture

I focus on four sets of presuppositions that print culture entails:[4]

- Durability of a text
- Conditions for reading
- Value of books
- Navigation tools

These four were selected because new media technologies that enable us to read on-screen present challenges to these assumptions.

Durability of a Text   The first set of assumptions involves the durability of a text: once a written copy exists, readers can physically return to it. Given this durability, readers can (and do) annotate their copy of a work by writing in a page's margins, underlining, or otherwise highlighting text.

Annotating texts has a long history, predating the appearance of printing in the West (Jackson 2001; Caxton Club 2011). Annotation may be for the original reader's own benefit (for example, to record thoughts on an issue the author has addressed or to select materials that might be useful to review at a later point). In books passed down to family members or sold to other owners, marginalia offers new readers insight into the minds of earlier readers or owners. Regardless of who does the rereading, the assumption behind such annotation is that the potential exists for someone to subsequently return to that text.

Conditions for Reading   Print culture brought with it assumptions about the conditions under which we read. Two of these assumptions were that people predominantly read silently and that they read to themselves. Historically, reading was done aloud—either reading so others could hear or essentially mumbling to oneself (Parkes 1993; Saenger 1997). In fact, in twelfth-century cloister libraries in France and England, the space was divided into carrels, separated by stone walls, so that monks could read aloud softly to themselves (or dictate to secretaries) without disturbing others (Saenger 1982, 396). Silent reading did not become commonplace until the mid- and late fourteenth century, but has largely been taken for granted ever since. Similarly, although reading aloud to others—both literate and nonliterate audiences—was common historically, reading strictly by oneself became the norm by the time print culture was established (Baron 2000, 32–33, 85–87).

Another condition for reading that emerged as a cornerstone of print culture was the rise of libraries: both personal (generally for the well-to-do) and public (Baron 2000, 87–91). Increasingly, reading became an activity that could be done in places specially designed for that purpose: not only were large numbers of books available from which to choose, but there was also an ambiance (generally one in which silence was observed) that invited mental concentration.

A natural corollary of a library (or library-like) environment is the assumption that when a person is reading, he or she focuses on the text at hand. Obviously, readers stand up and stretch, pause to think about how the present text fits into larger mental schemes, daydream, or fall asleep over the book. However, paradigmatically, the assumption is that the reader is not simultaneously paying bills, conversing about an upcoming trip, or playing solitaire.

Value of Books   The third set of assumptions about print culture involves the value we place on books, including their contents. Consider the ideas that books should have something original to say, that authors of books have legal rights, and that the prose in which books are written should be well crafted. Although the concept of plagiarism dates back at least to Roman times, legal notions of copyright are relatively modern. Copyright laws are largely an eighteenth-century invention (Rose 1993; Woodmansee and Jaszi 1994). Similarly, careful editing of books (a process that was difficult at best in handwritten manuscripts and not widely practiced in the early days of printing—Price 1939; Simpson 1935) became the norm only in the seventeenth and eighteenth centuries. Moreover, emerging copyright laws included the presumption that unless you were writing fiction, what you wrote was true. Even today some book contracts call for authors to attest to the truth of what appears in their nonfiction works.

With the rise of wealth in England (and growth of the middle and upper-middle classes), printed books increasingly became prized possessions. Sets of volumes were elegantly bound in Moroccan leather; first editions and autographed copies of books held special value. Libraries created rare book rooms, where manuscript—and print—treasures were housed. The public came to see tangible books as having both aesthetic and economic value.

At the same time, literacy rates began to rise. During the middle ages, royalty generally felt little need to learn to read and write—one hired other people to perform those chores. But with the expansion of printed works and gradual increase in education levels in Europe and America (Baron 2000, 79–85), basic literacy skills came to be expected of everyone. As opportunities for higher education multiplied in the twentieth century, reading books—and many of them—became a socially defined goal.

Navigation Tools   Our last set of assumptions regarding print culture concerns tools for navigating within a text. These devices include now-familiar publishing elements such as a title page, a table of contents, section divisions within a book, an index, and page numbers.

None of these conventions existed in early manuscripts. They emerged gradually, largely as a result of printing. Consider the title page, which began to appear between 1475 and 1480. In very early printed books, text began on the first page (which was on the right-hand [recto] side). Understandably, that initial page tended to get dirty. To help keep the text clean, printers began adding an additional sheet to the front of the book and starting the text on the left-hand [verso] side. As a result, there was an empty recto page when the book was opened. To fill that page, printers initially inserted titles to the works, eventually adding such information as the publisher and the date and place of publication (Febvre and Martin 1976, 84).

Paul Saenger (2010) suggests that printing had substantial impact on the very way in which people read, even in the early years of the technology. For example, he argues that printing facilitated faster reading than was possible when readers were confronted with manuscripts. One reason was that abbreviations tended to become standardized in print, reducing the ambiguity that had resulted from the sometimes idiosyncratically created abbreviations found in manuscripts (Saenger 2010, 392). Speed was further enhanced by replacing low-quality Gothic cursive script (often used in inexpensively produced manuscript copies) with clearer, standardized type fonts (Saenger 2010, 394–97). A third tool that facilitated reading was the introduction of round parentheses for setting off a clause from the rest of a sentence or for distinguishing biblical text from commentary (397–401).

Saenger also explores the effect of printing on use of page numbers. In earlier Latin manuscripts that had been copied in the British Isles (as far back as the eighth or ninth centuries), numbering had sometimes been used to ensure that individual sheets of parchment were collated in the correct order. Sometimes numbers appeared on both recto and verso pages, but other times only one side of the leaf bore a number. Still, use of any numbering was rare. It has been estimated that around 1450, less than 10 percent of manuscript books contained such numbers (Saenger 2010, 255).

Fifty years later (at the close of the first half century of Western printing), the proportion of printed works with pagination was "far higher" (Saenger 2010, 256). Part of this change reflected the new role that page numbers were playing. By the 1510s, scholars were starting to "refer to folio numbers of specific editions to designate loci within printed texts" (Saenger 2010, 405). Since the early sixteenth century, readers have relied on page numbers to find their way in books, whether in using tables of contents or indexes, or in referring to specific locations of text.

Although it is not a textual navigation tool per se, another important development coterminous with the rise of print culture was the emergence of dictionaries and reference works that helped readers cope with the expansion of information (and knowledge) that characterized the sixteenth and seventeenth centuries in western Europe (Blair 2003, 2010; Rosenberg 2003; Yeo 2002). Highly reminiscent of modern complaints about information overload, intellectuals in early modern Europe complained there was literally too much to know. This abundance of knowledge (or, in many cases, undigested information) resulted from a variety of sources: the growth of trade and subsequent empire, increased communication across national boundaries, and the expanding numbers of comparatively inexpensive books available.

The solution was production of various types of compendia: from universal bibliographies to dictionaries, book reviews, and encyclopedias. The best-known examples of this last genre are Ephraim Chamber's *Cyclopaedia* (1728) and Denis Diderot's *Encyclopédie* (1751–1772). Did these compendia reduce the amount that people read? There is no evidence of it. Rather, such reference works enabled those who wanted to read to better find their way among the multiplying options of printed works.

Challenges to Print Culture

Print culture flourished for roughly two centuries. However, for varied reasons and in differing degrees, challenges began to arise to some of the presuppositions of print culture I examine. Such challenges often predated the online and mobile media revolution of the late twentieth and early twenty-first centuries, although it is the challenges generated by digital reading platforms that are the focus of this chapter.

Durability of a Text   As literacy rates began to soar by the mid- to late nineteenth century, the expanding population of readers sought inexpensive reading material. Publishers responded by producing more and more newspapers (London had over two dozen daily papers by the early 1890s [Shaw 1985, xi]) and cheap paperback books (Feather 1988). Many of these publications were intended to be read once and then abandoned. A century later, so-called quality paperbacks emerged (largely for the college-going or college-educated market), which were, in principle, destined for personal libraries along with hardbound books (Epstein 2002). However, as contemporary readers can attest, all manner of printed material—newspapers and magazines, trade paperbacks, and even hardbacks—were landing in the trash heap even before the proliferation of personal computers that began in the 1980s.

However, the explosion in personal computing and use of the internet, along with marketing strategies of contemporary booksellers and publishers, has magnified challenges to the presupposition of durability of text. On the one hand, readers who print text available online (whether a Shakespearean play or a book chapter for a college reading assignment) are more likely to toss those materials when they are finished reading (or being tested) than to discard their codex counterparts. On the other hand, bookstores (particularly college bookstores) do a brisk business in buying used books or renting out hard copies (such as www.rent-a-text.com). Similarly, publishers (such as www.efollett.com) now rent out electronic downloads of books that expire at the end of a contracted time period. Such books are not durable for the original reader and obviously are not destined for a personal library.

Conditions for Reading   The conditions under which reading is done have also been undergoing shifts. During the later decades of the twentieth century, public libraries expanded their function as repositories for printed volumes by purchasing large amounts of video material and providing social gathering spaces. In the age of new media, reading still tends to be individual and silent, but the profusion of personal computers and mobile phones has introduced a phenomenon that earlier was largely unknown: multitasking while reading. Such multitasking—searching for inexpensive plane fares while reading, changing one's Facebook status while reading, sending and receiving text messages while reading—is radically altering our understanding of what it means to attend to a text.

Value of Books   Lest we romanticize the notion of attentively focusing on a text, we should remind ourselves that skimming, flipping the pages of a book or magazine, and speed reading have long been practices associated with reading. Reading onscreen is hardly the source of such behavior.

However, the coming of computers and the internet has altered a number of assumptions from print culture about the value of books (and of reading them). The fact that academic libraries are increasingly removing their hard-copy collections in favor of online access (or offsite storage) sends a clear message to everyone in the academic community that hard copies and electronic versions are in essence interchangeable—an assumption that obviously needs to be examined (for examples of discussions comparing reading on the two platforms, see Cull 2011; Levy 2001; Marmarelli and Ringle 2009; Rich 2008). Wherever truth lies in the debate, there are diminishing opportunities for encountering those earlier Moroccan leather-bound volumes and shrinking impetus for building personal hardcopy libraries.

A further consequence of the online revolution has been to democratize production of and access to text. Democratization has brought undeniable benefits, but it has also helped usher in a cluster of attitudes that question some of the earlier assumptions of print culture. These include the right of authors to own their texts if they so choose (copyright) and the assumption (part of copyright) that—unless authors say they are writing fiction—what they write needs to be not only properly edited but also true.

In the age of blogs and online self-publishing, these earlier assumptions (admittedly sometimes honored in the breach) may be increasingly difficult to uphold. What appears online without formal vetting is sometimes closer to what the comedian Stephen Colbert has called "truthiness"—truth that "comes from the gut not books" (Comedy Central's *The Colbert Report,* October 17, 2005). In January 2006 the American Dialect Society, which named "truthiness" its word of the year, defined the word this way: "The quality of preferring concepts or facts one wishes to be true, rather than concepts or facts known to be true." Farhad Manjoo (2008) illustrated how a truthiness mindset is propagated through online venues such as political blogs. To the extent that reading is increasingly done online, and given the growing blurring of lines regarding who constitutes an author and what responsibilities authors have for veracity, readers potentially lower their own bar regarding the accuracy of the written word.

Navigation Tools   We saw earlier that textual navigation tools developed (some before the advent of print and others after) to aid readers in finding their way through a text. There is an interesting conundrum in this concept. On the face of things, many books are designed (at least in the eyes of their authors) to be read from start to finish. This concept clearly applies to novels or detective stories, but many (perhaps most) works of nonfiction are not read this way. In fact, since the development of the codex, perhaps they never have been (Stalleybrass 2002). Those of us raised on tables of contents and indexes understood the concept of random access long before the development of textual search functions on computers.

Yet with the coming of these computer tools, we have reached something of an apotheosis in random access, generating a process I have called "snippet literacy" (Baron 2008, 204–6). Students (and often their professors) are increasingly prone to use the "find" function to zero in on just the phrase or sentence they think they need to know, rather than reading larger passages or entire works.

The possibilities of random access may also be responsible for the undoing of one of the important cornerstones of print culture: the use of page numbers. Page numbers have been valuable not simply for individual readers to find their place in a text but for readers to share such loci with others. Page numbers have long been a sine qua non in scholarly references, but they have also enabled two lay readers (say, talking on the phone from different physical locations) to share the hilarious scene on page 146 of the novel they are both reading.

Several years ago I began noticing a change in my university students' attitudes toward page numbers: most students were no longer inserting them into their written assignments, no matter how explicitly I had requested numbering. I knew that page numbers are not inserted automatically in Microsoft Word. Yet my students were otherwise quite savvy regarding Word's functionality. What was going wrong?

The answer appears to be that given the students' wealth of online (and, more generally, onscreen) reading experience, page numbers for documents created on a computer (such as their written assignments) seem irrelevant. When readers access newspapers online, there are no page numbers. (Significantly, more people now get their news online than from printed newspapers [State of the News Media 2011].) Some of the scholarly articles they are assigned come as unpaginated PDFs. Documents native to the Web are overwhelmingly unpaginated, as are the texts of many ebooks. Since the assignments in question were created on computers—and sometimes submitted electronically—surely (so the logic apparently goes) if I, the reader, want to locate a place in students' texts, I should use the "find" function.

We saw earlier how, with the initial emergence of print technology, the way people read changed in concrete ways. Just so, with the availability of "find" in navigating online reading, the notion of reading is potentially being redefined from linear activity to a random-access process.

Our discussion thus far has articulated both a conceptual and a historical framework for thinking about the potential effects of technology upon our encounters with the written word. We turn now to empirical data on ways in which contemporary technologies may be reshaping the way we read—and what the reading enterprise is about.

Pilot Study: Reading in Print and Onscreen

In the research described below, I asked a group of university students to describe their literacy practices and weigh the pros and cons of traditional print versus onscreen text.

Research Questions

Drawing upon our discussion of assumptions underlying print culture, the research addressed four main issues:

- Durability of a text
  Does the durable (print) versus ephemeral (onscreen) nature of a reading platform matter to users (for example, with respect to rereading works or annotating works)?

■ Conditions for reading
On which platform is multitasking more likely to occur?
■ Value of books
Does the physicality of books matter (including the literal feel of a book and desire to retain a book once it has been read)?
■ Navigation tools
What do students feel about the relative usability of print versus onscreen platforms?

In addition, I considered two further dimensions (the first of which overlaps with conditions for reading):

■ Cognitive/pedagogical issues
On which platform do users perceive they learn more? remember more?
■ Resources
What do students feel about the advantages or disadvantages of the two platforms regarding the environment or monetary resources?

Study Design

A questionnaire was mounted on SurveyMonkey, a commercial online survey instrument. The survey, which was administered in Fall 2010, took approximately seven to eight minutes to complete. Using a convenience sample, eighty-two undergraduate students at a midsized private university in the United States were surveyed. All were between the ages of eighteen and twenty-four. In the sample 68 percent were female and 32 percent male, an imbalance that reflects both the undergraduate population of the institution and the greater willingness of females to complete surveys.

Two types of questions were presented. In the first set, subjects were asked to choose from possible alternatives provided. For example, students were asked how often ("most of the time," "sometimes," "occasionally," or "never") they annotated their textbooks by highlighting, underlining, or making notes in the books themselves. The second set of questions solicited open-ended responses. These questions inquired what students liked most (and what they liked least) about reading onscreen or reading in hard copy. Additionally, students were invited at the end of the survey to make any additional comments they wished.

Results: Questions Involving Choice of Answers

The larger study included a range of questions regarding

■ The kinds of personal technology students owned;
■ Whether they purchased their textbooks in hard copy or as digital downloads, whether they rented textbooks, and whether they sold books at the end of the semester;
■ What their book annotation habits were;
■ How many books they personally owned;
■ How much reading they did;

- Their preference regarding platform (hard copy or onscreen) for reading a range of genres either for academic purposes or for pleasure;
- Habits regarding rereading;
- The extent to which they felt they remembered what they had read;
- Multitasking habits while reading; printing habits;
- Preferences regarding online assignments and online grading; and
- Use of library ebooks.

My analysis focuses on the issues most relevant to this chapter.

Results from the "choice of answers" questions clustered into four conceptual categories:

- Relationship to textbooks,
- Preferred mode for reading,
- Doing assigned reading, and
- Cognitive or pedagogical issues.

Relationship to Textbooks   The first set of questions concerned students' relationships with their textbooks. When asked whether they sold their texts (generally back to the campus bookstore), 61 percent said, "most of the time." In response to a separate question, 51 percent indicated they were renting hard copies of some of their textbooks during the semester the survey was conducted. (The university's campus store had heavily advertised this option. Students received 50 percent of the purchase price at the end of the semester, even if they had written in the book.) Seven percent of students indicated they had "leased" at least one short-term electronic download of a textbook that semester, and 10 percent had purchased outright at least one textbook.

A separate question inquired how often subjects annotated their textbooks. Given the options of "most of the time," "sometimes," "occasionally," and "never," 29 percent said "occasionally" and 18 percent said "never." Those two percentages combined (48 percent—because of rounding) begin to approach the 61 percent who responded that "most of the time" they sold their textbooks at the end of the semester. There is, perhaps, a certain logic at work here: If one will be disposing of a book anyway, why bother writing in it—particularly because traditional resale value often depends upon how clean the book is?

Preferred Mode for Reading   Another series of items queried students' preferred platform for reading different genres. Table 12.1 summarizes the results for doing academic reading. The only genres for which reading onscreen showed slight preference were reading academic journals and reading newspapers. Neither of these results was surprising. Nearly all the students' assignments from academic journals were for reading electronic copies. In fact, the university had recently removed nearly all its bound journals to an offsite location to create more space. Regarding newspapers, we have already noted that accessing news online rather than in hard copy is a national trend.

Table 12.1
Preferred platform for academic reading (%)

	Hard copy	Onscreen	Don't read this genre
Course text	98	2	0
Nonfiction (serious)	89	7	4
Nonfiction (light)	88	7	5
Fiction (serious)	94	5	1
Fiction (light)	94	4	2
Academic journal	44	56	0
Newspaper	46	54	0

As shown in table 12.2, when the same questions (minus the ones relating to textbooks and academic journals) were asked regarding reading for pleasure, the results were barely distinguishable from responses for academic reading. In evaluating the results regarding both academic and pleasure reading, it is important to keep in mind that only 35 percent of the subjects owned smart phones and only 5 percent owned devices that could conveniently function as ereaders (such as a Kindle, Nook, or iPad). Similarly, only 12 percent had ever checked out an ebook from the university library for academic work, and 12 percent had checked out one (although only one) ebook for pleasure reading. At the same time, the university library owned both Kindles and iPads that students could borrow, if they wished.[5]

Doing Assigned Reading   Two questions probed how students approached reading assignments. The first asked in what format did students prefer to read if academic reading was available online. The second inquired as to the likelihood of students reading an assigned article, depending upon the format in which it was available. Table 12.3 summarizes these results.

Although 55 percent of students in the study indicated they usually read an academic assignment online if it was available on that platform, the other 45 percent responded that usually they printed out a hard copy, either before or after they had

Table 12.2
Preferred platform for pleasure reading (%)[a]

	Hard copy	Onscreen	Don't read this genre
Nonfiction (serious)	85	2	12
Nonfiction (light)	82	7	11
Fiction (serious)	84	7	9
Fiction (light)	89	7	4
Newspaper	40	52	7

[a]Because of rounding, some rows do not add up to 100%.

■ Table 12.3
How students approach reading assignments (%)

If academic work is available online, do you usually

read it onscreen	print it out and read it	read it and print it out
55	39	6

Are you more likely to read an assigned article if

it is available online	you are handed a copy	difference
6	56	38

read the piece. More than half (56 percent) responded they were more likely to read an assigned article if they were handed a copy, compared with 6 percent who favored reading it online and 38 percent who said they were indifferent to platform. Taken together, these questions suggest that many of today's undergraduates—who are digital natives—still favor the printed word. The second question may also offer an object lesson to faculty members about the pedagogical efficacy of physically putting assigned reading in the hands of their students.

Cognitive and Pedagogical Issues   A final group of four questions involved cognitive and pedagogical issues relating to rereading, memory, and multitasking. The first of these questions asked how often students reread academic materials. Given the choices of "most of the time," "sometimes," "occasionally," and "never," 49 percent said "occasionally" and another 10 percent said "never." Recall that 48 percent of students indicated that they "occasionally" or "never" wrote in their textbooks. It stands to reason that if students have not annotated their books, rereading can be quite time consuming, since it essentially entails beginning afresh rather than focusing on the issues the student has already marked out.

Table 12.4 summarizes the questions and responses to the other three issues. Responses to the questions on platform and the likelihood of rereading indicated that students themselves believed they were more likely to reread a hard copy of academic materials (66 percent) than an online copy (24 percent). Similarly, half of the students (51 percent) believed they remembered more when they read in hard copy. (A bit fewer than half believed the medium made no difference.) Most dramatic, though, were responses to the questions on multitasking: 90 percent of subjects reported, they were more likely to multitask when reading onscreen, whereas only 10 percent said either the medium made no difference or—in the case of just one subject—that multitasking was more likely to occur when reading hard copy.

Results: Open-Ended "Like Most"/"Like Least" Questions
The eighty-two subjects were asked four open-ended questions:

- ■ What is the one thing you like *most* about reading *onscreen?*
- ■ What is the one thing you like *least* about reading *onscreen?*

■ Table 12.4
Cognitive/pedagogical issues (%)

Are you more likely to reread academic materials if the materials are available

onscreen	in hard copy	don't reread
24	66	10

Compare your memory for what you read in different media: I remember more if I read

onscreen	in hard copy	about the same
2	51	46

Are you more likely to be multitasking when reading

onscreen	in hard copy	about the same
90	1	9

[a]Because of rounding, the memory question does not add up to 100%.

■ What is the one thing you like *most* about reading in *hard copy?*
■ What is the one thing you like *least* about reading in *hard copy?*

Coding Open-Ended Responses   After all the open-ended responses were collected, coding schemes were created for categorizing replies to the four "like most"/"like least" questions.[6] The same four primary categories were used in coding all data sets, although there were some differences in the coding of subcategories. Figure 12.1 summarizes the composite major coding categories, along with examples of the types of responses in each category.

Major Findings   Table 12.5 summarizes all "like most"/"like least" responses with respect to the four primary coding categories. Examining the open-ended responses regarding likes and dislikes, four trends emerge. The first two point to advantages of reading in hard copy. Although the numbers are small, some students (10 percent) appreciated the physicality of printed works ("Hard Copy: Like Most"). More notably, reading in hard copy was clearly perceived as having better cognitive or pedagogical outcomes than reading onscreen. That is, free to respond to all four open-ended questions however they chose, 78 percent of the subjects specifically addressed the cognitive and pedagogical benefits as what they "liked most" about reading in hard copy. At the same time, 91 percent spontaneously mentioned cognitive or pedagogical drawbacks as what they "liked least" about reading onscreen.

Two trends highlight the advantages that subjects saw to reading onscreen. Reading onscreen was generally viewed as more accessible or convenient than reading in hard copy (48 percent of all "Onscreen: Like Most" responses and 50 percent of all "Hard Copy: Like Least" responses). When it came to resource issues (both ecological and monetary), onscreen reading was again the preferred medium. Of the "Onscreen: Like Most" responses referring to resources (30 percent of total "Onscreen:

Abbreviations:

| Onscreen: Like Most | OS: LM | Hard Copy: Like Most | HC: LM |
| Onscreen: Like Least | OS: LL | Hard Copy: Like Least | HC: LL |

Physicality

e.g.,   "lack of physical interaction with reading material" (OS: LL)

"having a tangible copy of the text" (HC: LM)

"tactile interaction with reading material" (HC: LM)

Cognitive/Pedagogical Issues

Related academic tasks

e.g.,   "you can easily look up words you don't know" (OS: LM)

"easy to look up additional information" (OS: LM)

Readability/usability

e.g.,   "it's harder to keep your place online" (OS: LL)

"I hate not being able to dog-ear pages and flip

back and forth!!!!!!" (OS: LL)

"it hurts my head" (OS: LL)

"I can write in it" (HC: LM)

"harder to find specific details. Ctrl+F doesn't work for

hard copies!" (HC: LL)

Cognitive focus/cognitive outcome/multitasking

e.g.,   "I can multitask when I read it" (OS: LM)

"I get distracted" (OS: LL)

"I don't absorb as much" (OS: LL)

"necessary for focus" (HC: LM)

"It takes me longer because I read more carefully" (HC: LL)

Access/Convenience

Physical convenience of access

e.g.,   "portability" (OS: LM)

"easy access to the document" (OS: LM)

"it's easy to take it with me" (HC: LM)

"it's a hassle to carry around a lot of books" (HC: LL)

Convenience

e.g.,   "more convenient" (OS: LM)

Resources

Ecological

e.g.,   "not wasting resources" (OS: LM)

"kills trees" (HC: LL)

Monetary

e.g.,   "don't have to pay to print stuff out" (OS: LM)

"cost" (HC: LL)

▪ Figure 12.1 Composite major coding categories for "like most"/"like least" questions.

■ Table 12.5
Tabulation of "like most"/"like least" responses (%)[a]

	Onscreen		Hard copy	
	Like most	Like least	Like most	Like least
Physicality	0	2	10	0
Cognitive and pedagogical issues	18	91	78	13
Access/convenience	48	5	11	50
Resources	30	0	0	28

[a]Some columns do not add up to 100%, either because responses were not codable or because subjects had nothing of substance to say (e.g., "Not applicable").

Like Most" responses), two-thirds specified ecological resources (the rest involved money or were not clearly codable, such as "conserves"). Of the "Hard Copy: Like Least" responses referring to resources (28 percent of all such responses), slightly more than half involved ecological issues.

Results: Other Comments
At the end of the survey, subjects were invited to offer additional comments. Many of these observations reinforced themes already reported in the "like most"/"like least" discussion. For example, with regard to physicality, one subject wrote,

I like the experience of holding a book and flipping the pages.

On the issues of memory and efficiency (which are cognitive and pedagogical issues), two relevant comments were

I . . . seem to remember things more accurately from printed text.

I'm more productive and efficient with my time by far if I'm reading in hard copy.

Yet others commented regarding ease or difficulty in navigating a text:

Love electronic reading for shorter articles . . . but hate e-anything for school work. Too hard to flip through.

There were also comments that were economically driven:

Cash rules everything for me.

Others reflected practical considerations of balancing school work with paid employment:

For those of us spending most of our time in a job, pulling out a book is unacceptable, while pulling up an article online is more acceptable.

Interestingly, a number of comments revealed personal conflicts in making choices between reading platforms. In nearly all cases, these conflicts pitted individual preference against environmental issues:

> I prefer hard copies, but think they're bad for the environment.

> I know it's a waste of paper, but I really prefer reading a physical book or article to reading it online.

> While I prefer reading things in Hard Copy, I can't bring myself to print out online material simply for the environmental considerations. However, I highly highly prefer things in Hard Copy—just to clarify.

Discussion and Conclusions

Against the backdrop of circumstances that have led readers to question the presuppositions of print culture—both before and following the advent of online computing—I focused on the issue of reading onscreen versus in hard copy, using data from a pilot study of university undergraduates in the United States. To introduce that study, I returned to the four central presuppositions discussed in my analysis of print culture: durability of a text, conditions for reading, value of books, and navigation tools, to which I added cognitive and pedagogical issues and resources. To analyze responses to questions for which subjects were asked to choose among possible answers, I divided the discussion into four areas: relationship to textbooks, preferred mode for reading academic work, doing assigned reading, and cognitive or pedagogical issues. In my analysis of the open-ended data, the coding scheme naturally broke down into four primary categories: physicality, cognitive or pedagogical issues, access or convenience, and resources. Although the use of three separate (though overlapping) schemes does not make for elegant analysis, each scheme suits the task it was designed to serve.

In the discussion that follows, I begin by asking what the data suggest regarding the question contained in the title of this chapter: Is reading in hard copy better, worse, or about the same as reading onscreen? I then turn to the issue of whether onscreen reading platforms affect how we read and what it means to read in the first place.

Better, Worse, or About the Same?

Reflecting upon the three sets of data (questions involving choice of answers, open-ended "like most"/"like least" questions, and additional comments), a clear picture emerges.

Better   Reading in hard copy was seen by the subjects as differing in a number of ways from reading onscreen. The most important of these involved issues associated with learning (hence, my logical leap to "better"). These included

- A greater likelihood of rereading a text,
- A greater likelihood of remembering what has been read,
- A much lower likelihood of multitasking while reading,

- A greater ability to focus on and absorb what is being read,
- Greater ease in annotating, and
- Preferred media for reading course texts (for academic work) and for reading fiction and nonfiction—both for academic work and for pleasure.

Some subjects noted they valued the physicality of books ("tactile interaction with reading material"). In the section for additional comments, one student remarked on the importance of marginalia (an issue of textual durability) when a book is passed from one reader to the next: "Even if I get a library book, it's a great experience to see what someone else underlined and found significant."

Reading onscreen was also seen as having some advantages. These included

- Greater ease in finding a specific word or passage,
- The ability to look up additional information (on the internet) while reading,
- Portability, and
- Being more resource friendly (both ecologically and monetarily).

Worse   The attributes that subjects disliked about each reading platform were generally mirror opposites of those affordances they liked most. However, a few of the responses to the "like least" questions are worthy of note here. Responding to the "like least" question about reading in hard copy, one subject replied, "It takes me longer to read because I read more carefully." Given higher education's premise that careful reading is a hallmark of learning, this comment seems a surprising response to the "like least" question. Implied in the answer is the assumption that having to spend time reading may be a more important desideratum than how carefully that reading is done.

Negative comments about reading onscreen were sometimes related to limitations of the hardware ("It hurts my head"). Subjects also commented on navigation issues. In contrast to students favoring reading onscreen because of such features as the "find" function, one subject replied to the "like least" question about reading onscreen, "I hate not being able to dog-ear pages and flip back and forth!!!!!!" Clearly, there are alternative senses to the notion of ease of navigation.

About the Same   Some of the questions involving choice of answers gave subjects the option of indicating they viewed both reading platforms as equivalent. We saw, for example, that when asked to choose between reading in hard copy or onscreen, preferences for reading academic journals or for reading newspapers (either for academic work or for pleasure) were roughly the same. Similarly, when asked about their printing habits for materials available online, 45 percent printed such material out, whereas 55 percent exclusively read it onscreen.

Reading Redefined?

Gauging likes and dislikes regarding reading platforms is a first step toward understanding the potential impact of new media technology on reading. But are these preferences (and practices) leading to a changed notion of reading itself? Our discussion focuses on two central domains: cognitive and pedagogical issues on the one hand, and resources (environmental and monetary) on the other.

Cognitive and Pedagogical Issues   It has been suggested (Goody and Watt 1968; Havelock 1963; Olson 1994) that the emergence of writing (whether writing in general or alphabetic writing in particular) made possible fundamental shifts in the way people think. Being able to literally see one's own words or those of other writers allows for rereading and encourages (so it is argued) a level of mental reflection and logical discourse that is difficult to attain without the durability of linear, written text. Elizabeth Eisenstein (1979) makes the case that with the coming of print in the West, scholarship and critiques of other authors' works blossomed in part because it was now possible to physically compare multiple texts (rather than, for example, having to travel from one monastic library to another to read manuscripts *seriatim*). In short, first writing and then the appearance of print—both made possible by the existence of durable texts—encouraged a particular kind of analytical thought. The notion of reading became deeply entwined with the ideas of contemplation, comparison, and reflection.

What happens to our concept of reading when written material is no longer accessed on a durable platform? We have seen three areas in which some students in our pilot study reported engaging in practices that may undermine the idea of reading as a deliberative activity.

First, the study offered hints at the erosion of texts being durable. Many students do not view textbooks (or at least some texts) as continuing parts of their mental lives once a school term has ended. Such students sell back their books or do short-term rentals. Moreover, many students do not annotate their books, and many do not reread them.

Second, the overwhelming majority of subjects in the study indicated they multitasked while reading onscreen, but very few reported multitasking while reading in hard copy. Without rehearsing the myriad of data indicating that multitasking degrades cognitive performance (see Baron 2008, 36–40, 216–19; Carr 2010), suffice it to say that trying to perform two or more cognitive tasks simultaneously (or even quickly shifting back and forth between cognitive tasks) generally diminishes cognitive outcomes. As increasing amounts of text that are part of the pedagogical enterprise are available onscreen, it stands to reason that the amount of multitasking done while reading can be expected to increase as well. The negative prognosis for contemplation and serious analysis of texts should give educators pause.

The third issue concerns linearity of text. Although writing is designed to be read from beginning to end, in practice it is often accessed in chunks: a single chapter, the dozen pages referenced in the index, and so on. However, with onscreen navigation tools it is possible to hone in on a single word or sentence, obviating the need to read much more (including the surrounding context that often makes that word or sentence properly interpretable). In the "like most"/"like least" questions in the survey, 6 percent of the "Onscreen: Like Most" responses specifically mentioned the concept of the "find" function, and 4 percent of the "Hard Copy: Like Least" responses were specific complaints about the lack of this function. My personal observations regarding a growing indifference among university students toward page numbers further

suggest that experience with networked computing is helping shift the traditional notion of reading as a linear activity to one that is increasingly random access.

Resources   In the pilot study, 30 percent of the "Onscreen: Like Most" responses and
28 percent of the "Hard Copy: Like Least" responses concerned environmental or
monetary resources. At the same time, though, several students noted feeling conflicted regarding environmental issues: although they preferred reading in hard copy,
they also felt environmental guilt.

Given what would appear to be some educational advantages for reading in hard
copy, the question becomes this: Is pedagogy potentially being held hostage by environmental agendas and financial realities?

Particularly over the past two decades, Americans have become increasingly sensitive to the reality of limitations on natural resources. Many students have grown up
in school or community settings that promote green practices, and university cam-
puses appropriately reinforce this message. However, discussions of environmental
awareness almost never include consideration of possible educational consequences.
There are possible pedagogical advantages of reading in hard copy—along with most
students' preference to do so when reading anything except newspapers and academic
journal articles. It is time to objectively assess where legitimate ecological considerations might be at loggerheads with pedagogical agendas. (Parenthetically, paper is
a renewable resource.)

Monetary considerations are also nuanced. It is true that students are peren-
nially looking for ways to manage their (often) limited financial resources. It is
equally true that textbook costs have soared, and that some of the books students
are asked to read probably will not prove useful in later life. Yet at the same time,
companies that produce computers (or ereaders or the iPad), along with publishers creating online books as a source of new revenue, are aggressively marketing
their hardware and software to readers. There have been few scholarly attempts to
compare cognitive outcomes for reading in hard copy versus onscreen with respect
to conceptual depth. We need to go beyond such relatively straightforward issues
as ease of annotation or basic processing of information, which can be assessed
with traditional testing.

It seems highly likely that onscreen reading will continue to grow apace, significantly driven by environmental and monetary considerations, but also by the very
welcome affordances praised by students in the study. Given this reality, we need to
remain mindful that reading as a reflective, cognitive activity—made possible by
durable, linear texts—has, over the millennia, been a critical component in the growth
of civilizations, societies, and individuals.

Technologies have consequences, some of which may not materialize until long
after those technologies have been widely embraced. (Think of current challenges
such as the diminishing supply of fossil fuels or needing to reduce the massive pol-
lution generated by automobiles.) It therefore behooves us to seriously examine the
directions in which our model of reading may be heading and to weigh both positive
and negative consequences, rather than find ourselves with an altered notion of reading by default.

Whether reading in hard copy is better, worse, or about the same as reading on-screen remains an empirical issue. The data presented herein generate questions that can be addressed only with broader empirical study. Unless we undertake such studies, we can hardly hope for meaningful answers to these queries.

NOTES

1. Carr has been accused by some of succumbing to technological determinism, that is, of assuming that new technologies necessarily bring about particular individual or social changes. This chapter will not address this debate; see Baym (2010) for useful discussion of the issues.
2. For more information on the history of writing, see Coulmas (1999), Gaur (1985), and Robinson (1999).
3. For discussions of print culture, see Chartier (1989), Eisenstein (1979), and *Transactions of the Book* (2001).
4. For fuller discussion regarding the presuppositions of print culture, see Baron (2005).
5. According to some reports, both academic and public libraries are reporting fairly minimal use of (and satisfaction with) books available on ereaders (Huthwaite et al. 2011; Lund 2011).
6. I am grateful to Michal Panner for assistance in constructing the coding categories and in coding the data.

REFERENCES

Aboujaoude, Elias. 2011. *Virtually you: The dangerous powers of the e-personality.* New York: W. W. Norton.
Baron, Naomi S. 2000. *Alphabet to email: How written English evolved and where it's heading.* London: Routledge.
———. 2005. The future of written culture. *Ibérica* 9: 7–31.
———. 2008. *Always on: Language in an online and mobile world.* New York: Oxford University Press.
Baym, Nancy. 2010. *Personal connections in a digital age.* Boston: Polity.
Blair, Ann. 2003. Reading strategies from coping with information overload, c. 1550–1700. *Journal of the History of Ideas* 64, no. 1:11–28.
———. 2010. *Too much to know: Managing scholarly information before the modern age.* New Haven, CT: Yale University Press.
Carr, Nicholas. 2008. Is Google making us stupid? *Atlantic Monthly,* July/August. www.theatlantic .com/magazine/archive/2008/07/is-google-making-us-stupid/6868/.
———. 2010. *The shallows: What the internet is doing to our brains.* New York: W. W. Norton.
Caxton Club. 2011. *Other people's books: Association copies and the stories they tell.* New Castle, DE: Oak Knoll Press.
Chadwick, John. 1959. A prehistoric bureaucracy. *Diogenes* 26:7–18.
Chartier, Roger, ed. 1989. *The culture of print: Power and the uses of print in early modern Europe.* Trans. Lydia G. Cochrane. Princeton, NJ: Princeton University Press.
Clanchy, M. T. 1993. *From memory to written record: England, 1066–1307.* 2nd ed. Oxford: Blackwell.
Coulmas, Florian. 1999. *The Blackwell encyclopedia of writing systems.* Oxford: Wiley-Blackwell.
Cull, Barry W. 2011. Reading revolutions: Online digital text and implications for reading in academe. *First Monday* 16, no. 6. firstmonday.org/htbin/cgiwrap/bin/ojs/index.php/fm/article/view/3340/2985.
Eisenstein, Elizabeth. 1979. *The printing press as an agent of change.* Cambridge: Cambridge University Press.
Epstein, Jacob. 2002. *Book business: Publishing past, present, and future.* New York: W. W. Norton.
Feather, John. 1988. *A history of British printing.* London: Croom Helm.
Febvre, Lucien, and Henri-Jean Martin. 1976. *The coming of the book: The impact of printing, 1450–1800.* London: NLB.
Gaur, Albertine. 1985. *A history of writing.* London: British Library.
Goody, Jack, and Ian Watt. 1968. The consequences of literacy. In *Literacy in traditional societies,* ed. Jack Goody, 27–68. Cambridge: Cambridge University Press.

Hallowell, Edward. 2006. *CrazyBusy: Overstretched, overbooked, and about to snap! Strategies for coping in a world gone ADD.* New York: Ballantine.

Harris, William. 1989. *Ancient literacy.* Cambridge: Cambridge University Press.

Havelock, Eric. 1963. *Preface to Plato.* Cambridge, MA: Harvard University Press.

Huthwaite, Ann, Colleen E. Cleary, Brendan Sinnamon, Peter Sondergeld, and Alex McClintock, Alex. 2011. Ebook readers: Separating the hype from the reality. In *Proceedings of the 2011 ALIA Information Online Conference and Exhibition.* Sydney: Sydney Convention and Exhibition Centre. eprints.qut.edu.au/41132/.

Jackson, H. J. 2001. *Marginalia: Readers writing in books.* New Haven, CT: Yale University Press.

Johns, Adrian. 1998. *The nature of the book: Print and knowledge in the making.* Chicago: University of Chicago Press.

Levy, David M. 2001. *Scrolling forward: Making sense of documents in the digital age.* New York: Arcade Publishing.

Lund, James. 2011. E-books: Little use so far. *The Bottom Line: Managing Library Finances* 24, no. 2:122–24.

Manjoo, Farhad. 2008. *True enough: Learning to live in a post-fact society.* Hoboken, NJ: John Wiley.

Marmarelli, Trina, and Martin Ringle. 2009. The Reed College Kindle study. *Reed College Computing and Information Services.* www.reedcollege.com/cis/about/kindle_pilot/Reed_Kindle_report.pdf.

Olson, David. 1994. *The world on paper: The conceptual and cognitive implications of writing and reading.* Cambridge: Cambridge University Press.

Parkes, M. B. 1993. *Pause and effect: An introduction to the history of punctuation in the west.* Berkeley: University of California Press.

Price, Hereward. 1939. Grammar and the compositor in the sixteenth and seventeenth centuries. *Journal of English and Germanic Philology* 38:540–48.

Rheingold, Howard. 1999. Look who's talking. *Wired* 7, no. 1. www.wired.com/wired/archive/7.01 /amish_pr.html.

Rich, Motoko. 2008. Literacy debate: Online, R U really reading? *New York Times,* July 27. www.nytimes.com/2008/07/27/books/27reading.html.

Roberts, Colin, and T. C. Skeat. 1983. *The birth of the codex.* London: Oxford University Press for the British Academy.

Robinson, Andrew. 1999. *The story of writing.* London: Thames and Hudson.

Rose, Mark. 1993. *Owners and authors: The invention of copyright.* Cambridge, MA: Cambridge University Press.

Rosenberg, Daniel. 2003. Early modern information overload. *Journal of the History of Ideas* 64, no. 1:1–9.

Saenger, Paul. 1982. Silent reading: Its impact on late medieval script and society. *Viator* 13:367–414.

———. 1997. *Space between words: The origins of silent reading.* Stanford, CA: Stanford University Press.

———. 2010. The impact of the early printed page on the history of reading. In *The History of the Book in the West,* vol. 2, *1455–1700,* ed. Ian Gadd, 385–449. Surrey, UK: Ashgate.

Scragg, D. G. 1974. *A history of English spelling.* Manchester, UK: Manchester University Press.

Shaw, George Bernard. 1985. *Agitations: Letters to the press, 1875–1950.* Ed. Dan H. Laurence and James Rambeau. New York: Frederick Ungar.

Simpson, Percy. 1935. *Proof-reading in the sixteenth, seventeenth, and eighteenth centuries.* Oxford: Oxford University Press.

Sparrow, Betsy, Jenny Liu, and Daniel Wegner. 2011. Google effects on memory: Cognitive consequences of having information at our fingertips. *Science* 333, no. 6040:776–78.

Stalleybrass, Peter. 2002. Books and scrolls: Navigating the bible. In *Books and readers in early modern England,* eds. Jennifer Andersen and Elizabeth Sauer, 42–79. Philadelphia: University of Pennsylvania Press.

The state of the news media 2011: An annual report on American journalism. 2011. *Pew Research Center's Project for Excellence in Journalism.* stateofthemedia.org/overview-2011.

Transactions of the book. 2001. Conference, Folger Shakespeare Library, Washington, DC, November 1–3. www.folger.edu/template.cfm?cid=399.

Turkle, Sherry. 1995. *Life on the screen: Identity in the age of the internet.* New York: Simon and Schuster.

————. 2011. *Alone together: Why we expect more from technology and less from each other.* New York: Basic Books.

Umble, Diane. 1996. *Holding the line: The telephone in Old Order Mennonite and Amish life.* Baltimore: Johns Hopkins University Press.

Woodmansee, Martha, and Peter Jaszi, eds. 1994. *The construction of authorship: Textual appropriation in law and literature.* Durham, NC: Duke University Press.

Yeo, Richard 2002. Managing knowledge in early modern Europe. *Minerva* 40:301–14.

13

Fakebook

Synthetic Media, Pseudo-sociality, and the Rhetorics of Web 2.0

CRISPIN THURLOW
University of Washington

Figure 13.1

> Social media applies contradictory, yet intertwined ideals of counterculture and capitalism to the self, friends, relationships, and interpersonal interactions. People can spread ideas and creations to a formerly inconceivable mass audience, but in ways bounded and influenced by the confines of modern neoliberal capitalism. (Marwick 2010, 11)

"THE DIGITAL MEDIA REVOLUTION is here. Are you?"[1] This bold challenge (or threat) is lifted from publicity materials used by the masters of communication in digital media program at my university. In its publicity, this "self-sustaining" program sells itself by promising "professionals the necessary tools to understand and exploit the fast changing world of media technology." Elsewhere, in North Africa and the Middle East, a very different kind of fast-paced revolution has been happening. The determined, often violently opposed uprisings of the so-called Arab Spring have meanwhile been excitedly recast by many Western newsmakers and commentators as the "Facebook Revolution," "Revolution 2.0," and "Tanks versus Twitter." And then there's the Queen of England—the revolution that never happened. With the 2010 launch of a new corporate profile on Facebook, the British monarchy joined the ranks of politicians around the world, from Barack Obama and Nicolas Sarkozy to Nelson Mandela and Mahmoud Ahmadinejad. It certainly seems that everyone and everything is nowadays positioned in relation to social media. We are everywhere incited to use them, to discuss them, and to reconceive our lives around them.

This chapter is intended not so much as a corrective as it is a considered response to these wide-sweeping incitations, from someone who has himself always been enthusiastic about the possibilities or opportunities of new media and who has been fiercely critical of public discourse that hastily or ignorantly dismisses new media (see, for example, Thurlow 2001, 2003, 2006, 2009; Thurlow, Lengel, and Tomic 2004; Thurlow and Mroczek, 2011). To be clear, I am still very enthusiastic about new media and remain critical of knee-jerk, end-of-the-world reactions to them. This should not, however, preclude me from keeping a watchful eye on my excitement, on my own professional or scholarly investments, and on those often hyperbolic claims about social media made in the context of education, the media, commerce, and politics. In fact, it is these invested claims—or *rhetorics*—about Web 2.0 that I want to examine a little more carefully.

To this end, and with reference to the language and new media theme of the current volume, my chapter aligns itself most closely with critical discourse studies, that branch of language study that pays special (but not exclusive) attention to matters of ideology. Grounded in the work of linguistically oriented discourse analysts (notably Fairclough 1992; Cameron 2000) as well as broader sociological perspectives on discourse (notably Bourdieu 1991; Foucault 1980), the chapter also draws heavily on allied cultural critiques coming from within new media studies itself (specifically Jarrett 2008; Scholz 2008; van Dijck and Nieborg 2009; Marwick 2010; Turkle 2011). My objective here, then, is to review some of the ways influential, institutional domains—or discourses—work to produce a pointedly synthetic media based on highly stylized, commoditized notions of language and communication. In doing so, I want to suggest that the heated, excitable rhetorics of Web 2.0 often have little to do with the everyday social uses of new media, and everything to do with the kind of pseudo-sociality favored by advertisers and other agents (or beneficiaries) of neoliberal capital. This distinction between the social and the pseudo-social is a crucial one for sociolinguists and discourse analysts.

My story begins, as all good Labovian stories do, with a complicating action.

Complicating Action

In figure 13.2 I present a behind-the-scenes look at the mundane realities of my life; specifically, my family's breakfast table. In the foggy stupor of one weekday morning several months ago, I was struck by the injunction on the back of a milk carton to "follow us on Twitter." A little grumpily (to be honest), I found myself wondering why. Why would I want to follow my milk? Why would anybody want to follow their milk? It all begged the bigger the question: What does it mean to be hailed by my milk in this way?

The fact is, so-called Web 2.0 and so-called social media are everywhere and there is talk of them everywhere. The real questions reach far beyond my milk carton, of course. How are we, as citizens and as scholars, to understand ourselves in a world where, as US presidential candidate Mitt Romney (*New York Times* 2011) has proposed, corporations are people and where products want to be our friends? What are

■ Figure 13.2

we to make of widespread discourses about this latest round of new media? Are we making anything of them? Are we simply buying [*sic*] into cultural-corporate discourses of Web 2.0 and social media, or have we reserved spaces in which to reflect critically on the many ways we are hailed or positioned by these discourses?

This is the story I want to tell here. It is a story about my initial attempt to address these kinds of questions, to find some sort of resolution for the initial complicating action of my breakfast table. But first some theoretical orientation.

Orientation: Discourse and Social Change

One finds techniques for efficiently and nonchalantly "handling" people wherever one looks in the public institutions of the modern world. Equally, one finds what I shall refer to as *synthetic personalization,* a compensatory tendency to give the impression of treating each of the people "handled" en masse as an individual. (Fairclough 1989, 62 [my emphasis])

A central argument in favour of "better communication" . . . is that the ability to talk in certain ways *empowers* people. Developing their communication skills enables them to realize their goals and take charge of their own destinies. . . . But what is called *empowerment* . . . has little to do with liberating people from existing constraints on their agency and freedom. In many cases it has more to do with teaching them to discipline themselves so they can operate more easily within those constraints: become more flexible, more team-oriented, better at resolving conflicts and controlling the emotions that threaten to disrupt business as usual. (Cameron 2000, 179 [my emphasis])

In pursuing a story such as this one, I find myself obviously following the lead of critical discourse analysts such as Norman Fairclough and Deborah Cameron, who have for some time been documenting (and critiquing) the relationship between widespread social changes and everyday discourse. Particularly in the contexts of postindustrial, neoliberal societies like Britain, these scholars have presented detailed analyses of the rise of enterprise culture and the extrapolation of business models and commercial priorities to otherwise noneconomic areas of life. Examples of this include the centripetal spread of such corporate practices as branding, risk management, advertising, and customer care to the public spaces of higher education. This colonization of public life is also often accompanied by a centrifugal incorporation of such essentially social notions as empowerment, sustainability, diversity (as in management), and—indeed—communication (as in skills). Inevitably it is against this backdrop that the rhetorics of Web 2.0 emerge and take shape; indeed, public discourse about new media appears merely to intensify the blurring of the boundaries between the corporate world and what Jürgen Habermas (1984) has famously called the "lifeworld."[2]

Not least given the increasing importance of service-based labor in contemporary economies, language and communication have become key targets of—and vehicles for—these dual processes of corporate colonization and incorporation (cf. Heller 2003; Jaworski and Thurlow 2010). In this regard both Fairclough and Cameron have been particularly concerned with the commodification and technologization of "ordinary" discursive practices. This is especially noticeable in the case of "discourse technologies" (Fairclough 1989, 216), where otherwise informal and/or interpersonal communicative genres are strategically recontextualized for instrumental (and usually economic) purposes. What I want to suggest here is that the production and promotion of social media sites such as Facebook, Twitter, and Foursquare present yet another manifestation of the ongoing commodification of communication. For new media critics such as Alice Marwick (2010), David Silver (2008), and Kylie Jarrett (2008), social media take things to new heights by incorporating even the most banal areas of everyday (inter)personal life. Along similar lines, I too am concerned with the ways new media language is often taken up as a resource for constructing identities of difference and ideologies of control (see Thurlow 2007, 2011). These metadiscursive processes see new media being doubly technologized; they are managed and regulated for commercial gain, but are also deployed in the stylization of Self and Other (cf. Foucault 1988, on technologies of self). One of the most common examples of this is the use of social media like Twitter or Facebook by politicians and celebrities for the purposes of styling themselves as interactive—available to, and in communication with, their publics. But I get ahead of myself.

Abstract: Web 2.0 Mythologies

Before looking more carefully and critically at some of its domain-specific rhetorics, I begin with an abridged account (or abstract) of the underlying mythologies of Web

2.0. Although our lives are saturated with taken-for-granted talk about social media and the like, there remains very little consensus about what exactly constitutes the "2" in "2.0," and whether, for all its hype, there is anything qualitatively different from *old* new media. Like many others, danah boyd (2009) locates the origin of the term "Web 2.0" in a 2004 marketing ploy aimed at re-energizing enthusiasm (and presumably sales) for digital technologies following the 1990s dot.com boom and bust. From the outset, stakeholders were invested in characterizing the distinguishing features of Web 2.0, and—as shown in table 13.1—these typically coalesced around the putative newness of content creators (as opposed to users); of content sharing and collaboration; and, of course, of social media such as social networking (e.g., Facebook) and microblogging (e.g., Twitter).[3] Other technologies commonly awarded the Web 2.0 title include blogs, wikis, virtual worlds, and news aggregators. Given its specious origins, most characterizations of Web 2.0 continue to be wedded to exaggerated, binarized accounts of old (the implied Web 1.0) and new, with a heavy stress on the latest and "the newest of new media (van Dijck and Nieborg 2009). This kind of presentism (Sterne 2003) invariably means that there is a noticeable lack of consideration for historicity and precedent. So, for example, whereas the single-agent broadcast potential of the internet is undeniably new and represents a major (revolutionary, even) change, the technological affordances of networking, sharing, multimodality, and user-generated content are not without precedent. The newness of new media is, therefore, typically a fabrication; it is almost always a discursive construction and deeply ideological (van Dijck and Nieborg 2009; Thurlow and Mroczek 2011).

One way to abstract and foreground the underlying mythologies of Web 2.0 is to head straight to an example of the newest of the new media (always a foolhardy moment given the incompatible pace of technological change vis-à-vis academic publishing). In this regard, the locational, GPS-based social-networking technology Foursquare epitomizes the much talked-about convergence of web-based media and mobile media, and nicely fulfills the romantic geek-in-a-garage fantasy of Web 2.0 development. Conceived by two college friends, it purports to have 20 million members worldwide (including President Barack Obama) and to be valued at over $600 million (as of April 2012). This company or technology also epitomizes the commodification of communication at the heart of my story.

Table 13.1

Web 1.0	Web 2.0
Web 1.0 was about reading	Web 2.0 is about writing
Web 1.0 was about home pages	Web 2.0 is about blogs
Web 1.0 was about lectures	Web 2.0 is about conversation
Web 1.0 was about advertising	Web 2.0 is about word of mouth
Web 1.0 was about companies	*Web 2.0 is about communities*
Web 1.0 was about client-server	Web 2.0 is about peer to peer

The transcription in extract 1, for example, comes from a short Flash video for Foursquare newcomers, boldly and somewhat presumptuously titled "How to Unlock Your World with Foursquare." Briefly, I want to draw attention to the telling recontextualization of social and interpersonal priorities and the reproduction of the consumer-citizen (Bauman 2007), a figure central to the neoliberal, postindustrial state.

Extract 1: Planned serendipity

Transcript of voiceover from Foursquare's "learn more" presentation (emphasis mine)

1. *Wish you were more aware* of all the incredible things around you? *With*
2. *foursquare you can unlock your world and find happiness just around the*
3. *corner!* You will need foursquare, a cell phone, and a *passion for*
   exploration.
4. Step 1. Download the foursquare app to your cell phone and instantly link
5. to address book, facebook, and twitter accounts to *discover where your*
6. *friends are hanging out.* See if they're near you by looking at where
7. they've recently checked in. . . .
8. Step 2. *Tell your friends where you* are by checking in at one of thousands
9. of locations of places foursquare lists automatically based on your GPS
10. locations. Leave tips on special features you find around town and don't
11. skimp on the details. Inside information is one of foursquare's best
12. features. If the place you are at isn't listed you can add it to foursquare.
13. Step 3. Check out tips from your friends and from the hundreds of
14. thousands of other users. Find recommendations on your specific location
15. or suggestions for things to do or avoid nearby.
16. Step 4. *The more you use foursquare, the more you'll get out of it.* Unlock
17. badges and earn points based on where, when, and how often you check
    in.
18. See how many you can rack up in any given month and check out your
19. stats at foursquare.com
20. Step 5. *Check in at a location more than anyone else and become the*
21. *mayor. You don't get a key to the city but you might get rewards from*
    certain
22. *businesses just for being a loyal customer.* Even if you're not the mayor,
23. *look out for specials offered to foursquare users.*
24. Step 6. Use foursquare wherever you go. In museums, at airports, on
25. public transportation, during concerts. *You never know when you might*
26. *come across* a little planned serendipity.

In an excited, conversational style a female voiceover promises those with "a passion for exploration" (line 3) the chance to "unlock your world and find happiness" (line 2) and to "discover where your friends are hanging out" (lines 5–6) as well as "hundreds of thousands of other users" (lines 13–14). As such, *Foursquare* neatly repeats the glib, self-sustaining definition of Web 2.0 (see table 13.1) which is, apparently, committed to communities not companies. However, and even allowing for a little tongue-in-cheek fun, what looks like friendship and social intercourse is inevitably predicated on, and driven by, a concern for the demands of commerce: lines 21–23 exhort the user to "get rewards from certain businesses for being a loyal customer" and "look out for specials." This is, after all, how Foursquare comes to be valued at over $600 million. In other words, and as Cameron notes above, it is all really business as usual. Just as we are persuaded to apply interpersonal notions of loyalty in our dealings with businesses (e.g., Thurlow and Jaworski 2006, on frequent flier programs), Foursquare services a straightforward marketing strategy (the promise of "specials") by weaving it into a personalized message of self-actualization and civic engagement.

The point I mean to make with this initial example is a simple one, and one that several new media scholars have made elsewhere. Completely consistent with the technologizing discourses of "enterprise culture" (see Fairclough 1989; Cameron 2000), social media are inevitably—perhaps even unavoidably—caught up in their own romantic mythologies and in the neoliberal ideologies of commerce. Alice Marwick (quoted at the start of the chapter) observes that the emergence of social media is rooted in the "intertwined ideals of counterculture and capitalism;" not surprisingly, therefore, a corporate venture such as Foursquare finds itself caught up in its own mythologies of "social liberation." As a community of scholars concerned with discourse—with the daily life of language and communication—it is important that we remain vigilant of the ways everyday communicators are positioned and persuaded by this type of new media (meta)discourse, especially those that purport to be inherently and principally committed to the social. In these terms, our work should always be concerned as much with Foucauldian discourses as it is with the linguistic specificities of discourse (Thurlow and Mroczek 2011). With this in mind, I continue my story with reference to five key discourse domains: commerce, politics, media, education, and scholarship.

The Rhetorics of Web 2.0: A Story in Five Parts

Following Gunther Kress and Shakuntala Banaji and their colleagues (Kress et al. 2001; Banaji, Burn, and Buckingham 2006), I have chosen to organize my critique of these different discourse domains by highlighting some of the apparently persuasive (and often nonchalant) claims made about Web 2.0 and especially social media. Deploying a range of communicational means, these rhetorics invariably also present themselves as "plausible, integral, coherent accounts of the world" (Kress et al. 2001, 20) more generally. In a series of briefly sketched vignettes, I point to some of the most frequent rhetorics of Web 2.0—those typically articulated through excited claims for collaboration, participation, interactivity, empowerment, social inclusion, networking, relationship, creativity, liberation, transparency, and so on.

Corporate Rhetorics: "Plugging In" the Social

These days, the obvious needs saying: Don't believe corporate hype. Corporations exist to make profits, not public goods. Usually, when they say "community" they mean "commerce," and when they say "aggregation" they mean "advertising." (Silver 2008)

I hope it is already clear from my Foursquare example that the line between commerce and the rest of life is often blurred—and, indeed, strategically blurred—in the rhetoric of social media. Nowhere is this more apparent than in Facebook, where the meaning (and spaces) of social networking have been so fully co-opted (and colonized) by corporations such as Coca-Cola (see www.facebook.com/cocacola), which currently stands as the number one brand on Facebook, with more than 35 million "fans" worldwide (see table 13.2). Coke has, of course, been in the business of positioning itself as a company with noble social aspirations for some time, most notably with its famous jingle proclaiming, "I'd like to teach the world to sing (in perfect harmony)." As new media scholar David Silver reminds us, however, the bottom line is that "corporations exist to make profits, not public goods" (2008).

At the epicenter of Web 2.0, corporate discourse is in many ways an all-too-obvious site for critique. Certainly, it is received wisdom in critical discourse studies that what looks or sounds like conversation often is not (Cameron 2000). This is most strikingly evident in the pseudo-social performances of automated customer services such as Continental Airlines' virtual expert. In extract 2 my staged interaction with Alex™ (embodied, as it were, by a racially ambiguous but distinctively—and reassuringly—American-looking and -sounding avatar) entails a series of synthetic niceties and my being perfunctorily directed to a number of web pages. (Note also the italicized "Alex" is styled to look like a handwritten signature.) Here technological interactivity—in the guise of online chat—functions as a metaphor for social interaction (Jensen 1999). Alex™ is nothing more than an imposter!

■ Table 13.2
Those other "social" voices on Facebook: A snapshot (October 2011) of fanbase statistics from socialbakers.com

	Top 10 brands		Top 10 public figures	
1.	Coca-Cola	35 mil	Eminem	48 mil
2.	Disney	29 mil	Rihanna	46 mil
3.	Starbucks	26 mil	Lady Gaga	45 mil
4.	Oreo	23 mil	Michael Jackson	42 mil
5.	Red Bull	23 mil	Shakira	41 mil
6.	Converse All Star	21 mil	Justin Bieber	37 mil
7.	Converse	20 mil	Cristiano Ronaldo	35 mil
8.	Skittles	19 mil	Lil Wayne	32 mil
9.	PlayStation	18 mil	Bob Marley	32 mil
10.	iTunes	17 mil	Megan Fox	29 mil
19.	—	—	Barack Obama	24 mil

Extract 2: Interactivity as pseudo-social interaction

An exchange with Continental Airlines' virtual expert Alex

■ Figure 13.3

Alex: Hi, I'm Alex, your continental.com virtual expert. Type in a short
      question, keyword or phrase below, and I can help you find the information
      on our website.

Me: lost baggage

Alex: We apologize for any inconvenience you have experienced concerning
      your baggage. If you haven't already filed a report, please follow the
      instructions on this page. *View Page* [*html link*] Here's more:
      Tracking Delayed Baggage [*html link*]
      Delivery Release Form for Delayed Baggage PDF [*html link*]
      Baggage Allowances and Policies [*html link*]

Me: is continental a good airline

Alex: We are proud of our outstanding customer service and operational
      excellence. Take a look at this Web page for some of the awards we have
      received. *View Page* [*html link*]

Me: what's the meaning of life

Alex: That's a question that only you can answer for yourself.

Elsewhere, on Flickr (see below), what looks like multilingualism and a celebration of cultural diversity really is not. When a user logs into a personal Flickr account, a small, supposedly personalized welcome message appears in a different language each time: "**Sawubona crispinthurlow!** Now you know how to greet people in Zulu." Needless to say, visual multiplicity and a formulaic greeting ritual do not a polyglot (or a global citizen) make. This kind of "fake multilingualism" (Kelly-Holmes 2005) is something Aoife Lenihan (2011) tracks nicely in her essay about the practical and political realities of translating Facebook into Irish, where an ostensible commitment to social inclusion is inextricably caught up in an underlying concern for corporate reach. What is more, efforts such as these to translate Facebook also rely on the enthusiasm of unpaid Facebook members rather than any serious financial commitment by Facebook Incorporated. Indeed, cloaked in a participatory rhetoric of creators and contributors, most social media companies grow their profits by piggybacking on user-generated content and the "immaterial labor" of their members. For Søren Petersen (2008), it is not only people's content that is thus commodified, but also the people themselves.

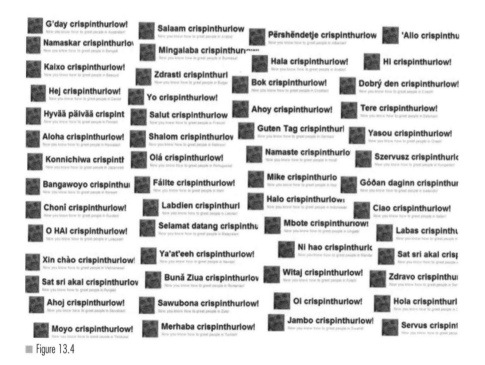

Figure 13.4

Extract 3: Plugging in the social

Facebook's "core concepts" for commercial developers

Social Design . . . is a product strategy that builds upon users' trusted communities, encourages conversation between them and ultimately creates a stronger sense of identity for everyone.

Social Plugins . . . enable you to provide engaging social experiences to your users with just a line of HTML.

Social Channels . . . lets you integrate with social channels such as News Feed and Requests to help you drive growth and engagement with your app, site or content.

It is part of the marketing acumen (and success) of a social media site such as Facebook that the term "Facebook" typically signifies its members and their social networking practices rather than the profit-making corporation. Nor is the rhetorical confusion merely accidental. In its own terms, Facebook, Inc., is ultimately in the business of "driving growth and engagement" and not making friends. While Facebook's suite of "social plugins" (see extract 2) appears to engage the social, it does so with quite apparently instrumental ends: what nowadays is labeled "monetization" but

what used to be called "profit." Personalization here is, of course, synthetic personalization (Fairclough 1989) that insinuates itself into members' trusted communities
(their friendships and other interpersonal relations). This is niche marketing that de-
liberately means to persuade customers that an "engaging social experience" may be
had just as easily with a product as with a friend or family member. By the same token, a company that plugs in with a Facebook profile or a Twitter feed persuades its
customers that it is somehow intimately and sincerely engaged with them—just as
Alex™ wants to persuade us of her eagerness to chat, or Coke that it is ultimately
concerned with world peace.

Political Rhetorics: "Like"

> To understand modern forms of rule, we suggest, requires an investigation not
> merely of grand political schemata, or economic ambitions, . . . but apparently
> humble and mundane mechanisms which appear to make it possible to
> govern. . . . (Miller and Rose 2008, 32)

The colonization of the lifeworld is of course not simply a matter of commerce and
the spread of enterprise culture; it is also realized through the increasing and changing influence of the State. As Nikolas Miller and Peter Rose note, governments too
are working their way into everyday discourse and relying more and more on "humble and mundane" mechanisms for exercising their influence and control. New media lend themselves nicely to this end. Politicians are, needless to say, all over new
technologies, often talking about them with the heightened, liberatory rhetoric of a
Foursquare marketer:

> The internet has already been a source of tremendous progress in China, and it
> is fabulous. . . . Information freedom supports the peace and security that
> provides a foundation for global progress. (From speech by Hilary Clinton,
> Newseum, Washington, DC, January 21, 2010)[4]

Politicians are also frantically looking to use social media—and, more importantly,
to be seen using social media—in order to plug themselves into our lives (Crawford
2009). Sadly, for them, the fan-base figures in table 13.2 alert us to the relative stand-
ing of politicians in the grander scheme of Facebook, especially vis-à-vis multina-
tional brands and celebrities. In terms of his supporters, President Obama weighs in
alongside Oreo cookies and well behind Justin Bieber and Lady Gaga. This relative
lack of reciprocity makes politicians no less eager to exploit the discursive—or,
rather, metadiscursive—potential of social media. Indeed, much like marketers (see
above) and celebrities (see below), the use of social media by politicians hinges on
a strategic blurring of public and private, formal and informal, local and nonlocal,
rhetorical and conversational. These "banal and humble" (Miller and Rose 2008, 32)
tools of the people are perfect for staging participatory democracy.

This brings me to the Facebook profile of Elizabeth Windsor (www.facebook
.com/TheBritishMonarchy). You know something is afoot when one of the most
detached, removed figureheads or institutions on the planet takes up social networking. This simply cannot be social media as we know it. Indeed, the British

monarchy's, White House's, and Ten Downing Street's use of Facebook, Twitter, or Foursquare is primarily a performance of open government—of access and of relevance. The limitations of this kind of access are exposed in the relational choices made available to followers: You cannot friend the queen (or Barack Obama, Sarah Palin, David Cameron, and Nicolas Sarkozy); you may only like her. Nor, for that matter, can you dislike her. This is still a largely one-way street, a metasemiotic resource for appearing to talk (with the people). In other words, the medium is the message: look how cool I am (I'm on Foursquare); look how in touch I am (I use Twitter); look how much I care (I have a Facebook profile). In practice, of course, the president and the queen are rendered no more (or less) real to me than Alex™. At least Alex™ answers my questions.

Once again we see how, in the hands of politicians, as with corporations, technology is easily used as a stand-in for talk. Put simply, we are encouraged to regard interactivity (the technological affordance) and interaction (the social process) as synonymous (Jensen 1999). Social media are most useful to politicians because the *appearance* of interaction may be achieved by the apparent use of interactive technologies. Politicians may strategically deploy the informal, conversational aura of social media. The same is true of newspaper blogs, which are only interactive or participatory if readers post and if journalists listen and respond. A technology is only social if people use it for social purposes. Besides, and following Norman Fairclough's (1992) earlier observations, it is also a pragmatic point of fact that "informal" does not equal "democratic"—a point that is often lost, it seems, on both politicians and the journalists who write about them. During the excited run-up to Barack Obama's presidential candidacy in August 2008, much was made of his campaign's use of new media, including this excited hyperbole from the *New York Times:* "Mr Obama's use of the newfound medium is the widest use of texting by a presidential candidate in history." Which brings me nicely to the rhetorics of Web 2.0 in media discourse.

Media Rhetorics: "Tanks versus Twitter"

> The dynamics of online modalities and new media technologies have reinforced, erased, or altered assumptions about what can be viewed as journalism, what counts as news, who can participate, and how a news story should be read. (Cotter 2011)

Perhaps more than most, journalists are in a state over new media. As Colleen Cotter notes, the entire business of newsmaking is, thanks in large part to digital media, currently under review—or under threat, depending on one's point of view. Journalists constitute a community of professional "language workers" (Thurlow 2007) that also seems truly conflicted by—but no less complicit in—the rise of Web 2.0. It certainly seems they have something of a love-hate relationship with the poster children of this latest generation of new media: blogging (and microblogging) and especially news aggregators. Social media advocates often maintain that these new technologies promise greater access, more transparency, and more creativity in the processes of newsmaking. To be sure, Web 2.0 media have certainly gone some way toward undermining—and even bankrupting—the traditional Big Media status of conventional newspapers and news broadcasters (Scholz 2008). For example, the kind of first-person reporting afforded by social (and mobile) media has contributed greatly to a significant role slippage between professional journalists and lay reporters, as well as a concomitant transformation in the nature of newsworthiness. Not least in an effort to mitigate these challenges to their authority and established practices, most newsmakers have sought to incorporate and capitalize on the affordances and opportunities of Web 2.0 technologies.[5]

While social media have undoubtedly facilitated the gathering and dissemination of news, reader engagement and the status of sources are slower to change. This is summed up nicely in a regular feature in Britain's *Independent* newspaper titled "The News in 140 Characters." This column comprises a seemingly arbitrary selection (made by a freelance reporter) of tweets from a range of British and global (mostly US American) celebrities or politicians. This kind of "informal syndication" (Thurlow 2006) hardly lives up to the kinds of reporting standards by which serious newsmakers (or so-called newspapers of record) usually like to hold themselves accountable; nor, for that matter, does the retweeting of elites do much to democratize the sourcing of news. It is in this way that heritage newsmakers like the British broadsheets and the BBC are, in effect, reincorporating any potential freedoms from Big Media afforded by social media. The usual Web 2.0 ideals of information democratization (and other participatory rhetorics) are imperfectly (if at all) realized in practice. The same is true for folksonomies and wikis where, for example, the sourcing, evaluation, and presentation of knowledge in Wikipedia can prove to be quite conservatively policed (see, for example, Johnstone 2011 on Wikipedia's restrictive preference for scholarly or print sources for knowledge about Pittsburghese). By the same token, reader responses at the end of online news articles do not a transparent people's press make, just as Facebook and Twitter do not a revolution make. Speaking of which. . . .

Alongside these not-always-successful attempts to keep up with social media, newsmakers are also complicit in perpetuating or even amplifying some of the principle rhetorics of 2.0, most notably technologically deterministic claims for the countercultural and revolutionary potential of social media (Marwick 2010). Perhaps the most blatant case of this was some of the framing of the Arab Spring uprisings of 2010 and 2011, as in these headlines: "Egypt's Youth Conducted a Facebook Revolution," "Here Comes the Wiki Revolution," the tabloidesque "Tanks versus Twitter in Egypt," and "Revolution 2.0: The Social Media Uprising."

These headlines epitomize the rather privileged, self-referential exaggeration of the facts by many Western journalists clearly enthralled with the undeniable role of social and mobile media in these events.[6] Where Web 2.0 is co-opted as a token of interaction, access, and "customer care" by marketers and politicians, newsmakers can greatly overplay the deterministic role of social media as instruments of liberation or as participation in the newsmaking process itself. Sometimes, their enthusiasm borders on the silly (see the *New York Times* comment about Obama's texting above) or tasteless. On the morning that I presented my initial version of this essay at the Georgetown Round Table, the west coast of Japan had just been struck by a

Figure 13.5

devastating earthquake and tsunami. Almost before the tsunami had exhausted itself across the lives of millions of people, the *LA Times* (see below) hastily chose to reframe the disaster as a social media story: "Just as Egypt has been cast as the Twitter Revolution, so Friday's massive Japanese earthquake and tsunami was destined to become the Twitter disaster" (*Los Angeles Times* 2011).

Always in search of a good—which is to say, compelling and easy to tell—story, journalists seem to be enthralled with the power of social media; although, it has to be said, not when it is in the hands of young people (Thurlow 2006, 2007). Perhaps caught up with the prominence of social media in their own lives, news-

Figure 13.6

makers (and others) appear to lose sight of the privilege of living in such media-rich environments, and of the fact that communication technologies may just as likely be co-opted as instruments of oppression and surveillance as they are instruments of liberation and transparency (see Morozov 2010 on "internet-centrism" and the authoritarian uses of technology). Along similar lines, Henry Giroux (2011, 23) reminds (or warns) us that the new media "can only be judged within the power relations and dominant ideologies and values that frame how they are defined and used within the larger society."

Educational Rhetorics: "Lighting the Flame of Learning"

> We need to move the discussion forwards, beyond the superficial fascination with technology for its own sake, towards a more critical engagement with questions of learning, communication and culture. (Buckingham 2007, 13)

It is now time to come closer to home with my critique. It is here also that I run the greatest risk of sounding like a complete Luddite.

Seemingly out of nowhere there has emerged an enormous industry of books, manuals, consultancies, government policies, and online resources on technology in the classroom. Everywhere teachers are persuaded that new media will enable them to "release their own potential," to "emancipate their students," and to "transform the future" (real soundbites from various educational resources on the Web). Those educators who do not respond to these new media imperatives are warned that they will simply be left behind. No wonder teachers, professors, and educational policymakers are scrambling to finds ways to tweet, post, and podcast. As David Buckingham argues, however, our fascination with "technology in the classroom" is too often superficial; shiny new technologies are taken up precisely because they are shiny and new, and invariably in an effort to appear current and/or attentive to our students.

If politicians' and marketers' uses of social media might provocatively be characterized as "wolves in sheep's clothing," then the growing presence of social media in the classroom might well be construed as "mutton dressed as lamb"—something tired and old being superficially altered to look fresh, new, and appealing. There is certainly relatively little effort made to test and validate the uptake of, say, podcasting, blogging, or tweeting in terms of teaching practice or learning outcomes. One exception is a recent study by Reynol Junco and his colleagues (Junco, Heiberger, and Loken 2010), which claims empirical evidence for the beneficial effects of using Twitter in the teaching of first-year medical students in the United States of America. (Notably, the findings of this study were taken up with enthusiasm in the press; see for example, *Times Higher Education* 2011). As if drawing from a received Web 2.0 lexicon, the authors concluded the following: "This study provides experimental evidence that Twitter can be used as an educational tool to help *engage* students and to *mobilize* faculty into a more active and *participatory* role" (119; my emphasis). The rhetoric aside, and as the authors concede, it is more than possible that it is the novelty and a sense of being *en vogue* that stimulates student

Figure 13.7

engagement—not that this is necessarily a bad thing. In either case, the technology per se cannot ensure learning. Indeed, social media may even prove to hinder the very learning outcomes that motivate their incorporation into our teaching (see my earlier reference to Johnstone 2011 and the surprisingly conservative sourcing of knowledge in Wikipedia).

The rhetorics of Web 2.0 in educational discourse typically hinge on the pedagogical-cum-countercultural ideal of empowerment, in much the same way that troubles Cameron and Fairclough. As Cameron observes, what is called empowerment often has more to do with *disciplining* people into ways of being, ways of behaving, that are suitable to commerce (2000; see also Jarrett 2008). It comes as no surprise, therefore, to see how a corporation such as Intel promotes its investment in education (see fig. 13.7). Backgrounded by romantic images of shiny, happy learners with laptops—the machine privileged over its actual uses—Intel's vision slides seamlessly from "empowering teachers to change lives" to "empowering the next generation of innovators" to "inspiring innovators, enabling entrepreneurs." (Note also how innovation is visually coded with the scientific-looking lab glasses.) In this regard, the educational rhetorics of Web 2.0 are more of the same. This is business as usual.

These largely unreflected rhetorics of emancipation (and participation) are also convenient to neoliberal agendas within academia, and many educators and their managers are hurriedly buying in. Certainly the technologization (or industrialization)

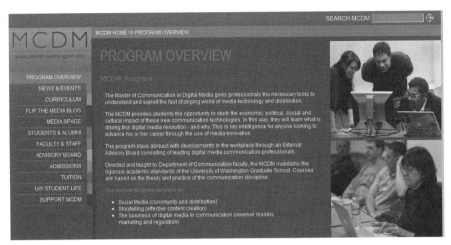

Figure 13.8

of education (aka the so-called learning industry) sees many of us rhetorically busy capitalizing on Web 2.0; we too are often heavily invested in the newness of things or in constructing things as new and cutting edge. In this regard, the self-sustaining (for-profit) master's program in digital media at my own university is a case in point (see fig. 13.8, with its similarly centered computers and glossy, stylized visions of engagement and collaboration). This is an educational venture where knowledge and understanding are explicitly rendered in the service of career advancement. Students pay for the chance to exploit "the digital media revolution." It also appears to be a far cry from the important—and, it has to be said, unavoidable—role Henry Giroux (2011; see also Buckingham 2007) envisions for new media in generating a critically informed public pedagogy.

Scholarly Rhetorics: "Discourse 2.0"

As scholars interested in—and often earning our salaries from being interested in—new media, we too must come under scrutiny and be subject to our own or others' critiques. Not that this is a call for some half-baked, name-and-shame exercise. Besides—far be it from me to appear to stand above the fray; I am, after all, someone who landed his first job because he offered to teach a course on computer-mediated communication (CMC [see also Thurlow, Lengel, and Tomic 2004]). We are, nonetheless, beholden to monitor the ways we too are positioned and persuaded by the rhetorical appeal of 2.0 and the ways we choose to represent the nature or extent of changes in, say, linguistic or discursive practice (fig. 13.9). If, as Marwick suggests, "Web 2.0 discourse is a conduit for the materialization of neoliberal ideology" (2010, 13), it behooves us to monitor our own assumptions about social media and the uses, however erudite, to which we put them.

All I can propose at this stage are a few pointers. To start, however, I am not saying that Web 2.0 doesn't exist (for tech specialists, for business people, for

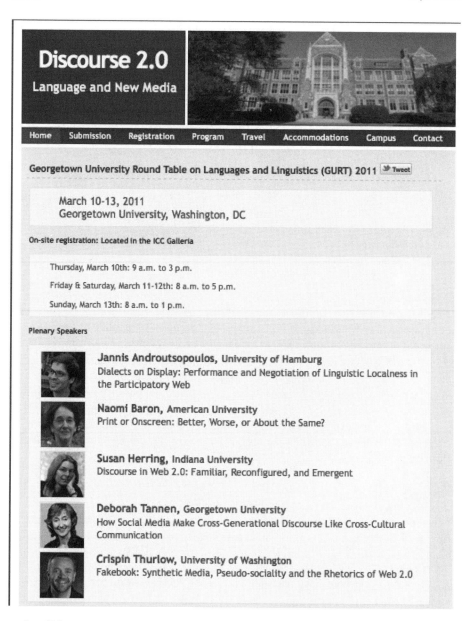

Discourse 2.0
Language and New Media

Home   Submission   Registration   Program   Travel   Accommodations   Campus   Contact

Georgetown University Round Table on Languages and Linguistics (GURT) 2011 🐦 Tweet

March 10-13, 2011
Georgetown University, Washington, DC

On-site registration: Located in the ICC Galleria

Thursday, March 10th: 9 a.m. to 3 p.m.

Friday & Saturday, March 11-12th: 8 a.m. to 5 p.m.

Sunday, March 13th: 8 a.m. to 1 p.m.

Plenary Speakers

Jannis Androutsopoulos, University of Hamburg
Dialects on Display: Performance and Negotiation of Linguistic Localness in the Participatory Web

Naomi Baron, American University
Print or Onscreen: Better, Worse, or About the Same?

Susan Herring, Indiana University
Discourse in Web 2.0: Familiar, Reconfigured, and Emergent

Deborah Tannen, Georgetown University
How Social Media Make Cross-Generational Discourse Like Cross-Cultural Communication

Crispin Thurlow, University of Washington
Fakebook: Synthetic Media, Pseudo-sociality and the Rhetorics of Web 2.0

▦ Figure 13.9

everyday users) or that there are no significant differences between, say, email and microblogging. By the same token, I am not meaning to suggest that there is nothing new—indeed, there is: for example, novel networking practices, extensive content creation and sharing, and even more confused public/private boundaries. Finally, I am definitely not meaning to imply that Web 2.0 technologies are the work of the devil or the ruin of culture. To do so would implicate me in precisely the kind of technological determinism that runs through the rhetorics of Web 2.0. What I am proposing are the following general guidelines:

1. We need constantly to challenge the misrepresentation (or simplistic representation) of new media discourse—whether it concerns processes of language change (always a case of evolution, not revolution); the interactional nature of all texts (not just those with comment boxes); the inherent multimodality of all reading/writing practices (not just those with videos and audio); and the heteroglossic, multivoiced nature of all communicative practice (not just the ones with friendship walls).

2. We must, in the spirit of critical discourse analysis, target for critique all discourse-based claims; for example, instances where media producers or promoters make promises regarding the interactive, communal, participatory, social, or relational affordances of their companies or technologies. In this sense, while attending to "user-centered" heteroglossia (cf. Androutsopoulos 2011) we should also be mindful of the other big social voices speaking through new media texts—specifically, the institutional voices of commerce, politics, and education, and so on.

3. We ought to monitor the reflexes of, for example, customer care (student-oriented teaching), participatory politics, engaged learning, and empowerment as they sometimes appear in our own research and teaching rationales. In tracking the "colonization of the lifeworld" (Habermas 1984), we should also be upholding the truly social—often banal, always embedded—practices of ordinary communicators. For Buckingham (2007) this means attending to communication and culture rather than technologies per se.

4. Just as others have sought to highlight the importance of attending to the contextual and particularistic nature of new media language (see Georgakopoulou 2006), it is essential that we locate our work in the histories of (new) media and not simply attend—or attend exclusively—to the latest and the newest. Equally, we need to keep asking what is really new—not shiny, surface new (or 2.0 new), but fundamentally new. Perhaps this is how we avoid reinventing the discourse wheel every time a new technology emerges. It might also hold us back from overstating the binaries (new versus old), from buying into neoliberal hype, and from unwittingly perpetuating another wave of technological determinism.

Like all good stories—or, at least, all good Labovian narratives—I will finish where I started, with a coda that sums up the point of my story.

Coda: Synthetic Media and Pseudo-sociality

Is it not ironic that a culture so overtly concerned with communication, so willing to expend thought, time and money on the subject, should have such limited and limiting ideas about what makes it good to talk? (Cameron 2000, 183)

I have always liked this thought-provoking conclusion (actually a searing critique) at the end of Deborah Cameron's wonderful *Good to Talk?* It is completely astute of course: the contemporary technologizing of language and communication—their scripting, regulation, and commodification—invariably hinges on ways of talking that have very little to do with the everyday practices and essentially social functions of talk. This is most apparent in the instrumental approach to communication skills training in schools or in call centers. Viewed differently, however, there is a sense that many so-called communication experts, professionals, or consultants know precisely what makes it good to talk. Perhaps it is this that makes their strategic deployment of social media so effective. Knowing that it is good to talk—and, to some extent, why it is good to talk—has enabled a whole range of neoliberal agents/beneficiaries to "collapse the social plane" and to skillfully persuade us that technology is talk (cf. Thurlow and Bell 2009; Thurlow and Mroczek 2011). After all, at least 213,972 people have chosen to follow my milk carton, even if I have not.[7]

For at least two good reasons, I see the rhetorics of Web 2.0 producing a decidedly synthetic kind of media. First, they collapse the social plane by combining (or synthesizing) and blurring the public and private, the personal and institutional, and the corporate and social (Habermas 1984; Marwick 2010). Second, and following Norman Fairclough, they are synthetic (i.e., artificial or feigned) insofar as they readily enable corporations, politicians, professors, and others to fabricate a sense of personal concern or attention for—and intimate interaction with—customers, voters, students, etc. All of which effectively produces a kind of intense *pseudo-sociality* by which institutional agents are able to stylize themselves as participatory, interactive, or accessible simply by using (or appearing to use) a social media such as Facebook, Twitter, or Foursquare—or, in the case of President Obama, all three. More often than not these institutional uses of social media are instances of communicative condescension akin to those that concerned Pierre Bourdieu (1991): powerful agents concealing their desire to influence and manage people by invoking apparently interpersonal gestures of informality and familiarity. Indeed, for Kylie Jarrett, this is the underlying issue with all Web 2.0 interactivity: "It is a disciplining into a liberal ideal of subjectivity based around notions of freedom, choice and activity. . . . As a seductive expression of power, [it] is based on condescension: a deliberate masking of power in order to effect control" (2008, n.p.). Whatever opportunities for agentful, creative practice they may enable, social media always have the potential for influencing the actions of ordinary users; in fact, the playful, seductive appeal of social media may make them even more suited to regulatory and self-regulatory exercises of power.

One domain or discourse where we witness most clearly the synthetic affordances of social media and the condescending exercise of social control is with celebrities. Of course, the use of ghost writers (one of the worst-kept secrets in Hollywood) by celebrity tweeters, bloggers, and social networkers complicates notions of authorship and authenticity in interesting ways: It is seldom clear, for example, who is doing the tweeting or posting and who fans are actually interacting with. Nonetheless, as another high-profile constituency of social media users, celebrities are certainly well served by the capacity of new media to blur the boundary between commerce and social life. Like politicians, celebrities deploy social media as a means of insinuating themselves into the lives of their mass audiences through an appearance of personal interaction and by strategically weaving together the public and private, the formal and informal. In her work, Alice Marwick (2010) focuses on celebrity discourse as a particularly powerful domain for the reproduction of neoliberal fantasies about Web 2.0. Far beyond the tweets and posts of actual celebrities (or their people), however, the affordances and typical uses of social media foster a microcelebrity mindset of extreme self-referentiality and self-promotion. It is in this way, too, that new technologies (and social media, in particular) are constantly held up as instruments of/for fame and success. Central to this celebritization of everyday life is the aggressive neocolonization of the lifeworld in the form of what Marwick calls "lifestreaming": the constant presentation and publication (or broadcasting) of oneself and one's private information to others. This is a phenomenon that is clearly role-modeled and stoked by celebrities themselves, but one that is also being taken up much more widely as we are all of us persuaded to codify and—in many cases—commodify previously ephemeral material from our ordinary, private lives. Our friends and family are thus transformed into our own little audience, our own fan base.

None of which is to suggest that intended audiences are necessarily unaware, or that individual social agents are complete dupes. As Kate Crawford nicely observes, "If networked technologies in general, and social media in particular, generate ideal listening subjects of the twenty-first century—for individuals, politicians, consumers, parents and corporations—they also reveal the human limits of attention" (2009, 532). This is something Alicia Keyes and her Hollywood friends discovered to their great embarrassment when they presumed to know their fans. In December 2010, and in somewhat poor taste, Keyes and others (including Elijah Wood, Jennifer Hudson, and Justin Timberlake) announced their so-called digital deaths in an effort to raise money for AIDS charities. Presented with a series of highly aestheticized, glamorized images of dead celebrities (fig. 13.10), the rationale behind this campaign was that desperate fans would be only too eager to donate money in order to resuscitate their idols' stream of supposedly behind-the-scenes posts and the-real-me tweets.

> The world's most followed celebrity Tweeters are sacrificing their digital lives to help save millions of real lives affected by HIV/AIDS in Africa and India. That means no more Twitter or Facebook updates from any of them. . . . But they don't have to die in vain. And they don't have to stay dead for long. Just watch their Last Tweet and Testaments, and buy their lives back. . . . And when $1,000,000 is reached, everyone will be back online and tweeting in no time. (buylife.org/about.php)

Within only a few weeks, it transpired that few fans were that interested in bringing these celebrities back to life after all; celebrity tweets and posts were possibly entertaining but certainly something they (the fans) could live without. For several days following their demise, the Digital Death celebrities discovered that donations were only trickling in; fans were, it seems, largely unimpressed by this presumptuous campaign and disinclined to bring any of the celebrities back to life after all. Keyes and the others were eventually rescued from their embarrassment only after a substantial

■ Figure 13.10

donation (initially anonymous) of $500,000 by pharmaceuticals billionaire Stewart Rahr. While the condescension of celebrities (those twits who tweet) may be without bounds, and the condescending uses of social media unavoidable, it appears that everyday communicators do know a thing or two about communication and are capable of seeing through some of the most clumsy, disingenuous uses of social media. Sometimes.

ACKNOWLEDGMENTS

I am grateful for all sorts of constructive feedback from participants who approached me after I had presented this material at GURT in April 2011. In preparing for the GURT presentation and, therefore, for this chapter, I am very grateful for the help of an undergraduate research assistant, Dale Coleman, and for conversations with my UW graduate colleague Kate Bell. My most special thanks go to Alice Marwick (previously of New York University) and David Silver (currently of University of San Francisco) for gifting me some cool ideas, keeping me (more or less) on track, and generally continuing to inspire me. I am grateful to Sinnan for permission to reproduce his "Facebook Queen" cartoon. Other images are either my own or those used fairly for the purposes of scholarly comment and criticism.

NOTES

1. The cartoon "Facebook Queen," is reprinted by permission of the artist, Sinnan (www.houseofcheah .com/images/editorialcartoons/facebookqueen_fc.jpg_).
2. Table 13.1 is based on lindsay-goodier.suite101.com/what-is-web-20-a51022.
3. There are, of course, other important examples of this kind of "domain bleed," such as the strategic uptake of video gaming technologies by the military (see Allen 2011).
4. As a telling insight into her imagined or desired audience—and into the geopolitical force of a talk like this—Clinton's speech is available on the State Department website in Arabic, Chinese, French, Persian, Russian, Spanish, and Urdu (www.state.gov/secretary/rm/2010/01/135519.htm).

5. In September 2011, at the International Broadcasting Convention, Kevin Bakhurst, deputy head of the BBC Newsroom, outlined the BBC's use of social media and the challenges they pose to a traditional news organization like his. A transcript of his speech is available online at www.bbc.co.uk/blogs/theeditors/2011/ 09/ibc_in_amsterdam.html.

6. To be fair, the *New Yorker's* Malcolm Gladwell (2010) was unequivocal in his criticism of the media's exaggerated social media framing of the Arab Spring (but see also *Guardian* 2010).

7. This is the number of Facebook members who had liked Organic Valley as I was finishing revisions of this chapter.

REFERENCES

Allen, Robertson. 2011. The unreal enemy of America's army. *Games and Culture* 6, no. 1:38–60.

Androutsopoulos, Jannis. 2011. From variation to heteroglossia in the study of computer-mediated discourse. In *Digital discourse: Language and the new media,* ed. Crispin Thurlow and Kristine Mroczek, 277–98. New York: Oxford University Press.

Banaji, Shakuntala, Andrew Burn, and David Buckingham. 2006. The rhetorics of creativity: A literature review. *Creativity, culture and education.*www.creativitycultureeducation.org/the-rhetorics-of-creativity-a-literature-review.

Bauman, Zygmunt. 2007. *Consuming life.* London: Polity.

Bourdieu, Pierre. 1991. *Language and symbolic power.* Ed. John B. Thompson. Trans. Gino Raymond and Matthew Adamson. Cambridge: Polity Press.

boyd, danah. 2009. Social media is here to stay . . . now what? *Danah boyd,* www.danah.org/papers /talks/MSRTechFest2009.html.

Buckingham, David. 2007. *Beyond technology: Children's learning in the age of digital culture.* Cambridge: Polity.

Cameron, Deborah. 2000. *Good to talk? Living and working in a communication culture.* London: Sage.

Cotter, Colleen. 2011. Journalists and linguists: Ways with words online. Panel organized for the Georgetown University Round Table on Languages and Linguistics, March 10–13, Washington, DC.

Crawford, Kate. 2009. Following you: Disciplines of listening in social media. *Journal of Media and Culture Studies* 23, no. 4:525–35.

Fairclough, Norman. 1989. *Language and power.* London: Longman.

———. 1992. *Discourse and social change.* Cambridge: Polity Press.

Foucault, Michel. 1980. *Power/knowledge: Selected interviews and other writings, 1972–1977.* Ed. and trans. Colin Gordon. New York: Pantheon.

———. 1988. Technologies of the self. In *Technologies of the self: A seminar with Michel Foucault,* ed. L. H. Martin, H. Gutman, and P. H. Hutton, 16–49. Amherst: University of Massachusetts Press.

Georgakopoulou, Alexandra. 2006. Postscript: Computer-mediated communication in sociolinguistics. *Journal of Sociolinguistics* 10, no. 4:548–57.

Giroux, Henry A. 2011. The crisis in public values in the age of new media. *Critical Studies in Media Communication* 28, no. 1:8–29.

Gladwell, Malcolm. 2010. Small change: Why the revolution will not be tweeted. *New Yorker,* October 4. www.newyorker.com/reporting/2010/10/04/101004fa_fact_gladwell.

Guardian. 2010. Sorry, Malcolm Gladwell, the revolution may well be tweeted. October 2. www.guardian.co.uk/commentisfree/cifamerica/2010/oct/02/malcolm-gladwell-social-networking-kashmir.

Habermas, Jürgen. 1984. *The theory of communicative action.* Trans. Thomas McCarthy. Boston: Beacon Press.

Heller, Monica. 2003. Globalization, the new economy and the commodification of language and identity. *Journal of Sociolinguistics* 7, no. 4:473–98.

Jarrett, Kylie. 2008. Interactivity is evil! A critical investigation of Web 2.0. *First Monday* 13, no. 3. www.firstmonday.org/htbin/cgiwrap/bin/ojs/index.php/fm/article/view/2140/1947.

Jaworski, Adam, and Crispin Thurlow. 2010. Language and the globalizing habitus of tourism: A sociolinguistics of fleeting relationships. In *The handbook of language and globalisation,* ed. Nikolas Coupland, 256–86. Oxford: Blackwell.

Jensen, Jens F. 1999. "Interactivity": Tracking a new concept in media and communication studies. *Nordicom Review* 19:185–204. www.nordicom.gu.se/common/publ_pdf/38_jensen.pdf.

Johnstone, Barbara. 2011. Making Pittsburghese: Communication technology, expertise, and the discursive construction of a regional dialect. *Language & Communication* 31, no. 1:3–15.

Junco, Reynol, Greg Heiberger, and Eric Loken. 2010. The effect of Twitter on college student engagement and grades. *Journal of Computer Assisted Learning* 27:119–32. onlinelibrary.wiley.com/doi/10.1111/j.1365-2729.2010.00387.x/full.

Kelly-Holmes, Helen. 2005. *Advertising as multilingual communication.* Basingstoke, UK: Palgrave Macmillan.

Kress, Gunther, Carey Jewitt, Jon Ogborn, and Charalampos Tsatsarelis. 2001. *Multimodal teaching and learning: The rhetorics of the science classroom.* London: Continuum.

Lenihan, Aoife. 2011. "Join our community of translators": Language ideologies and Facebook. In *Digital discourse: Language and the new media,* ed. Crispin Thurlow and Kristine Mroczek, 48–64. New York: Oxford University Press.

Los Angeles Times. 2011. Twitter response to Japan earthquake, tsunami is fast, widespread. March 11. articles.latimes.com/2011/mar/11/world/la-fg-japan-quake-twitter-20110312.

Marwick, Alice. 2010. Status update: Celebrity, publicity and self-branding in Web 2.0. PhD diss., New York University. www. tiara.org/blog/wp-content/uploads/2010/09/marwick_dissertation_statusupdate.pdf.

Miller, Peter, and Nikolas Rose. 2008. *Governing the present: Administering economic, social and personal life.* Cambridge: Polity.

Morozov, Evgeny. 2010. *The net delusion: The dark side of internet freedom.* New York: Public Affairs.

New York Times. 2011. "Corporations are people," Romney tells Iowa hecklers angry over his tax policy. August 11. www.nytimes.com/2011/08/12/us/politics/12romney.html.

Petersen, Søren M. 2008. Loser generated content: From participation to exploitation. *First Monday* 13, no. 3. firstmonday.org/htbin/cgiwrap/bin/ojs/index.php/fm/article/view/2141/1948.

Scholz, Trebor. 2008. Market ideology and the myths of Web 2.0. *First Monday* 13, no. 3. firstmonday.org/htbin/cgiwrap/bin/ojs/index.php/fm/article/view/2138/1945.

Silver, D. 2008. History, hype, and hope: An afterward. *First Monday* 13, no. 3. firstmonday.org/htbin/cgi-wrap/bin/ojs/index.php/fm/article/viewArticle/2143/1950.

Sterne, Jonathan. 2003. *The audible past: Cultural origins of sound reproduction.* Durham, NC: Duke University Press.

Thurlow, Crispin. 2001. Language and the internet. In *Concise encyclopedia of sociolinguistics,* ed. Raj Mesthrie, 287–89. London: Pergamon.

———. 2003. Generation Txt? The sociolinguistics of young people's text-messaging. *Discourse Analysis Online* 1, no. 1. extra.shu.ac.uk/daol/articles/v1/n1/a3/thurlow2002003-paper.html.

———. 2006. From statistical panic to moral panic: The metadiscursive construction and popular exaggeration of new media language in the print media. *Journal of Computer-mediated Communication* 11, no. 3, article 1. jcmc.indiana.edu/vol11/issue3/thurlow.html.

———. 2007. Fabricating youth: New-media discourse and the technologization of young people. In *Language in the media: Representations, identities, ideologies,* ed. Sally Johnson and Astrid Ensslin, 213–33. London: Continuum.

———, ed. 2009. Young people, mediated discourse and communication technologies. Special issue, *Journal of Computer-Mediated Communication* 14, no. 4. onlinelibrary.wiley.com/doi /10.1111/jcmc.2009.14.issue-4/issuetoc.

———. 2011. Determined creativity: Language play in new media discourse. In *Discourse and creativity,* ed. Rodney Jones, 169–90. London: Pearson.

Thurlow, Crispin, and Kate Bell. 2009. Against technologization: Young people's new media discourse as creative cultural practice. *Journal of Computer-mediated Communication* 14, no. 4:1038–49. onlinelibrary.wiley.com/doi/10.1111/j.1083-6101.2009.01480.x/full.

Thurlow, Crispin, and Adam Jaworski. 2006. The alchemy of the upwardly mobile: Symbolic capital and the stylization of elites in frequent-flyer programmes. *Discourse and Society* 17, no. 1:131–67.

Thurlow, Crispin, Laura Lengel, and Alice Tomic. 2004. *Computer-mediated communication: Social interaction and the internet.* London and Thousand Hills, CA: Sage.

Thurlow, Crispin, and Kristine Mroczek. 2011. Fresh perspectives on new media sociolinguistics. In *Digital discourse: Language and the new media,* ed. Crispin Thurlow and Kristine Mroczek, xix–xliv. New York: Oxford University Press.

Times Higher Education. 2011. Twitter can improve student performance, study says. February 3. www.timeshighereducation.co.uk/story.asp?storycode=415060.

Turkle, S. 2011. *Alone together: Why we expect more from technology and less from each other.* New York: Basic Books.

van Dijck, José, and David Nieborg. 2009. Wikinomics and its discontents: A critical analysis of Web 2.0 business manifestos. *New Media and Society* 11, no. 5:855–74.

Index

taciturnity, 107–8, 109, 111
Tagesschau (news program), 57
tagging: on Facebook, 139–40, 149–52; on
    Flickr, 75–76
Tannen, Deborah, x, 9, 99, 158, 170, 172, 174
Taxi Driver (movie), 35–36
"techniques of the body," 34
technological determinism, 222*n*1, 243
telephone calls, 102, 105, 113
television-mediated conversation, 5, 6
temporality of mobile device usage, 126
text-based CMC, 155–56, 157, 164
textbooks, 212
text messages: as asynchronous, 126; and face-
    to-face interactions, 102; intensity markers
    in, 112. *See also* mobile devices
"A Theory of Play and Fantasy" (Bateson), 101
three-way interactions, 130*n*2
Thüringisch dialect, 52, 68*n*7
Thurlow, Crispin, xii, 67, 75, 90, 100, 115,
    225
Timberlake, Justin, 245
Tiny Prints, 87–91
topical coherence, 13
tourism, 90–91
Trester, Anna Marie, xi, 117*n*3, 133, 146,
    148–49, 150
"truthiness," 209
Turkle, Sherry, 201–2
turn-taking, 110–11, 129–30. *See also*
    asynchronous communication
Twitter, 6, 11–12, 244

uniqueness, 89
user-generated content, 2

vacation postcards, 90
Vaisman, Carmel, 8, 9
value of books, 206, 208–9
van Leeuwen, Theo, 54
Varenne, Hervé, ix, 27, 40
Vázquez, Camilla, 167–68, 169
video: and media convergence, 16; text
    embedding in, 18. *See also* YouTube
video games: assessments in, 27–45; controllers
    for, 33–34, 43*n*14; multiplayer online
    games, 4–5, 6; scoring issues for, 33
Viégas, Fernanda B., 15
viral marketing, 2
Virtanen, Tuija, xi, 155

Virtually You (Aboujaode), 202
virtual worlds, 229
Visual Dynamic Topic Analysis, 13
Viswanath, Bimal, 137
volubility, 107–8, 111
Vygotsky, L. S., 184

Wallat, Cynthia, 158, 174
Waseleski, Carol, 106
Washington Post on Facebook interactions, 139,
    140
Wattenberg, Martin, 15
Web 2.0, 1–26; and complicating action, 226–27;
    corporate rhetorics of, 231–35; defined, 2–4;
    educational rhetorics of, 239–41; emergent
    aspects of discourse in, 14–20; familiar
    aspects of discourse in, 8–10; genre
    classification for, 6–8; and media
    convergence, 4–6; media rhetorics of,
    236–39; medium choice in, 99–117;
    mythologies of, 228–31; political rhetorics
    of, 235–36; and pseudo-sociality, 243–46;
    reconfigured aspects of discourse in, 10–14;
    rhetorics of, 231–43; scholarly rhetorics of,
    241–43; and social change, 227–28; and
    synthetic media, 243–46; temporal
    perspective of, 3
Weigert, Astrid, 187
Wessler, Sarah, ix, 27, 30, 31
West, Emily, 88
West, Laura, xi, 133, 150
White, P. R. R., 190
Wikipedia, 15
wikis: collaborative environment of, 6, 15; and
    nonbona fide participants, 19; as Web 2.0
    technology, 229
Williams, Michelle, 1, 6–7, 8
Wood, Elijah, 245

Xie, Ying, 186

Ybañez, Kathy, 170
YouTube: CMCMC on, 4; collaborative
    environment of, 18; comments on videos,
    62–66; dialect analysis on, 47–71;
    leadership roles in community of, 49;
    linking to, 110; and media convergence, 16;
    participatory culture of, 48–50

Zelenkauskaite, Asta, 105–6